THE YEARBOOK
OF
EDUCATION LAW
1997

Edited by

CHARLES J. RUSSO

UNIVERSITY OF DAYTON

EDUCATION LAW ASSOCIATION
DAYTON, OHIO

ABOUT THE EDITOR

Charles J. Russo is the Professor and Chair of the Department of Educational Administration in the School of Education at the University of Dayton. Dr. Russo is Vice President of the Education Law Association. He is a co-author of *The Law of Home Schooling* (1994), and *Special Education Law: Issues & Implications for the '90s* (1995). Dr. Russo has been a member of the Author's Committee of West's *Education Law Reporter* since 1987, and in 1996 he was appointed to the editorial advisory committee. He is a past regional reporter for the *School Law Reporter* and author of the *Law Review Digest* in *NOLPE Notes*. He has authored more than 150 articles and presented numerous papers at national and regional conferences.

CONTRIBUTORS

William E. Camp
Professor
Department of Advanced Studies
Cal State San Bernandino
San Bernandino, California

Gus Douvanis
Assistant Professor
University of West Georgia
Carrolton, Georgia

Paul R. Downing
Instructor
Department of Sport Science
Ashland University
Ashland, Ohio

William J. Evans, Jr.
Teacher and Administrator
Smithtown Central School District
Smithtown, New York

Robert M. Hendrickson
Professor
Higher Education Program
Pennsylvania State University
University Park, Pennsylvania

Ralph D. Mawdsley
Professor
Counseling, Administration, Supervision and Adult Learning
Cleveland State University
Cleveland, Ohio

Julie F. Mead
Assistant Professor
Department of Administrative Leadership
University of Wisconsin-Milwaukee
Milwaukee, Wisconsin

Allan G. Osborne, Jr.
Assistant Principal
Snug Harbor Community School
Quincy, Massachusetts
Visiting Associate Professor
Bridgewater State College
Bridgewater, Massachusetts

Charles J. Russo
Professor and Chair
Department of Educational Administration
School of Education
University of Dayton
Dayton, Ohio

Linda A. Sharp
Consultant
Sharp Consulting
Fort Collins, Colorado

Donald F. Uerling
Associate Professor
University of Nebraska - Lincoln
Department of Educational Administration
Lincoln, Nebraska

CONTENTS

1 EMPLOYEES

Ralph D. Mawdsley

2 SCHOOL GOVERNANCE

Donald F. Uerling

3 PUPILS

William E. Camp

4 BARGAINING

Julie F. Mead

5 STUDENTS WITH DISABILITIES

Allan G. Osborne, Jr.

6 TORTS

William J. Evans, Jr.

7 SPORTS

Linda A. Sharp

8 HIGHER EDUCATION

Robert M. Hendrickson

9 FEDERAL AND STATE LEGISLATION

Gus Douvanis

10 EDUCATION RELATED

Paul R. Downing

1
EMPLOYEES

Ralph D. Mawdsley

Introduction

Almost two hundred cases involving public K-12 education were reported last year. Although no new decisions relevant to employees were handed down by the Supreme Court in 1996, important precedent-setting rulings from past years are cited where appropriate. Litigation that is more properly the subject of other chapters is excluded as are actions that focus primarily on procedural matters. Consistent with the pattern in previous years, the majority of cases in this chapter examine dismissal, nonrenewal, demotion, and discipline, as many court actions addressed school board compliance with district and state policies.

Discrimination in Employment

Discrimination claims can arise under state or federal statutes. Even so, the overwhelming number of cases in this section were litigated under federal law. The most commonly applied statute, title VII of the Civil Rights Act of 1964,[1] prohibits public and private educational institutions from discriminating on the basis of race, color, religion, sex, and/or national origin. Discrimination based on national origin and race is also forbidden by section 1981 of the Civil Rights Act of 1866.[2] The Americans with Disabilities Act (ADA),[3] which applies to both public and private schools, has begun to generate case law. Suits continue to be brought under section 504 of the Rehabilitation Act of 1973, which prohibits discrimination against "otherwise qualified individuals."[4] Gender-based discrimination, including sexual harassment, is proscribed by title IX of

---

[1] 42 U.S.C. § 2000 *et seq.*
[2] 42 U.S.C. § 1981.
[3] 42 U.S.C. § 12101 *et seq.*
[4] 29 U.S.C. § 794.

the Educational Amendments of 1972,[5] while gender-based wage discrimination is prohibited by the Equal Pay Act of 1963.[6] Employees forty years of age and older are safeguarded by the Age Discrimination in Employment Act of 1973 (ADEA).[7] Moreover, discrimination claims can be pursued under section 1983 of the Civil Rights Act of 1871 which protects federal constitutional and statutory rights.[8]

A suit from California involved charges of both age and race discrimination. An appellate court reversed and held that proof of satisfactory job performance was not part of a former superintendent's prima facie case. In applying the Supreme Court decision, *McDonnell Douglas Corporation v. Green,*[9] the panel ruled that whether an employee who has been discharged has met this burden of proof is a question of law for the trial court.[10]

In upholding an arbitrator's award on behalf of a bus mechanic, an appeals court ruled that the Veteran Preference Act of Pennsylvania applied only to job appointments, not promotions. The court reasoned that since awarding the mechanic a job as school bus driver constituted a promotion, not an appointment, it fell outside of the statute.[11]

Race

School districts prevailed in the first six cases in this section. The Eighth Circuit upheld a determination by a district court that a school board in Missouri had a legitimate, nondiscriminatory reason for terminating the employment of a black public safety officer.[12] The court found that there was no racial discrimination under title VII in the black officer's dismissal nor in other district actions against him that occurred after he filed his discrimination suit.

In a second case from Missouri, a federal district court granted summary judgment for a board of education in a case where a teacher alleged racial discrimination.[13] The court reasoned that since the teacher failed to raise the discrimination claim before the board during her

---

[5] 20 U.S.C. § 1681 *et seq.*
[6] 29 U.S.C. § 206(d)(1).
[7] 29 U.S.C. § 621 *et seq.*
[8] 42 U.S.C. § 1983.
[9] 411 U.S. 792 (1973).
[10] Caldwell v. Paramount Unified Sch. Dist., 48 Cal. Rptr. 2d 448 [105 EDUC. L. REP. 652] (Cal. Ct. App. 1995).
[11] Belle Vernon Area Sch. Dist. v. Teamsters Local Union No. 782, 670 A.2d 1201 [106 EDUC. L. REP. 1203] (Pa. Commw. Ct. 1996).
[12] Ruby v. Springfield R-12 Pub. Sch. Dist., 76 F.3d 909 [107 EDUC. L. REP. 71] (8th Cir. 1996).
[13] Thomas v. St. Louis Bd. of Educ., 933 F. Supp. 817 [112 EDUC. L. REP. 169] (E.D. Mo. 1996).

termination proceeding, she was precluded from doing so in her federal title VII action.

A federal trial court in New York held that a teacher whose job was terminated in January 1991 did not have a section 1981 action against the board of education.[14] The court found that even though the interpretation by the Supreme Court of the Civil Rights Act of 1991 in *Rivers v. Roadway Express, Inc.*[15] extended section 1981 to contract terminations, it did not apply retroactively to actions arising before the change went into effect on November 21, 1991.

The only white public school teacher in an otherwise all Hispanic bilingual education department provided statistical evidence to establish a prima facie case of racial discrimination in violation of title VII and section 1981. However, when the school district proffered anticipated budget cuts as a legitimate, nondiscriminatory reason for not promoting him to a supervisory position, the federal trial court in Colorado granted summary judgment in favor of the system. On further review, the Eighth Circuit affirmed that the teacher failed to produce evidence that the prospect of budget cuts was a sham for eliminating the position.[16]

An appellate court in Pennsylvania reversed in favor of a school board in a dispute over who could be hired as a superintendent.[17] The court held that black parents lacked standing to contest the allegedly discriminatory hiring of a white woman as superintendent.

In Florida, an appellate court reinstated a hearing officer's finding that a school board did not discriminate against teachers in performing their evaluations.[18] In so doing, the panel overruled a trial court judgment because it was of the opinion that the hearing officer's finding was supported by competent substantial evidence that neither the superintendent nor other school officials took any discriminatory action against teachers due to their race.

Employees won four other decisions. In a case of remedial significance, the Seventh Circuit reversed a grant of summary judgment on behalf of a school board in a title VII sex discrimination claim.[19] The court maintained that the teacher's success in her title VII claim before

[14] Smith v. New York City Bd. of Educ., 918 F. Supp. 130 [108 EDUC. L. REP. 130] (S.D.N.Y. 1996).
[15] 114 S. Ct. 1510 (1994).
[16] Reynolds v. School Dist. No. 1, Denver, Colo., 69 F.3d 1523 [104 EDUC. L. REP. 1004] (10th Cir. 1995).
[17] Board of Educ. of Sch. Dist. of Pittsburgh v. Pennsylvania Human Relations Comm'n, 682 A.2d 1345 [113 EDUC. L. REP. 339] (Pa. Commw. Ct. 1996).
[18] Bay County Sch. Bd. v. Bryan, 679 So. 2d 1246 [113 EDUC. L. REP. 518] (Fla. Dist. Ct. App. 1996).
[19] Waid v. Merrill Area Pub. Sch., 91 F.3d 857 [111 EDUC. L. REP. 644] (7th Cir. 1996).

the Wisconsin Equal Rights Division did not preclude her intentional sex discrimination charge against school officials pursuant to section 1983 and the district under title VII.

The Third Circuit upheld a ruling that the affirmative action plan of a board of education in New Jersey violated title VII. The plan gave preference to minority over nonminority teachers in layoff decisions.[20] Pursuant to a claim filed by a white teacher, the court stated that the plan violated title VII because it had been adopted to promote diversity rather than to remedy discrimination or its past effects.

A federal district court in Florida denied a school board's motion for summary judgment where a black assistant principal alleged racial discrimination when she was not restored to her administrative position following a reduction-in-force.[21] The court found that the administrator introduced evidence that could form the basis for a finding of facts that could allow a jury to decide that the actions of the board were a pretext for discrimination.

In a second case from Florida, an appellate court reversed in favor of a black middle school teacher who sued his school board for racial discrimination.[22] The court found that genuine issues of material fact over the teacher's claims that the board had paid him inadequately, transferred him to less favorable classes, not renewed his contract, and failed to hire him for vacant positions precluded summary judgment for the school system.

Religion

In a nonschool case with possible implications for public education, the Ninth Circuit held that rules of the California Department of Education violated the right to free speech. The rules forbade employees from engaging in any oral or written religious advocacy in the workplace and displaying any religious artifacts, tracts, or materials outside of their offices or cubicles. In rejecting the Establishment Clause concerns of the state, the court concluded that " . . . nothing [that the employee] says about religion in his office is likely to cause a reasonable person to believe that the state is speaking or supports his views."[23]

---

[20] Taxman v. Board of Educ. of Township of Piscataway, 91 F.3d 1547 [111 EDUC. L. REP 696] (3d Cir. 1996).

[21] Perkins v. School Bd. of Pinellas County, 902 F. Supp. 1503 [104 EDUC. L. REP. 1121] (M.D. Fla. 1995).

[22] Weaver v. School Bd. of Leon County, 661 So. 2d 335 [104 EDUC. L. REP 530] (Fla. Dist. Ct. App. 1995).

[23] Tucker v. California Dep't of Educ., 97 F.3d 1204, 1213 [113 EDUC. L. REP. 102] (9th Cir. 1996).

Two former school bus drivers failed in a title VII discrimination suit against their district on the ground that the district refused their request for an eight-day leave so that they could participate in a religious observance.[24] A federal trial court in Texas reasoned that the district did not have to make the accommodation since it would have faced an undue hardship by having to hire more drivers at higher pay and require supervisors or mechanics to drive buses.

Sex

Gender-based discrimination cases presented a range of issues. In West Virginia, a female county board of education finance department employee stated a cause of action for sex discrimination under state law. The West Virginia Supreme Court of Appeals agreed as it reversed and remanded an earlier judgment that her claim was without merit.[25] The court ruled that the board failed to provide a legitimate explanation for nondiscrimination in salary differentials where a male coworker had received a pay cut in the year preceding the woman's and her salary had been reduced in successive years while his was left unchanged.

In vacating and remanding a finding of discrimination against female cafeteria workers under the Equal Pay Act, the Supreme Judicial Court of Massachusetts held that the wrong standard had been applied at trial.[26] The court reasoned that in determining whether the jobs of cafeteria workers and male custodians were comparable in content and common characteristics, the judge needed to take evidence regarding fringe benefits and other forms of remuneration into account when calculating wages.

The Tenth Circuit upheld the dismissal of a title VII sex discrimination claim against the Utah Department of Corrections by a teaching assistant who had been hired by a school district to work in an academy for inmates at a correctional facility.[27] The court found that the Department of Corrections did not employ the teaching assistant even though it regulated physical entry and security to the facility where the teacher worked.

A female principal in Arkansas failed to show that she was dismissed in retaliation for filing a gender discrimination claim. Reversing in favor of the school system, the Eighth Circuit observed that there were legitimate, nondiscriminatory reasons for the principal being discharged.

---

[24] Favero v. Huntsville Indep. Sch. Dist., 939 F. Supp. 1281 [113 EDUC. L. REP. 747] (S.D. Tex. 1996).

[25] Martin v. Randolph County Bd. of Educ., 465 S.E.2d 399 [105 EDIC. L. REP. 1306] (W. Va. 1995).

[26] Jancey v. School Comm. of Everett, 658 N.E.2d 162 [105 EDUC. L. REP. 265] (Mass. 1995).

[27] Lambertsen v. Utah Dep't of Corrections, 79 F.3d 1024 [108 EDUC. L. REP. 58] (10th Cir. 1996).

The court was of the opinion that the former principal had spread outrageous rumors about the new superintendent, including comments that the superintendent was involved in drugs, was a womanizer, had a drinking problem, had financial problems, and was often absent from the school district.[28]

Age

School districts prevailed in all three of the age claims this year. The Seventh Circuit affirmed that the the state did not aid and abet local school districts to violate the ADEA when it failed to repeal a provision of the Illinois school code that requires teachers to retire at age seventy.[29] The court reasoned that because local districts held the key employment powers, there was no evidence that the state extensively controlled the employment of teachers. The court concluded that mandates in the code could not be treated as firing directives.

The federal trial court in Wyoming held that school employees failed to state a claim under the ADEA or section 1983 when their district awarded early retirement benefits to some, but not all, staff members.[30] The court held that the ADEA was not violated because the benefits had been disbursed according to a negotiated agreement.

A federal district court in New York dismissed ADEA and title VII claims against a supervisor that were filed by a cook who had occasionally served as a child care worker in a special education school. The court ruled that an individual does not qualify as an employer under either statute. Following the lead of four federal circuits, the court agreed that "a supervisor cannot be sued in his or her individual capacity under title VII or the ADEA."[31]

National Origin

The federal district court in Colorado granted a motion by a school system to strike a demand for a jury trial and a request for compensatory damages in an action by one of its employees who alleged that he was suspended because of his race and ethnic origin.[32] The court held that the Civil Rights Act of 1991, which amended title VII to permit compensa-

---

[28] Jackson v. Delta Special Sch. Dist. No. 2, 86 F.3d 1489 [110 EDUC. L. REP. 574] (8th Cir. 1996).

[29] Equal Employment Opportunity Comm'n v. State of Ill., 69 F.3d 167 [104 EDUC. L. REP. 578] (7th Cir. 1995).

[30] Bozner v. Sweetwater County Sch. Dist. No. One, 935 F. Supp. 1230 [112 EDUC. L. REP. 880] (D. Wyo. 1996).

[31] Storr v. Anderson Sch., 919 F. Supp. 144, 146 [108 EDUC. L. REP. 267] (S.D.N.Y. 1996).

[32] Sena v. Denver Sch. Dist. No. 1, 902 F. Supp. 218 [104 EDUC. L. REP. 768] (D. Colo. 1995).

tory damages and a jury trial, could not be applied retroactively where the charges arose before the changes in law went into effect.

Disability

School employees lost all but the last of the four cases reviewed in this section. In Utah, the federal district court ruled that a private school did not violate the association provision of ADA when it decided not to renew the contract of a teacher due to the misconduct of his son who had a bipolar disorder.[33] The child had made serious threats against the headmaster and his family over an extended period. The court found no evidence that the nonrenewal was based on unfounded stereotypes about the son's disorder. The court concluded that the association provision did not protect the son's disability-induced misconduct.

The federal district court in Colorado held that an assessment psychologist who was unable to perform the essential testing functions of her position was not otherwise qualified as disabled under the ADA.[34] Consequently, the court concluded that she was not entitled to a transfer to another position as a regular school psychologist.

In Texas, a federal district court granted a motion by a board of education to dismiss an ADA claim filed by a former employee who inspected schools for asbestos.[35] The worker's employment was terminated due to his alleged disability. The court dropped the claim against district officials in both their individual and official capacities

A teacher who was also a volunteer trainer of helping dogs for the disabled prevailed in her claim that she be permitted to bring an animal that she was working with into her classroom. In affirming a preliminary injunction on behalf of the teacher, the Supreme Court of Nevada noted that as a place of public accommodation under state law, the school owed the same duty of protection to a volunteer as it did to an employee.[36] The court added that where teachers brought pets to class for educational purposes and other schools in the system permitted training dogs in their buildings, the district's refusal to negotiate a compromise solution was unreasonable.

---

[33] Den Hartog v. Wasatch Academy, 909 F. Supp. 1393 [106 EDUC. L. REP. 520] (D. Utah 1995).

[34] Dyer v. Jefferson County Sch. Dist. R-1, 905 F. Supp. 864 [105 EDUC. L. REP. 154] (D. Colo. 1995).

[35] Jenkins v. Board of Educ. of Houston Indep. Sch. Dist., 937 F. Supp. 608 [113 EDUC. L. REP. 142] (S.D. Tex. 1996).

[36] Clark County Sch. Dist. v. Buchanan, 924 P.2d 716 [113 EDUC. L. REP. 930] (Nev. 1996).

Substantive Constitutional Rights

This section not only includes discussions of the First Amendment rights of free speech and association but also examines the constitutional rights of persons who have liberty and property interests that cannot be treated arbitrarily or capriciously by the government. Cases involving the state arise under the Fourteenth Amendment while those concerning the federal government are brought under the Fifth Amendment.

Speech

School employees prevailed in six claims involving free speech. The Eighth Circuit upheld a jury award of approximately $240,000 for humiliation and injury to reputation to a school counselor in Wisconsin whose employment was terminated. It agreed that his articles in a local newspaper on such topics as school-based violations of the open meeting law and sharing household tasks by working couples were on matters of public concern. The court observed that the counselor's " . . . speech was not placed outside [the] orbit of protection by facts that the public was not large, that issues were not of global significance, and that [his] participation was not vital to [the] survival of Western civilization."[37]

A federal district court in Pennsylvania permitted the retaliation claim of an independent bus contractor to proceed.[38] The court found that the contractor had a viable free speech cause of action where his employment was terminated after he criticized the chief executive officer of his service unit for using a former official of the system as a scapegoat.

In a second case from Pennsylvania, teachers successfully challenged a policy that prohibited school employees from engaging in political activities on district property at any time.[39] A federal trial court reasoned that the policy violated the free speech rights of off-duty teachers to solicit votes for candidates at official polling places located on school property.

A federal district court in Virginia held that a teacher had presented a matter of public concern after she was fired for allegedly using a racially derogatory word during a discussion on interracial dating.[40] The court stated the teacher could go to trial to decide whether her dismissal was motivated by retaliation when she exercised her right to protected speech.

---

[37] Dishnow v. School Dist. of Rib Lake, 77 F.3d 194, 197 [107 EDUC. L. REP. 98] (8th Cir. 1996).
[38] Labalokie v. Capitol Area Intermediate Unit, 926 F. Supp. 503 [110 EDUC. L. REP. 146] (M.D. Pa. 1996).
[39] Castle v. Colonial Sch. Dist. 933 F. Supp. 458 [112 EDUC. L. REP. 120] (E.D. Pa. 1996).
[40] Scruggs v. Keen, 900 F. Supp. 821 [104 EDUC. L. REP. 611] (W.D. Va. 1995).

In Wyoming, a special education teacher challenged her being disciplined for violating a district policy that did not allow critical remarks to be made about staff members, administrators, or the school board members, unless the remarks were made directly to the person being criticized. In granting a permanent injunction on behalf of the teacher, the federal district court found not only that the policy was facially over broad and vague but also that it was invalid under the First Amendment as an appropriate time, place, and manner restriction on free speech.[41]

A teacher had partial success in a free speech case not involving a matter of public concern. The Supreme Judicial Court of Massachusetts reversed a grant of summary judgment in favor of a school district.[42] The district suspended the nontenured teacher for two days and later did not renew his contract following a brief classroom discussion with three thirteen-year-old male special education students over vulgar words. The court concluded that since the district violated the teacher's free speech rights, it had to pay him damages and reappoint him for a third year. However, the court refused to order the teacher's further reappointment since, under state law, individuals who successfully complete three years of teaching are entitled to tenure and the court would not make the decision as to whether the teacher would qualify for tenure.

School districts prevailed in five cases where speech was not of public concern or where discipline was for reasons unrelated to speech. The Fifth Circuit upheld the dismissal of a maintenance director in Texas.[43] The court agreed that the director failed to produce evidence that his discharge was motivated by his speech against privatization of his department and records indicated that there was sufficient reason to believe that he had engaged in misconduct.

In a second case from Texas, a federal trial court granted a school district's motion for summary judgment. A coach employed by the district claimed he was reassigned to teaching after he made comments on matters of public concern about expenditures on and abuses of the district tobacco policy.[44] The court held that the coach's free speech rights were not infringed upon and he was reassigned for making a derogatory remark about a former athletic director.

A federal district court in Illinois dismissed the claim of a female coach who was fired for making comments that male colleagues recruited

---

[41] Westbrook v. Teton County Sch. Dist. No. 1, 918 F. Supp. 1475 [108 Educ. L. Rep. 215] (D. Wyo. 1996).

[42] Hosford v. School Comm. of Sandwich, 659 N.E.2d 1178 [106 Educ. L. Rep. 313] (Mass. 1996).

[43] Fowler v. Smith, 68 F.3d 124 [104 Educ. L. Rep. 86] (5th Cir. 1995).

[44] Hill v. Silsbee Indep. Sch. Dist., 933 F. Supp. 616 [112 Educ. L. Rep. 150] (E.D. Tex. 1996).

her players into other sports. It decided that her right to free speech was not violated because her remarks were not on a matter of public concern.[45] However, the court permitted her title VII and equal protection charges to remain intact since there were issues of fact as to whether she had been treated differently from other coaches.

In Pennsylvania, a federal district court held that a teacher did not have a free speech right to use a motivational technique called Learnball in her classroom at an alternative high school for at-risk students.[46] It reasoned that because a classroom is a nonpublic forum, the school board needed only a reasonable basis for banning Learnball as an instructional technique. In addition, the court found that there was no credible evidence supporting the teacher's claim that the board's action was an attempt to stifle her viewpoint.

An appellate panel in New Jersey upheld a ruling that the statutory oath for teachers was constitutional. The court decided that the oath, which requires teachers to support the state and federal constitutions, did not impinge on free speech because both documents assured rights of expression.[47]

Citizens in California successfully challenged a school board policy against making comments at open meetings, including charges or complaints against any district employee, identified or not.[48] In enjoining the enforcement of the policy as a violation of free speech, a federal trial court observed that the interests of the district to prevent the defamation of its employees could not outweigh the right of citizens to express themselves freely to their elected officials at open sessions of board meetings.

Association

A probationary teacher's aide in Alabama unsuccessfully claimed that a board of education violated her First Amendment right to association. An appellate court affirmed that although there was conflicting testimony over why the aide's contract was terminated, there was sufficient evidence that the decision was based on financial reasons rather than on her relationship with a board member.[49]

---

[45] Davis v. McCormick, 898 F. Supp. 1275 [104 Educ. L, Rep. 151] (C.D. Ill. 1995).

[46] Murray v. Pittsburgh Bd. of Pub. Educ., 919 F. Supp. 838 [108 Educ. L. Rep. 593] (W.D. Pa. 1996).

[47] Gough v. State of N.J., 667 A.2d 1057 [105 Educ. L. Rep. 584] (N.J. Super. Ct. App. Div. 1995).

[48] Baca v. Moreno Valley Unified Sch. Dist., 936 F. Supp. 719 [112 Educ. L. Rep. 917] (C.D. Cal. 1996).

[49] Milligan v. Albertville City Bd. of Educ., 661 So. 2d 254 [104 Educ. L. Rep. 526] (Ala. Civ. App. 1995).

In California, an appellate court upheld a school board policy prohibiting district employees from wearing political buttons in instructional settings. The court reasoned that since state support " . . . gives teacher[s] the opportunity and authority to mold young and impressionable minds . . . public school authorities may reasonably conclude it is not possible to both permit instructors to engage in classroom advocacy and at the same time successfully disassociate the school from such advocacy."[50]

Religion

The Ninth Circuit upheld the dismissal of a section 1983 suit filed by the coordinator of the Native American Bilingual Program.[51] The coordinator claimed that religious and racial discrimination led to his dismissal by a county superintendent. The court held that since the superintendent had been sued in his official capacity, he was a state agent who was entitled to immunity under the Eleventh Amendment.

According to the Seventh Circuit, the removal of a teacher's name from a list of approved substitutes in a school district in Indiana did not violate his rights under title VII or the Religious Freedom Restoration Act.[52] The teacher had read from the Bible in front of middle and high school students, distributed biblical pamphlets, and professed his belief in the biblical version of creation to a fifth-grade science class. The court affirmed that the removal of the teacher's name from the list was the least restrictive way to further a compelling governmental interest to avoid the unconstitutional interjection of religion into public school classrooms.

Privacy

A federal district court in Alabama ruled that a county board of education did not conduct an unreasonable search under the Fourth Amendment when it conducted a random drug test of a mechanic's helper who inspected, repaired, and drove school buses. In considering the safety risk to children, the court held that " . . . the [b]oard's intrusion on [the helper's] privacy interests were minimal . . . [and requiring] individual suspicion would severely undercut the utility of the tests."[53]

---

[50] California Teachers Ass'n v. Governing Bd. of San Diego Unified Sch. Dist., 53 Cal. Rptr.2d 474, 479 [109 EDUC. L. REP. 1335] (Cal. Ct. App. 1996).

[51] Eaglesmith v. Ward, 73 F.3d 857 [106 EDUC. L. REP. 104] (9th Cir. 1995).

[52] Helland v. South Bend Community Sch. Corp., 93 F.3d 327 [111 EDUC. L. REP. 1108] (7th Cir. 1996).

[53] English v. Talladega County Bd. of Educ., 938 F. Supp. 775, 783 [113 EDUC. L. REP. 291] (N.D. Ala. 1996).

Substantive Due Process

All four of the cases claiming substantive due process violations were resolved in favor of school districts. In upholding a superintendent's dismissal, an appellate court in Oklahoma found that the superintendent failed to state a prima facie case of a violation of his right to substantive due process.[54] The court pointed out that the superintendent's allegation that board members not only campaigned to terminate his employment but also undertook a campaign to vilify him publicly by making untrue charges failed to specify what claims were allegedly specious, how they were so, and by what authority the claims may have been actionable.

An appellate court in Indiana reversed an award in favor of a teacher who was fired after drinking a pitcher of beer in front of students before driving them home.[55] The former teacher argued that she was treated differently from a colleague who had been given a warning and received a one-year suspension for twice having alcohol on his breath. The court held that the incidents were dissimilar because having alcohol on one's breath did not violate school policy, no students saw the other teacher drink alcohol, and there was no evidence that the other teacher operated a motor vehicle.

In North Carolina, an appellate court upheld the firing of a teacher for immorality despite his claim that the statute used to dismiss him was unconstitutionally vague.[56] The court concluded that any reasonable public school teacher of ordinary intelligence would understand that approaching a crowded pool room with a loaded shot gun and violent intent, as the teacher had done, would place one's professional position in jeopardy.

Three teachers in Alabama who faced disciplinary action and the possible revocation of their teaching licenses unsuccessfully claimed that statutory grounds of immoral conduct and unbecoming behavior were constitutionally vague.[57] The federal district court reasoned that the statute did not violate due process as long as the superintendent or others enforcing the law related its terms to fitness to teach.

Procedural Due Process

Except in emergency suspensions with pay, the United States Constitution mandates that procedural due process must be followed before

---

[54] Hoerman v. Western Heights Bd. of Educ., 913 P.2d 684 [108 EDUC. L. REP. 395] (Okla. Ct. App. 1995).
[55] Dickson v. Aaron, 667 N.E.2d 759 [111 EDUC. L. REP. 475] (Ind. Ct. App. 1996).
[56] Barringer v. Caldwell County Bd. of Educ., 473 S.E.2d 435 [111 EDUC. L. REP. 994] (N.C. Ct. App. 1996).
[57] Alford v. Ingram, 931 F. Supp 768 [111 EDUC L. REP. 793] (M.D. Ala. 1996).

adverse employment actions can be taken against personnel who have liberty and property interests in their jobs.[58] Although the type of due process varies depending upon the nature and severity of the anticipated consequences, its essence is notice and a fair opportunity to respond to the charges.

Liberty and Property Interests

The first two actions in this section, both won by school districts, illustrate that liberty and property interests can be involved in the same case. According to an appellate court in Colorado, placing permanent letters of reprimand in the personnel file of a middle school assistant principal did not implicate liberty interests. The court denied the principal's claim because he failed to allege specifically how his professional status had been affected by the letters. The court found that the principal's interest in his good name did not impinge upon his property interest in continued employment[59].

Similarly, in upholding the dismissal of a school district cleaner who had an unclassified, at will position, an appellate court in New York found that he did not have a property interest that entitled him to pre-termination or post-termination hearings. Likewise, the court maintained that the cleaner did not have a liberty interest claim because there had been "no public disclosure of any allegations affecting [his] good name or reputation."[60]

A school district prevailed in only the first of four cases implicating liberty interests. A federal district court in New York granted a motion by a school board for judgment in a case filed by a former nontenured teacher.[61] The court found that since the teacher failed to challenge the substantial truth of her attendance record on which her dismissal was based, she lacked a liberty interest and a name-clearing hearing was not required.

The Second Circuit reversed in holding that the dismissal of an assistant principal in New York implicated her liberty interests.[62] The assistant principal received strongly negative evaluations in the areas of discipline, staff relations, educational and instructional supervision,

---

[58] *See* Cleveland Bd. of Educ. v. Loudermill, 470 U.S. 532 [23 Educ. L. Rep. 473] (1985).

[59] Perez v. Denver Pub. Sch., 919 P.2d 960 [111 Educ. L. Rep. 537] (Colo. Ct. App. 1996).

[60] Macina v. North Salem Cent. Sch. Dist., 633 N.Y.S.2d 596, 597 [104 Educ. L. Rep. 1273] (N.Y. App. Div. 1995).

[61] Cohen v. Litt, 906 F. Supp. 957 [105 Educ. L. Rep. 515] (S.D.N.Y. 1995).

[62] Donata v. Plainview-Old Bethpage Cent. Sch. Dist., 96 F.3d 623 [112 Educ. L. Rep. 624] (2d Cir. 1996).

administrative responsibilities and leadership. The court stated that the comments were so harsh that they would be likely to persuade other school boards not to hire her as a supervisor. The court also found that the evaluations were publicized by being placed in the assistant principal's personnel file. The court concluded that putting stigmatizing charges in the personnel file warranted a name-clearing hearing because the records were likely to be disclosed to prospective employers.

A trial court in New York found that the liberty interest of a former Director of Operations was violated.[63] The Director was discharged after the release of a report that suggested he had mismanaged funds. The court offered that since the Director was fired due to allegations that placed his name, reputation, honor and integrity at stake, he was entitled to a name-clearing hearing.

In a case of first impression from Illinois, an appellate court decided that administrative procedures used to place the names of persons suspected of child abuse on a state register violated due process. The court ruled that the Department of Children and Family Services (DCFS) violated a teacher's liberty interest when it failed to conduct a hearing and render a timely decision following a finding that he sexually abused a student.[64] Moreover, the court posited that the statutory standard of credible evidence was constitutionally infirm. The court was of the opinion that since a finding of child abuse indicated in the register may deprive a teacher of his right to work and cause great damage to his reputation, DCFS was obligated to prove its case by a preponderance of the evidence.

Five courts found that school employees lacked property interests. The Eighth Circuit upheld the dismissal of a principal in Arkansas when it found that the Teacher Fair Dismissal Act did not create a constitutionally protected property interest in the renewal of the former administrator's contract.[65]

In New York, a federal district court decided that the due process rights of a former school nurse who was employed under an at-will contract were not violated.[66] The court found that the nurse did not have a cognizable property interest in her employment, that no property interest was created by a collective bargaining agreement, and that the school district satisfied all due process requirements.

---

[63] Okebiyi v. Cortines, 641 N.Y.S.2d 791 [109 Educ. L. Rep. 334] (N. Y. Sup. Ct. 1996).
[64] Cavarreta v. Department of Children and Family Servs., 660 N.E.2d 250 [106 Educ. L. Rep. 834] (Ill. App. Ct. 1996).
[65] Piggee v. Jones, 84 F.3d 303 [109 Educ. L. Rep. 622] (8th Cir. 1996).
[66] Recchia-Hansemann v. BOCES, 901 F. Supp. 107 [104 Educ. L. Rep. 670] (E.D.N.Y. 1995).

Based on state law, a federal district court in Mississippi granted a motion for summary judgment for a school board.[67] The board did not renew the contract of a librarian who slapped a student. The court observed that because the law did not require the board to demonstrate good cause in the nonrenewal of a contract, the librarian did not have a property interest in her job that would have entitled her to a hearing.

In Alabama, an appellate court upheld the denial of a probationary teacher's request for a writ of mandamus ordering her reinstatement.[68] The court agreed that since probationary teachers in the state do not have a property interest entitling them to contract renewal, the writ could not be granted.

An appellate court in Arizona affirmed that under state law, nontenured teachers and administrators do not have a property right in continued employment.[69] When a nontenured administrator was offered a teaching position, the court found that the nonrenewal of her contract and her reassignment to a classroom did not implicate a property interest.

Aspects of Notice

All four courts that addressed the issue of notice were satisfied that the rights of school employees were not violated. In interpreting the leading case of *Cleveland Board of Education v. Loudermill*,[70] the federal district court for Puerto Rico decided that a teacher who had been relieved of her duties and had her certificate suspended had received appropriate pretermination procedures.[71] It found that *Loudermill* does not require a person to have advanced knowledge of all charges since notice and the opportunity to respond can be provided concurrently. The court added that either oral or written notice is acceptable under *Loudermill*.

The Supreme Court of Mississippi affirmed the dismissal of a teacher despite her claims of lack of notice.[72] The court ruled that under state law, once the teacher insisted on a hearing, she waived any defect in the notice of her dismissal.

In Missouri, a federal district court upheld the termination of a tenured teacher's contract even though he claimed that he was not properly notified because the suspension letter he received prior to his hearing did

---

[67] Pruett v. Dumas, 914 F. Supp. 133 [107 EDUC. L. REP. 120] (N.D. Miss. 1996).

[68] Lawrence v. Birmingham Bd. of Educ., 669 So. 2d 910 [108 EDUC. L. REP. 455] (Ala. Civ. Ct. App. 1995).

[69] Wallace v. Casa Grande Union High Sch. Dist. No. 82 Bd. of Governors, 909 P.2d 486 [106 EDUC. L. REP. 352] (Ariz. Ct. App. 1995).

[70] 470 U.S. 532 [23 EDUC. L. REP. 473](1985).

[71] Reyes-Pagan v. Benitez, 910 F. Supp. 38 [106 EDUC. L. REP. 546] (D.P.R. 1995).

[72] Young v. Jefferson Davis County Sch. Bd., 672 So. 2d 1219 [109 EDUC. L. REP. 515] (Miss. 1996).

not state a right to counsel.[73] The court observed that the teacher had been notified orally and could have had an attorney present before discussing his alleged inappropriate disciplining of students.

Pursuant to state law, an appellate court in California affirmed that a principal's right to notice was not violated when he was transferred to another building.[74] In upholding the denial of a writ of mandate for reinstatement, the court held that the statute applied only to discharge or demotions.

Aspects of Hearing

Failure to conduct a hearing may be appropriate in some situations, but not in others. For example, in affirming the nonrenewal of a teacher's contract in North Dakota, the Eighth Circuit found that a pretermination hearing satisfied due process even though the board did not produce any witnesses to substantiate its action and the principal allegedly relied on hearsay evidence in recommending the nonrenewal.[75]

An appellate court in Minnesota agreed that placing a teacher on partial medical leave did not trigger her due process right to a hearing.[76] The court noted that since the district's action was neither a discharge nor a demotion, a hearing was not required.

On the other hand, an appellate court in Pennsylvania reversed in favor of a Director of Data Processing who was denied a hearing because the board deemed itself biased.[77] The court ruled that even though the Director allegedly had an affair with a board member, the entire board could determine its ability to be impartial only after a hearing on the record. The court concluded that an alternate resolution process should be used only if the record demonstrated bias or impartiality.

In Texas, an appellate court affirmed that a teacher was not entitled to a hearing before the school board over the nonrenewal of her contract.[78] The court found that the teacher's right to due process was not violated since she had two hearings, one on the issue of bias and the other on her deficiencies as a teacher. The court added that the teacher

---

[73] Clark v. Board of Dirs. of Sch. Dist. of Kansas City, 915 S.W.2d 766 [107 Educ. L. Rep. 368] (Mo. Ct. App. 1996).

[74] Gilliam v. Moreno Valley Unified Sch. Dist., 55 Cal Rptr 2d 695 [111 Educ. L. Rep 919] (Cal. Ct. App. 1996).

[75] Flath v. Garrison Pub. Sch. Dist. No. 51, 82 F.3d 244 [108 Educ. L. Rep. 1113] (8th Cir. 1996).

[76] Palmer v. Independent Sch. Dist. No. 917, 547 N.W.2d 899 [109 Educ. L. Rep. 941] (Minn. Ct. App. 1996).

[77] Foster v. Board of Sch. Directors of Keystone Oaks Sch. Dist., 678 A.2d 1214 [111 Educ. L. Rep. 350] (Pa. Commw. Ct. 1996).

[78] Gilder v. Meno, 926 S.W.2d 357 [111 Educ. L. Rep. 1031] (Tex. Ct. App. 1996)

had been represented by counsel at both hearings and chose not to present any evidence herself or through witnesses at either one.

Dismissal, Nonrenewal, Demotion, and Discipline

Issues in this area include judicial intervention and exhaustion of remedies, immunity, arbitrary and capricious behavior, and burden of proof. In the first of two federal cases from New York, a district court refused to reinstate a superintendent's salary and benefits pending a disciplinary hearing. Under the abstention doctrine of *Younger v. Harris*,[79] the court stayed the superintendent's claims for monetary damages until state proceedings were completed.[80]

The same federal district court in New York held that members of the disciplinary hearing panel that suspended a teacher for misconduct and insubordination were performing a judicial function.[81] As such, it found that panel members were entitled to absolute immunity from a section 1983 claim.

The Supreme Court of Alaska partially reversed in favor of a former Reserve Officer Training Corps instructor who was dismissed for the alleged sexual abuse of students even though he had not exhausted contractual remedies.[82] The court reasoned that since the board that suspended the teacher without pay was also the body to whom an appeal of last resort would have been made the grievance process was futile.

The Supreme Court of Idaho upheld an award in favor of a teacher who was dismissed for furnishing a court with information during a sentencing hearing.[83] The court concluded that the superintendent violated public policy in punishing the teacher for providing information that led to a reduced sentence for a convicted felon.

In upholding a decision by a school board to transfer a teacher, an appellate court in Maryland affirmed that the teacher was not entitled to a full evidentiary hearing because the transfer was neither arbitrary nor capricious.[84] The court pointed out that the teacher failed to identify any

---

[79] 401 U.S. 37 (1971).
[80] Pinckney v. Board of Educ. of the Westbury Union Free Sch. Dist., 920 F. Supp. 393 [108 EDUC. L. REP. 664] (E.D.N.Y. 1996).
[81] Taylor v. Brentwood Union Free Sch. Dist., 908 F. Supp. 1165 [106 EDUC. L. REP. 108] (E.D.N.Y. 1995).
[82] Romulus v. Anchorage Sch. Dist., 910 P.2d 610 [106 EDUC. L. REP. 1332] (Alaska 1996).
[83] Hummer v. Evans, 923 P.2d 981 [113 EDUC. L. REP. 452] (Idaho 1996).
[84] Hurl v. Board of Educ. of Howard County, 667 A.970 [105 EDUC. L. REP. 565] (Md. Ct. Spec. App. 1995).

specific facts to support her claim that the superintendent had singled her out unjustly.

An appellate court in Florida reversed and remanded a school board's decision to terminate the employment of a teacher for allegedly sexually abusing his daughter.[85] The court maintained that pursuant to state law, the board had to prove the grounds for dismissal by a preponderance of evidence.

Similarly, an appeals court in Michigan reversed the termination of a teacher's contract for allegedly using excessive force because the board failed to produce substantial and material evidence of a violation of the corporal punishment statute.[86]

Other issues involving discipline related to access to records, adequate notice of charges, and justifiable causes of action. The Supreme Court of Wisconsin reversed an earlier ruling and held that all disciplinary or personnel records of public employees are subject to the state's open records law.[87] At the same time, the court affirmed that since a letter to a school district from its attorney fell within the scope of the attorney-client privilege, access to it was properly denied.

In New York, an appellate court confirmed a ruling that a teacher was not prejudiced by the inclusion of additional charges at a hearing.[88] The hearing was conducted by the board of education over an allegation that the teacher had altered student answer sheets on a Regents examination. The court reasoned that the modified charge was acceptable because it did not differ significantly from the original one.

An appellate court in Louisiana affirmed that a principal who voluntarily resigned without coercion could not sue for wrongful termination. The court was of the opinion that the principal's voluntary resignation and retirement, even though undertaken without consulting an attorney, rendered his cause of action moot.[89]

Insubordination

Courts are frequently divided on issues concerning employee conduct that constitutes insubordination and school district assessments of

[85] Sublett v. Sumter County Sch. Bd., 664 So. 2d 1178 [105 EDUC. L. REP. 1339] (Fla. Dist. Ct. App. 1995).
[86] Widdoes v. Detroit Pub. Sch., 553 N.W.2d 688 [113 EDUC. L. REP. 432] (Mich. Ct. App. 1996).
[87] Wisconsin Newspress v. School Dist. of Sheboygan Falls, 546 N.W.2d 143 [108 EDUC. L. REP. 922] (Wis. 1996).
[88] Wohlleb v. Board of Educ. of Bridgehampton Union Free Sch. Dist., 647 N.Y.S.2d 801 [113 EDUC. L. REP. 383] (N.Y. App. Div. 1996).
[89] Smith v. Evangeline Parish Sch. Bd., 663 So. 2d 281 [105 EDUC. L. REP. 353] (La. Ct. App. 1995).

appropriate penalties. For example, an appellate court in Illinois found that a teacher who refused to request an unpaid medical leave of absence to determine her psychological fitness to continue teaching was not insubordinate.[90] The court agreed that the teacher could ignore an order by the board of education to take unpaid leave and wait for a dismissal hearing at which she could defend herself.

Similarly, an appellate court in New York reversed the dismissal of a bus driver for insubordination following physical contact with students.[91] The court found that the penalty was disproportionate in light of the driver's above average overall performance evaluations.

On the other hand, another appellate court in New York upheld the two-year suspension of a faculty member for insubordination and conduct unbecoming a teacher.[92] The court observed that the penalty was not disproportionate where the teacher failed to use the established system of grading her pupils' Regents examinations and communicated test answers to three students.

The Supreme Court of Mississippi upheld the nonrenewal of a high school principal's contract for insubordination.[93] The court found that the superintendent was the appropriate person to give the principal his notice of nonrenewal. It added that the principal had been informed in advance of the statutory deadline.

Unprofessional Conduct, Unfitness, Willful Neglect of Duty

Conduct related to medical certification and sick leave was the subject of two cases from New York involving school bus drivers. In the first, an appellate court upheld the discharge of a driver for misrepresenting the extent of her disability and for continuing sick leave when she was no longer disabled.[94] The court noted that surveillance tapes depicted the driver playing golf while she was supposedly disabled.

Similarly, a trial court in New York confirmed the suspension of a driver for failing to obtain medical certification of his fitness to operate a bus.[95] The court determined that the driver had unilaterally discontinued

---

[90] Board of Educ. of City of Chicago v. Weed, 667 N.E.2d 627 [111 Educ. L. Rep. 1306] (Ill. App. Ct. 1996).

[91] Smith v. Board of Educ., Onteora Cent. Sch. Dist., 633 N.Y.S.2d 625 [104 Educ. L. Rep. 1279] (N.Y. App. Div. 1995).

[92] Earles v. Pine Bush Cent. Sch. Dist., 638 N.Y.S.2d 163 [107 Educ. L Rep. 252] (N.Y. App. Div. 1996).

[93] Ford v. Holly Springs Sch. Dist., 665 So. 2d 840 [105 Educ. L. Rep. 1374] (Miss. 1995).

[94] D'Aurizio v. Greece Cent. Sch. Dist., 645 N.Y.S.2d 363 [111 Educ. L. Rep. 450] (N.Y. App. Div. 1996).

[95] Marcottte v. Corinth Cent. Sch. Dist., 635 N.Y.S.2d 1021 [106 Educ. L. Rep. 287] (N.Y. Sup. Ct. 1995).

his participation in a six month counseling/rehabilitation program for alcoholismeven though it was a condition for his continued employment.

Another issue is the relationship between an employee's conduct and how a school system imposes an appropriate penalty. An appellate court in Florida reversed a seventeen month suspension, without pay, of an employee who brandished a pocket knife to a fellow worker in a joking manner.[96] The court found that the conduct was not unbecoming a board employee because there was no dispute that he was joking and neither he nor or his fellow worker took the act seriously.

The use of vulgar words or profanity also can be the subject of litigation. A federal district court in Missouri ordered the reinstatement, with full back pay and attorneys fees, of a teacher who permitted her students to use profanity in creative activities where such language was part of the assigned class materials.[97] The court found that since teachers did not clearly understand the district policy regarding profanity in course materials, her conduct did not constitute willful violation of school board regulations.

In Louisiana, an appellate court upheld the termination, without remediation, of a tenured teacher's contract.[98] The teacher had read a narrative with sexually suggestive words to her seventh-grade class. The court maintained that while remediation is necessary prior to dismissal for incompetence, it is not required for willful neglect of duty.

An appellate court in Illinois upheld the termination of a tenured teacher's contract for unsatisfactory performance under a remedial plan.[99] It observed that the teacher admitted to his lack of having the defined standard for student assessment and could not produce legible records of their performance. The court added that the teacher's evaluations during the remediation period mirrored his earlier unsatisfactory performance and his deficiencies correlated directly with his inability to do his job.

In Alabama, an appellate court upheld the cancellation of the contact of a teacher with twenty-six years of experience after he slapped female students who had been involved in an altercation.[100] The court acknowl-

---

[96] Collins v. School Bd. of Dade County, 676 So. 2d 1052 [111 Educ. L. Rep. 599] (Fla. Dist. Ct. App. 1996).

[97] Lacks v. Ferguson Reorganized Sch. Dist., 936 F. Supp. 676 [112 Educ. L. Rep. 907] (E.D. Mo. 1996).

[98] Williams v. Concordia Parish Sch. Bd., 670 So. 2d 351 [108 Educ. L. Rep. 466] (La. Ct. App. 1996).

[99] Davis v. Board of Educ. of Chicago, 659 N.E.2d 86 [105 Educ L. Rep. 1175] (Ill. App. Ct. 1995).

[100] Alabama State Tenure Comm'n v. Morrow, 662 So.2d 284 [104 Educ. L. Rep. 957] (Ala. Civ. App. 1995).

edged that the board's action to cancel the contract was permissible because it was not against the overwhelming weight of the evidence.

Immorality

Four of the five decisions in this section supported the efforts of districts to discipline or terminate the contracts of employees who engaged in immorality, a concept that can include behavior either on or off of school premises. In the first of two cases from Missouri, an appellate court upheld the revocation of an educator's teaching certificate after she engaged in sexually explicit conversations with some of her students. The court, in reversing an earlier decision in favor of the teacher, agreed that the state law required intent to harm students in immorality. Even so, the court found that intent was unnecessary here because the state licensing board had presented proof of immorality and " . . . condon[ing] the teacher's conduct . . . would thwart the protections to which these children are entitled."[101]

The second case from Missouri involved a teacher who shot her estranged husband's girlfriend. An appellate court in Missouri agreed that the teacher's behavior constituted immoral conduct and supported the school board's finding that she was unfit to teach.[102]

An appellate court in Pennsylvania upheld the dismissal of a tenured teacher who pled guilty to trafficking in counterfeit goods and services.[103] The court found that his federal conviction warranted the termination of his employment.

In Louisiana, an appellate court affirmed the dismissal of a tenured bus driver who had been convicted of attempted obscenity.[104] It reasoned that because the driver's action was prohibited by state statute, the decision to dismiss the driver was justified.

A case in Ohio dealing with behavior modification and discipline of multihandicapped children was decided in favor of the teacher.[105] An appellate court found that since placing hot sauce in a student's mouth, tipping a student backwards while strapped to a chair, and putting a towel over a student's head neither violated school board rules nor harmed any of the students, the teacher's employment should not have been terminated.

---

[101] Howard v. Missouri State Bd. of Educ., 913 S.W.2d 887, 893 [106 Educ. L. Rep. 942] (Mo. Ct. App. 1995).

[102] In re Thomas, 926 S.W.2d 163 [111 Educ. L. Rep. 1023] (Mo. Ct. App. 1996).

[103] Kinniry v. Abington Sch. Dist., 673 A.2d 429 [108 Educ. L. Rep. 312] (Pa. Commw. Ct. 1996).

[104] Allo v. Horne, 672 So. 2d 961 [109 Educ. L. Rep. 504] (La. Ct. App. 1996).

[105] James v. Trumbull County Bd. of Educ., 663 N.E.2d 1361 [109 Educ. L. Rep. 349] (Ohio Ct. App. 1995).

Incompetence

Incompetence necessarily relates to an employee's performance on the job. In one case, the Supreme Court of Mississippi reversed in favor of a school board in finding that a teacher's decision to show the movie, *Silence of the Lambs*, to students under seventeen constituted misconduct.[106] The court pointed out that the teacher disregarded an earlier warning from his principal that films needed to relate to subject matter. The court also found the teacher ineligible for unemployment compensation.

A school secretary in New York unsuccessfully sought to regain her job after being dismissed for making false entries on her time sheets. An appellate court confirmed that the school district had evidence to support its dismissal of the secretary, and the actions of the board were not so disproportionate as to shock one's conscience.[107]

In Missouri, an appellate court upheld the firing of a tenured teacher where there were numerous complaints about disruptions in her classroom.[108] The court rejected the teacher's argument that the district caused the disorder by putting together a class of twenty-six boys and six girls.

One ruling on behalf of a school administrator examined facts in light of a definition of incompetence. An appellate court in Nebraska reversed the cancellation of a superintendent's contract by a school board because evidence failed to substantiate incompetence or neglect of duty.[109] Even though the superintendent was a probationary certificated employee, the court found that he was entitled to a showing of specific grounds before his contract could be canceled. The court added that such conduct as errors in draft budget documents and missing the filing deadline for a Chapter I application did not meet the standard for termination.

Compliance with Board Policies and State Statutes

In the first of four cases where employees prevailed because supervisors did not follow statutory requirements, the Supreme Court of Ohio reversed in favor of a teacher whose board decided not to award her a continuing contract after two evaluations.[110] The court held that the

---

[106] Mississippi Employment Security Comm'n v. Harris, 672 So. 2d 739 [109 EDUC. L. REP. 498] (Miss. 1996).
[107] Roach v. Plainedge Union Free Sch. Dist., 646 N.Y.S.2d 704 [112 EDUC. L. REP. 417] (N.Y. App. Div. 1996).
[108] Newcomb v. Humansville R-IV Sch. Dist., 908 S.W.2d 821 [104 EDUC. L. REP. 928] (Mo. Ct. App. 1995).
[109] Boss v. Fillmore County Sch. Dist. No. 19, 548 N.W.2d 1 [109 EDUC. L. REP. 949] (Neb. Ct. App. 1996).
[110] Snyder v. Mendon-Union Local Sch. Dist. Bd. of Educ., 661 N.E.2d 717 [107 EDUC. L. REP. 268] (Ohio 1996).

state law, which required four classroom observations of at least thirty minutes each, rather than the terms of the operative collective bargaining agreement, which called for only two evaluations, controlled. The court found that the district failed to conduct the correct number of evaluations.

The Supreme Court of Arkansas reversed in favor of a high school teacher whose contract was terminated for using inappropriate language in class.[111] It found that the teacher's letter asking for a hearing before the board as soon as possible did not waive the five to ten-day period required by law between the request and the hearing. The court held that the board violated the statute when it conducted the hearing four days after the request.

An appeals court in Illinois reversed in favor of a teacher who was dismissed as the principal did not provide her with an evaluation required under state statute.[112] The court found that the principal failed to complete the evaluation review form of a remediation plan that the teacher had been following.

In a case in Texas involving the Term Contract Nonrenewal Act, an appellate court reversed the nonrenewal of a teacher's contract.[113] The court ruled that the board failed to review any of the teacher's written evaluations prior to making its decision. The court stated that this failure clearly violated the Act and was evidence of a predetermination not to renew the teacher's contract prior to a hearing.

As illustrated by a case from the Tenth Circuit, school board charges over employee conduct must comply with state law.[114] The court reversed the nonrenewal of a teacher's contract which contained a provision waiving due process protections under Oklahoma statute. It decided that language in the contract, permitting her summary removal, violated due process protections designed to prevent the removal of capable and experienced educators based solely on political or personal whims.

In New York, an appellate court reversed the twenty-day suspension of a school bus driver for misconduct and/or incompetence because the board of education failed to present substantial evidence of a statutory violation.[115] The court observed that the driver's expert testimony that a

---

[111] Lester v. Mount Vernon-Enola Sch. Dist., 917 S.W.2d 540 [108 Educ. L. Rep. 438] (Ark. 1996).

[112] Chicago Bd. of Educ. v. Smith, 664 N.E.2d 113 [109 Educ. L. Rep. 863] (Ill. App. Ct. 1996).

[113] Wilmer-Hutchins Indep. Sch. Dist. v. Brown, 912 S.W.2d 848 [106 Educ. L. Rep. 408] (Tex. Ct. App. 1996).

[114] Parker v. Independent Sch. Dist. No. 1-003 of Okmulgee County, Okla., 82 F.3d 952 [109 Educ. L. Rep. 45] (10th Cir. 1996).

[115] DeVito v. Leone, 639 N.Y.S.2d 223 [107 Educ. L. Rep. 956] (N.Y. App. Div. 1996).

railroad guard arm descended and hit the top of her bus may have resulted from a malfunction of the guard and was sufficient to offset the charges made by the board.

Compliance issues can be tied to certification. For example, an appellate court in Texas reversed a grant of summary judgment in favor of a school district that dismissed an English as a Second Language (ESL) teacher who failed to complete her certification.[116] The court reasoned that the teacher's other certification entitled her to due process under state law.

The Supreme Court of Arkansas reversed in favor of a teacher whose employment as a part-time, long-term substitute was terminated without notice.[117] The court found that since the teacher was required to have a valid teaching certificate, she met the criteria under the Fair Dismissal Act entitling her to notice of nonrenewal.

One case in which a teacher prevailed addressed a question of suspension with pay. A trial court in New York upheld a state statute that required school boards to pay suspended teachers their full salaries while proceedings were pending.[118] In so doing, it rejected a state constitutional claim that payment of salary and benefits was an improper gift of public monies. The court also dismissed a federal constitutional charge that such payment impaired a collective bargaining agreement with the teachers under Article I, section 10.

A second case from New York reiterated the importance of specific statutory requirements regarding causes of action and limits on claims. An appellate court affirmed in favor of a school system where a former employee had not challenged the termination of her contract within the statutory four month period.[119] The court agreed that the appeal lacked merit because the employee failed to demonstrate the existence of fraud, misrepresentation, or deception which induced her to refrain from challenging her termination in a timely manner

In Utah, a provisional teacher alleged that the guidelines of the Educator Evaluation Act (EEA), which established procedures for provisional teachers, were not followed.[120] An appellate court found that the EEA did not give the teacher a private right of action to enforce its provision.

---

[116] Carrillo v. Anthony Indep. Sch. Dist., 921 S.W.2d 800 [109 EDUC. L. REP. 1007] (Tex. Ct. App. 1996).

[117] Love v. Smackover Sch. Dist., 907 S.W.2d 136 [104 EDUC. L. REP. 513] (Ark. 1995).

[118] Brady v. A Certain Teacher, 632 N.Y.S.2d 418 [104 EDUC. L. REP. 459] (N.Y. Sup. Ct. 1995).

[119] Vanmaenen v. Hewlett-Woodmere Pub. Sch., 640 N.Y.S.2d 95 [108 EDUC. L. REP. 841] (N.Y. App. Div. 1996).

[120] Broadbent v. Board of Educ. of Cache County Sch. Dist., 910 P.2d 1274 [106 EDUC. L. REP. 1373] (Utah Ct. App. 1996).

Further, in upholding the teacher's dismissal, the court reasoned that the EEA had not altered her employment status and that the school board could decide not to renew her contract with any or no reason.

An appellate court in Connecticut affirmed in favor of a board of education in a dispute with a teacher whose contract was not renewed.[121] The court held that since the teacher failed to challenge her nonrenewal, the Teacher Tenure Act precluded her from bringing a separate action to dispute the board's allegedly wrongful conduct.

Statutory requirements concerning evaluations also have been litigated. For example, an appellate court in Indiana found that a principal complied with a state law that required him to provide a written evaluation of a nonpermanent teacher before January 1.[122] In upholding the dismissal, the court determined that the teacher failed to invoke her statutory right to additional observations by the principal by simply making a notation to that effect on the evaluation form.

In a second case from Indiana, the same court affirmed the denial of a nonpermanent teacher's request for reinstatement even though she had not been provided with her statutory right to a conference prior to her dismissal.[123] The court decided that the appropriate remedy was a remand for a conference rather than the teacher's reinstatement.

As illustrated by a case from California, state law can relate to a reduction in hours and the need for a hearing. An appellate court upheld the reduction of hours of two teachers when it reasoned that they were not entitled to statutory notice and an opportunity for a hearing because they were not subject to a partial termination as defined by state law.[124]

Compliance with state notice requirements can become an issue. In Texas, a teacher received oral notice that her superintendent was recommending the nonrenewal of her contract.[125] However, the school board minutes were silent concerning the recommendation of her nonrenewal. In upholding the nonrenewal of the contract, an appellate court in Texas ruled that the oral notice was admissible as parol evidence, and that where minutes are silent, parol evidence could be used to prove compliance with state law.

---

[121] Drahan v. Board of Educ. of Regional Sch. Dist. No. 18, 680 A.2d 316 [111 EDUC. L. REP. 1237] (Conn. Ct. App. 1996).

[122] Vukovits v. Board of Sch. Trustees of the Rockville Community Sch. Corp., 659 N.E.2d 174 [105 EDUC. L. REP. 1214] (Ind. Ct. App. 1995).

[123] Lewis v. Board of Sch. Trustees of Charles A. Beard Memorial Sch. Corp., 657 N.E.2d 180 [104 EDUC. L. REP. 1294] (Ind. Ct. App. 1995).

[124] Black v. Board of Trustees of Compton Unified Sch. Dist., 54 Cal. Rptr.2d 140 [110 EDUC. L. REP. 263] (Cal. Ct. App. 1996).

[125] Hext v. Central Educ. Agency, 909 S.W.2d 252 [104 EDUC. L. REP. 946] (Tex. Ct. App. 1995).

An appellate court in Missouri upheld the dismissal of a teacher who alleged that she had not received the statutory one semester notice of charges.[126] The court agreed that the eighteen week notice that the teacher received satisfied the law because it was equivalent to one semester.

Compliance with state law can relate to an individual's expectation of employment. The Supreme Judicial Court of Massachusetts affirmed that the statute governing the employment of teachers who served as coaches permitted the termination of their athletic contracts for reasons other than good cause.[127] In upholding the nonrenewal of a teacher's athletic contract, the court reasoned that state law permitted coaches to sign stipendiary contracts not to exceed three years that were readily terminable upon their expiration.

The Supreme Court of Ohio upheld the rejection of a mandamus claim filed by a superintendent whose contract was not renewed.[128] The court offered that even though the school board failed to provide timely notice of nonrenewal as required by its own evaluation procedures, the former superintendent still had not established a clear right to re-employment.

An appellate court in Louisiana affirmed a school district's decision not to appoint a probationary bus driver with seniority to a route that was not chosen by any of its tenured drivers.[129] The court found that state law granted districts discretion in assigning routes among probationary bus drivers.

State law governs the standard for appropriate conduct. An appellate court in Florida upheld a teacher's suspension despite the failure of the school board to make a statutorily mandated finding that his conduct impaired his effectiveness.[130] The court maintained that the record clearly showed the teacher's conduct impaired his effectiveness.

In Ohio, an appellate court affirmed the dismissal of a custodian who had been convicted of public indecency.[131] The court based its decision on a state statute that prohibits a board of education from employing an individual who is responsible for the care, custody, or control of a child if the person has been convicted of certain offenses, one of which is

---

[126] Soward v. Mahan, 926 S.W.2d 138 [111 Educ. L. Rep. 1017] (Mo. Ct. App. 1996).

[127] School Comm. of Natick v. Education Ass'n of Natick, 666 N.E.2d 486 [110 Educ. L. Rep. 784] (Mass. 1996).

[128] State *ex rel.* Stiller v. Columbiana Exempted Village Sch. Dist. Bd. of Educ., 656 N.E.2d 679 [104 Educ. L. Rep. 475] (Ohio 1995).

[129] Huszar v. Tangipahoa Parish Sch. Bd., 681 So.2d 60 [113 Educ. L. Rep. 1021] (La. Ct. App. 1996).

[130] Summers v. School Bd. of Marion County, 666 So.2d 175 [106 Educ. L. Rep. 442] (Fla. Dist. Ct. App. 1996).

[131] Prete v. Akron City Sch. Dist. Bd. of Educ., 667 N.W.2d 73 [110 Educ. L. Rep. 1226] (Ohio Ct. App. 1995).

public indecency. The court concluded that since the custodian had regular contact with children, and had been convicted of public indecency, he could be dismissed.

Professional employees unsuccessfully sought further review of their suspensions after a district moved an elementary school into the same building as a middle and high school. The school was then able to change the schedules of certain staff members, thereby reducing the number of professional staff needed. An appellate court in Pennsylvania ruled that the consolidation constituted a statutory cause justifying the suspensions.[132]

An appellate court in New York upheld the discharge of a bus driver for speeding while on duty even though she had already signed an agreement consenting to a twenty-day suspension.[133] The court stated that the action of the board was justified because the driver had been warned prior to signing the agreement that she could be subject to an additional penalty.

In Kansas, an appellate court affirmed the dismissal of a tenured teacher for failing to provide an orderly learning environment.[134] The court found that the board had substantial evidence constituting good cause for acting as it did.

Reduction-in-force and
Involuntary Leaves of Absence

Reorganization or consolidation of a school system, declining enrollment, or fiscal restraints may require a board to institute a reduction-in-force (RIF). As illustrated in the cases in this section, the sufficiency of the reasons for a RIF, which employees are to be laid off, the realignment or reassignment of staff members, and call-back rights are ordinarily governed by state tenure statutes, local board policies, and collective bargaining agreements.

In California, an appellate court ruled that restructuring to accommodate budget reductions does not necessarily constitute a RIF.[135] The court upheld the restructuring of a psychological services program of a

[132] Bricillo v. Duquesne City Sch. Dist., 668 A.2d 629 [105 Educ. L. Rep. 1121] (Pa. Commw. Ct. 1995).
[133] Herbison v. Board of Educ. of Carmel Cent. Sch. Dist., 638 N.Y.S.2d 678 [107 Educ. L. Rep. 926] (N.Y. App. Div. 1996).
[134] Unified Sch. Dist. No. 500, Kansas City, Wyandotte County v. Robinson, 924 P.2d 651 [113 Educ. L. Rep. 920] (Kan. Ct. App. 1996).
[135] Gallup v. Alta Loma Sch. Dist. Bd. of Trustees, 49 Cal. Rptr. 289 [106 Educ. L. Rep. 266] (Cal. Ct. App. 1996).

school district even though three elementary school psychologists were replaced by an administrative psychologist and independent psychologists. In overruling a mandamus order to reinstate the psychologists, the panel reasoned that the state's economic layoff statute was inapplicable since it did not require services to be provided in only one way.

Necessity for Reduction-in-force

The Supreme Court of North Dakota reversed a grant of summary judgment on behalf of a school district in dispute over a RIF.[136] In remanding, the panel ordered the trial court to determine, as a matter of law, whether the RIF was based on declining enrollment as stated by the district and whether the district met its contractual obligation.

Two cases from Pennsylvania illustrate the type of evidence that is appropriate in demonstrating the need for a RIF. In the first case, an appellate court upheld a teacher's suspension for declining enrollment after the joint operating committee of a vocational-technical school presented evidence that general cumulative enrollment would decline 36.6% over a ten-year period.[137]

Similarly, an appellate court found that evidence from the prior three years of declining attendance in a school business program and courses was sufficient to predict enrollment and the need for teachers. The court decided that because the district had enough data to comply with a Pennsylvania statute that required decisions on eliminating courses or programs to be based on current evidence of decline in enrollment, the suspensions of the teachers were justified.[138]

A third case from Pennsylvania demonstrated that a determination of whether a RIF is necessary can be subject to contractual interpretations. An appellate court upheld an arbitrator's decision that a music teacher's union contract, which expressly incorporated the statutory requirement that a school district must show a substantial decrease in enrollment before furloughing an employee, meant that the question of substantiality was arbitrable.[139]

---

[136] Borr v. McKenzie County Pub. Sch. Dist. No. 1, 541 N.W.2d 681 [105 Educ. L. Rep. 1235] (N.D. 1995).
[137] Newell v. Wilkes-Barre Area Vocational Technical Sch., 670 A.2d 1190 [106 Educ. L. Rep. 1198] (Pa. Commw. Ct. 1996).
[138] Shegelski v. Mid Valley Sch. Dist., 677 A.367 [110 Educ. L. Rep. 218] (Pa. Commw. Ct. 1996).
[139] Ambridge Area Sch. Dist. v. Ambridge Area Educ. Ass'n, PSEA/NEA, 670 A.2d 1207 [106 Educ. L. Rep. 1208] (Pa. Commw. Ct. 1996).

Elimination of Position

A federal district court in Texas affirmed a school board's decision to eliminate seventy-four supervisory positions in special education as part of a $20,000,000 reduction.[140] In response to the claims of two former supervisors that they were reassigned to teaching in retaliation for their ongoing complaints about low pay, the court found that the action of the board was based on legitimate, nondiscriminatory reasons.

In New York, a part-time teacher unsuccessfully petitioned for reinstatement after the board of education eliminated her position. An appellate court in New York observed that the board did not have to follow the seniority rule because in determining positions to abolish, the statute did not protect part-time teachers.[141]

Selection of Employees

School districts were not successful in all RIF decisions regarding the selection of employees who would be furloughed. For example, the Supreme Court of Oklahoma reversed a RIF plan that resulted in the release of a career teacher who was qualified to fill a position held by a nontenured faculty member.[142] The court reasoned that state law required the district to make a reasonable accommodation for a career teacher, including possible reassignment of classes.

In Pennsylvania, an appellate court reversed in favor of a school nurse who was demoted from full-time to part-time status. The district employed one other full-time nurse. The court found that 1,631 students needed to be serviced and state law required that no more than 1,500 students could be serviced by one nurse. The court concluded that when the part-time nurse was not on duty, the full-time nurse would be serving more than the 1,500 students in violation of state law.[143]

A tenured assistant superintendent for instructional services regained his position after it was eliminated for budgetary reasons. An appellate court in New York agreed that he should have been retained because he was in the same tenure area as, and was senior to, the assistant superintendent for personnel and administration who was retained.[144]

---

[140] Johnson v. Houston Indep. Sch. Dist., 930 F. Supp. 243 [111 EDUC. L. REP. 243] (S.D. Tex. 1996).

[141] Van Derzee v. Board of Educ. of Odessa-Montour Cent. Sch. Dist., 644 N.Y.S.2d 847 [110 EDUC. L. REP. 1178] (N.Y. App. Div. 1996).

[142] Barton v. Independent Sch. Dist. No. I-99 Custer County, 914 P.2d 1041 [108 EDUC. L. REP. 1291] (Okla. 1996).

[143] Battaglia v. Lakeland Sch. Dist., 677 A.2d 1294 [110 EDUC. L. REP. 745] (Pa. Commw. Ct. 1996).

[144] Schlick v. Board of Educ. of Mamaroneck Union Free Sch. Dist., 642 N.Y.S.2d 64 [109 EDUC. L. REP. 346] (N.Y. App. Div. 1996

Realignment/Reassignment

Realignment/reassignment involves two kinds of legal questions: the appropriate remedy for employees affected by a RIF and the nature of the reassignment/realignment. An appellate court in Massachusetts rejected a teacher's attempt to assert her right under state law to bump a colleague who lacked professional teacher status.[145] The court ruled that the teacher's sole remedy was arbitration under her collective bargaining agreement.

Results vary as to whether school districts have correctly complied with state law in reassigning faculty. An appellate court in Pennsylvania affirmed that a teacher's demotion from full-time to part-time status due to the reorganization of her school district constituted a "realignment-demotion" under state statute.[146] As such, the court required the district to realign its staff in such a way that less senior certificated teachers were demoted.

An appellate court in California interpreted state law as requiring a school district to assign coaching positions to teachers in its own system before filling jobs with individuals who were not already on its staff. In reversing an earlier judgment on behalf of the district, the court found that the statutory language was manifestly clear in expressing legislative intent.[147]

On the other hand, teachers in New York who were tenured in the specialized area of remedial reading unsuccessfully sought reinstatement after they were laid off. An appellate court affirmed that the remedial reading teachers could be replaced by more senior teachers because remedial reading was included in the general elementary tenure area.[148]

A dispute in Minnesota focused on a senior furloughed faculty member who had been assigned two additional study halls so that she would have a full teaching assignment. An appellate court affirmed that the district was not required to assign the teacher extra study halls because study hall was not an area of certification and the district's practice was to assign only one such period per faculty member.[149]

---

[145] Turner v. School Comm. of Dedham, 670 N.E.2d 202 [112 EDUC. L. REP. 1019] (Mass. Ct. App. 1996).

[146] Boris v. Saint Clair Sch. Dist., 668 A.2d 264 [105 EDUC. L. REP. 642] (Pa. Commw. Ct. 1995).

[147] California Teachers Ass'n v. Governing Bd. of Rialto Unified Sch. Dist., 47 Cal. Rptr.2d 795 [105 EDUC. L. REP. 227] (Cal. Ct. App. 1995).

[148] Demo v. Sachem Cent. Sch. Dist., 638 N.Y.S.2d 715 [107 EDUC. L. REP. 928] (N.Y. App. Div. 1996).

[149] Kvernmo v. Independent Sch. Dist. No. 403, 541 N.W.2d 620 [105 EDUC. L. REP. 1231] (Minn Ct. App. 1996).

In New Jersey, an appellate court found that a school district could fill vacancies in an elementary school by hiring nontenured teachers.[150] A secondary teacher who was laid off as part of a RIF subsequently obtained an endorsement on her teaching certificate for elementary education. The teacher claimed that she was entitled to preference in re-employment, but the court disagreed by stating that preferred re-employment rights were determined on the date of layoff, not after.

Call-back Rights

In the first of two cases from New York, an appeals court affirmed a decision by the Commissioner of Education that a faculty member who was laid off from a business education position should have been given priority in filling a job teaching classes about computers.[151] The court reasoned that for the purposes of a call-back, the Commissioner was better qualified to determine whether the position teaching about computers was in the same tenure area as business education.

A trial court in New York held that a tenured teacher who was discharged after her part-time position was abolished was entitled to regain her job.[152] It decided that since the teacher's job had been abolished, she had the same reappointment rights as if the position had been full-time.

Contract Disputes

Among the many types of problems that can arise concerning employment contracts are the inclusion of ancillary administrative, collective bargaining, and other provisions, as well as questions regarding breach. Like other legally binding agreements, employment contracts require an offer, consideration, and acceptance.

Board Policies and Contract Stipulations

As illustrated by a case from Louisiana, a breach of contract action requires a complainant to have an appropriate employment status. When a tenured high school teacher resigned after being threatened with criminal charges because he grabbed a student, an appellate court maintained that he could not subsequently sue the board for breach of contract. The

---

[150] Francey v. Board of Educ. of City of Salem, Salem County, 669 A.2d 282 [106 EDUC. L. REP. 246] (N.J. Super. Ct. 1996).
[151] Hessney v. Board of Educ. of Pub. Sch. of the Tarrytowns, 644 N.Y.S.2d 826 [110 EDUC. L. REP. 1182] (N.Y. App. Div. 1996).
[152] Avila v. Board of Educ. of North Babylon Union Free Sch. Dist., 647 N.Y.S.2d 923 [113 EDUC. L. REP. 389] (N.Y. Sup. Ct. 1996).

court held that the teacher's claim was without merit since he had voluntarily resigned.[153]

In Arkansas, an appellate court upheld the termination of a custodian's contract.[154] The court pointed out that the action was consistent with the terms of what amounted to an employment at will contract. The agreement contained provisions stating that the custodian would work for a maximum of 233 days and was terminable at any time by either party.

The Supreme Judicial Court of Maine held that a Director of Special Education was not a teacher as defined by the state Teacher Employment Statute.[155] As such, the court affirmed that the Director was not entitled to the due process protections that the law provided teachers.

Whether breach of contract actions are successful can depend on such factors as grievance procedures under collective bargaining agreements. For example, a teacher who was hired as a basketball coach was replaced after several practices. The teacher sought further review of a grievance proceeding where the assistant who took his place as coach prevailed. In affirming that the coach did not have a breach of contract claim, the West Virginia Supreme Court of Appeals found that the school district acted in good faith in hiring the teacher but was justified in replacing him because it could not ignore the result of the grievance process.[156]

In a suit filed by taxpayers against a school district and the unions of its employees, an appellate court in New York upheld a provision in a collective bargaining contract that called for a cash payment to individuals for unused accumulated sick leave.[157] The court reasoned that since, under state law, the provision related to a term or condition of employment, the district had the statutory authority needed to negotiate the matter.

A case from Illinois tied a contract with certification. An appellate court reversed a damages award in favor of a teacher who won a breach of contract suit after her employment was terminated because her certification expired.[158] The court maintained that insofar as certification was an essential condition of employment, the teacher's failure to maintain it

---

[153] Johnson v. Vernon Parish Sch. Bd., 670 So. 2d 373 [108 EDUC. L. REP. 470] (La. Ct. App. 1996).

[154] Kimble v. Pulaski County Special Sch. Dist., 921 S.W.2d 611 [109 EDUC. L. REP. 988] (Ark Ct. App. 1996).

[155] Cook v. Lisbon Sch. Comm., 682 A.2d 672 [113 EDUC. L. REP. 317] (Me. 1996).

[156] Copley v. Mingo County Bd. of Educ., 466 S.E.2d 139 [106 EDUC. L. REP. 915] (W. Va. 1995).

[157] Perrenod v. Liberty Bd. of Educ., 636 N.Y.S.2d 210 [106 EDUC. L. REP. 302] (N.Y. App. Div. 1996).

[158] Lewis-Connelly v. Board of Educ. of Deerfield Pub. Sch., Dist. 109, 660 N.E.2d 283 [106 EDUC. L. REP. 850] (Ill. App. Ct. 1996).

meant that her contract was no longer binding. The court concluded that the school board in permitting the educator to continue to teach for a short period of time after her certification expired was ultra vires and she could not rely upon this under an estoppel theory.

As illustrated by a case from New York, contracts and tenure can be related. An appellate court affirmed that a school counselor who had contracts to work in a federally funded position for three years did not acquire tenure rights.[159] The court held that each of the contracts contained a provision indicating that tenure did not apply to the position.

In New York, an appellate court ruled that the statutory tenure rights of noncertificated school employees are not retroactive. In reversing in favor of a school board, the court observed that the termination provisions in employees' contract were in effect prior to the effective date of an amendment to the School Personnel Act that would have given noncertificated employees tenure, therefore the amendment did not apply.[160]

A third case from New York demonstrated that contracts can require school employees to develop special skill levels. An appellate court upheld the dismissal of a probationary faculty member who, upon being hired, was notified that she had to implement the master teacher concept.[161] It found that despite being given special training in the concept, the teacher failed to increase her communication skills to the level that was required to fulfill her employment requirement.

Calculation of salaries can present contract issues. An appellate court in Missouri upheld the way in which a school board used conversion tables to determine teachers' salary schedules.[162] The court was of the opinion that since the board had the authority to deviate from past custom and practice, its calculations were neither arbitrary nor capricious.

A release granted in exchange for benefits also can be a contract. The federal trial court in Nebraska stated that a superintendent's contract was not breached when she executed a release of her claims against a school district in exchange for a monetary payment and an agreement that the district would not participate in any investigation against her by the state Professional Practices Commission (PPC).[163] The case arose when the former superintendent subsequently became the subject of a

---

[159] Yastion v. Mills, 645 N.Y.S.2d 585 [111 EDUC. L. REP. 940] (N.Y. App. Div. 1996).
[160] Gadsden Fed'n of Teachers v. Board of Educ. of Gadsden Indep. Sch. Dist., 920 P.2d 1052 [111 EDUC. L. REP. 978] (N.M. Ct. App. 1996).
[161] Kurey v. New York State Sch. for Deaf, 642 N.Y.S.2d 415 [109 EDUC. L. REP. 900] (N.Y. App. Div. 1996).
[162] Hagely v. Board of Educ. of Webster Groves Sch. Dist., 930 S.W.2d 47 [113 EDUC. L. REP. 509] (Mo. Ct. App. 1996).
[163] Watts v. Butte Sch. Dist. No. 5, 939 F. Supp. 1418 [113 EDUC. L. REP. 800] (D. Neb. 1996).

PPC investigation and the district provided it with information. The court concluded that the district was unaware of the PPC investigation at the time of the release and an agreement not to voluntarily provide information to a state investigatory body is not against public policy.

Failure of a party to honor a provision in an agreement can result in separate actions for interference with or breach of contract. The Supreme Judicial Court of Maine reversed in favor of a teacher in finding that the teacher stated a claim that his superintendent interfered with his contractual relationships.[164] The court agreed that the superintendent used fraud and intimidation to interfere with the teacher's job and attempted to force the teacher to resign or face grounds for dismissal created by the superintendent.

An appellate court in California affirmed that a school district did not breach a teacher's contract in a dispute over a nondisclosure provision in an agreement between the parties.[165] The court found that such a nondisclosure was illegal as a matter of public policy where the nondisclosure concerned a student's allegations that she had been raped by the teacher.

Administrative Regulations and Statutory Provisions

Contract status may be related to school board action. An appellate court in Pennsylvania upheld the rejection of a salary increase that a retired superintendent claimed he was owed based on an amendment to his contract.[166] The court found that the former administrator was not entitled to the salary increase since it had neither been placed before the school board at a public session nor approved by a majority vote at that meeting.

The Supreme Court of Ohio upheld a guidance counselor's claim that even though it had not been reduced to writing, her supplemental agreement to work extra days during the school year was automatically renewed when she was awarded a continuing contract.[167] The court decided that pursuant to state law, a supplemental contract, once awarded, automatically remains in effect until the board notifies an employee that it has not been renewed.

---

[164] Shaw v. Southern Aroostook Community Sch. Dist., 683 A.2d 502 [113 Educ. L. Rep. 855] (Me. 1996).

[165] Picton v. Anderson Union High Sch. Dist., 57 Cal. Rptr.2d 829 [113 Educ. L. Rep. 869] (Cal. Ct. App. 1996).

[166] Preston v. Saucon Valley Sch. Dist., 666 A.2d 1120 [104 Educ. L. Rep. 818] (Pa. Commw. Ct. 1995).

[167] Hara v. Montgomery County Local Vocational Sch. Dist., 661 N.E.2d 711 [107 Educ. L. Rep. 264] (Ohio 1996).

An appellate court in Florida reversed a school board's reinstatement of a painter whose contract was not renewed by the superintendent.[168] The court observed that under state statute, a board cannot hire an individual who lacks the superintendent's recommendation.

Teacher status under state law can influence contract litigation. An appellate court in Pennsylvania upheld a school board's decision that the individual who replaced a permanent science teacher who ultimately resigned was a substitute teacher, not a temporary professional employee.[169] The court found that since the replacement had not taught for two years, he failed to qualify as a temporary professional employee. Therefore, the court concluded that the operative collective bargaining agreement did not automatically entitle him to be offered a permanent position when one became available.

A teacher who was reassigned from his coaching duties unsuccessfully challenged the school district. The Supreme Court of Arkansas affirmed that by signing a new contract that reduced his coaching duties and compensation, the teacher waived the notice requirements under the Fair Dismissal Act that otherwise would have been applicable.[170]

A district sought further review of a judgment that a teacher who worked for ninety-three days during a school year was entitled to probationary status for purposes of statutory termination rights. The Supreme Court of Nevada reversed in favor of the school district.[171] It reasoned that the teacher did not meet the requirements for a probationary employee because he had been present for only one of the three performance evaluations required for each year.

One case tied a contract to tenure under state law. An appellate court in Tennessee reversed an award of tenure to supervisors who had been returned to the classroom with salary reductions.[172] The court held that a grandfather clause that gave tenure to teachers who were supervisors at the time the law went into effect did not apply to teachers who were appointed as administrators after the law went into effect.

Whether staff members are eligible for unemployment compensation continues to generate case law. The Supreme Judicial Court of

---

[168] Cox v. School Bd. of Osceola County, 669 So. 2d 353 [107 EDUC. L. REP. 1066] (Fla. Dist. Ct. App. 1996).
[169] Kielbowick v. Ambridge Area Sch. Bd., 668 A.2d 1228 [106 EDUC. L. REP. 227] (Pa. Commw. Ct. 1995).
[170] McCaskill v. Fort Smith Pub. Sch. Dist., 921 S.W.2d 945 [109 EDUC. L. REP. 1392] (Ark. 1996).
[171] Clark County Sch. Dist. v. Harris, 913 P.2d 1268 [108 EDUC. L. REP. 942] (Nev. 1996).
[172] Teague v. Campbell County, 920 S.W.2d 219 [109 EDUC. L. REP. 448] (Tenn. Ct. App. 1995).

Massachusetts affirmed that a teacher who asked for a one-year leave of absence for personal reasons was not entitled to unemployment compensation even though she changed her mind and unsuccessfully sought to return to her job.[173]

A private school in Pennsylvania sought further review of a ruling that granted unemployment compensation to an assistant house manager who was demoted. An appellate court affirmed that because the manager's demotion was accompanied by a substantial reduction in pay, he had a necessitous and compelling reason for voluntarily leaving his job.[174] As such, the court concluded that he was eligible for unemployment compensation benefits.

In New York, an appellate court upheld the denial of unemployment benefits during summer months to a substitute teacher.[175] The court reasoned that because the teacher received a letter from her school district advising her that her name would be placed on a list of substitutes, she had a reasonable assurance of continued employment and was ineligible for benefits.

Tenure

Tenure Status

Acquisition of tenure status requires compliance with the appropriate state law on tenure. For example, an appellate court in New York reversed an award of tenure to a special education teacher.[176] The court pointed out that the teacher's work as a per diem replacement for a faculty member who had been reassigned for an indeterminate period of time was not the equivalent to work as a regular substitute teacher.

In Missouri, an appellate court affirmed that a Vocational Program Coordinator who was occasionally assigned instructional duties was not a teacher.[177] Accordingly, it decided that the Coordinator was not entitled to the procedural protection under the Teacher Tenure Act of the state when his contract was not renewed because of budgetary difficulties.

An appellate court in Pennsylvania upheld a decision by a school district that a substitute who received a three-year appointment as a full-

---

[173] LeBeau v. Commissioner of the Dep't of Employment and Training, 664 N.E.2d 21 [109 EDUC. L. REP. 362] (Mass. 1996).

[174] Allegheny Valley Sch. v. Unemployment Compensation Bd. of Review, 666 A.2d 1144 [104 EDUC. L. REP. 827] (Pa. Commw. Ct. 1995).

[175] Claim of Papageorge, 632 N.Y.S.2d 687 [104 EDUC. L. REP. 474] (N.Y. App. Div. 1995).

[176] Speichler v. Board of Cooperative Educ. Servs., Second Supervisory Dist., 643 N.Y.S.2d 193 [110 EDUC. L. REP. 333] (N.Y. App. Div. 1996).

[177] Mitchell v. Board of Educ. of Normandy Sch. Dist., 913 S.W.2d 130 [106 EDUC. L. REP. 423] (Mo. Ct. App. 1996).

time second-grade teacher had not attained the status of a professional employee.[178] The court was of the opinion that the teacher did not acquire the rights of full-time reassignment and could be returned to a position as a day-to-day substitute.

One of the benefits of tenure is usually statutory protection regarding dismissal. A federal district court in Virginia decreed that a continuing contract teacher retained her right to notice and a hearing even though she had been placed on probation.[179] The court stated that the school board could not reclassify a continuing contract teacher without following the express terms of state law.

Tenure by Default or Acquiescence

Results varied as to whether employees successfully acquired tenure by default or a school district's acquiescence. The Court of Appeals of New York affirmed that an administrator who served as acting principal for one year and as principal for three years was entitled to tenure by estoppel at the beginning of her fourth year.[180] The court held that the year as acting principal counted toward the three years because the administrator had assumed the responsibilities of the position.

On the other hand, another appellate court in New York agreed that an assistant principal was not entitled to tenure by estoppel.[181] The court decided that he was not qualified for tenure because when he was on assignment to the central office for more than one year of his probationary term, he did not perform the duties of an assistant principal.

Similarly, in the first of two cases from New Jersey, an appellate court affirmed a ruling of the Commissioner of Education.[182] The court agreed that an educator cannot combine teaching service under permanent and emergency certificates to acquire tenure.

The Supreme Court of New Jersey upheld the denial of tenure to an assistant superintendent who claimed that the nonrenewal of his contract prevented him from acquiring tenure.[183] The court found that since it is

---

[178] Franson v. Bald Eagle Area Sch. Dist., 668 A.2d 633 [105 EDUC. L. REP. 1125] (Pa. Commw. Ct. 1995).

[179] Williams v. Charlottesville Sch. Bd., 940 F. Supp. 143 [113 EDUC. L. REP. 813] (W.D. Va. 1996).

[180] McManus v. Board of Educ. of Hempstead Union Free Sch. Dist., 638 N.Y.S.2d 411 [107 EDUC. L. REP. 919] (N.Y. 1995).

[181] Feldman v. Community Sch. Dist. 32, 647 N.Y.S.2d 805 [113 EDUC. L. REP. 385] (N.Y. App. Div. 1996).

[182] Breitwieser v. State-Operated Sch. Dist. of Jersey City, 670 A.2d 73 [106 EDUC. L. REP. 751] (N.J. Super. Ct. App. Div. 1996).

[183] Picogna v. Board of Educ. of Cherry Hill, 671 A.2d 1035 [107 EDUC. L. REP. 859] (N.J. 1996).

governed solely by statute, an administrator who failed to serve the requisite number of years could not obtain tenure in a breach of contract suit.

Certification

Certification Standards

A state must apply its certification standards in a reasonable manner. The Supreme Court of Appeals of West Virginia upheld the decision of a board of education to require district employees who applied for a position that was posted as a sixth-grade teacher to have certification for grades six through eight.[184] At the same time, the court reversed and remanded in holding that the board had to allow teachers sufficient time to obtain the appropriate certification. The court ruled that the refusal to give teachers more time to complete certification was arbitrary and capricious because it previously assured applicants that certification for grades one through six would suffice but changed its mind without affording them adequate time to procure the additional course work.

The relationship between a university and the state certification authority was at issue where an appellate court in Pennsylvania interpreted the effective date of new regulations. The court upheld the application of the regulations to a teacher with provisional certification who submitted his papers to a university two days before they went into effect.[185] The court reasoned that the acceptance of an incomplete application by the university could not estop the enforcement of the regulations since the institution was not an agent of the state for certification purposes.

Certification can also relate to state licensing requirements for certain professions. An appellate court in North Carolina upheld a claim of the Board of Examiners for Speech and Language Pathologists and Audiologists that the Licensure Act was the sole qualification.[186] The court remanded for a determination of whether the State Board of Education had issued certificates to language pathologists and audiologists who did not meet the requirements of the Act.

A federal district court in California found that under title VII, the state test for certification had an adverse discriminatory impact on Hispanic, Afro-American, and Asian teachers. The court rejected the argument

---

[184] Cowen v. Harrison County Bd. of Educ., 465 S.E.2d 648 [106 EDUC. L. REP. 383] (W. Va. 1995).
[185] Logsdon v. Department of Educ., 671 A.2d 302 [106 EDUC. L. REP 1253] (Pa. Commw. Ct. 1996).
[186] North Carolina Bd. of Examiners for Speech and Language Pathologists and Audiologists v. North Carolina State Bd. of Educ., 468 S.E.2d 826 [108 EDUC. L. REP. 995] (N.C. Ct. App. 1996).

by the state " . . . that adverse impact should be assessed in light of cumulative rather than first-time, pass rates [because] . . . [t]he law of an employment opportunity occurs each and every time a candidate fails the test."[187]

Decertification, Revocation, or Suspension

States have considerable latitude in determining whether certificates should be denied and courts will intervene only in rare cases. An appellate court in Wisconsin ruled against a superintendent who revoked a teacher's certificate.[188] The court agreed that the superintendent used an improper role model standard where there was no clear and convincing evidence that a teacher's two acts of a homosexual nature had a nexus to the physical health, welfare, or safety of any student.

In Florida, an appellate court overturned a final order of the Education Practices Commission that suspended a principal's teaching certificate, an act that would have permanently barred him from serving as a building level administrator.[189] The court held that the administrator had not violated a state requirement to keep medication under lock and key. The court reasoned that although the school vault that had historically been used to store student medications was open during the day, there was no evidence that it was left unsupervised at any time.

A former elementary school principal in Kentucky sought further review of the dismissal of her libel and wrongful use of civil proceedings after her superintendent forwarded her evaluations to the Education Professional Standard Board. In affirming that the superintendent had absolute immunity, the court observed that the reporting requirement included nonrenewed employees, especially where their conduct might warrant consideration for the revocation of their certificates.[190]

In the first of three cases involving sexual misconduct, the Supreme Court of Minnesota upheld the revocation of a teacher's license by the Board of Teaching.[191] The teacher's contract was terminated for improper contact with a student. Even though the teacher died during the pendency of the appeal, the court retained jurisdiction because the case involved an issue of public concern that was capable of repetition.

---

[187] Association of Mexican-American Educators v. State of Cal., 937 F. Supp. 1397, 1409 [113 Educ. L. Rep. 199] (N.D. Cal. 1996).
[188] Thompson v. Wisconsin Dep't of Pub. Instruction, 541 N.W.2d 182 [105 Educ. L. Rep. 746] (Wis. Ct. App. 1995).
[189] McKinney v. Castor, 667 So. 2d 387 [107 Educ. L. Rep. 402] (Fla. Dist. Ct. App. 1995).
[190] Matthews v. Holland, 912 S.W.2d 459 [106 Educ. L. Rep. 398] (Ky. Ct. App. 1995).
[191] Falgren v. State Bd. of Teaching, 545 N.W.2d 901 [108 Educ. L. Rep. 890] (Minn. 1996).

A teacher in New York unsuccessfully challenged the decision of the Commissioner of Education. An appellate court rejected the argument that the statutory authority of the Commissioner to annul teaching licenses was an unconstitutional delegation of legislative power.[192] It concluded that the authorization to annul for cause set forth adequate standards.

In the extension of the same case, another appellate court in New York upheld the annulment of the teacher's certification on the ground of moral character.[193] The court agreed that a hearing panel had sufficient evidence to conclude that the teacher had committed acts of sexual abuse and misconduct against his nieces.

Revocation also can involve procedural questions. An appellate court reasoned that the Pennsylvania Professional Standards and Practices Commission was entitled to revoke a teacher's certificate after he failed to file a responsive answer to a notice of charges.[194] The court found that the teacher's failure to respond in a timely manner permitted the Commission to deem the charges against him admitted after he plead guilty to an offense of trafficking in counterfeit goods and services.

An appellate court in Florida reversed a decision of the Education Practices Commission and upheld a hearing officer's determination that disciplinary action should have been taken against a teacher.[195] In reinstating the hearing officer's decision, the court ruled that under state law the Commission can overturn a finding only if it is unsupported by substantial evidence.

Conclusion

Issues addressed by courts relating to employment law have not changed appreciably over the past decade. Employee discipline continues to dominate the picture, probably reflecting the increased emphasis by school districts on evaluation. The relative dearth of case law dealing with constitutional, as opposed to statutory, concerns suggests a greater involvement by state legislatures and administrative agencies in addressing questions relating to education.

---

[192] Welcher v. Sobol, 636 N.Y.S.2d 421 [106 EDUC. L. REP. 306] (N.Y. App. Div. 1995).
[193] Welcher v. Sobol, 642 N.Y.S.2d 370 [109 EDUC. L. REP. 896] (N.Y. App. Div. 1996).
[194] Kinniry v. Professional Standards and Practices Comm'n, 678 A.2d 1230 [111 EDUC. L. REP. 355] (Pa. Commw. Ct. 1996).
[195] Brogan v. Carter, 671 So. 2d 822 [108 EDUC. L. REP. 1365] (Fla. Dist. Ct. App. 1996).

2
SCHOOL GOVERNANCE

Donald F. Uerling

Introduction

School Governance is a new chapter in the *Yearbook of Education Law*. This chapter reports on cases that address issues pertaining to the exercise of authority in directing the affairs of public elementary and secondary education.

State Education Agencies and Officials

State education agencies and officials are instrumental in the governance of public schools. This section examines cases involving state boards, commissioners, and departments of education.

State Boards of Education

A federal district court held that officials violated the Voting Rights Act by failing to obtain preclearance for a change from staggered to concurrent terms for members of the State Board of Education.[1] The court decided that section 5 of the Act requires certain jurisdictions, including

---

[1] Shuford v. Alabama State Bd. of Educ., 920 F. Supp. 1233 [108 EDUC. L. REP. 705] (M.D. Ala. 1996).

Alabama, to obtain preclearance of any change in a standard, practice, or procedure with respect to voting that has the potential to discriminate against African-Americans.

The New Jersey State Board of Education refused to permit a teacher to acquire tenure for work performed under a permanent certificate by tacking on an earlier period of service pursuant to an emergency credential in a different field. On further review, an appellate court affirmed.[2] It noted that the State Board is charged with implementing school laws and that its decision is entitled to considerable weight.

The North Carolina State Board of Education, after conducting public rule-making procedures, chose not to amend its rules to allow chiropractic doctors to perform required annual physical examinations of prospective interscholastic athletes. An appellate court agreed that pursuant to state statute, the board's decision was a rule-making decision and, as such, was not subject to judicial review.[3]

State Commissioners of Education

The Supreme Court of Wisconsin entertained an original action by the governor to determine the legality of a state law designed to strip constitutional power from the Superintendent of Public Instruction. The court indicated that the party challenging a law must prove its unconstitutionality beyond a reasonable doubt.[4] In construing the pertinent provision of the law, the court turned to the plain meaning of the words in context, the debates and practices in existence at the time of the writing of the constitution, and the earliest legislative interpretation of the provision as manifested in the first law passed following its adoption. The court concluded that because the law gave the powers of the elected superintendent of public instruction to other appointed officers at the state level who were not subordinate to the superintendent, it was unconstitutional.

A superintendent of schools in New York brought suit in federal district court against a board of education and its trustees seeking compensatory and punitive damages for alleged violations of his rights to due process. In addition, he sought a preliminary injunction to reinstate his salary and benefits until a decision was reached on pending disciplinary charges. The board asserted that the court should abstain from hearing the case because the administrator had an action pending before the State

---

[2] Breitwieser v. State-Operated Sch. Dist. of Jersey City, 670 A.2d 73 [106 EDUC. L. REP. 751] (N.J. Super. Ct. App. Div. 1996).

[3] North Carolina Chiropractic Ass'n v. North Carolina State Bd. of Educ., 468 S.E.2d 539 [108 EDUC. L. REP. 972] (N.C. Ct. App. 1996).

[4] Thompson v. Craney, 546 N.W.2d 123 [108 EDUC. L. REP. 904] (Wis. 1996).

Commissioner of Education. The court ruled that under state law, since judicial review of the Commissioner's decision included the power to hear constitutional claims in state court, abstention was properly invoked to the extent that the charges for money damages were stayed, rather than dismissed, until those proceedings were over.[5] Consequently, the court denied the request for a preliminary injunction.

An appellate court in Texas addressed whether the Term Contract Nonrenewal Act required the state Commissioner to conduct a new evidentiary hearing in reviewing every local school board's decision to not renew a teacher's contract. In sustaining a board's dismissal of a teacher, the court maintained that the evidentiary hearing conducted by the board was sufficient and that there was no need for the Commissioner to conduct a new hearing since the teacher who was dismissed failed to show "good cause" for presenting evidence to the Commissioner.[6]

The California Superintendent of Public Instruction was accused of four counts of violating the state conflict of interest laws by making official contracts in which he had a financial interest. He was charged with causing the state Department of Education to reimburse local districts for keeping employees on their payrolls while they were working for a nonprofit corporation in which he had a financial interest. The superintendent sought further review of his conviction that sentenced him to probation on the condition that he complete community service and make restitution. An appellate court affirmed the conviction and the sentence of probation, but remanded on the issue of restitution.[7]

State Departments of Education

The Pennsylvania Department of Education challenged a determination of the United States Secretary of Education that a job training program in the state dealt with vocational education for the purpose of Perkins Act funding. The Third Circuit affirmed that the Secretary's decision not to require an evidentiary hearing was neither arbitrary nor capricious.[8] It contended that the state's characterization of the program as nonvocational was irrelevant because federal law characterized vocational education under the Perkins Act. The court added that the Secretary's application of federal law to a set of undisputed facts did not impinge on the state's sovereign authority.

---

[5] Pinckney v. Board of Educ. of the Westbury Union Free Sch. Dist., 920 F. Supp. 393 [108 Educ. L. Rep. 664] (E.D.N.Y. 1996).
[6] Gilder v. Meno, 926 S.W.2d 357 [111 Educ. L. Rep. 1031] (Tex. Ct. App. 1996).
[7] People v. Honig, 55 Cal. Rptr.2d 555 [111 Educ. L. Rep. 870] (Cal. Ct. App. 1996).
[8] State of Pa. v. Riley, 84 F.3d 125 [109 Educ. L. Rep. 614] (3rd Cir. 1996).

In a second case from Pennsylvania, a teacher unsuccessfully questioned new regulations of the Department of Education that required applicants for permanent certificates to pass state teaching examinations. An appellate court upheld the regulations, noting that a state agency has wide discretion in establishing standards. In addition, the court stated that although neither the university nor the Department had specifically informed the teacher about the test, he did not establish the necessary elements of estoppel where there was no evidence of misrepresentation and he knew of the certification requirements.[9]

The California State Department of Education forbid employees to engage in any oral or written religious advocacy in the workplace or to display any religious artifacts, tracts, or materials outside their offices or cubicles. A computer analyst alleged that the orders violated his First Amendment rights to freedom of speech. After a federal trial court ruled in favor of the Department, the Ninth Circuit reversed.[10] In balancing the interests of the employee and the state, the court determined that the state failed to demonstrate its concerns outweighed those of the staff member. The court took into account the government's greater interest in controlling the posting of materials on its property than in regulating the private speech of employees, but decreed that the Department's order was not a reasonable means of achieving a legitimate end because it was overbroad.

State Funding

An important topic within school governance is the role of state government in providing funding for public education. The following cases address issues related to state funding.

State Finance Plans

An appellate court in North Carolina refuted a challenge to the state system of financing public schools. The plaintiffs alleged that the state failed to satisfy its obligations to maintain a funding system that would take sufficient account of the substantial disparities in wealth among school districts. The court, in rejecting the claim, held that the "general and uniform" provision in the state constitution required uniformity in the system of schools across the state, not spending or program uniformity in individual buildings or districts.[11] It pointed out that the fundamental

---

[9] Logsdon v. Department of Educ., 671 a.2d 302 [EDUC L. REP. 1253] (Pa. Commw. Ct. 1996).
[10] Tucker v. California Dept. of Educ., 97 F.3d 1204 [113 EDUC. L. REP. 102] (9th Cir. 1996).
[11] Leandro v. State, 468 S.E.2d 543 [108 EDUC. L. REP. 975] (N.C. Ct. App. 1996).

educational right under the state constitution was limited to one of equal access and did not embrace any qualitative standard.

Two school districts in Arizona and several of their students sued state and county officials alleging that a plan for equalization of funding involving the redistribution of Federal Impact Aid violated the Supremacy Clause. The Ninth Circuit affirmed that the suit had properly been dismissed because the districts lacked standing to bring suit against the state and the students failed to allege particularized harm or distinct injury that would afford them the opportunity to sue.[12]

Desegregation Plans

School districts sued the State of Arkansas and its Department of Education alleging that they violated the Little Rock Schools Desegregation Settlement Agreement. The Eighth Circuit agreed the state's formula for calculating the disbursement of workers' compensation "seed money" violated the agreement.[13] The court further maintained that the state had to exclude from the average daily membership base used to calculate lost funding those students who voluntarily transfered from districts where they were a majority race to districts where they were a minority race. The court concluded that the state was not required to pay districts that did not participate in the Arkansas Public School Computer Network program an amount equivalent to what it would have paid the districts had they participated.

After a city school district in Pennsylvania was ordered to remedy racial disparities and unequal educational opportunities, a trial was conducted on the issue of liability on the part of the state and city to pay the extra costs for compliance. The court noted that public education is a fundamental right under the state constitution and that the commonwealth retained the ultimate power and authority over the district, irrespective of the legislature's delegation of limited authority to the city. As such, the court ruled in favor of the district.[14] It posited that the district met its burden of proof that funding was inadequate to meet the obligations of the order. The court was of the opinion that the state and governor failed to show either that the district had the capacity to comply or that existing funding levels were sufficient.

---

[12] Indian Oasis-Baboquivari Unified Sch. Dist. No. 40 v. Kirk, 91 F.3d 1240 [111 Educ. L. Rep. 655] (9th Cir. 1996).
[13] Little Rock Sch. Dist. v. Pulaski County Special Sch. Dist. No. 1, 83 F. 3d 1013 [109 Educ L. Rep. 590] (8th Cir. 1996).
[14] Human Relations Comm'n v. School Dist. of Philadelphia, 681 A.2d 1366 [112 Educ. L. Rep. 957] (Pa. Commw. Ct. 1996).

Special Education

Virginia unsuccessfully challenged a decision by the United States Department of Education to withhold funding for special education. The Fourth Circuit maintained that a state risks losing all or part of its Individuals with Disabilities Education Act, Part B funds if it refuses to provide educational services to a disabled student who has been expelled or suspended for conduct unrelated to his or her disability.[15] The court added that the Department's action was not unconstitutional coercion and that since the Department was issuing an interpretive, rather than a legislative, rule it was not required to abide by the notice and hearing provisions of the Administrative Procedures Act.

A school district filed a petition for declaratory judgment against a state agency arguing that it was not responsible for special education costs when a student was placed at a youth center under a delinquency statute. The district based its claim on the notion that the costs of the placement were not covered by state law since they were not authorized by the student's original Individualized Education Program (IEP). The Supreme Court of New Hampshire disagreed.[16] The court judged that the district was liable for the disputed costs up to the statutory limit, regardless of whether a new IEP was in place.

Allocation of State Funds

The Supreme Court of North Carolina affirmed that monies paid by a company to the state Department of Environment, Health and Natural Resources constituted a penalty, forfeiture, or fine under a provision of the state constitution that required all such monies to be used exclusively for public schools.[17] The court found that since the monies were paid to settle the assessment of a penalty for violations of environmental standards, the trial court properly granted a motion for summary judgment by the board of education that entitled the board to the funds.

In Texas, a school district unsuccessfully challenged the state Comptroller's valuation of its property. The taxable value of property in the district directly determined how much state funding it received. An appellate court agreed that the clear language of the statute governing valuation of district property required the Comptroller, in conducting the 1991 study, to apply an old method that used comparable sales and other

---

[15] Commonwealth of Va. Dep't of Educ. v. Riley, 86 F.3d 1337 [110 EDUC. L. REP. 552] (4th Cir. 1996).
[16] Ashland Sch. Dist. v. New Hampshire Div. for Children, Youth, and Families, 681 A.2d 71 [112 EDUC. L. REP. 284] (N.H. 1996).
[17] Craven County Bd. of Educ. v. Boyles, 468 S.E.2d 50 [108 EDUC. L. REP. 409] (N.C. 1996).

generally accepted techniques, rather than a local value presumption method provided for in an amendment that was to be used beginning in 1992.[18]

Taxpayers and a school district unsuccessfully claimed that a tax act violated the Equal Protection provisions in both the state and federal constitutions. The act required county districts that received assessment reductions for nuclear power facilities located within their boundaries to be responsible for school tax refunds. The court interpreted legislative intent as not requiring other districts to pay the refund since they did not share in the benefit of the initial overassessment. An appellate court in New York affirmed that the plaintiffs failed to establish that the legislature discriminated invidiously.[19]

Special Schools and School Districts

Some of the following cases addressing special governance structures for public education involved the authority of the state while others examined decisions at the local level.

Charter Schools

Hispanic parents accused a board of education of discrimination when it opened a charter school and closed two elementary schools. Based on the Colorado Charter Schools Act, the Tenth Circuit affirmed a ruling in favor of the board.[20] It agreed that the board did not intentionally discriminate in violation of the Equal Protection Clause. At the same time, the court decided that neither the opening of the charter school nor the closing of the two elementary schools violated title VII of the Civil Rights Act of 1964 by having a negative disparate impact on the Hispanic population.

An appellate court in Michigan affirmed that the Academy Schools Act violated the state constitution because academy schools were not public institutions.[21] The court viewed the key issue as whether academy schools are under the exclusive control of the state. It found that since the Act allowed entities with privately selected boards of directors to control academies, they did not meet the common understanding of a public school.

---

[18] El Paso Indep. Sch. Dist. v. Sharp, 923 S.W.2d 844 [110 EDUC. L. REP. 489] (Tex. Ct. App. 1996).

[19] Prodell v. State, 645 N.Y.S.2d 589 [111 EDUC. L. REP. 1314] (N.Y. App. Div. 1996).

[20] Villanueva v. Carere, 85 F.3d 481 [110 EDUC. L. REP. 38] (10th Cir. 1996).

[21] Council of Orgs. v. Governor of Mich., 548 N.W.2d 909 [110 EDUC. L. REP. 402] (Mich. Ct. App. 1996).

Special School Districts

In *Board of Education of Kiryas Joel Village School District v. Grumet*,[22] the Supreme Court held that a statute permitting the creation of a special school district violated the Establishment Clause. Immediately after this decision, the legislature passed, and the governor signed into law, a new bill that accomplished the same purpose as the old act. A trial court sustained the law but on further review the law was struck down. An appellate court in New York held that the new statute merely resurrected the prior one by achieving the same result through carefully crafted indirect means.[23] The court noted that while each criteria of the new law might be viewed as neutral and legitimately be given general application when standing alone, when considered together the criteria simply identified the Village of Kiryas Joel. As such, the court thought it necessary to look beyond the words of the current law which, it said, were no more than camouflage for the true purpose.

Special Schools

Taxpayers sued a district for opening a special elementary school at the request of a religious group known as the Brethren. Even though religion was not going to be taught, the school intended to limit the use of electronic technology to the extent legally permissible because it was offensive to the beliefs of the Brethren. The Brethren were to provide the facility while the district was to provide the teacher and books. The federal district court in Minnesota rebuffed the contention that the school was going to accommodate religious beliefs.[24] The court indicated that the district could neither open such a school nor modify its curriculum based solely on the request of a religious group.

Special Governance Arrangements

In the spring of 1989, Boston University and the School Committee of Chelsea entered into an agreement whereby the univeristy would participate in managing the educational system of Chelsea. In response to a suit to stay the implementation of the agreement, the Supreme Judicial Court of Massachusetts held that allowing the university to participate in the management of schools did not violated the anti-aid amendment of the state constitution. It also held that the committee had not impermissibly

---

[22] 114 S. Ct. 2481 [91 Educ. L. Rep. 810] (1994).
[23] Grumet v. Cuomo, 647 N.Y.S.2d 565 [113 Educ. L. Rep. 362] (N.Y. App. Div. 1996).
[24] Stark v. Independent Sch. Dist. No. 640, 938 F. Supp. 544 [113 Educ. L. Rep. 274] (D. Minn. 1996).

delegated its powers to a private entity.[25] The court reasoned that since the committee retained extensive supervisory control over the university, the university was acting as the agent of the public entity.

School District Boundary Changes

When territory is transferred from one school district to another, disputes are not uncommon. Six cases resolved issues associated with the detachment and annexation of district property.

After a hearing on a petition filed by two families, a county commissioners court ordered twenty-five square miles to be detached from one school district and annexed to another. The district from which the land was to be detached appealed the order to the Commissioner of Education, claiming that the size of the area transferred was grossly disproportionate to the number of children living there. The Commissioner refused to hear evidence on the issue because the district failed to raise it in the county commissioners court. The Supreme Court of Texas reversed.[26] It held that by not hearing the evidence, the Commissioner committed an error of law by ignoring facts that could have affected his substantial evidence de novo review.

A district petitioned for review of a determination by the School District Boundary Appeal Board (SDBAB). The district contended that SDBAB exceeded its authority by detaching an "island" parcel of land from one district and attaching it to an adjoining district. On appeal, the Supreme Court of Wisconsin affirmed.[27] The court held that the provision allowed for the detachment and attachment of such a parcel of property even if the land did not adjoin the district to which it was being added.

In a second cases from Wisconsin, an appellate panel reinstated a decision of the SDBAB that had been reversed as arbitrary and capricious. It explained that the merits of a district reorganization are a legislative determination and do not raise justiciable issues of fact or law. The court observed that the only questions to be considered are whether the reorganization authority acted within its jurisdiction and if its determination was arbitrary or capricious.[28] The court upheld the action of the SDBAB because the board engaged in a rational process of considering

---

[25] Fifty-One Hispanic Residents v. School Comm. of Chelsea, 659 N.E.2d 277 [105 Educ. L. Rep. 1223] (Mass. 1996).
[26] Nueces Canyon Consol. Indep. Sch. Dist. v. Central Educ. Agency, 917 S.W.2d 773 [108 Educ. L. Rep. 447] (Tex. 1996).
[27] Stockbridge v. Department of Pub. Instruction Sch. Dist. Boundary Appeal Bd., 550 N.W.2d 96 [110 Educ. L. Rep. 847] (Wis. 1996).
[28] School Dist. of Waukesha v. School Dist. Boundary Appeal Bd., 548 N.W.2d 122 [109 Educ. L. Rep. 967] (Wis. Ct. App. 1996).

the evidence, applied the requisite legal standards, and arrived at a well reasoned decision.

An appellate court in Illinois affirmed a regional board's denial of a petition for detachment and annexation.[29] The tribunal rejected the residents' argument that approval of the petition was required under a section of the school code that stated territory "shall" be detached and annexed on request. The court found that the residents' argument was not properly before the court because the residents had explicitly chosen to proceed under a different section of the school code before the regional board.

Property owners in Michigan sought further review after their petitions for transfers into an adjacent district were denied. An appellate court addressed the question of the appropriate standard of review to be applied by the state board. The court found that judicial review is limited to the question of whether the board's decision was authorized by law, and if so, was it arbitrary and capricious or an abuse of discretion.[30] In the absence of any evidence that the board acted improperly, the court affirmed the denials.

An appellate court in New York resolved a dispute between two school districts over a parcel of land. In 1991, apparently relying on a 1943 atlas map, the Lisbon district laid claim to land which had long been considered part of Ogdensburg. On further review, an appellate court affirmed the decision by the Commissioner of Education to reject the claim of the Lisbon district.[31] The court noted that there was evidence in the record to show that Ogdensburg provided services to residents on the land for ninety years; that the people living on the land voted in Ogdensburg elections; and that the property had been on the tax-exempt rolls of Ogdensburg since 1927. The court stated that in light of history and the fact that the 1943 atlas was not an official school district map, the Commissioner's determination should be left in place since it was logical, supported by the evidence, and was neither arbitrary nor capricious.

School District Board Membership

Boards of education are responsible for school governance at the local level. How a board's membership is determined was the subject of six cases from five states.

---

[29] Jackson v. Cook County Regional Bd. of Sch. Trustees, 667 N.E.2d 1335 [112 Educ. L. Rep. 365] (Ill. App. Ct. 1996).
[30] McBride v. Pontiac Sch. Dist., 553 N.W.2d 646 [113 Educ. L. Rep. 426] (Mich. Ct. App. 1996).
[31] Board of Educ. of Lisbon Cent. Sch. Dist. v. Sobol, 641 N.Y.S.2d 168 [108 Educ. L. Rep. 1241] (N.Y. App. Div. 1996).

Selection of Board Members

In the first of two cases from North Carolina, voters challenged a plan for the reapportionment of electoral districts for county commissioners and school board members. The voters claimed the plan violated the one-person, one-vote principle because it used the total, rather than the voting age, population as a base and the two were not substantially equal. A federal district court held that the plan violated the Equal Protection Clause, but the Fourth Circuit vacated and remanded. The Fourth Circuit discussed the distinction between electoral equality, which is tied to voter strength, and representational equality, which is based on total population, and found that "electoral equality is not necessarily superior to representational equality."[32] The court also noted that a ten percent deviation is a guide, rather than an absolute benchmark, for placing burden of proof.

White voters moved for a temporary restraining order against conducting a school board election pursuant to a merger plan that included race-based voting districts. In noting that the evidence suggested racial gerrymandering that would be extremely difficult for the state to justify, a federal district court in North Carolina considered the balance of hardships and likelihood of success on the merits in granting the requested relief.[33]

In a voting rights case from Texas, the Fifth Circuit agreed that plaintiffs failed to prove a district's at-large system diluted the voting strength of black voters.[34] The court acknowledged that there was historical discrimination in the district and that few minorities had been elected to the board. However, the appellate panel found no merit to the assignments of error over the legal standard used by the district court, the adequacy of the detail in its opinion, or abuse of discretion in refusing to consider evidence from an election that took place after the trial.

African-American voters in Missouri appealed the dismissal of their claim that the at-large, multimember system used to elect members of a board of education violated the Voting Rights Act by diluting their ballots. The Eighth Circuit affirmed that the African-Americans voters failed to establish that a White voting bloc defeated the minority-preferred candidate, one of three preconditions for a violation of the Voting Rights Act.[35]

---

[32] Daly v. Hunt, 93 F.3d 1212 [111 EDUC. L. REP. 1126] (4th Cir. 1996).
[33] Cannon v. North Carolina State Bd. of Educ., 917 F. Supp. 387 [107 EDUC. L. REP. 825] (E.D.N.C. 1996).
[34] Rollins v. Fort Bend Indep. Sch. Dist., 89 F.3d 1205 [111 EDUC. L. REP. 68] (5th Cir. 1996).
[35] Clay v. Board of Educ. of St. Louis, 90 F.3d 1357 [111 EDUC. L. REP. 183] (8th Cir. 1996).

According to an appellate court in New Jersey, a board of education acted properly in striking the nominating petition of a candidate.[36] The board rejected the petition when the signature of an unregistered voter was removed and the petition no longer had the minimum number of signers. The court found that the legislature intended the recently enacted law governing such elections to have retroactive effect and that the board secretary had the inherent authority to verify whether each petition conformed with statutory requirements.

Taxpayers unsuccessfully challenged the appointment of a school board member by the presiding judge of a county court. An appellate court in Pennsylvania affirmed that the judge did not have to recuse himself even though his daughter worked for the district because nothing in state law precluded him from making the appointment.[37]

Removal of Board Members

Two school board members appealed a judgment that two charges in recall petitions were legally and factually sufficient for submission to the voters. One charge alleged that board members violated the Open Meeting Act by conspiring to compel the superintendent to accept a modification of his employment status. Alternatively, the superintendent alleged that the board failed to notify him that his contract would not be extended. The second charge was that two school board members began an investigation to retaliate against other board members and the superintendent. The Supreme Court of Washington reversed, finding that both charges were factually and legally insufficient to submit to the voters.[38] It declared that the first was inadequate since the petitions stated no facts, only conclusory allegations. The court reasoned that the second was insufficient because it was conjectural and failed to provide sufficient detail to enable the electorate to make an informed decision.

Board members challenged a recall petition that alleged they had violated the Open Meetings Act. An appellate panel in Michigan held that once the lower court decided that the petitions were clear, it should have ended its review since it had no authority to review the statements in the petitions for truth or falsity.[39] The court added that the validity of the petition was moot because a recall election must pertain to conduct

---

[36] Saunders v. Toms River Regular Sch. Bd. of Educ., 673 A.2d 804 [108 EDUC. L. REP. 755] (N.J. Super. Ct. App. Div. 1996).

[37] *In re* Appointment of a Sch. Director for Region No. 9 of Keystone Cent. Sch. Dist., 682 A.2d 871 [113 EDUC. L. REP. 327] (Pa. Commw. Ct. 1996).

[38] *In re* Recall of Beasley, 908 P.2d 878 [105 EDUC. L. REP. 1267] (Wash. 1996).

[39] Meyers v. Patchkowski, 549 N.W.2d 602 [110 EDUC. L. REP. 810] (Mich. Ct. App. 1996).

that occurred after the start of a public official's current term and here the dispute was over one that took place before the board members started their current terms of office.

School board members who were suspended by a Chancellor sought to vacate the order on the ground that the Chancellor exceeded his authority. A trial court granted the board members' petition, but an appellate tribunal in New York reversed.[40] The panel was of the opinion that the trial court improperly exercised its jurisdiction by erroneously concluding that the board members were not required to exhaust remedies prior to bringing suit and this undermined the administrative review provisions of state law.

Miscellaneous Election Issues

A statute providing that school-based decision-making councils consist of two parents, three teachers, and an administrator, expressly prohibited district employees or their spouses from serving as parent members. Two parents who were ineligible to serve on the council because they were married to board employees contended that the anti-nepotism provision violated their rights to equal protection as it discriminated against only them and not other members. An appellate court struck the statute down, but the Supreme Court of Kentucky reversed.[41] In applying the rational basis test, the court held that the law did not violate equal protection because it was clearly related to the legitimate goal of avoiding the appearance of nepotism.

In Michigan, a resident alleged that irregularities in school board and bond elections violated her rights under both federal and state law. A federal district court in Michigan dismissed her complaint for failure to state cognizable federal claims.[42] The court indicated that since no federal case was pending, there was no basis for jurisdiction over the state charge.

School District Board Meetings

School boards can perform their governance functions only when gathered as a body. When board meetings are required, how they are convened, and the way in which they are conducted were among the issues addressed by the courts.

---

[40] Community Sch. Bd. Nine v. Crew, 648 N.Y.S.2d 81 [113 EDUC. L. REP. 877] (N.Y. App. Div. 1996).

[41] Kentucky Dept. of Educ. v. Risner, 913 S.W.2d 327 [106 EDUC. L. REP. 938] (Ky. 1996).

[42] Willing v. Lake Orion Bd. of Trustees, 924 F. Supp. 815 [109 EDUC. L. REP. 1204] (E.D. Mich. 1996).

When a Meetings is Required

A school district challenged the denial of its petition to conduct a special meeting to approve a renegotiated collective bargaining agreement. The Supreme Court of New Hampshire dismissed the appeal as moot because district voters approved the agreement at a subsequent annual meeting.[43]

In New York, a school administrator petitioned for reinstatement on the ground that his unilateral dismissal by the Chancellor violated state law. A trial court granted the petition when it found that the purpose of the statute was to protect persons from being unilaterally deprived of their employment without ratification by the board of education.[44] The court directed the board to comply with the law by convening a regular public meeting at which the administrator's retention or dismissal could be put to a formal vote.

Open Meetings

A school committee opted out of the Early Retirement Act at a meeting that was not in compliance with the state's Open Meeting Law because no adequate notice of the meeting was published in a newspaper. Subsequently, an intermediate appellate court declared the vote null and void. On further review, the Supreme Court of Rhode Island affirmed that the Open Meeting Law had been violated, but vacated the remedy.[45] The court concluded that the committee and superintendent had not acted in bad faith because the teachers knew of the meeting and the remedy had the effect of penalizing the taxpayers. As such, the school system was permitted to opt out of the Early Retirement Act.

A teacher unsuccessfully tried to compel a school board to issue him a supplemental coaching contract. The Supreme Court of Ohio agreed that when the board voted three-to-one with one abstention to reject the issuance of the supplemental coaching contract, it did not violate the statute requiring a roll-call vote to hire a teacher.[46]

In a second case from Ohio, a board of education sought a temporary restraining order to limit picketing by striking employees. At the same time, the union requested declaratory and injunctive relief to invalidate a resolution that would have created a contract with an outside source for

---

[43] *In re* Mascoma Valley Regional Sch. Dist., 677 A.2d 679 [110 Educ. L. Rep. 722] (N.H. 1996).

[44] Okebiyi v. Cortines, 641 N.Y.S.2d 791 [109 Educ. L. Rep. 334] (N.Y. Sup. Ct. 1996).

[45] Edwards v. State *ex rel.* Attorney Gen., 677 A.2d 1347 [110 Educ. L. Rep. 756] (R.I. 1996).

[46] State *ex rel.* Savarese v. Buckeye Local Sch. Dist. Bd. of Educ., 660 N.E.2d 463 [106 Educ. L. Rep. 871] (Ohio 1996).

bus transportation services. The union alleged that the resolution was the result of deliberations in executive session that violated the state's Sunshine Law. An appellate court held that the union's evidence about the board's deliberations raised the inference that the board improperly made the resolution.[47]

In Louisiana, a federal district court that maintained jurisdiction over a desegregation case for forty years responded to a request from a newly elected board of education that wanted to formulate a plan to end the litigation. The court issued two orders to help ensure confidentiality of the deliberations. The first prohibited educators from discussing any aspects of the plan with anyone other than the parties to the litigation. The second required the board to meet in private sessions and to keep preliminary versions of the plan confidential. On further review, the Fifth Circuit vacated both orders.[48] The court pointed out that both orders were unconstitutional because they intruded severely on the First Amendment right of a news agency to gather information and the orders did not protect a countervailing governmental interest. The appellate panel added that the trial court abused its discretion in the second order by not considering the relationship between conducting private sessions and the Open Meeting Law.

A board of education challenged a holding that it violated the Open Meeting Law when it voted in a closed session to terminate a construction contract. An appellate tribunal in North Carolina affirmed that while the board violated the law, the trial court did not abuse its discretion by declining to void the board's action.[49] However, the court also agreed that the contractor was entitled to an award of attorney fees because the firm prevailed on the Open Meeting Law issue.

A school district in Texas challenged the reinstatement of a student it expelled for assaulting a teacher. Prior to reaching a final decision on whether to exclude the student, the board recessed into executive session. Upon returning to open session, the board upheld the expulsion but shortened it to the remainder of the semester. After a trial court declared the expulsion void, the district sought further review. In reversing, an appellate court found that the expulsion was appropriate, the student received due process, and the board did not violate the Open Meeting Law.[50]

---

[47] Springfield Local Sch. Dist. Bd. of Educ. v. Ohio Ass'n of Pub. Sch. Employees, Local 530, 667 N.E.2d 458 [111 EDUC. L. REP. 463] (Ohio Ct. App. 1996).

[48] Davis v. East Baton Rouge Parish Sch. Bd., 78 F.3d 920 [107 EDUC. L. REP. 540] (5th Cir. 1996).

[49] H.B.S. Contractors v. Cumberland County Bd. of Educ., 468 S.E.2d 517 [108 EDUC. L. REP. 965] (N.C. Ct. App. 1996).

[50] United Indep. Sch. Dist. v. Gonzalez, 911 S. W.2d 118 [105 EDUC. L. REP. 341] (Tex. Ct. App. 1995).

In California, a school district policy prohibited individuals from complaining about district employees during open sessions of board meetings, regardless of whether the person was identified by name or position. A federal district court enjoined the enforcement of the policy.[51] It reasoned not only that such speech, even if defamatory, was protected by the state and federal constitutions, but also that the policy was not narrowly drawn to effectuate a compelling state interest. The court concluded that the policy could not be justified on grounds of secondary effects of speech or of protecting unwilling listeners from hearing negative comments.

Powers of School District Boards

School governance depends on the authority that legislatures grant to local boards. The extent of these powers and how they may be exercised are often at issue.

Statutory Authority

A county board of education argued that because it was prohibited from making expenditures for items other than those expressly authorized by statute, it could not be subject to a municipal service fee. The Supreme Court of Appeals of West Virginia agreed that a board of education can only exercise power that is explicitly conferred on it by statute.[52] However, the court affirmed that state law authorized the board to pay a municipal service fee for fire and flood protection to safeguard the health of its pupils and to keep school grounds and buildings in good order.

Delegation of Authority

Much of the authority granted by legislatures to school boards may not be delegated to others. Thus, courts must sometimes decide whether it is permissible for a board to delegate specific authority.

A school board member obtained a copy of a field-tested version of a test that eleventh-graders had to take as a graduation requirement. When the board member was enjoined from procuring copies of test that would be administered the following fall, a trial court denied relief on the basis of confidentiality. On appeal, the Supreme Court of Iowa held that the test was excluded from disclosure under the examination exception to the Open Meetings Law.[53] In addition, the court ruled that even though board members generally should be allowed access to both public and

---

[51] Baca v. Moreno Valley Unified Sch. Dist., 936 F. Supp. 719 [112 EDUC. L. REP. 917] (C.D. Cal. 1996).

[52] City of Huntington v. Bacon, 473 S.E.2d 743 [111 EDUC. L. REP. 1001] (W. Va. 1996).

[53] Gabrilson v. Flynn, 554 N.W.2d 267 [113 EDUC. L. REP. 894] (Iowa 1996).

private records that are necessary for the proper discharge of their duties, they did not have the right to copy, disseminate, or publish the contents of the records because of the confidentiality provisions of the Open Records Law.

A school district sought further review of an order by the state labor relations board. The board found that the district committed an unfair practice by refusing to arbitrate a grievance after it suspended a teacher without pay for one day. An appellate court in Illinois affirmed that arbitration of the dispute neither violated nor was inconsistent with any other statutory provisions.[54] The court reasoned that while the board had statutory authority to impose a temporary disciplinary suspension, arbitration did not interfere with the overarching statutory framework for teacher dismissals.

Board Policy

One of the basic functions of a governing board is the adoption of policy. The validity of board policy was at issue in the following cases.

A teacher who volunteered as a trainer of helping dogs for the disabled challenged her district's denial of her request to bring a trainee dog to school so that the dog could become acclimated to the demands of accompanying its future master in public places. The teacher alleged that the district violated a state statute that made it unlawful for a place of public accommodation to refuse admittance or service to a person training a helping dog. The Supreme Court of Nevada affirmed a preliminary injunction in favor of the teacher.[55] The court concluded that since the school was a place of public accommodation, the statute entitled the teacher to be admitted with whatever helping dog she was training.

Teachers in Pennsylvania sought declaratory and injunctive relief against a board policy that prohibited employees from engaging, at any time, in political activities on district property. A federal trial court agreed that the policy violated the First Amendment because it was invoked to prevent off-duty employees from soliciting votes for board members at official polling places on school property.[56] The court observed that the speech involved a matter of public concern and implicated a fundamental First Amendment interest. The court held that there was no evidence to reasonably indicate that the interests of the board in the operation of the

---

[54] Granite City Community Unit Sch. Dist. #9 v. Illinois Educ. Labor Relations Bd., 664 N.E.2d 1060 [109 EDUC. L. REP. 1343] (Ill. App. Ct. 1996).

[55] Clark County Sch. Dist. v. Buchanan, 924 P.2d 716 [113 EDUC. L. REP. 930] (Nev. 1996).

[56] Castle v. Colonial Sch. Dist., 933 F. Supp. 458 [112 EDUC. L. REP. 120] (E.D. Pa. 1996).

district outweighed those of the teachers in exercising their First Amendment rights.

A teacher in Wyoming challenged a policy that limited and restricted criticism. Staff members could address critical remarks only directly to the person being criticized, to the building principal, to the superintendent, or at a regular board meeting. The federal district court maintained that the policy violated the First Amendment because it was impermissibly overbroad, void for vagueness, and not a permissible content-neutral time, place, and manner restriction.[57]

In California, a teachers' union questioned a policy that prevented district employees from wearing political buttons at work sites during school hours. An appellate court affirmed that the district had the power to disassociate itself from controversy by preventing its employees from wearing political buttons in class or when otherwise engaged in providing instruction.[58] At the same time, the court pointed out that the district did not have such power when its employees expressed their political viewpoints to each other in noninstructional settings on school property.

The Michigan State Tenure Commission upheld a board's termination of a teacher's contract because the teacher used excessive force against a student. On further review, the appellate court reversed in ruling that the teacher's dismissal was not supported by competent, substantial, and material evidence that he violated the law on corporal punishment.[59] The court added that while the teacher's actions may not have violated the corporal punishment statute, they may have transgressed the board's excessive use of force policy. The court remanded for further consideration of whether the teacher violated such a policy.

A teacher in Tennessee unsuccessfully appealed her dismissal on grounds of unsatisfactory performance. The court offered that the board of education did not violate her due process rights by failing to comply with its own policy of providing a written warning from the superintendent if a teacher's performance was so unsatisfactory that it could lead to dismissal.[60] The court acknowledged that the principal had given the teacher numerous written notices of unsatisfactory performance that were sufficiently specific and serious enough to warn her that she had to improve her performance or risk the loss of her job.

---

[57] Westbrook v. Teton County Sch. Dist. No. 1, 918 F. Supp. 1475 [108 Educ. L. Rep. 215] (D. Wyo. 1996).

[58] California Teachers Ass'n v. Governing Bd. of San Diego Unified Sch. Dist., 53 Cal. Rptr.2d 474 [109 Educ. L. Rep. 1335] (Cal. Ct. App. 1996).

[59] Widdoes v. Detroit Pub. Sch., 553 N.W.2d 688 [113 Educ. L. Rep. 432] (Mich. Ct. App. 1996).

[60] Childs v. Roane County Bd. of Educ., 929 S.W.2d 364 [113 Educ. L. Rep. 505] (Tenn. Ct. App. 1996).

In a wrongful death action arising from a student's at-home suicide, an appellate court in Minnesota held that discretionary function immunity protected a school district from liability for not adopting a suicide prevention policy.[61] The court concluded that discretionary function immunity protected the district over both the development and the nondevelopment of a policy.

An appellate panel in New York affirmed that a trial court lacked jurisdiction to review a resolution that was passed by a board of education.[62] The court determined that insofar as a state statute vested original jurisdiction over such disputes in the Commissioner of Education, the law precluded recourse to the judiciary until such review was complete.

School District Financial Affairs

Cases involving the financial affairs of school districts can be organized into two categories: how they acquire funds and how they use funds. This section includes actions involving the taxing authority of districts and disputes over the ways in which they put their financial resources to use.

Taxing Authority

Pennsylvania alone generated four cases on taxing authority. All of the cases, the first three of which were decided in favor of the school districts, turned on the application of a state statute authorizing local taxation.

Tavern owners unsuccessfully sought to enjoin an Across-the-Bar Tax to help fund public schools. An appellate court in Pennsylvania affirmed that it was a valid and enforceable ordinance granting a school board ongoing authority to levy a tax that did not have to be renewed by annual vote of the city council.[63]

An appellate court ruled that a six percent tax imposed by a school district on all parking lot fees collected within its boundaries was statutorily permissible.[64] As a transaction tax, rather than a statutorily prohibited business privilege tax, the court decided that the district neither

---

[61] Killen v. Independent Sch. Dist. No. 706, 547 N.W.2d 113 [109 EDUC. L. REP. 387] (Minn. Ct. App. 1996).

[62] Schulz v. Galgano, 637 N.Y.S.2d 797 [106 EDUC. L. REP. 1291] (N.Y. App. Div. 1996).

[63] Licensed Beverage Ass'n of Phila. v. Board of Educ. of Sch. Dist. of Phila., 680 A.2d 1198 [111 EDUC. L. REP. 1275] (Pa. Commw. Ct. 1996).

[64] Airpark Int'l I v. Interboro Sch. Dist., 677 A.2d 388 [110 EDUC. L. REP. 222] (Pa. Commw. Ct. 1996).

violated the Equal Protection Clause nor imposed an excessive tax because it was not subject to statutory caps.

A city in Pennsylvania challenged a tax imposed by a school district on the privilege of leasing tax-exempt realty. In reversing a decree nisi invalidating the tax, an appellate court held that since the tax was a true privilege tax, it was a proper subject under the Local Tax Enabling Act and did not contravene the General County Assessment Law.[65] The court added that the because the tax applied uniformly to all and involved a reasonable classification, it did not violate either the uniformity clause of the state constitution or the Equal Protection Clause of the Fourteenth Amendment.

In the only case that a district in Pennsylvania lost, a school system unsuccessfully sought further review of its being enjoined from implementing a resolution that imposed a one percent wagering tax on gambling done at an off-track betting establishment created by a harness racing corporation. An appellate court affirmed that the tax was duplicative.[66] It reasoned that the resolution was pre-empted pursuant to the Local Tax Enabling Act because an existing state tax dealt with wagers and both were measured on the same base - the amount of the bets being placed.

Other states also witnessed litigation over property taxes. Most of these cases turned on whether a district had the ability to levy the tax in question or if its authority was being implemented in a legally permissible way.

When a taxpayer challenged a Tax Relief Act, a special referee found that it did not violate the state constitution. On further review, the Supreme Court of South Carolina affirmed.[67] It observed that the Act was not taxation without representation because the legislation authorized the school district to impose a sales tax upon the approval of the electorate of the entire county. Further, the court was of the opinion that the Act was not prohibited special legislation since it imposed a lawful tax limited in application and incidence to persons or property in one county.

The Supreme Court of Georgia affirmed that an agreement between a city and its school district, under which the school district received an amount equal to thirty percent of the local option sales tax receipts, was prohibited by the state constitution.[68] The court decreed that a constitutional provision established an exclusive financing method,

---

[65] City of Harrisburg v. School Dist. of Harrisburg, 675 A.2d 758 [109 Educ. L. Rep. 788] (Pa. Commw. Ct. 1996).

[66] Pocono Downs v. Catasauqua Area Sch. Dist., 669 A.2d 500 [106 Educ. L. Rep. 261] (Pa. Commw. Ct. 1996).

[67] Bradley v. Cherokee Sch. Dist. No. One, 470 S.E.2d 570 [109 Educ. L. Rep. 981] (S.C. 1996).

[68] Atlanta Indep. Sch. Sys. v. Lane, 469 S.E.2d 22 [108 Educ. L. Rep. 1297] (Ga. 1996).

providing that each school system in the state was prohibited from receiving funds from any local tax source other than ad valorem taxes. The court concluded that mandamus to compel the district to return the funds it received from the city under the agreement was not available because such relief only applies prospectively and does not require the undoing of acts that already have been completed.

A board of education sought further review after an appellate court ruled in favor of a county sheriff in a disagreement about the proper fee that he was entitled to for collecting school taxes. The Supreme Court of Kentucky affirmed.[69] It pointed out that the allocation of expenses associated with tax collection based on a percentage of total revenues, rather than a division of the cost equally among districts, did not violate the state constitutional provision requiring educational taxes to be appropriated to common schools and no other purpose.

In the first of two cases from Illinois, a federal district court held that the local government tort immunity act authorized a board of education to level taxes to pay for the cost of remedying alleged racially discriminatory practices.[70] The court acknowledged that the tort immunity act specifically authorized payment of compensatory damages for constitutional injuries. The court decided that the costs incurred in complying with a mandatory injunction to remedy racial discrimination were authorized.

Taxpayers requested further review of a ruling in favor of a school district in a dispute over their real estate taxes. An appellate court in Illinois affirmed.[71] It maintained that the tax was proper since the objectors had an opportunity to be heard prior to the formal adoption of proposed multipliers and the objectors were unable to demonstrate that the assessment of nonfarm property increased substantially more than the assessment of farm property so as to violate equal protection.

Bonds and Leases

A consolidated school district sought both to compel the board to issue refunding bonds and to order the county clerk to levy taxes to help do so. When the county clerk sought further review, an appellate court in Illinois affirmed.[72] The court agreed that because the district had the power

---

[69] Board of Educ. of Calloway County Sch. Dist. v. Williams, 930 S.W.2d 399 [113 EDUC. L. REP. 977] (Ky. 1996).

[70] *In re* County Collector of County of Winnebago, Ill., 918 F. Supp. 235 [108 EDUC. L. REP. 145] (N.D. Ill. 1996).

[71] People *ex rel.* Bonefeste v. B.D.H. Rentals, 660 N.E.2d 1012 [106 EDUC. L. REP. 1271] (Ill. App. Ct. 1996).

[72] Lemont-Bromberek Combined Sch. Dist. No. 113(A), Cook and DuPage Counties v. Walter, 665 N.E.2d 548 [110 EDUC. L. REP. 292] (Ill. App. Ct. 1996).

to issue refunding bonds to cover its own obligations and those of its predecessor, the district had the authority to issue bonds not only to cover the liabilities incurred by its previous system but also to spread the obligation to repay the money to all of its taxpayers.

Taxpayers challenged a decision of the State Board of Tax Commissioners that approved a lease-purchase agreement to build a new high school, arguing that the commission was required to conduct an additional public hearing. The Tax Court of Indiana affirmed that the Commissioners did not err in deferring to a letter from the Department of Education stating that the additional hearing was not required. [73]

Use of School District Funds

Cases from three different states involved disputes over the use of school district funds. The Supreme Court of Connecticut decided that a board of education did not have authority to reallocate capital funds that were appropriated to it by the board of aldermen.[74] The court distinguished between the power of the board of education over the operating budget and the power of the board of aldermen over capital construction.

Parents and others appealed the dismissal of their claims against two school districts for illegal management of public funds and against the county attorney for not prosecuting the administrators who were responsible. The Supreme Court of Montana held that the trial court erred in dismissing the first count for lack of standing because the parents alleged an injury personal to themselves as distinguished from one suffered by the community in general.[75] The court was of the opinion that the parents did not need to claim that they suffered exclusively. However, it added that the trial court properly dismissed the action against the county attorney since a decision as to whether to prosecute is discretionary. The court concluded that the county attorney had common law immunity from civil liability for conduct within the scope of his duties.

In Illinois, parents charged that a board of education violated the law by using Chapter 1 funds to cover general costs rather than pay for supplemental programs designed to assist poor children. An appellate panel reasoned that the trial court erred in finding that the state school

---

[73] Riley at Jackson Remonstrance Group v. State Bd. of Tax Comm'r, 663 N.E.2d 802 [108 Educ. L. Rep. 881] (Ind. Tax Ct. 1996).
[74] Board of Educ. of New Haven v. City of New Haven, 676 A.2d 375 [109 Educ. L. Rep. 1277] (Conn. 1996).
[75] Helena Parents Comm'n v. Lewis and Clark County Comm'r, 922 P.2d 1140 [112 Educ. L. Rep. 1051] (Mont. 1996).

code implied no private right of action with regard to the Chapter 1 funds.[76] It posited that the parents, as representatives of disadvantaged children, could bring suit because they were the class of persons for whose benefit the legislation was written.

School District Employment Affairs

School governance necessarily includes the employment of personnel who carry out a school district's mission. Therefore, this section reports on cases involving the employment of administrators, teachers, and support staff.

Administrators

The Supreme Court of Pennsylvania held that annuity payments to a school superintendent were not compensation for the purposes of computing final average salary under the state retirement code.[77] In this instance, the court viewed the payments as nonstandard remuneration, distinguishable from annuity contracts purchased under a deferred compensation program that would be included in a retirement program. The court noted that the code and regulations included a restrictive definition of compensation that was intended to preserve the actuarial integrity of the retirement fund by excluding an employee's final average salary from the computation that tended to artificially inflate pay for the enhancing retirement benefits.

In a second case from Pennsylvania, an appellate court ruled that a payment for unused sick, vacation, and compensatory days made pursuant to a negotiated agreement leading to a superintendent's resignation, was severance pay that could not be included in calculating his final average salary.[78] The court decided that there had not been any commingling of prosecutorial and adjudicative functions within the retirement system agency in violation of the former administrator's constitutional due process rights.

After a board of education terminated the employment of an assistant superintendent approximately two months before the expiration of his three-year contract, he brought suit alleging breach, denial of tenure, and other claims. An appellate court affirmed a finding of liability and awarded

---

[76] Noyola v. Board of Educ. of Chicago, 671 N.E.2d 802 [113 EDUC. L. REP. 1287] (Ill. App. Ct. 1996).
[77] Christiana v. Public Sch. Employees' Retirement Bd., 669 A.2d 940 [106 EDUC. L. REP. 705] (Pa. 1996).
[78] Wyland v. Public Sch. Employees' Retirement Bd., 669 A.2d 1098 [106 EDUC. L. REP. 718] (Pa. Commw. Ct. 1996).

punitive and emotional distress damages. The Supreme Court of New Jersey disagreed.[79] It held that stress induced by litigation is not recoverable as a separate component of emotional distress. The court vacated the punitive award damages and remanded for a new trial on the issue of damages only. The court further pointed out that the administrator did not acquire tenure since he was not employed for at least one additional day after working in the district for three consecutive calendar years.

After a school committee voted not to extend the contract of a Director of Special Education, the Director alleged violations of her statutory and constitutional rights. The Supreme Judicial Court of Maine held that as an administrator, the Director was neither entitled to the statutory protections afforded teachers nor did she have a property interest in continuing employment that was safeguarded by the Due Process Clause.[80] The court added that the committee's failure to respond to the Director's request for documents was a sanctionable violation of the Freedom of Access Act. The court concluded that even though the eventual production of the requested documents did not alter the results of the case, the Director was entitled to court costs on this claim.

The Seventh Circuit affirmed the dismissal, for lack of standing, of a section 1983 action brought by parents who alleged that a board of trustees discriminated against African-Americans in hiring a superintendent.[81] The court decided that the parents' inability to establish standing rested squarely on one false proposition they alleged, namely that they had a constitutional right to have an African-American considered for the job. The court stated that if the board had engaged in discrimination, it was the applicants rather than the parents who had been injured.

A superintendent whose contract was canceled on grounds of neglect of duty, incompetency, and unprofessional conduct appealed the dismissal of his suit for reinstatement. An appellate court in Nebraska reversed.[82] The court indicated that since there was insufficient evidence as a matter of law to support any of the grounds for dismissal, the board's action was arbitrary and capricious.

In the first of two cases from New York, an appellate court affirmed in favor of a tenured assistant superintendent for instructional services who was discharged when his position was eliminated for budgetary reasons.[83] The court agreed that since he had seniority rights over the

[79] Picogna v. Board of Educ. of Cherry Hill, 671 A.2d 1035 [107 EDUC. L. REP. 859] (N.J. 1996).
[80] Cook v. Lisbon Sch. Comm., 682 A.2d 672 [113 EDUC. L. REP. 317] (Me. 1996).
[81] Clay v. Fort Wayne Community Sch., 76 F.3d 873 [107 EDUC. L. REP. 64] (7th Cir. 1996).
[82] Boss v. Fillmore County Sch. Dist. No. 19, 548 N.W.2d 1 [109 EDUC. L. REP. 949] (Neb. Ct. App. 1996).

assistant superintendent for personnel and administration and because both positions were in the same tenure area, the employee with less seniority should have been discharged first.

After a school district negotiated contracts with various employees, including the superintendent, other administrators, and their unions that included provisions allowing accumulated sick days to be converted into cash upon retirement or dismissal, a resident challenged the contract provisions. A trial court refused to declare that the provisions violated the state constitution, that they were contrary to public policy, and that the money should have been returned to the district. An appellate court in New York affirmed.[84] It offered that the board had statutory authority to bargain and include such provisions in its contracts.

When a board of education tried to dismiss an administrator for engaging in a sexual affair with one of its members, the whole board did not believe that it could provide an unbiased hearing. When the administrator refused to submit the matter to an arbitrator, the board voted to terminate the administrator's employment without giving him notice. After a trial court ordered the administrator's reinstatement, an appellate panel in Pennsylvania vacated and remanded.[85] It directed the board to conduct a hearing and to determine on the record whether the proceeding could be impartial. The court found that where the board had taken a personnel action without affording the required due process, the proper remedy was a remand for a hearing, not reinstatement.

Teachers

The Supreme Court of Alaska affirmed the dismissal of a Reserve Officers Training Corps instructor for sexual abuse of students.[86] It held that the board of education was not bound to follow a hearing officer's findings in favor of the instructor because the board's decision was supported by substantial evidence in the record. However, the court declared that since the instructor was not required to have exhausted his contractual remedies before pursuing judicial review, his predismissal suspension should have been with pay.

Pursuant to a new funding scheme that made it more attractive for school systems to operate their own special education programs, districts

---

[83] Schlick v. Board of Educ. of Mamaroneck Union Free Sch. Dist., 642 N.Y.S.2d 64 [109 EDUC. L. REP. 346] (N.Y. App. Div. 1996).
[84] Perrenod v. Liberty Bd. of Educ., 636 N.Y.S.2d 210 [106 EDUC. L. REP. 302] (N.Y. App. Div. 1996).
[85] Foster v. Board of Dirs. of Keystone Oaks Sch. Dist., 678 A.2d 1214 [111 EDUC. L. REP. 350] (Pa. Commw. Ct. 1996).
[86] Romulus v. Anchorage Sch. Dist., 910 P.2d 610 [106 EDUC. L. REP. 1332] (Alaska 1996).

hired teachers who had worked for intermediate units. An issue arose as to whether the teachers would retain their seniority for years of service in those units. The Supreme Court of Pennsylvania affirmed that state law required districts both to credit the teachers with years of service from their intermediate units and to accept the years of experience that they gained prior to working in those positions.[87] The court noted that the Pennsylvania Department of Education also interpreted the statute to mean that whatever service was credited by the intermediate unit must also be recognized by a school district.

In a second case from Pennsylvania, a teacher disputed an order of the public school employees' retirement board that denied his request to purchase credit for service rendered as an instructor at a juvenile detention center. An appellate court reversed in favor of the teacher.[88] It found that his service as a teacher of school-age students in a youth detention center was in a "public education institution" within the meaning of the state school employees' retirement code.

The Supreme Court of Appeals of West Virginia prohibited a board of education from abolishing the positions of full-time homebound teachers and replacing them with hourly employees absent a showing of the need to reduce such instruction.[89] The court stated that such a plan clearly contravened the contractual scheme of employment contemplated by state law.

A board of education and a teachers association entered into a collective bargaining agreement that afforded probationary employees more protection than state law. Subsequently, an arbitrator found in favor of a teacher when the board did not follow the procedures set out in the agreement. On appeal, the Supreme Court of California held that state law pre-empted the bargaining agreement as to procedures governing the re-election of probationary teachers.[90] The court concluded that since decisions about re-employing probationary teachers are vested in the board, they are not subject to bargaining.

According to a second appellate court in California, a school district's replacement of three elementary school psychologists with an administrative psychologist and independent contractors constituted a

---

[87] Allegheny Intermediate Unit #3 Educ. Ass'n v. Bethel Park Sch. Dist., 680 A2d 827 [111 EDUC. L. REP. 1257] (Pa 1996).
[88] Hopkins v. Public Sch. Employees' Retirement Bd., 674 A.2d 1197, [109 EDUC. L. REP. 271] (Pa. Commw. Ct. 1996).
[89] State *ex rel.* Boner v. Kanawha County Bd. of Educ., 475 S.E.2d 176 [112 EDUC. L. REP. 504] (W. Va. 1996).
[90] Board of Educ. of Round Valley Unified Sch. Dist. v. Round Valley Teachers Ass'n, 52 Cal. Rptr.2d 115 [108 EDUC. L. REP. 947] (Cal. 1996).

reduction or discontinuation of a particular kind of service.[91] The court found that the board's action was permissible pursuant to the economic layoff provision of the state education code.

A school board in Mississippi suspended a first-year teacher for the duration of the school year for slapping a student. The board later voted not to offer the teacher a contract for the ensuing year. Although the teacher did not avail herself of the hearing, she brought a section 1983 action in federal district court alleging that the nonrenewal of her contract violated her right to due process. The court granted the board's motion for summary judgment.[92] It agreed that the nonrenewal of the teacher's contract implicated neither a protected property interest in continued employment nor a protected liberty interest in her reputation.

Legislation in New York authorized an early retirement incentive program that allowed public employers to offer designated employees up to three years of additional service credit if they retired during a specified open period. When a board of education that set its own open period refused to grant credit to two teachers who resigned prior to the stated time, the teachers filed suit. A trial court rejected the teachers' petition that sought to certify them as eligible.[93] The court mandated that the board's interpretation of the law as permitting it the discretion to select which employees were eligible for early retirement was rational.

In North Carolina, a teacher who was involved in a firearms incident at a pool hall challenged his dismissal for immorality. An appellate court affirmed.[94] The court agreed that the statute under which the teacher was released was not unconstitutionally vague either as written or as applied by the board of education.

Support Staff

The constitutional rights of a school bus driver were at issue in Kentucky where a board of education and superintendent suspended and ultimately dismissed the driver after he appeared at a board meeting and espoused his pro-union views. The driver's suit in federal district court alleged violations of freedom of speech and association, due process, and equal protection. A federal trial court decreed that the driver did not have a property interest in continued employment to support a due process charge.[95]

---

[91] Gallup v. Alta Loma Sch. Dist. Bd. of Trustees, 49 Cal. Rptr.2d 289 [106 EDUC. L. REP. 266] (Cal. Ct. App. 1996).

[92] Pruett v. Dumas, 914 F. Supp. 133 [107 EDUC. L. REP. 120] (N.D. Miss. 1996).

[93] Dodge v. Board of Educ. for Schodack Cent. Sch. Dist., 638 N.Y.S.2d 288 [107 EDUC. L. REP. 256] (N.Y. Sup. Ct. 1996).

[94] Barringer v. Caldwell County Bd. of Educ., 473 S.E.2d 435 [111 EDUC. L. REP. 994] (N.C. Ct. App. 1996).

However, the court offered that the driver could pursue a claim based on his liberty interest because the district did not address it in its motion.

In the first of three cases in New York, a former temporary full-time cleaner brought a title VII suit against a school district alleging that she had been subject to unlawful employment discrimination. The cleaner asserted that the board acted improperly, first when she was not hired for a permanent position because she was a woman, and again when she was fired in retaliation for complaining about this discrimination. A federal district court ordered the woman's reinstatement as a full-time permanent cleaner after she offered direct evidence of discriminatory intent on the part of board and her employment was terminated in retaliation for complaining about the way she had been treated.[96] The court added that the woman was entitled to back pay from the date of her dismissal until the date of judgment, reduced by interim earnings.

A former school employee challenged the dismissal of her claim for reinstatement. An appellate court in New York affirmed that the board did not act arbitrarily or capriciously in refusing to request a review of her status by the civil service commission since her claim was time barred.[97]

The third case from New York involved an appellate court's affirmation in favor of a school board.[98] The court agreed that since the board's determination that a secretary made false entries on her time sheets was supported by substantial evidence, the penalty of dismissal was not so disproportionate to the offenses as to be shocking to one's sense of fairness.

In Texas, a former groundskeeper/custodian brought a retaliatory termination suit against a school district, alleging that he was discharged for having filed a worker's compensation claim. Following a jury verdict in favor of the employee, the district sought further review on the basis of sovereign immunity. An appellate court affirmed.[99] The court concurred that the legislature waived district immunity in retaliatory discharge cases but modified to the extent that it acknowledged that there was a statutory cap on the damages that may be awarded.

---

[95] Creager v. Board of Educ. of Whitley County, Ky., 914 F. Supp. 1457 [107 EDUC. L. REP. 195] (E.D. Ky. 1996).

[96] Brooks v. Fonda-Fultonville Cent. Sch. Dist., 938 F. Supp. 1094 [113 EDUC. L. REP. 676] (N.D.N.Y. 1996).

[97] Vanmaenen v. Hewlett-Woodmere Pub. Sch., 640 N.Y.S.2d 95 [108 EDUC. L. REP. 841] (N.Y. App. Div. 1996).

[98] Roach v. Plainedge Union Free Sch. Dist., 646 N.Y.S.2d 704 [112 EDUC. L. REP. 417] (N.Y. App. Div. 1996).

[99] Canutillo Indep. Sch. Dist. v. Olivares, 917 S.W.2d 494 [108 EDUC. L. REP. 422] (Tex. Ct. App. 1996).

An amendment to the New Mexico School Personnel Act extended tenure rights to almost all public school employees by providing that a board could not terminate, without just cause, the employment of a staff member who had been employed for three consecutive years. An appellate court posited that the amendment did not protect noncertified staff members whose employment was terminated shortly after the effective date of the amendment, because their dismissals were authorized by the terms of contracts that predated the change in the law.[100] Finding no clear legislative intent to apply the amendment retroactively, the court presumed that the statute did not impair the term of the contract that permitted the board to dismiss the employees on ten-days notice.

In Pennsylvania, a district disputed an arbitration award that granted a mechanic a job as a school bus driver. An appellate court affirmed that since the driving position was a promotion, rather than an appointment governed by the seniority position in a collective bargaining agreement, it was not subject to a state veteran's preference act that would have given the position to another driver.[101]

A school custodian brought a wrongful discharge action against his district, contending that his employment was not terminable at will. On further review of a grant of summary judgment in favor of the district, an appellate court in Arkansas affirmed.[102] It held that although the custodian's contract was for a definite term, it was terminable at will by either party for any reason as long as notice and hearing were provided. The court based its decision on the custodian's admission that he had been given notice of the reason for his termination and a hearing.

In the first of three cases from Florida, an appellate court offered that, pursuant to state statute, a school board did not have authority to reinstate a painter who had been employed under annual contracts.[103] The court found that the painter lacked the nomination of the superintendent that was required by statute and that even if the nomination rule was improper, the board still did not have the authority to act.

A materials handler questioned a school board's decision to suspend him for seventeen months without pay for brandishing a pocket knife at a fellow worker in a joking manner. The board considered the behavior to be conduct unbecoming one of its employees. An appellate court in

---

[100] Gadsden Fed'n of Teachers v. Board of Educ. of Gadsden Indep. Sch. Dist., 920 P.2d 1052 [111 EDUC. L. REP. 978] (N.M. Ct. App. 1996).

[101] Belle Vernon Sch. Dist. v. Local Union 782, 670 a.2d 1201 [106 EDUC. L. REP. 1203] (Pa. Commw. Ct. 1996).

[102] Kimble v. Pulaski County Special Sch. Dist., 921 S.W.2d 611 [109 EDUC. L. REP. 988] (Ark. Ct. App. 1996).

[103] Cox v. School Bd. of Osceola County, 669 So. 2d 353 [107 EDUC. L. REP. 1066] (Fla. Dist. Ct. App. 1996).

Florida affirmed that the incident constituted conduct unbecoming a board employee but reversed the penalty as disproportionate to the offense in light of the individual's long service and good record.[104]

In the third case from Florida, a board dismissed a custodian for having sexual relations with his girlfriend on school premises during evening hours when the children were gone. An appellate court of Florida affirmed the board's finding of conduct unbecoming an employee, but concluded that dismissal was unwarranted.[105] The court acknowledged that a collective bargaining agreement incorporated the concept that discipline should be reasonably related to the seriousness of the offense and that the longtime employee had no prior infractions.

In Louisiana, an appellate court upheld a school board's termination of the employment of a tenured bus driver who had been convicted of attempted obscenity, a clearly immoral act.[106] The court found that the board had a rational basis supported by substantial evidence in dismissing the driver.

A personnel commission and state school employees association in California sought a writ of mandate to compel a district to vacate its decision to layoff transportation workers and contract with a private firm for services. Rather than reach the substantive issue of the legality of the district's decision, an appellate court held that the personnel commission failed to demonstrate the required beneficial interest to merit standing.[107] Further, the court posited that the employees' association had to exhaust administrative remedies through the unfair labor practice charge it had pending before the state public employment relations board.

School District Contracts

Ten cases resolved disputes involving contracts between school districts and outside entities. These decisions are organized into two sections: the first includes general contracts for goods and services while the second examines agreements involving the New York City School Construction Authority.

---

[104] Collins v. School Bd. of Dade County, 676 So. 2d 1052 [111 EDUC. L. REP. 599] (Fla. Dist. Ct. App. 1996).
[105] Bell v. School Bd. of Dade County, 681 So. 2d 843 [113 EDUC. L. REP. 1351] (Fla. Dist. Ct. App. 1996).
[106] Allo v. Horne, 672 So. 2d 961 [109 EDUC. L. REP. 504] (La. Ct. App. 1996).
[107] Personnel Comm'n of Barstow Unified Sch. Dist. v. Barstow Unified Sch. Dist., 50 Cal. Rptr.2d 797 [107 EDUC. L. REP. 892](Cal. Ct. App. 1996).

Goods and Services

After an independent transportation contractor with an intermediate unit in Pennsylvania made critical remarks about the director at a board meeting, his contract was terminated. In the face of the district's motion to dismiss the contractor's suit, a federal trial court ruled that the contractor had stated a viable First Amendment free speech claim, but not a Fourteenth Amendment due process charge.[108] The court judged that since the contractor raised an inference that the director was acting outside of his role as an agent of the unit, his claims of conspiracy and tortious interference with contract survived.

An appellate court in California decided that city school districts were not bound to honor an exclusive franchise for trash hauling awarded by the municipality.[109] The court concluded that since districts, as state agencies, were immune from city trash collection regulations, they were free to contract independently with other haulers pursuant to the competitive bidding provisions of state law.

In Florida, an appellate court held that a school board failed to demonstrate how staying the awarding of a contract for a telecommunications system, pending its final action on a protest by an unsuccessful bidder, would pose an immediate and serious danger to public health, safety, or welfare.[110] The court decided the stay had to be reimposed.

In Ohio, a teacher challenged his board's rejection of his low bid for a contract to paint its schools. An appellate court agreed that the board did not abuse its discretion by enforcing its own adminisrative directive that prohibited it from purchasing goods or services from employees.[111]

In Pennsylvania, an appellate tribunal upheld a judgment that substantially lessened an arbitration award to an architect who requested remuneration for services not covered by the base contract fee.[112] The court observed that an affirmative vote of a majority of board members was required by statute because the modification would increase the school district's indebtedness. The court noted that since the architect failed to adduce any proof that a majority had approved his performance, he was not entitled to pay for any additional services that he may have provided.

---

[108] Labalokie v. Capitol Area Intermediate Unit, 926 F. Supp. 503 [110 Educ. L. Rep. 146] (M.D. Pa. 1996).

[109] Laidlaw Waste Sys. v. Bay Cities Servs., 50 Cal. Rptr.2d 824 [107 Educ. L. Rep. 906] (Cal. Ct. App. 1996).

[110] NEC Business Communication Sys. v. Seminole County Sch. Bd., 668 So. 2d 338 [107 Educ. L. Rep. 424] (Fla. Dist. Ct. App. 1996).

[111] Darnell Painting Co. v. Toledo Bd. of Educ., 669 N.E.2d 311 [111 Educ. L. Rep. 1354] (Ohio Ct. App. 1995).

[112] Hazelton Area Sch. Dist. v. Krasnoff, 672 A.2d 858 [107 Educ. L. Rep. 886] (Pa. Commw. Ct. 1996).

An appellate court in New York affirmed that a contractor was entitled to compensation on a unit cost basis for repairing any area of school roof that was over and above the original estimate of square footage.[113] The court noted that the unambiguous terms of the contract obligated the contractor to repair any areas of the roof where moisture was present in the insulation and directed that the firm would be paid on a unit cost basis for spots not covered by the base amount of the bid. However, insofar as an issue remained as to how many square feet of roof were actually repaired, the case was remitted for a determination of damages.

School Construction Authority

All four of the cases involving the New York City School Construction Authority (NYCSCA), which was created by the legislature in large part to address corruption in the construction industry, were resolved in favor of the NYCSCA. In the first, an appellate court reasoned that the NYCSCA had the authority to withdraw its approval of a subcontractor after the firm's president was arrested for bid rigging.[114]

An assignee of construction contracts sought further review of the dismissal of its petition to compel the NYCSCA to make payment on contracts. An appellate court affirmed that mandamus was appropriate only where the right to relief is clear and the duty sought to be compelled is the performance of an act required by law.[115] The court concluded that since contracts that fraudulently have been procured from the NYCSCA are subject to recision and restitution and there were substantial questions about whether the agreement in question had been obtained improperly, the duty to make payment was clearly not a ministerial act.

After noting that the policy of the NYCSCA to award contracts in excess of $1,000,000 only to bidders who participate in state-approved apprenticeship programs was authorized by state law, an appellate court in New York affirmed that it was neither arbitrary nor capricious for the authority to refuse to award the contract at issue to a petitioner.[116] The court based its judgment on the fact that two of the petitioner's subcontractors were not participants in state-approved apprenticeship programs when the bid was opened.

---

[113] Hygrade Insulators v. Board of Educ., Middle County Cent. Sch. Dist., 646 N.Y.S.2d 382 [111 EDUC. L. REP. 1330] (N.Y. App. Div. 1996).
[114] Wolff & Munier v. New York City Sch. Constr. Auth., 639 N.Y.S.2d 429 [108 EDUC. L. REP. 354] (N.Y. App. Div. 1996).
[115] Citywide Factors v. New York City Sch. Constr. Auth., 644 N.Y.S.2d 62 [110 EDUC. L. REP. 360] (N.Y. App. Div. 1996).
[116] Astro Waterproofing v. New York City Sch. Constr. Auth., 643 N.Y.S.2d 165 [113 EDUC. L. REP. 344] (N.Y. App. Div. 1996).

Aftr the NYCSCA terminated a contract for being in default, the contractor unsuccessfully challenged the dismissal of his claim. An appellate court agreed that the contractor should have initiated an Article 78 proceeding to dispute the administrative determination in a timely fashion rather than pursue a collateral attack on the default committee's determination.[117]

School District Facilities

After school officials in Denver refused a request to host a youth forum rally in a high school auditorium, members of a local committee associated with the Million Man March brought suit in federal district court alleging violations of their constitutional rights. School officials had denied the request as not being in the best interests of the district, claiming that committee members had been associated with a student walkout and had made disparaging public remarks about the system. The district court in Colorado granted the committee's motion for a preliminary injunction.[118] It held that the district's permission requirement was an unconstitutional form of prior restraint since it went beyond content-neutral time, place, and manner restrictions by not including procedural protections against unlawful censorship. The court added that since the denial of the permit to use a designated public forum was based on anticipated comments and potential student response, it was unjustified because it was not narrowly tailored to achieve a compelling governmental interest.

The Equal Access Act came into play where high school students in New York wanted to form an after school Bible club. Administrators refused to recognize the club because they felt that the students' insistence that only Christians could serve as officers violated the district's nondiscrimination policy. A federal trial court ruled in favor of the district. On further review, the Second Circuit reversed.[119] It stated that in requiring officers to be Christian, the club was protected by the Act because it was essential to the expressive content of its meetings and to the group's preservation of its purpose and identity. The court added that this application of the Act was constitutional because the district's recognition of the club would neither have drawn it into an establishment of religion nor impaired its efforts to prevent invidious discrimination.

---

[117] Abiele Contracting, Inc. v. New York City Sch. Constr. Auth., 648 N.Y.S.2d 468 [113 EDUC. L. REP. 891] (N.Y. App. Div. 1996).
[118] Local Org. Comm., Denver Chapter, Million Man March v. Cook, 922 F. Supp. 1494 [109 EDUC. L. REP. 223] (D. Colo. 1996).
[119] Hsu v. Roslyn Union Free Sch. Dist. No. 3, 85 F.3d 839 [109 EDUC. L. REP. 1145] (2nd Cir. 1996), *cert. denied*, 117 S. Ct. 608 (1996).

In the first of two cases involving the purchase and sale of real estate, a board of education settled an eminent domain action by agreeing to buy property at more than twice its appraised value. However, the board approved the transaction by a bare majority vote rather than by the extraordinary majority required by statute when a sales price exceeds appraised value. After a trial court ruled in favor of the board, a taxpayer sought further review. An appellate court in Florida reversed.[120] The court posited that the board's action with less than the requisite vote was of sufficient public importance that an aggrieved taxpayer had standing to bring a mandamus claim.

A school district challenged a permanent injunction that prohibited it from selling surplus land to the highest bidder on the basis that there was an irregularity in the bid process because the published call for bids included a typographical error in the closure date. On further review, an appellate court in Texas reversed on the ground that the typographical error was de minimis.[121] The court stated that since the error neither caused harm to any person nor interfered with the transaction, it should not have been used to stop the sale of property that went through what was otherwise a correct, competitive bidding process.

Student Claims of Mistreatment

General Claims

In a case of questionable merit, parents in Texas appealed the dismissal of their section 1983 suit against a school district for failure to state a claim. The parents alleged violations of their son's constitutional rights because a band director and school officials did not respond adequately to their complaints. In affirming, the Fifth Circuit concluded that since the appeal was frivolous, the parents had to show cause why reasonable attorney fees and double costs should not be awarded to the district.[122]

A second case demonstrated that school officials must be sensitive to the privacy rights of students. A student in Kentucky brought suit in federal district court against the board of education and others alleging violations of her state and federal rights to privacy after they released information that appeared in a newspaper about the girl being a

---

[120] Clayton v. School Bd. of Volusia County, 667 So. 2d 942 [107 EDUC. L. REP. 410] (Fla. Dist. Ct. App. 1996).

[121] West Orange-Cove Consol. Indep. Sch. Dist. v. Smith, 928 S.W.2d 773 [112 EDUC. L. REP. 1090] (Tex. Ct. App. 1996).

[122] Shinn v. College Station Indep. Sch. Dist., 96 F.3d 783 [112 EDUC. L. REP. 646] (5th Cir. 1996).

hermaphrodite. The court rejected a motion to dismiss in finding that the Eleventh Amendment did not bar actions against the board and its members in their official capacities.[123] Yet, it added that sovereign immunity precluded state tort claims against the board and its members as well as the superintendent in their official capacities. Finally, because it believed that a question of fact remained as to whether the information that was released allowed the child to be identified personally, the court denied the motion to dismiss based on violations of the state and federal family education rights and privacy acts.

Sexual Harassment and Abuse

Four cases dealt with the troublesome issue of sexual harassment and abuse of students by professional staff. The first two analyzed where liability rests in such litigation.

In Missouri, a high school student sued her school district and others alleging misconduct by a teacher with whom she had a sexual relationship. After the student reached a settlement with the teacher, a federal trial court largely rejected the defendants' motions for summary judgment.[124] The court ruled that the teacher's intentional misconduct was imputed to the district under respondeat superior and under title IX where the staff member intentionally discriminated against the student on the basis of sex. The court also stated that individual defendants could be liable on a section 1983 claim for violations of constitutional rights under a failure to train theory and that state official immunity did not protect the superintendent or principal from negligence claims premised on failure to maintain a safe environment. However, the court concluded that a board member had immunity since his involvement dealt with discretionary rather than ministerial acts.

A student in Michigan brought a hostile environment sexual harassment suit under title IX, state civil rights charges, and negligence and gross negligence claims against his district, high school, administrators, and teacher. The litigation grew out of an alleged improper relationship between the male high school student and his female teacher that ultimately lead to his attempted suicide. A federal district court in Michigan dismissed claims against the school because it was not a separate entity subject to suit under state law.[125] The court denied a motion for

[123] Doe v. Knox County Bd. of Educ., 918 F. Supp. 181 [108 Educ. L. Rep. 134] (E.D. Ky. 1996).
[124] Bolon v. Rolla Pub. Sch., 917 F. Supp. 1423 [108 Educ. L. Rep. 101] (E.D. Mo. 1996).
[125] Nelson v. Almont Community Sch., 931 F. Supp. 1345 [111 Educ. L. Rep. 799] (E.D. Mich. 1996).

summary judgment on the district's liability under title IX and state sexual harassment charges premised on intentional discrimination when it decided that questions of fact remained about what the principal knew, if he acted reasonably, and whether the relationship was consensual. The court added that since the daily operations of a school are within the state governmental immunity statute, both the district and the principal, but not the teacher, were immune from negligence charges. At the same time, the court concluded that since genuine issues of material fact remained, the teacher and principal were not immune from claims of gross negligence.

Two state cases involving the important concept of when an act is actually in the course of employment addressed the duty of districts to defend staff against charges of sexual misconduct. In the first, a school board in New Jersey challenged a ruling because a kindergarten teacher successfully defended himself against criminal charges of sexually abusing young students. An appellate court affirmed.[126] The court reasoned that where the claims arose out of and in the course of the performance of his duties, the teacher was entitled to indemnification.

A former truant officer and the law firm that had been appointed to defend him sued a board of education. The action sought to recover attorney fees and costs incurred by the firm in successfully representing the officer in a civil rights action against him by a student who alleged that she was a victim of sexual abuse. An appellate court in Illinois concurred that while the board's obligation to defend and indemnify had to be determined solely on the allegations in the complaint, the fact that the officer's sexual assault of the student was outside the scope of employment meant that the board did not have the duty to defend the officer in the lawsuit.[127]

General Tort Liability

Defamation

School board trustees sued a superintendent for slander and defamation after the superintendent claimed that the board authorized him to procure a credit card in the district's name during his tenure. Based on a sworn affidavit, the superintendent asserted immunity on the basis that he made the statement in the course of his duties. After a trial court denied the superintendent's motion for summary judgment, an appellate

---

[126] Bower v. Board of Educ. of the City of East Orange, 670 A.2d 106 [106 Educ. L. Rep. 760] (N.J. Super. Ct. App. Div. 1996).
[127] Deloney v. Board of Educ. of Thornton Township, 666 N.E.2d 792 [111 Educ. L. Rep. 1297] (Ill. App. Ct. 1996).

panel in Texas affirmed.[128] The court viewed the affidavit as a conclusory and self serving statement that did not conclusively establish whether the superintendent's statements were made within the scope of his employment.

Negligence

The tragedy of student death can lead to negligence suits against districts. All three of the cases this year were decided in favor of the school systems. A mother sought further review of the dismissal of her wrongful death and negligence action against a city and its board of education over the death of her son who was shot by a fellow student while on the premises of his high school. An appellate court in Illinois affirmed that the mother failed to state a cause of action for premises liability since she was unable to allege that the board created or facilitated the condition that caused the death of her son or that it had actual or constructive knowledge of criminal conduct.[129] The court added that the board did not owe the deceased student a special duty because his mother had not alleged awareness of a particular threat or specific danger.

Parents disputed a jury verdict after they unsuccessfully sued a board of education and its employees over their allegation that the system's failures to address their son's academic deficiencies led to his suicide. After receiving a call that someone at the son's address was in danger of committing suicide, police came to the house, questioned him, conducted a cursory search for weapons, and, before leaving, left a message for the parents to call the department. About an hour later, the boy shot himself to death. The parents claimed that the trial court improperly instructed the jury on intervening cause. An appellate court in Connecticut affirmed that the dismissal was appropriate because there was sufficient evidence from which the jury could have reasonably concluded that the police department's negligence was an intervening cause.[130]

In Georgia, parents challenged the dismissal of their wrongful death suit after their daughter was murdered when she was let out of school early. An appellate court affirmed that the members of the board, the superintendent, and the vocational secretary were protected from individual liability by official immunity because their acts were discretionary, not ministerial.[131] The court also noted that the defendants

---

[128] Gallegos v. Escalon, 918 S.W.2d 62 [108 EDUC. L. REP. 452] (Tex. Ct. App. 1996).

[129] Lawson v. City of Chicago, 662 N.E.2d 1377 [108 EDUC. L. REP. 814] (Ill. App. Ct. 1996).

[130] Brown v. Board of Educ. of Milford, 681 A.2d 996 [112 EDUC. L. REP. 953] (Conn. App. Ct. 1996).

[131] Perkins v. Morgan County Sch. Dist., 476 S.E.2d 592 [113 EDUC. L. REP. 498] (Ga. Ct. App. 1996).

would not have been liable under the theory of intervening cause based on the unforeseen criminal act of the third party.

Three cases reflected special concerns regarding students with disabilities. In the first, the Supreme Court of Nebraska declared that a school district contracting with a private service provider cannot be held liable for damages due to the contractor's negligence in failing to provide agreed upon physical therapy mandated by law.[132] The court indicated that in the absence of allegations that the board's supervisory personnel knew of the potential dangers of continuance or discontinuance of such a program, the suit failed. However, the court pointed out that the students should be granted leave to amend their petition.

The mother of a six-year-old student with osteoporotic and brittle leg bones appealed a jury verdict in favor of a school district's insurer when her son suffered a broken leg after his wheelchair tipped over while being pushed by another pupil during the teacher's absence from the room. The Supreme Court of Arkansas reversed.[133] It observed that the trial court committed reversible error in refusing to instruct the jury on the "egg shell" plaintiff rule. The court maintained that the child's condition was not only relevant to damages but also embraced aspects of proximate causation in light of his existing condition and predisposition to injury.

Where a platform fell on and injured a special education student, his family challenged a ruling in favor of the board of education. An appellate court in New York reversed and granted a new trial.[134] The court found both that the jury verdict in favor of the district was against the weight of evidence and that the trial court had erred in dismissing the negligent supervision claim because the child's attorney had made out a prima facie case.

An appellate court in Florida reversed in favor of a school where a mother filed suit after a teacher accidentally shut a door on her one-year-old son's finger.[135] It decided that genuine issues of material fact about the teacher's alleged failure to exercise reasonable care when she accidentally shut the door precluded summary judgment. The court reflected that absent some evidence of wrongdoing, the fact that an injury occurs in the presence of a teacher does not establish negligent supervision.

---

[132] Crider v. Bayard City Sch., 553 N.W.2d 147 [112 Educ. L. Rep. 1023] (Neb. 1996).
[133] Primm v. United States Fidelty & Garanty Ins., 922 S.W.2d 319 [110 Educ L. Rep. 460] (Ark. 1996).
[134] Farrukh v. Board of Educ. of the City of N.Y., 643 N.Y.S.2d 118 [110 Educ. L. Rep. 323] (N.Y. App. Div. 1996).
[135] La Petite Academy v. Nassef *ex rel*. Kniffel 674 So. 2d 181 [110 Educ. L. Rep. 497] (Fla. Dist. Ct. App. 1996).

School Transportation

As reflected by the following two cases involving the accidental deaths of young children and claims of negligence against schools, the safety of transportation services has practical and legal implications. The family of a six-year-old boy, who was killed when hit by a motorcycle while crossing the street after getting off a school bus, requested further review of a grant of summary judgment in favor of the defendants in their wrongful death suit against the school district, the bus driver, and a monitor. An appellate court in Texas affirmed.[136] The court held that the employees were covered by official immunity for not escorting the boy across the street since such a practice was not required and they were exercising their discretion in deciding not to do so. It added that the district was protected by sovereign immunity from not having a stop arm on the bus since a stop arm was optional on such older buses at that time.

After a five-year-old boy exited a school bus, reached the steps to his house, dashed back into the street, and was struck by the bus, his parents unsuccessfully sued the driver, board, and insurance carrier. An appellate court in Louisiana affirmed that the accident was unavoidable and that the driver did not breach his duty of care.[137] It stated that although the driver owed young passengers the highest duty of care, once the child reached a place of safety, the driver's duty became that of an ordinary motorist. As to allegations that the bus was defective because it did not have a second globe mirror on its right fender, the court concluded that the evidence did not support a finding that this equipment would have mattered.

In order to recover in a negligence suit against a school district, an injured party must establish that a bus driver is actually one of its employees. In the first of two cases illustrating this point, an appellate court in Texas affirmed that since a bus driver was not acting as an employee of a school district at the time of an accident, the district was not liable.[138] The court acknowledged that the driver was employed both as a driver by the transportation department of a county school system that comprised thirteen districts and as a teacher by the district that owned the bus in question. Although there was some conflicting evidence, the court contended that the jury could reasonably have concluded that the driver was not under the control and direction of her district while on her regular bus route.

---

[136] Cortez v. Weatherford Indep. Sch. Dist., 925 S.W.2d 144 [110 Educ. L. Rep. 1298] (Tex. Ct. App. 1996).
[137] Brown v. United States Fire Ins. Co., 671 So. 2d 1195 [109 Educ. L. Rep. 474] (La. Ct. App. 1996).
[138] White v. Liberty Eylau Sch. Dist., 920 S.W.2d 809 [109 Educ. L. Rep. 464] (Tex. Ct. App. 1996).

An automobile owner prevailed in a negligence action against a district for damages that his car incurred in an incident involving a school bus, where the district sought further review. Even though the district owned the bus and there was evidence that the vehicle was being used to transport children home from school, the district did not admit to an agency relationship with the driver. An appellate panel in Kansas reversed in favor of the district.[139] It posited that since ownership of a vehicle alone is not enough to impute the negligence of the driver to the owner, the plaintiff failed to plead and prove an essential element of his case, namely that the bus driver was an employee of the school district.

School Premises

The need to maintain educational premises in a safe condition was illustrated by a case involving a police officer who was injured when he slipped and fell on an exterior stairway while responding to a burglar alarm at a school. After a trial court granted judgment in favor of the district even though the jury ruled in favor of the officer, an appellate tribunal reversed. On further review, the Supreme Court of North Carolina affirmed.[140] It mandated that the duty of care owed to the officer was the same as was due to an invitee, namely to keep the property reasonably safe and to warn of hidden perils or unsafe conditions that could be ascertained by reasonable inspection. The court concluded that the since the evidence was sufficient to raise a jury question that the district had constructive, if not actual, knowledge of the dangerous condition of the stairs and the district failed to correct the situation, its negligence was the proximate cause of the officer's injuries.

Two cases illustrated how school systems sometimes successfully raise an immunity defense based on the discretionary nature of their duties. A woman challenged a grant of summary judgment in favor of a district after she tripped over a damaged storm drain grate on school premises. An appellate court in Georgia affirmed that two school employees were immune from individual liability because their duties in inspecting and repairing the facilities were discretionary, not ministerial.[141]

A food service worker disputed a ruling in favor of her district after she brought suit to recover for personal injuries she sustained when she fell on an icy sidewalk at school. An appellate court in Connecticut, after

---

[139] Felix v. Turner Unified Sch. Dist., 923 P.2d 1056 [113 EDUC. L. REP. 460] (Kan. Ct. App. 1996).
[140] Newton v. New Hanover County Bd. of Educ., 467 S.E.2d 58 [106 EDUC. L. REP. 1392] (N.C. 1996).
[141] Hemak v. Houston County Sch. Dist., 469 S.E.2d 679 [109 EDUC. L. REP. 443] (Ga. Ct. App. 1996).

noting that the determination of whether official acts or omissions are ministerial or discretionary is a question of fact for the jury, affirmed.[142] The court reasoned that since district officials exercised considerable latitude in making decisions about removing snow and sanding, they were protected by governmental immunity.

Notice of Claims

States typically require plaintiffs to file timely notices of claims with school districts or risk that their suits are barred. The first five cases in this section illustrate the complexity of determining which claims may be barred and which defendants may be protected.

Landowners sued a board of education, a city, an architect, and a general contractor contending that they were liable for damages to their crops and farmland from flooding that was caused by the improper construction of a public school and an inadequate drainage system. At issue was whether a statutory notice of claim requirement and a six-year statute of limitations barred the suit against the board and city and if the same law and a ten-year statute of repose precluded an action against the architect and general contractor. The Supreme Court of New Jersey held that the claims against the city and board could be pursued to the extent that injuries were suffered within the relevant limitation period.[143] However, the court ruled that those against the architect and contractor were time barred.

A high school student in Utah who sued the state, his district, and the driver who drove a school bus over his foot filed notice of a claim with the state Office of Education and the attorney general's office. Yet, because the student did not file a notice with the district board, the trial court entered summary judgment for the defendants. On appeal, the Supreme Court of Utah affirmed.[144] It decided that because the student alleged injuries by a school employee, he was obligated by statute to file a notice of claim with the district board.

The suit of a student who suffered a serious skull fracture when pushed into a concrete wall during gym class was time barred because she failed to observe the statutory sixty-day waiting period following notice of the claim. On further review, an appellate court in Washington agreed.[145]

---

[142] Beach v. Regional Sch. Dist. No. 13, 682 A.2d 118 [112 EDUC. L. REP. 987] (Conn. App. Ct. 1996).

[143] Russo Farms v. Vineland Bd. of Educ., 675 A.2d 1077 [109 EDUC. L. REP. 800] (N.J. 1996).

[144] Shunk v. State of Utah, 924 P.2d 879 [113 EDUC. L. REP. 957] (Utah 1996).

[145] Pirtle v. Spokane Pub. Sch. Dist. No. 81, 921 P.2d 1084 [111 EDUC. L. REP. 1370] (Wash. Ct. App. 1996).

The court stated that the waiting period did not violate equal protection because it was reasonably related to the objective of negotiation and settlement while not creating an impediment for governmental tort victims.

Parents unsuccessfully sued a school district and teacher, asserting several tort claims arising from the teacher's alleged sexual abuse of their daughter. An appellate court in Oregon affirmed summary judgment for the district, but reversed as to the teacher.[146] The court reasoned that since sexual contact between a minor student and a teacher is not within the parameters of an educator's responsibilities, the parents were not required to provide tort claims notice to the teacher. The court also pointed out that summary judgment was precluded since there was a disputed issue of fact as to whether the teacher and student engaged in sexual intercourse.

A school counselor filed suit against a superintendent and principal alleging sexual harassment and retaliatory discharge in violation of title VII and the Kansas Act Against Discrimination (KAAD) as well as intentional infliction of emotional distress under state common law. The federal district court dismissed the title VII and KAAD claims against the administrators because they had been sued directly.[147] It rejected the common law tort claims because the counselor failed to comply with state law by providing notice of the claims before taking action.

In the first seven of nine cases from New York, failure to file a timely claim was fatal to the claims. A school district sought further review of a finding by the New York State Division of Human Rights that it committed an unlawful discriminatory practice based on the sexual harassment of a teacher. The district argued that the complaint should have been dismissed due to the teacher's failure to comply with the statutory notice of claim requirement. An appellate court agreed.[148] The court concluded that because the teacher sought to enforce a private right, rather than vindicate a public interest, a notice of claim was required.

Parents failed to submit evidence that a board of education had actual knowledge that a principal altered grades on standardized tests to improve the status of his school within ninety days of when the principal's alleged actions took place. An appellate court found that the petitioner should not have been granted leave to file a late notice of claim.[149] The court decided that the board would have been substantially prejudiced by

---

[146] Finney v. Bransom, 924 P.2d 319 [113 EDUC. L. REP. 486] (Or. Ct. App. 1996).

[147] Miller v. Brungardt, 916 F. Supp. 1096 [107 EDUC. L. REP. 794] (D. Kan. 1996).

[148] Saranac Lake Cent. Sch. Dist. v. New York State Div. of Human Rights, 640 N.Y.S.2d 303 [108 EDUC. L. REP. 849] (N.Y. App. Div. 1996).

[149] Sica v. Board of Educ. of N.Y., 640 N.Y.S.2d 610 [108 EDUC. L. REP. 854] (N.Y. App. Div. 1996).

permitting the late notice of claim to be filed because the tests that had allegedly been tampered with had been destroyed.

An appellate tribunal reversed in favor of a board of education after a petitioner was granted leave to serve a late notice of claim.[150] It ruled that because the board did not acquire actual notice of the facts within three months of its accrual, the petitioner's defense of ignorance of the statutory filing period was an unacceptable excuse.

According to an appellate court, a school nurse's report of an incident did not give a board of education actual notice of the essential facts of her negligence claim within three months of its accrual.[151] The panel held that the trial court improperly granted the nurse leave to serve a late notice of claim for her personal injuries.

A student was sexually abused by her former fourth-grade teacher in August 1992. Her proposed notice of claim was filed in March 1995. After meeting with the school psychologist and the teacher a month after the incident occurred, the student's father asked district employees not to question his daughter or to pursue the matter further. The father subsequently claimed he did not learn about the seriousness of the incident until May 1994 but did not offer a reasonable excuse for his delay in filing the claim. An appellate court affirmed the denial of the claim.[152] It offered that the delay would have seriously prejudiced the district's ability to defend itself against the claim that it improperly handled the allegation of sexual abuse.

A former school employee sought further review of the dismissal of her claim against a board of education on the basis that it was time barred because she did not file a notice of claim within the three months following the accrual of her cause of action. An appellate court in New York reasoned that while the failure to file a notice of claim would not have been fatal in an action to vindicate a public interest, her suit over lost retirement benefits was subject to the three month deadline.[153]

After a student was injured in an altercation at school, an appellate court found that he was improvidently granted leave to serve a late notice of claim on the board of education three and one-half years after the fact. The court indicated that since there was nothing in the record to indicate that the board had actual notice of the facts of the negligent supervision

---

[150] Jackson v. City of New Rochelle, 643 N.Y.S.2d 127 [110 EDUC. L. REP. 326] (N.Y. App. Div. 1996).

[151] Rusiecki v. Clarkstown Cent. Sch. Dist. 643, N.Y.S.2d 132 [110 EDUC. L. REP. 328] (N.Y. App. Div. 1996).

[152] Bordan v. Mamaroneck Sch. Dist., 646 N.Y.S.2d 373 [111 EDUC. L. REP. 1325] (N.Y. App. Div. 1996).

[153] Doyle v. Board of Educ. of Deer Park Union Free Sch. Dist., 646 N.Y.S.2d 842 [112 EDUC. L. REP. 419] (N.Y. App. Div. 1996).

claim within ninety days of its occurrence, it would have suffered prejudice if the claim had been permitted to proceed.[154]

The first of two cases in New York where injured parties were permitted to file late notices of claims involved an improper practice charge filed with the state public employment relations board. An appellate court permitted the suit to go forward.[155] The court declared that the board of education had been apprised of the facts constituting the charge less than one month after it accrued and was unable to demonstrate that it would have been prejudiced by permitting the late notice of claim to be served.

In the second case, an appellate court affirmed that a late notice of claim over a shooting incident at a high school was permissible.[156] The court posited that the school board knew the actual facts underlying the claim on the day that the shooting took place and failed to substantiate its assertion that it would have been prejudiced by late service of notice.

Conclusion

The cases discussed in this chapter address a wide range of school governance issues. Most observers probably believe that nearly all of the cases were decided correctly and that few, if any, of the decisions broke any new legal ground. However, a review of these cases does provide insight into the kinds of disputes that arise over the control of public elementary and secondary education and how these disagreements are resolved by the courts.

---

[154] Dunlea v. Mahopac Cent. Sch. Dist., 648 N.Y.S.2d 673 [113 EDUC. L. REP. 1273] (N.Y. App. Div. 1996).

[155] Beckerman v. Board of Educ. of Comsewogue Union Free Sch. Dist., 636 N.Y.S.2d 860 [106 EDUC. L. REP. 857] (N.Y. App. Div. 1996).

[156] Artis v. Board of Educ. of Amityville Union Free School Dist., 638 N.Y.S.2d 99 [107 EDUC. L. REP. 251] (N.Y. App. Div. 1996).

3

PUPILS

William E. Camp

Introduction

The courts continue to address complex and controversial issues concerning how to balance the rights of students, the interests of parents in raising their children, and the duty of the schools to maintain an orderly learning environment. Pupils have expectations of fairness, safety, and privacy when they enter school each day. Although courts have ruled that the rights of students may not be as extensive as those of adults, certain basic conditions must be observed. Over the past year a variety of courts defined and modified the balance between the rights of students and their schools.

Issues Relating to Public School Attendance

Compulsory Attendance

Hispanic parents unsuccessfully sought to enjoin a district from closing two neighborhood elementary schools and opening a charter school. The Tenth Circuit affirmed that the district did not act improperly and neither violated the parents' right to equal protection nor demonstrated discriminatory impact.[1] The court stated that the Colorado Charter Schools Act expressed a legitimate interest in encouraging innovation in education by increasing opportunities for at-risk students.

A student in Massachusetts enjoined a school committee's voluntary affirmative action program that set aside thirty-five percent of the seats available at three public schools for African-American and Hispanic pupils. The federal district court ruled that the program, which based admission on examination scores and sixth-grade marks, was not construed narrowly enough to escape an equal protection claim.[2]

In the first of two cases involving home schooling, a mother in Maryland who was home schooling her children filed a section 1983 action alleging that monitoring provisions in the Maryland compulsory education law violated the Free Exercise Clause of the First Amendment and the Religious Freedom Restoration Act. The mother asserted that since public schools indoctrinate children in atheistic views, they placed a substantial burden on her right to free exercise of religion. The mother refused to fill out a consent form, prepare a portfolio, or allow observation of her teaching. The federal trial court dismissed in favor of the district.[3] The court observed that if the district had tailored the home school curriculum to every parent's demand, it would have involved a greater entanglement with religion.

Parents claimed that their rights to procedural and substantive due process and to equal protection were violated when their seven-year-old was removed from home by county officials for almost a day to interview her over an allegation of sexual abuse. Insofar as the child was educated at home, the interview could not take place at school. Even so, the officials did not uncover evidence to support an abuse claim and returned the girl

---

[1] Villanueva v. Carere, 85 F.3d 481 [110 EDUC. L. REP. 38] (10th Cir. 1996).
[2] McLaughlin *ex rel.* McLaughlin v. Boston Sch. Comm., 938 F. Supp. 1001 [113 EDUC. L. REP. 624] (D. Mass. 1996).
[3] Battles v. Anne Arundel County Bd. of Educ., 904 F. Supp. 471 [105 EDUC. L. REP. 93] (D. Md. 1995).

to her parents. A federal district court decided that the parents' rights were protected but that the child could claim that her Fourth Amendment rights were violated.[4]

In the first of three cases from Ohio, students and parents brought a section 1983 action to enjoin a policy that prohibited white students from transferring. The school system had twice been declared unitary and developed a policy to maintain this status. A federal district court found that the policy was unconstitutional since it created a discriminatory racial classification and was not narrowly tailored to satisfy a compelling state interest.[5] It added that the policy violated the Equal Protection Clause of the Fourteenth Amendment by irreparably harming white students.

A father and his three children sought further review of the denial of a writ of mandamus to order administrators to issue grades and credits that were withheld because the father refused to pay instructional fees for the academic year. After an operating levy failed, the district imposed the fee system, but the father objected because he felt that his children were entitled to a free public education. The Supreme Court of Ohio affirmed that the schools could charge a fee for classroom materials.[6]

A grandmother challenged her conviction for contributing to the unruliness of children after her grandchildren, two high school students living with her, were declared truant. An appellate court in Ohio reversed.[7] It ruled that the state failed to establish that the grandmother caused the children to be truant habitually. The court observed that the state was unable to show that the students were absent with their grandmother's permission because she had encouraged her grandchildren to attend class and, on occasion, had driven them to school.

The Supreme Court of Michigan reversed in a dispute over a residency policy that allowed students to enroll in public schools only if they lived within the boundaries of a district with their legal guardians.[8] Where a student lived with an uncle, the lower courts ruled in favor of the district. However, the high court found that the district violated state law since the code did not require the appointment of a legal guardian as a condition of legal residency.

Educational organizations claimed that the Academy Schools Act of Michigan was unconstitutional because it failed to place the institutions

---

[4] J.B. v. Washington County, 905 F. Supp. 979 [105 EDUC. L. REP. 167] (D. Utah 1995).
[5] Equal Open Enrollment Ass'n v. Board of Educ. of Akron Sch. Dist., 937 F. Supp. 700 [113 EDUC. L. REP. 149] (N.D. Ohio 1996).
[6] State *ex rel.* Massie v. Bd. of Educ., 669 N.E.2d 839 [112 EDUC. L. REP. 421] (Ohio 1996).
[7] State of Ohio v. Michael, 670 N.E.2d 560 [113 EDUC. L. REP. 397] (Ohio Ct. App. 1996).
[8] Feaster v. Portage Pub. Sch., 547 N.W.2d 328 [109 EDUC. L. REP. 394] (Mich. 1996).

exclusively under the control of the state and open them to all children. An appellate court agreed.[9] The court held that the act was unconstitutional since it did not place charter schools under exclusive control of the state.

Students and parents disputed the denial of their request for a writ of mandate, an injunction, and declaratory relief over a district'a placement of late enrollees. An appellate court in California affirmed.[10] The court posited that the policy, which temporarily placed students in settings other than those nearest their residences, was not an abuse of discretion because it did not deny the children access to district schools.

Navajo parents sued a board of education in Utah to compel it to improve elementary education and to provide a secondary school at a remote area of their reservation.[11] The parents claimed that the district discriminated against their children by failing to provide them with educational opportunities equal to those of their peers. The court stated that since it was ill-equipped to answer difficult questions about how limited resources should best be allocated, the responsible parties should explore options before the court could impose a solution. The court denied both parties' motions for summary judgment and refused the parents' request to certify their action as a class action.

After a youth court enjoined the alcohol and absence policies of a district, it appealed. The Supreme Court of Mississippi affirmed in part, modified in part, and remanded.[12] Although the court stated that the youth court could order a student's enrollment in a school system, the panel found that the district's policies were not overbroad as applied to his conduct. The court added that the policy of treating suspensions as unexcused absences was arbitrary and capricious because the state's compulsory attendance law distinguished between days missed due to truancy and days missed due to suspension. The court ruled that the policy of refusing to grant credit for days of absence was enforceable because the policy was stated clearly in the student handbook.

Transfer of Students

A high school student enjoined the state high school athletic association from declaring him ineligible to play baseball following his transfer. The student was suspended from one high school, withdrew

---

[9] Council of Orgs. v. Governor of Mich., 548 N.W.2d 909 [110 Educ. L. Rep. 402] (Mich. Ct. App. 1996).

[10] Helena F. v. West Contra Costa Unified Sch. Dist., 57 Cal. Rptr.2d 605 [113 Educ. L. Rep. 862] (Cal. Ct. App. 1996).

[11] Meyers *ex rel.* Meyers v. Board of Educ. of San Juan Sch. Dist., 905 F. Supp. 1544 [105 Educ. L. Rep. 453] (D. Utah 1995).

[12] T.H., Jr. *ex rel.* T.H., III v. Board of Trustees of the Pascagoula Mun. Separate Sch. Dist., 681 So. 2d 110 [113 Educ. L. Rep. 1025] (Miss. 1996).

from that school, and enrolled in another school. An appellate tribunal affirmed the temporary injunction, but the Supreme Court of Kentucky dismissed.[13] The court reasoned that the case was moot because the baseball season had ended.

The Pennsylvania Interscholastic Athletic Association (PIAA) sought further review when a student obtained an injunction that permitted him to play basketball after he transferred from a public to a private school. The student argued that he changed schools not only due to financial problems, but also because his father had an altercation with his coach. The court noted that even though the student lacked a property interest in playing basketball, the PIAA arbitrarily and capriciously discriminated against the student because he did not violate the rule against recruitment.[14] In agreeing that the PIAA rules were inconsistent with their purpose, an appellate court affirmed a preliminary injunction in favor of the student.

In the first of three cases from Indiana, an appellate court struck down an order that enjoined the Indiana High School Athletic Association (IHSAA) from enforcing its eight semester rule against a senior who went over the semester limit when he repeated ninth-grade.[15] The court found both that the IHSAA did not violate the student's right to equal protection under the state constitution and that the Restitution Rule of the IHSAA that required schools to forfeit games in which ineligible players participated was appropriate and fair.

A student successfully challenged an IHSAA rule that would have prevented him from participating in varsity swimming for one year after he transferred.[16] The student had switched from a private to a public school even though his parents had not moved. An appellate court in Indiana affirmed that the rule violated the student's right to equal protection and it was overbroad because he transferred for reasons unrelated to sports.

A high school student was unable to enjoin the IHSAA from preventing her participation on a varsity interscholastic team for a year after she transferred from a public to a nonpublic school because she converted to Catholicism.[17] A federal district court in Indiana rejected the student's

---

[13] Kentucky High Sch. Athletic Ass'n v. Runyon, 920 S.W.2d 525 [109 Educ. L. Rep. 462] (Ky. 1996).

[14] Boyle v. Pennsylvania Interscholastic Athletic Ass'n, 676 A.2d 695 [109 Educ. L. Rep. 1310] (Pa. Commw. Ct. 1996).

[15] Indiana High Sch. Athletic Ass'n v. Reyes, 659 N.E.2d 158 [105 Educ. L. Rep. 1200] (Ind. Ct. App. 1995).

[16] Indiana High Sch. Athletic Ass'n v. Carlberg, 661 N.E.2d 833 [107 Educ. L. Rep. 961] (Ind. Ct. App. 1996).

[17] Robbins v. Indiana High Sch. Athletic Ass'n, 941 F. Supp. 786 [113 Educ. L. Rep. 1240] (S.D. Ind. 1996).

argument that the rule burdened her right to free exercise because it had not been enacted to interfere with religiously motivated transfers.

Black high school students alleged that a board of education policy violated their rights to equal protection. The policy required athletes who transferred under a majority to minority program to sit out a year. A federal district court ruled in favor of the board.[18] The court held that even though the board knew the policy would have a greater impact on black athletes, it was not enough to prove discriminatory intent based on race because the plan was designed to benefit predominately black schools.

Tuition and Fees

Two students challenged the admission policy of a school district in North Carolina. An appellate court vacated and dismissed the students' claims as moot because both students came to be qualified under the policy: the mother of one student had established residency in the district and the other student qualified on his own because he turned eighteen.[19]

A board of education unsuccessfully sought to compel parents to pay book user fees. The Supreme Court of Appeals of West Virginia maintained that since education is a fundamental right in the state, items necessary to accomplish the goals of the school system must be provided free of charge to students.[20] The court observed that because books and school supplies met the legal definition of essential parts of education, the payment of user fees was unconstitutional.

Private and Parochial Schools

A former student and his parent sued for the loss of parental consortium following the student's physical and sexual abuse by other students while attending a boarding school. The federal district court in Connecticut dismissed, finding that the state did not recognize such a cause of action.[21]

Former students filed charges of sexual abuse against the chaplain at their parochial school after the statute of limitations had expired. The Supreme Court of Maryland was asked to determine whether repressed and recovered memory can compel application of the discovery rule.

[18] Young v. Montgomery County Bd. of Educ., 922 F. Supp. 544 [109 Educ. L. Rep. 202] (M.D. Ala. 1996).
[19] Ballard v. Weast, 465 S.E.2d 565 [106 Educ. L. Rep. 376] (N.C. App 1996).
[20] Randolph County Bd. of Educ. v. Adams, 467 S.E.2d 150 [107 Educ. L. Rep. 324] (W. Va. 1995).
[21] Hyun v. South Kent Sch., 166 F.R.D. 272 [110 Educ. L. Rep. 705] (D. Conn. 1996)

The court agreed that since the mental process of repression did not activate the discovery rule, the claims were barred three years after the students reached their eighteenth birthdays.[22]

A former Catholic school student appealed the dismissal of her claim that a priest, guidance and licensed counselors, and others failed to report child abuse perpetrated by her father. The Supreme Court of Iowa affirmed that the priest did not have a duty to report.[23] It also found that a statement by a social worker who was involved in the case did not show that the guidance counselor knew of the abuse. Moreover, even though the licensed counselor knew of the abuse and was covered by the statutory reporting requirements, the court agreed that under respondeat superior, neither the church nor the social services agency that employed the counselor were liable for the counselor's failure to report child abuse.

The suit of parents that alleged a private school failed to provide an adequate education was consolidated with two identical claims. A federal district court in Alabama ruled in favor of the school.[24] The court dismissed when it found that the school was not a state actor as required for liability under section 1983. In the interests of economy, convenience, fairness, and comity, the court declined to exercise supplemental jurisdiction.

Substantive Rights of Students

First Amendment Religious Rights

Students appealed after a federal trial court in New York refused their request for an injunction that would permit them to include a bylaw setting eligibility requirements for their prayer and Bible study club. The parties agreed on all points except a provision that allowed only Christians to be officers. On further review, the Second Circuit reversed in favor of the students.[25] It reasoned that the students were likely to succeed at a trial on the merits of their claims that the conditional recognition of the club by the district violated the Equal Access Act. The court decided that applying the leadership provision to the club president, vice president, and music coordinator violated neither the Equal Access Act nor the Establishment Clause.

---

[22] Doe v. Maskell, 679 A.2d 1087 [111 EDUC. L. REP. 857] (Md. 1996).

[23] Wilson v. Darr, 553 N.W.2d 579 [113 EDUC. L. REP. 419] (Iowa 1996).

[24] Nobles v. Alabama Christian Academy, 917 F. Supp. 786 [107 EDUC. L. REP. 851] (M.D. Ala. 1996).

[25] Hsu v. Roslyn Union Free Sch. Dist. No. 3, 85 F.3d 839 [109 EDUC. L. REP. 1145] (2d. Cir. 1996), *cert. denied* 117 S. Ct. 608 (1996).

In a case from New Jersey, an en banc Third Circuit upheld an earlier judgment that a board policy allowing students to vote whether to have a prayer at a graduation ceremony violated the Establishment Clause.[26] The court agreed that the policy could not be accepted as promoting freedom of speech.

The Fifth Circuit affirmed the invalidation of a law in Mississippi that allowed students to initiate nonsectarian, nonproselytizing prayer at various compulsory and noncompulsory events.[27] The court said that except for a provision that allowed prayer at high school commencement ceremonies, the statute violated the Establishment Clause and should have been enjoined.

In another case from Mississippi, a mother asserted that district practices involving prayer and religious instruction violated the Establishment Clause. A federal trial court agreed.[28] The court ruled that permitting a religious club to make announcements involving prayers and Bible readings was unconstitutional. It also struck down the district's practice of offering classes taught by instructors who were hired by a Bible Committee that based its choices on religious beliefs. However, the court permitted student-initiated prayer before school to continue and refused to prohibit the hiring of an instructor who was paid by a local church to teach a Bible class as long as the course was aggressively monitored by the district.

Students and parents in Ohio appealed the dismissal of their claim that the use of the "Blue Devil" as a school mascot violated the Establishment Clause. The Sixth Circuit affirmed that no reasonable observer could believe that the mascot had the primary effect of endorsing religion.[29]

The Seventh Circuit reviewed a dispute involving a student's First Amendment rights to free exercise of religion and free speech.[30] The student and his family challenged a Wisconsin district's policy on the grounds that it restricted the student's ability to hand out invitations to a religious meeting. The court indicated that the district could require prior approval and screening of nonschool materials for offensive messages, set time and place restrictions for their distribution, and

---

[26] American Civil Liberties Union of N.J. v. Black Horse Pike Regional Bd. of Educ., 84 F.3d 1471 [109 Educ. L. Rep. 1118] (3rd Cir. 1996).

[27] Ingebretsen v. Jackson Pub. Sch. Dist., 88 F.3d 274 [110 Educ. L. Rep. 942] (5th Cir. 1996), *cert. denied sub nom.* Moore v. Ingebretsen, 117 S. Ct. 388 (1996).

[28] Herdahl v. Pontotoc County Sch. Dist., 933 F. Supp. 582 [112 Educ. L. Rep. 131] (N.D. Miss. 1996).

[29] Kunselman v. Western Reserve Local Sch. Dist., 70 F.3d 931 [105 Educ. L. Rep. 43] (6th Cir. 1995).

[30] Muller *ex rel.* Muller v. Jefferson Lighthouse Sch., 98 F.3d 1530 [113 Educ. L. Rep. 1085] (7th Cir. 1996).

require all such items to carry disclaimers that they were not endorsed by the school.

In a similar suit, a first-grade student alleged that his First Amendment and statutory rights were violated when he was told not to distribute religious tracts before a lunch break. Subsequently, the student challenged the new policy that the board developed for such a situation. A federal trial court in Indiana rejected the student's argument that the policy substantially burdened his free exercise of religion in violation of the Religious Freedom Restoration Act because the policy only set the required time and place for distribution of the pamphlets.[31] The court called for a briefing at which it would decide whether the school could require prior review of printed materials before their distribution.

A student in Utah filed a civil contempt petition asserting that his high school violated a court order to prevent a choir from singing religious songs at graduation ceremonies. After the Tenth Circuit precluded the use of the songs, the board agreed to substitute two other selections. However, when the choir's performance was done, the audience interrupted the ceremony by singing one of the prohibited songs. The federal trial court reasoned that district officials acted in good faith because they took reasonable steps to achieve compliance with the previous order.[32] The court added that the audience also acted properly since the injunction did not apply to its exercise of the constitutional right to express itself in song.

A federal trial court in Texas considered public right of access to testimony in a suit wherein adults and children sued a school district over alleged violations of the Establishment Clause. The court indicated that even though the public had First Amendment rights of access to attend the civil trial, the trial would be closed during testimony by the children to protect their identities.[33]

First Amendment Freedom of Speech

A school district in California appealed a judgment that a student, who received a three-day suspension for threatening to shoot a school counselor over a proposed schedule change, engaged in protected First Amendment speech. The Ninth Circuit reversed.[34] The court declared

---

[31] Harless *ex rel.* Harless v. Darr, 937 F. Supp. 1339 [113 Educ. L. Rep. 182] (S.D. Ind. 1996).

[32] Bauchman v. West High Sch., 906 F. Supp. 1483 [105 Educ. L. Rep. 543] (D. Utah 1995).

[33] Doe v. Santa Fe Indep. Sch. Dist., 933 F. Supp. 647 [112 Educ. L. Rep. 162] (S.D. Tex. 1996).

[34] Lovell v. Poway Unified Sch. Dist., 90 F.3d 367 [111 Educ. L. Rep. 116] (9th Cir. 1996), *cert. denied* 117 S. Ct. 27 (1996).

that the threats of violence made by the angry student were not protected speech.

The Tenth Circuit upheld the dismissal of all but one claim by a high school student from Utah over a hazing incident.[35] As the student was leaving a shower, teammates on the football team caught him, taped him to a towel rack, and brought his former girlfriend into the dressing room. The student was dismissed from the team for reporting the incident, yet his teammates were allowed to participate in the next game. The student charged that he was subjected to a hostile environment and transferred to another school at the recommendation of the principal. The appellate court affirmed that the student had no basis for state action, title IX, or due process claims. At the same time, it found that the student filed a proper claim for First Amendment protection and that school officials violated clearly established law. As such, the court remanded in stating that the officials could not rely on qualified immunity in the dismissal of this part of the case.

Students sought to enjoin a school committee from enforcing a dress code that prohibited them from wearing apparel that harassed, intimidated, or demeaned an individual because of sex, color, race, religion, handicap, national origin, or sexual orientation. The students alleged that the dress code violated their rights to free speech under the First Amendment and state law. The federal district court in Massachusetts upheld the dress code, but the First Circuit vacated on the basis of state law, deferred on the federal constitutional claim, and certified a question of law to the Supreme Judicial Court of Massachusetts.[36] On further review, the high court ruled that the students had freedom under state law to engage in nonschool sponsored expression that may reasonably be considered vulgar as long as it does not cause disruption or disorder in school.

A student brought a section 1983 suit against a school district and others alleging violations of the First, Fourth, and Fourteenth Amendments after he was disciplined and arrested following a search of his home. The student published a clandestine newspaper, and the case developed over the reactions of administrators and police. A federal trial court in New York denied the defendants' motion for summary judgment pending discovery.[37] The court stated that it could not act on the governmental immunity defense until pretrial discovery resolved issues regarding the officials' participation in the incident.

---

[35] Seamons v. Snow, 84 F.3d 1226 [109 EDUC. L. REP. 1103] (10th Cir. 1996).
[36] Pyle v. School Comm. of S. Hadley, 667 N.E.2d 869 [111 EDUC. L. REP. 481] (Mass. 1996).
[37] Herzog v. Will, 931 F. Supp. 276 [111 EDUC. L. REP. 768] (S.D.N.Y. 1996).

On remand from the Supreme Court of Oregon, an appellate tribunal reviewed a case involving a student's unsuccessful request for retrospective relief on his state and federal claims. The pupil charged that the school engaged in censorship when disciplining him over his involvement with a student publication. The court confirmed that the student's disciplinary record should be expunged under section 1983.[38]

The federal trial court in Kansas ordered a district to return to a school library a book depicting a romantic relationship between two girls.[39] The court found that the board and its superintendent violated the free expression rights of current students when, based on their own personal disapproval of the ideas expressed in the book, they improperly removed the book from the library. The court pointed out that the board and superintendent failed to follow the district policy for reviewing objectionable material and had not considered a less restrictive limitation on access.

Sexual Abuse and Harassment By Students

In the first of two cases from Texas, a mother who alleged that a school district condoned and caused a hostile environment involving the sexual assault of eighth-grade girls by a male student brought a title IX claim seeking declaratory and injunctive relief, compensatory damages, and attorney fees. After a federal trial court granted summary judgment in favor of the district, the Fifth Circuit affirmed.[40] It found that title IX does not impose liability on a district for sexual harassment between students if it does not directly discriminate on the basis of sex. The court stated that when peer sexual harassment is at issue, an injured party must demonstrate that a district responded differently to boys' claims than girls' claims.

A mother filed section 1983 and title IX charges against a district after her daughter allegedly was sexually harassed at school. A federal trial court in Texas rejected the mother's claims in declaring that the district did not have a constitutional duty to protect the pupil from the acts of other students.[41] Further, the court rebuffed the title IX charge on the basis that it could not be brought against individuals.

In Wisconsin, a homosexual student brought a section 1983 claim asserting that his school district violated his rights to equal protection

---

[38] Barcik v. Kubiaczyk, 912 P.2d 408 [108 Educ. L. Rep. 1282] (Or. Ct. App. 1996).
[39] Case v. Unified Sch. Dist. No. 233, 908 F. Supp. 864 [105 Educ. L. Rep. 1053] (D. Kan 1995).
[40] Rowinsky v. Bryan Indep. Sch. Dist., 80 F.3d 1006 [108 Educ. L. Rep. 502] (5th Cir. 1996), *cert. denied*, 117 S. Ct. 165 (1996).
[41] Garza v. Galena Park Indep. Sch. Dist., 914 F. Supp. 1437 [107 Educ. L. Rep. 193] (S.D. Tex. 1994).

and due process because educators failed to protect him from harassment and physical abuse by other pupils. After a federal trial court granted summary judgment to the defendants, the Seventh Circuit agreed that the evidence did not support the student's due process charge.[42] However, the court reversed in holding that there was sufficient evidence to permit the equal protection claim of discrimination based on gender and sexual orientation to proceed and that school officials were not entitled to qualified immunity on this charge.

A mother brought an Eighth Amendment claim of deliberate indifference against the Arkansas Department of Human Services, school principal, house parents, and administrator of a juvenile delinquents' residence when her son was physically assaulted by a classmate. The mother alleged that the administrator's failure to notify the school that the boy was a victim of a prior sexual assault by the classmate was an act of deliberate indifference to his safety. She also stated that the defendants' decision not to segregate her son from his abuser led to the physical assault. A federal trial court granted summary judgment in favor of the defendants and the Eight Circuit affirmed.[43] The court decided that since the facility notified the superintendent of the attack, the house parents and administrator acted appropriately. The court noted that the defendants' failures to provide information on the danger posed by the classmate might suggest negligence on the part of some but did not demonstrate deliberate indifference.

In Georgia, a mother brought suit on behalf of her fifth-grade daughter, who over a six month period, allegedly was sexually harassed and abused when a classmate fondled her and directed offensive language at her while in school. The mother asserted that even though she reported these actions, school officials did not take corrective steps. The mother appealed after a federal district court dismissed her claim. The Eleventh Circuit rejected the mother's accusation that educators violated the girl's due process and equal protection rights.[44] However, the court added that the mother had established a valid title IX claim since the board knowingly permitted a hostile environment to be created by the classmate's sexual harassment of the girl.

A former high school student and her parents sued a district and administrators for failing to prevent her from being sexually harassed at school. After the young woman told her parents the names of students who attended a party at her home and damaged it, the students retaliated

---

[42] Nabozny v. Podlesny, 92 F.3d 446 [111 EDUC. L. REP. 740] (7th Cir. 1996).

[43] Tribble v. Arkansas Dep't of Human Servs., 77 F.3d 268 [107 EDUC. L. REP. 104] (8th Cir. 1996).

[44] Davis v. Monroe County Bd. of Educ., 74 F.3d 1186 [106 EDUC. L. REP. 486] (11th Cir. 1996).

against her over a two-year period. Even though the girl and her parents reported the attacks regularly, administrators offered little protection. A federal trial court in Iowa ruled that the student could raise title IX claims over the defendants' failure to remedy the hostile sexual environment and over defendants' inaction to prevent the physical harm she suffered as a result of the assaults by her peers.[45] Further, the court denied the defendants' summary judgment on the negligent infliction of emotional distress claim but granted one for the charges of intentional infliction of emotional distress and violations of section 1983.

In a second case from Iowa, a federal trial court granted a school district a motion for judgment as a matter of law after a jury returned a verdict in favor of a pupil who had been raped.[46] The student had sought damages under title IX for peer-to-peer sexual harassment. The court found that the district had made efforts to separate the students by sending the boy to an alternative school and by making special arrangements for the girl's instruction. It reasoned that the student and her parents were unable to establish that the district intentionally failed to take proper remedial steps because of her sex.

In Missouri, a student and her mother filed suit under section 1983 and title IX claiming that a school district failed to protect the student from sexual harassment by her peers. A federal trial court granted the defendant's motion for summary judgment on the mother's sexual harassment claims under section 1983, title IX, and state law, but denied it on the student's title IX charge.[47]

Sexual Abuse and Harassment By Employees

A principal and athletic director in Texas appealed a ruling in favor of parents who brought a section 1983 claim over their daughter's alleged sexual molestation by a coach. After a district court denied the defendants' motions for summary judgment based on qualified immunity, the Fifth Circuit reversed.[48] The court found that since the defendants properly reported and acted on suspected child abuse, they were entitled to qualified immunity.

Administrators in Texas appealed the denial of their motion to dismiss a section 1983 claim after a thirteen-year-old student was raped by a

---

[45] Burrow v. Postville Community Sch. Dist., 929 F. Supp. 1193 [110 EDUC. L. REP. 1102] (N.D. Iowa 1996).

[46] Wright v. Mason City Community Sch. Dist., 940 F. Supp. 1412 [113 EDUC. L. REP. 1183] (N.D. Iowa 1996).

[47] Bosley v. Kearney R-1 Sch. Dist., 904 F. Supp. 1006 [105 EDUC. L. REP. 101] (W.D. Mo. 1995).

[48] John Doe v. Rains County Indep. Sch. Dist., 76 F.3d 666 [107 EDUC. L. REP. 44] (5th Cir. 1996).

school custodian. The Fifth Circuit affirmed.[49] It ruled that the section 1983 claim was adequately presented based on allegations of the inadequate hiring policies of the district and the district's failure to investigate or take action on reports that staff members were sexually abusing children. The court concluded that the educators violated the student's right to bodily integrity by instituting a process that placed her in harm's way.

In a third case from Texas, a mother sued a district and administrators charging that her son's substantive due process rights to bodily integrity and equal protection were violated when "troubled teachers" were transferred into predominately minority schools. The case arose when the student was sexually molested in his home by a former teacher approximately five months after the student withdrew from school. A federal trial court granted the defendants' motions for summary judgment.[50] It observed that the administrators could not be liable because they did not place the teacher in the child's home. The court added that the assaults were too remotely related to the transfer policy to hold the district liable.

The Sixth Circuit reviewed a case from Tennessee concerning a section 1983 action where a teacher was accused of sexually harassing and physically abusing children. The court asserted that the school district was not liable for the teacher's constitutional torts and that the teacher's single slap of a student combined with his rubbing another's stomach accompanied by a sexually suggestive remark did not violate their substantive due process rights.[51]

In a second case from Tennessee, students sued a board of education and school personnel alleging negligent supervision and hiring as well as false imprisonment after the children were sexually assaulted by a coach. The students claimed that the locks on the doors in the coach's room prevented them from escaping. A trial court entered judgment for the defendants and an appellate panel affirmed.[52] The court indicated that the students failed to show that the board violated its duty to provide a safe environment and that the change of locks was not the proximate cause of their injuries.

A teacher in New Mexico appealed the dismissal of his motion for summary judgment based on qualified immunity after he called a twelve-

---

[49] John Doe v. Hillsboro Indep. Sch. Dist., 81 F.3d 1395 [108 Educ. L. Rep. 1088] (5th Cir. 1996).

[50] Becerra v. Asher, 921 F. Supp. 1538 [109 Educ. L. Rep. 135] (S.D. Tex. 1996).

[51] Lillard v. Shelby County Bd. of Educ., 76 F.3d 716 [107 Educ. L. Rep. 49] (6th Cir. 1996).

[52] Doe v. Coffee County Bd. of Educ., 925 S.W.2d 534 [111 Educ. L. Rep. 569] (Tenn. Ct. App. 1996).

year-old student a prostitute in front of his class and continued to do so over a period of several weeks. The Tenth Circuit reversed.[53] Even though the court condemned the teacher's actions as a complete abuse of authority and an example of flagrant misconduct, the court stated that his behavior was not severe enough to violate the student's right to substantive due process. According to the court, the student should have sought relief under state tort law.

Students and their parents brought a section 1983 action against a teacher and district claiming religious, sexual, and family abuse over the teacher's off-campus relationships with the students and the teacher's reputation for imparting religious instruction. A federal trial court in Pennsylvania granted the district's motion to dismiss.[54] The court rejected the contention that the district owed the students an affirmative duty of care or that it had a right to intervene in an out-of-school relationship between the teacher and his former pupils.

In a second case from Pennsylvania, a student brought a section 1983 action against a teacher and two school districts over his alleged sexual assault. The student maintained that the first district had not only undertaken a cover-up of facts that allowed the teacher to obtain his current job but that it also used inadequate termination procedures that encouraged his abuse of children. The court granted the defendants' motions for summary judgment.[55] It stated that there was no direct causal connection between the supposed defective policy and the alleged constitutional deprivation.

The first of two cases from Michigan was a section 1983 suit brought by parents against a gym teacher in an elementary school. The parents claimed deprivation of their liberty interest in the creation and maintenance of the parent-child relationship arising out of the teacher's alleged exposure of his genitalia and other heinous acts that were directed toward several students on multiple occasions. A federal district court granted the teacher's motion to dismiss.[56] The court posited that the parents failed to state a claim for deprivation because they did not prove that governmental action was directed toward a protected aspect of the relationship and that any injury was merely incidental.

A high school student and his parents filed title IX and state law charges against a school district, principal, and teacher alleging the student

---

[53] Martinez *ex rel.* Abeyta v. Chama Valley Indep. Sch., 77 F.3d 1253 [107 EDUC. L. REP. 478] (10th Cir. 1996).
[54] Shepard v. Kemp, 912 F. Supp. 120 [106 EDUC. L. REP. 689] (M.D. Pa. 1995).
[55] Doe v. Methacton Sch. Dist., 914 F. Supp. 101 [107 EDUC. L. REP. 117] (E.D. Pa. 1996).
[56] Divergilio v. Skiba, 919 F. Supp. 265 [108 EDUC. L. REP. 273] (E.D. Mich. 1996).

was sexually harassed by the teacher. The relationship between the two did not involve sexual intercourse but lasted for six months and ended with the student's attempted suicide. A federal district court in Michigan dismissed negligence claims against all of the defendants, except the teacher, based on governmental immunity.[57]

In Oregon, a student and her mother brought a section 1983 suit against a district for alleged sexual abuse by a school janitor. They argued that the district violated the student's Fifth and Fourteenth Amendment rights by failing to protect her from sexual abuse when it had knowledge that the janitor was sexually abusing female students. The federal district court dismissed the tort claim due to the student's failure to meet appropriate deadlines.[58] Turning to the section 1983 claims, it granted the district's motion for summary judgment. The court found that the district neither created a policy or custom to establish liability nor had an affirmative duty to protect the student from criminal acts of its employee for the purpose of special relationship liability.

A principal, superintendent, and school board in Missouri filed motions for summary judgment in a case involving a teacher's sexual misconduct with a sixteen-year-old student. When the teacher reached a settlement with the student, all of the claims against him were dropped. One motion to dismiss was granted for a state law negligence charge against a board member. The court denied all other motions to dismiss. The court held that the board was subject to strict liability under title IX for intentional sexual discrimination by the teacher.[59] The court also permitted the student's section 1983 claim to proceed because the board had implied notice that its failure to train teachers about the need to safeguard students' constitutional rights to be free from sexual abuse and other violations of bodily integrity would be likely to result in its liability.

In Nevada, a student filed a civil rights action against a teacher, counselor, and school district, claiming that the instructor's criminal sexual attack violated his federal constitutional rights. The federal trial court ruled that since the counselor did not knowingly refuse to stop the teacher's sexual predations, the counselor was not liable under the civil rights law.[60] The court rejected the district motion to dismiss because there was a

---

[57] Nelson v. Almont Community Sch., 931 F. Supp. 1345 [111 EDUC. L. REP. 799] (E.D. Mich. 1996).

[58] Plumeau v. Yamhill County Sch. Dist. #40, 907 F. Supp. 1423 [105 EDUC. L. REP. 1006] (D. Or. 1995).

[59] Bolon v. Rolla Pub. Sch., 917 F. Supp. 1423 [108 EDUC. L. REP. 101] (E.D. Mo. 1996).

[60] Knackert *ex rel.* Doe v. Estes, 926 F. Supp. 979 [110 EDUC. L. REP. 171] (D. Nev. 1996).

legitimate question as to whether the district had developed a policy for which it could be held accountable.

Male elementary students brought section 1983 and state tort claims based on alleged sexual abuse and harassment by a teacher. A federal district court in Alabama allowed the students to supplement evidence before ruling on whether a title IX sexually hostile environment had been created. Even so, the court reserved judgment on the students' allegations that the board failed to satisfy title IX by not adopting and publishing procedures to receive and investigate complaints of sex discrimination.[61] The court decided that school officials were entitled to qualified immunity in all but the state tort charges and may have had substantive immunity if their actions fell within the exercise of their discretionary functions.

In California, male students sued a male principal who had sexually abused and harassed them, the school system, and the principal's former district that gave him a positive reference. After a trial court sustained the demurrers of the current district, the students amended their complaint to include the previous system and sought further review. An appellate court reversed in finding that administrators may be liable for negligent misrepresentation, fraud, and negligence when recommendations fail to disclose known or reasonably suspected acts of molestation and when no report had been made pursuant to the state child abuse and neglect statute.[62] The court added that the first district did not owe the students a duty under title IX.

A student challenged the denial of her petition to file a late notice of claim against a school district for its inadequate handling of an alleged act of sexual abuse by a teacher. An appellate court in New York affirmed.[63] It pointed out that the two- and one-half-year delay in filing the claim prejudiced the ability of the district to defend itself, especially since there was no reasonable excuse for the wait and it no longer employed the principal or the teacher who had been involved in the incident.

Privacy

The parents of a high school student who was not accepted as a member of the National Honor Society appealed the denial of their writ of mandate to direct the district to provide the voting records of teachers

---

[61] Does v. Covington County Sch. Bd. of Educ., 930 F. Supp. 554 [111 EDUC. L. REP. 265] (M.D. Ala. 1996).

[62] Randi W. v. Livingston Union Sch. Dist., 49 Cal. Rptr.2d 471 [106 EDUC. L. REP. 772] (Cal. Ct. App. 1995).

[63] Bordan v. Mamaroneck Sch. Dist., 646 N.Y.S.2d 373 [111 EDUC. L. REP. 1325] (N.Y. App. Div. 1996).

involved in the denial of their son's application. The parents based their claim on the right-to-know provision of the state constitution. The Supreme Court of Montana affirmed.[64] The court reasoned that even though the right-to-know provision applied to districts, the information requested in the petition was not subject to inspection under the statutes because the records of the National Honor Society are not considered public documents.

The Editor in Chief of a student newspaper challenged the dismissal of his petition for mandamus against a board and teacher to compel disclosure of the results of a high school election. The Supreme Court of Virginia affirmed that even if a candidate's individual vote total was an official record under the Freedom of Information Act, the data was excused from mandatory disclosure under the scholastic records exemption.[65]

In Louisiana, a student unsuccessfully sued for invasion of privacy when his records were seized without his permission and reviewed by a teacher, board member, and the state department of education. The issue arose over charges of grade changing by an administrator. An appellate court affirmed.[66] It held that the teacher had a legitimate concern to review records that he suspected had been altered, the board member could examine a copy of the grades for an alleged violation of school procedures, and the release of the information to the state department was appropriate. The court also noted that the student had not demonstrated actual damages for which he could recover even if his privacy was violated.

A student sued a board of education and others over alleged violations of her state and federal rights to privacy after they released information that appeared in a newspaper about her being a hermaphrodite. A federal district court rejected the board's motion to dismiss in finding that the Eleventh Amendment did not bar actions against the board and its members in their official capacities.[67] The court added that sovereign immunity precluded the state tort claims against the board and its members and the superintendent in their official capacities. The court denied the motion to dismiss based on violations of the federal Family Educational Rights and Privacy Acts and its state counterpart because a question of

---

[64] Becky v. Butte-Silver Bow Sch. Dist. 1, 906 P.2d 193 [105 EDUC. L. REP. 292] (Mont. 1995).
[65] Wall v. Fairfax County Sch. Bd., 475 S.E.2d 803 [112 EDUC. L. REP. 1084] (Va. 1996).
[66] Young v. St. Landry Parish Sch. Bd., 673 So. 2d 1272 [109 EDUC. L. REP. 1416] (La. Ct. App. 1996).
[67] Doe v. Knox County Bd. of Educ., 918 F. Supp. 181 [108 EDUC. L. REP. 134] (E.D. Ky. 1996).

fact remained as to whether the information that was released allowed the child to be identified personally.

Community Service

A student and his parents in New York appealed the dismissal of their section 1983 civil rights action that claimed the mandatory community service program of the school district violated the Thirteenth Amendment. They alleged that the community service program requiring students to perform forty hours of service during high school constituted involuntary servitude. The Second Circuit affirmed that the program violated neither the student's privacy rights by requiring him to disclose where he served nor his parents' liberty interests under the Fourteenth Amendment in raising their son.[68] The court indicated that the student was free to transfer to another public school, a private school, or participate in home schooling to avoid taking part in the program.

In a similar action, students and parents in North Carolina challenged a community service program that required pupils to perform fifty hours of community service in order to graduate. The Fourth Circuit affirmed summary judgment for the school district.[69] The court observed that the program neither violated the Thirteenth Amendment and its prohibition against involuntary servitude nor did it interfere with the parents' Fourteenth Amendment rights to direct the education of their children.

Search and Seizure

Parents in Rhode Island appealed the dismissal of section 1983 and state tort claims. The parents alleged that an illegal search had taken place following reports from a teacher and a crisis center counselor about possible child abuse. The parents charged that transporting one child to a separate school site so that siblings could be interviewed together amounted to an illegal search. The First Circuit agreed that transporting a child from one location to another did not violate the Fourth Amendment.[70]

In Alabama, parents sought further review of the dismissal of their claims after two teachers allegedly strip-searched eight-year-old girls based on a classmate's accusation that the girls had stolen seven dollars. The Eleventh Circuit upheld a grant of summary judgment in favor of all of the defendants on state tort charges and of the school board and officials

---

[68] Immediato v. Rye Neck Sch. Dist., 73 F.3d 454 [106 EDUC. L. REP. 85] (2nd Cir. 1996), *cert. denied* 117 S. Ct. 60 (1996).

[69] Herndon *ex rel.* Herndon v. Chapel Hill-Carrboro, 89 F.3d 174 [110 EDUC. L. REP. 1037] (4th Cir. 1996).

[70] Wojcik v. Town of N. Smithfield, 76 F.3d 1 [108 EDUC. L. REP. 1065] (1st Cir. 1996).

on the section 1983 claims.[71] However, the court reversed in holding that the educators who were involved in the search were not entitled to qualified immunity under section 1983.

Junior high school students in Indiana filed a section 1983 action claiming that a principal and teachers conducted an illegal strip-search for four dollars and fifty cents that was missing from a locker room after a physical education class. A federal trial court reasoned that because the principal was not the policymaker for the board, the board could not be held liable for his behavior.[72] At the same time, the court decided that since the search was not reasonable under the circumstances, the educators were not entitled to qualified immunity from the section 1983 action.

The Supreme Court of Illinois reinstated the conviction of a student with behavioral disorders who attended an alternative high school.[73] A police liaison officer at the school searched the student and found five bags of cocaine in his flashlight. In reversing, the court found that reasonable suspicion, rather than probable cause, applied to determine whether the search of the flashlight was permissible. As such, the court concluded that the officer's search was reasonable under the Fourth Amendment.

A second case from Illinois upheld two of three searches of high school students by educators or police liaison officers. There was individualized suspicion that the pupils were carrying contraband.[74] The searches resulted in the seizure of handguns. In the first search, the court ruled that use of a metal detector satisfied the reasonableness standard. The court found that the second search was permissible because it was based on an informant's tip to a police liaison officer who was in the same position as a school official for the purpose of the Fourth Amendment. The final search occurred when an administrator interviewed a student for almost an hour before asking him to empty his pockets. The court acknowledged that while there may have been reasonable suspicion when the interview began, the situation had changed such that by its end the administrator was acting on a mere hunch.

A student who was adjudicated a juvenile delinquent and placed on probation for possessing a knife in school claimed that the search that led to the discovery of the weapon was invalid. The student charged that

---

[71] Hall *ex rel.* Jenkins v. Talladega City Bd. of Educ., 95 F.3d 1036 [112 EDUC. L. REP. 90] (11th Cir. 1996).

[72] Hines *ex rel.* Oliver v. McClung, 919 F. Supp. 1206 [108 EDUC. L. REP. 619] (N.D. Ind. 1995).

[73] People v. Dilworth, 661 N.E.2d 310 [107 EDUC. L. REP. 226] (Ill. 1996).

[74] People v. Pruitt, 662 N.E.2d 540 [108 EDUC. L. REP. 329] (Ill. App. Ct. 1996).

the search was inappropriate because it was not based on individualized suspicion. An appellate court in Pennsylvania disagreed.[75] The court upheld the action as reasonable since all students were searched by officials in the same minimally intrusive manner upon entering school and that the search was justified due to the high rate of violence in area schools.

In the first of two cases from Oregon, an appellate court affirmed that a seventeen-year-old student who possessed marijuana was within its jurisdiction.[76] The student alleged that he had not voluntarily consented to the search of his backpack by his high school vice principal. The court relied on testimony that the educator had not originally searched the student's pockets since he had not agreed to this, but had examined the backpack. The court maintained that the facts of the case showed that the school complied with the state constitutional requirement that the student had to consent to a search before it could take place.

A sixteen-year-old student in Oregon challenged the discovery of drugs in his jacket. The student claimed that the drugs were discovered illegally by an assistant principal who searched his jacket after he went to the administrator's office following his involvement in a fight that took place off school property. When the administrator searched the jacket, because he thought that the student might be carrying a weapon, he discovered a bong and twenty grams of psilocybin mushrooms. An appellate court in Oregon reversed in favor of the student.[77] The court was of the opinion that the search of the jacket was impermissible because it had not been supported by reasonable suspicion.

Florida sought further review of an order quashing the discovery of a gun during a search for weapons at a high school. After an administrator searched a coat that was being passed through the room, he found a gun. The student who owned the coat not only denied that the gun was his but also charged that the search was unlawful. An appellate court reversed in favor of the state.[78] The court upheld the search on the ground that it was minimally intrusive and involved the legitimate school concern of safety.

After a security guard at a school noticed a bulge in a student's jacket that was shaped like a gun handle, a search led to the discovery of a loaded weapon. The student, who was suspended for a year, claimed that the gun was discovered in an illegal search. When a trial court rejected

---

[75] *In re* S.S., 680 A.2d 1172 [111 EDUC. L. REP. 1270] (Pa. Super. Ct. 1996).

[76] State *ex rel.* Juvenile Dep't v. Doty, 906 P.2d 299 [105 EDUC. L. REP. 298] (Or. Ct. App. 1995).

[77] State *ex rel.* Juvenile Dep't v. Finch, 925 P.2d 913 [113 EDUC. L. REP. 1315] (Or. Ct. App. 1996).

[78] State of Fla. v. J.A., 679 So. 2d 316 [112 EDUC. L. REP. 1107] (Fla. Dist. Ct. App. 1996).

the student's petition to dismiss, he sought further review. An appellate court in New York reversed.[79] The court reasoned that because the bulge was not remotely suspicious, the delinquency petition should have been dismissed since the discovery of the gun had to be suppressed.

Other

In the first of two cases from Texas, parents and a student sued a band director, school district, and others for emotional distress. They claimed that the educators violated the student's First and Fourteenth Amendment rights to be free from emotional harassment, punishment absent personal guilt, and retaliation for exercising free speech. A federal district court granted the defendants' motion to dismiss. On appeal, the Fifth Circuit affirmed that the case had been dismissed properly because it was frivolous.[80]

An elementary school student with a pony tail was suspended for three days, placed in an in-school suspension program for four months, and finally entered home schooling. Subsequently, his mother alleged that a school rule that limited the length of her son's hair violated the Equal Rights Amendment (ERA) and an antidiscrimination statute of the state. An appellate court affirmed an order enjoining enforcement of the rule.[81] It declared that the judiciary could not act on an ERA challenge to the length of a student's hair based on precedent from the Supreme Court of Texas.[82] However, in finding that the rule did discriminate against the student on the basis of gender, the court awarded him attorney fees.

A student, who was dismissed from school and found guilty of trespass when he tried to return, filed suit based on his Sixth Amendment right to effective assistance of counsel. The Supreme Court of Utah held that the student's rights were not implicated since he did not risk the chance of imprisonment.[83]

In Alabama, a student sued her high school and board of education claiming violations of her right to due process under the Fifth Amendment and equal protection pursuant to the Fourteenth Amendment after the cheerleader sponsor failed to follow procedures in the student handbook for the selection of head cheerleaders. The student argued that because

---

[79] Juan C. v. Cortines, 647 N.Y.S.2d 491 [113 Educ. L. Rep. 353] (N.Y. App. Div. 1996).

[80] Shinn v. College Station Indep. Sch. Dist., 96 F.3d 783 [112 Educ. L. Rep. 646] (5th Cir. 1996).

[81] Bastrop Bd. of Trustees v. Toungate, 922 S.W.2d 650 [110 Educ. L. Rep. 475] (Tex. Ct. App. 1996).

[82] *See* Barber v. Colorado Indep. Sch. Dist., 901 S.W.2d 447 [101 Educ. L. Rep. 1241] (Tex. 1995).

[83] Salt Lake City v. Grotepas, 906 P.2d 890 [105 Educ. L. Rep. 309] (Utah 1995).

the sponsor, not her peers, made the choice, her chances of obtaining a college cheerleading scholarship were harmed. A federal district court in Alabama dismissed.[84] The court found that since the student did not have a federally protected interest to be selected head cheerleader, she did not show that she was treated differently from similarly situated individuals.

A fifteen-year-old girl sought injunctive relief and monetary damages alleging that her title IX and Fourteenth Amendment equal protection rights were violated. The girl had been prohibited from participating on the high school wrestling team even though she had been allowed to be on the junior high school team. The federal district court in Kansas granted the student's request for a preliminary injunction permitting her to wrestle pending the resolution of her section 1983 claim.[85]

Sanctions for Student Misconduct

Generally

A principal sought further review of the denial of his motion for qualified immunity after three students in Idaho alleged that he used excessive force in slapping, punching, choking, and throwing one of them head first into a locker. On one occasion, the police even charged the principal with assault and battery for using excessive force on the students. The Ninth Circuit affirmed.[86] The court maintained that the students had a constitutional right to be free from the use of force and that a reasonable principal would not have engaged in this conduct.

The parents of a third-grade student who was transferred from one class to another due to disciplinary problems alleged that administrators violated their child's constitutional rights by not following proper expulsion procedures. The federal district court in Puerto Rico disagreed.[87] The court dismissed in noting that there was no basis for Fourteenth or Eighth Amendment claims based on harassment, humiliation, and wrongful expulsion.

A student who misbehaved while on a tour of a detention center during a field trip was placed in a holding cell for seven minutes. Subsequently, the student asserted that school officials violated her federal and state constitutional rights. A federal district court in North Carolina

---

[84] James v. Tallassee High Sch., 907 F. Supp. 364 [105 EDUC. L. REP. 559] (M.D. Ala 1995).
[85] Adams v. Baker, 919 F. Supp. 1496 [108 EDUC. L. REP. 637] (D. Kan. 1996).
[86] P.B. v. Koch, 96 F.3d 1298 [112 EDUC. L. REP. 687] (9th Cir. 1996).
[87] Gonzalez v. Torres, 915 F. Supp. 511 [107 EDUC. L. REP. 633] (D.P.R. 1996).

dismissed.[88] The court pointed out that the detention was a de minimis deprivation of the student's liberty and violated neither her procedural nor substantive due process rights.

In Pennsylvania, a student unsuccessfully filed federal civil rights and state law claims against a teacher who attempted to discipline him by grabbing his arm and pulling him across a desk. A federal district court granted the teacher's motion for summary judgment on the civil rights charge when it found that the punishment did not rise to the level of a constitutional claim because it would have had to involve more than an ordinary tort.[89] It dismissed the state law claims without prejudice.

A twelve-year-old student challenged her designation as delinquent after a jury found that she attempted to poison her homeroom teacher. The Supreme Court of Tennessee affirmed.[90] The court found that even though the teacher had intervened before the student could place rat poison in her cup, the child had taken a critical step and had tried to commit second degree murder when she placed her purse containing the poison on the teacher's desk.

A student appealed a ruling that permitted a district to deny him a semester of high school credit because he was absent excessively. The Supreme Court of Missouri reversed in favor of the student because it viewed the action as disciplinary rather than academic.[91] The court reasoned that since the student had a property interest in education under state law, he was entitled to a hearing before a serious penalty could be imposed.

In California, a student challenged his commitment to the Youth Authority because he violated the state penal code by bringing a pellet gun to school. An appellate court affirmed.[92] It rejected the student's contention that the operability of the gun did not matter. The court stated that any instrument resembling a firearm was not conducive to a school learning environment because it could be disruptive.

A high school student in Texas sued coaches and a district for use of excessive force in discipline. The student alleged that the coaches threatened to hang him and that one coach placed what he believed was a gun to his head, saying that they would kill him if he did not improve his grades. A trial court granted the district's, but not the coaches', motion for summary

---

[88] Tucker *ex rel.* Harris v. County of Forsyth, 921 F. Supp. 325 [108 EDUC. L. REP. 1139] (M.D.N.C. 1996).

[89] Jones v. Witinski, 931 F. Supp. 364 [111 EDUC. L. REP. 775] (M.D. Pa. 1996).

[90] State of Tenn. v. Reeves, 916 S.W.2d 909 [107 EDUC. L. REP. 1054] (Tenn. 1996).

[91] State *ex rel.* Yarber v. McHenry, 915 S.W.2d 325 [107 EDUC. L. REP. 361] (Mo. 1995).

[92] *In re* Arturo H., 51 Cal. Rptr.2d 5 [107 EDUC. L. REP. 914] (Cal. Ct. App. 1996).

judgement. An appellate tribunal affirmed but modified.[93] The court posited that it could not address the coaches' request for qualified immunity since they failed to address the student's Fourteenth Amendment equal protection and Fifth Amendment substantive due process claims. In addition, the court found that disputes over material issues of fact precluded summary judgment on the state law charges of excessive force.

In Alabama, a student challenged his ten-day suspension for leaving class without permission. The student asserted that he was not allowed to go to the restroom even though he was suffering from diarrhea. The teacher responded that the child simply misbehaved. An appellate court affirmed a grant of summary judgment in favor of the teacher and principal.[94] The court ruled that the teacher and principal were immune from state tort claims because they acted within their discretionary authority. The court added that the student failed to show that he was deprived of constitutional rights or that the educators demonstrated bad faith or deliberate indifference to his needs.

After a seventh-grader was suspended for fighting, administrators failed to notify his guardian of a meeting involving the administrators, guardian, and student. The following day, the student appeared in the administrator's office for the meeting, but when the meeting was cancelled the student went to class, intending to wait for the meeting to be rescheduled. Later that day, he was charged with trespassing on school grounds and adjudicated delinquent. On further review, an appellate court reversed in favor of the student.[95] The court pointed out that the student could not have been convicted of trespassing since he returned to school upon the express invitation of the educators and was there for legitimate business.

In South Carolina, a seventh-grade student who possessed a razor was convicted of carrying a weapon on school property. A trial court rejected the student's argument that the razor was exempt from state law because it was a knife with a blade less than two inches long. An appellate court affirmed.[96] The court reasoned that since the blade was an "other type weapon," his sentence of indefinite probation was appropriate.

---

[93] Spacek v. Charles, 928 S.W.2d 88 [112 EDUC. L. REP. 525] (Tex. Ct. App. 1996).
[94] Boyett v. Tomberlin, 678 So. 2d 124 [112 EDUC. L. REP. 547] (Ala. Civ. Ct. App. 1995).
[95] M.C. v. State, 677 So. 2d 1382 [112 EDUC. L. REP. 540] (Fla. Dist. Ct. App. 1996).
[96] *In re* Dave G., 477 S.E.2d 470 [113 EDUC. L. REP. 1334] (S.C. Ct. App. 1996).

Suspension and Expulsion

A superintendent, principal, and board of education appealed a $10,000 award plus attorney fees after a federal trial court found that a district in Arkansas violated a student's Fourth Amendment rights. The student was expelled after a search of all male pupils for dangerous weapons led to the discovery that he possessed cocaine. The Eighth Circuit reversed.[97] It found that since the exclusionary rule did not apply to school disciplinary hearings, the search was reasonable.

Two high school students in Georgia who were suspended for separate incidents sought further review of the dismissals of their section 1983 claims against the principal, superintendent, and board of education. The Eleventh Circuit affirmed.[98] In the first case, the court ruled that the student's substantive due process rights were not violated and that he had received appropriate procedural safeguards before being suspended for nine days for fighting, screaming obscenities, and assaulting a teacher. In the second case, the court decided that the principal had reasonable grounds to search the student based on a tip from a second student. The court added that the student's suspension and transfer to an alternative school for possessing a look-alike illegal substance did not violate his substantive due process rights.

In Massachusetts, a student alleged that his school district violated his right to due process when he lost his parking privileges and was suspended from the soccer team and from school for three days for confronting an administrator, coming to campus with alcohol on his breath, and leaving school without permission. The federal trial court granted the district's motion for summary judgment.[99] The court determined that the loss of parking was not grievous in any event, that participation in athletics was not a constitutionally protected activity, and that the suspension did not violate procedures in the student handbook.

A high school student who was suspended after a verbal altercation with another student unsuccessfully tried to enjoin a district from making her take second semester examinations that she would have been excused from if she had not been disciplined. According to a federal district court in Indiana, the student received adequate due process and was not denied equal protection even though the other student, who had a lengthy discipline

---

[97] Thompson v. Carthage Sch. Dist., 87 F.3d 979 [110 Educ. L. Rep. 602] (8th Cir. 1996).

[98] Breeding *ex rel.* C.B. v. Driscoll, 82 F.3d 383 [108 Educ. L. Rep. 1126] (11th Cir. 1996).

[99] Zehner v. Central Berkshire Regional Sch. Dist., 921 F. Supp. 850 [109 Educ. L. Rep. 90] (D. Mass 1995).

record, was given the same punishment.[100] In addition, the court concluded that a suspension for uttering an obscenity did not violate the First Amendment.

In a second case from Indiana, a student who tried to place rat poison in a classmate's drink was suspended, adjudicated delinquent, and released to the custody of her aunt on the condition that she attend school regularly. When the district tried to exclude the student from school, her probation officer obtained an injunction that prohibited her expulsion. On further review, the case was dismissed as moot.[101] An appellate tribunal noted that even though the juvenile court did not have authority to issue a permanent injunction, the case was moot because the student completed the semester without incident.

When a black student was suspended and expelled for possessing marijuana in class, he unsuccessfully filed civil rights and tort claims against administrators. A federal trial court in Alabama granted the administrators' motion for summary judgment.[102] It found that the student's due process rights had been protected because there was no evidence of discriminatory actions forming a conspiracy to violate his civil rights.

A student challenged his ten-day suspension for coming onto campus after having consumed alcohol. When the principal refused to reconsider the suspension, district officials notified the student's attorney that board policy did not allow appeals of alcohol-related offenses beyond the building level. On further review, the Supreme Court of South Carolina affirmed.[103] The court reasoned that state law permits appeals of expulsions but not suspensions.

Three middle school students who were caught with marijuana on school grounds were expelled for the rest of the year and placed on homebound services. Subsequently, the students unsuccessfully filed a section 1983 suit alleging that the board of education violated their due process rights since they and their parents had not been informed of the zero tolerance policy. The Supreme Court of Utah affirmed.[104] It stated that the board had not acted arbitrarily and capriciously since the students received homebound services.

Students lost all three cases where they claimed that discipline over school related offenses violated the Fifth Amendment prohibition against double jeopardy. Police and school officials who searched a tenth-grade

[100] Heller v. Hodgin, 928 F. Supp. 789 [110 Educ. L. Rep. 694] (S.D. Ind. 1996).
[101] *In re* H.L.K., 666 N.E.2d 80 [110 Educ. L. Rep. 383] (Ind. Ct. App. 1996).
[102] Arrington *ex rel.* L.Q.A. v. Eberhart, 920 F. Supp. 1208 [108 Educ. L. Rep. 680] (M.D. Ala. 1996).
[103] Byrd v. Irmo High Sch., 468 S.E.2d 861 [108 Educ. L. Rep. 1003] (S.C. 1996).
[104] S.M. *ex rel.* E.M. v. Briggs, 922 P.2d 754 [112 Educ. L. Rep. 472] (Utah 1996).

student's truck based on an anonymous tip found a semiautomatic pistol. The school expelled the student and police commenced a juvenile proceeding. A trial court agreed with the student's argument that prosecuting him for possessing a firearm after he had been expelled from school was double jeopardy. The Supreme Court of Kansas reversed.[105] The court ruled that the student's expulsion for possessing the gun on school property was not a serious enough offense to bar his prosecution on the ground of double jeopardy.

An appellate court in Minnesota affirmed that a student who was suspended for bringing a knife to school and later adjudicated delinquent did not face double jeopardy.[106] The court found that insofar as the remedial suspension met goals of safety, order, and protection of other students, it did not constitute double jeopardy.

In Georgia, an appellate court reviewed the question of double jeopardy when a seventeen-year-old student was suspended for ten days after being convicted of robbing a convenience store. The court affirmed that the suspension did not constitute a punishment for purposes of double jeopardy since it was a remedial act designed to ensure school safety.[107]

A second case from Georgia examined whether a twelve-year-old student could be permanently expelled for stabbing another pupil with a knife. An appellate court affirmed.[108] Even though the court questioned the shortsightedness of the district's action, it pointed out that the school system acted within the scope of its authority in expelling the student. Moreover, the court noted that since the student was placed on probation, the state did not have to provide her with an education. The court concluded that the student could not claim that the expulsion violated her right to an education or the compulsory attendance law.

In the first of two cases from Pennsylvania, a board of education sought further review of the reinstatement of a student it had expelled for supplying marijuana to a classmate. An appellate court reversed.[109] The court observed that the board had not abused its discretion since a one-year expulsion for selling drugs was a proper sanction.

Members of a softball team disputed their ten-day suspensions for consuming alcoholic beverages while on a school sponsored trip. An

---

[105] *In re* C.M.J., 915 P.2d 62 [109 EDUC. L. REP. 417] (Kan. 1996).
[106] *In re* E.R.D., 551 N.W.2d 238 [111 EDUC. L. REP. 512] (Minn. Ct. App. 1996).
[107] Clark v. State of Ga., 469 S.E.2d 250 [109 EDUC. L. REP. 428] (Ga. Ct. App. 1996).
[108] D.B. v. Clarke County Bd. of Educ., 469 S.E.2d 438 [109 EDUC. L. REP. 435] (Ga. Ct. App. 1996).
[109] Giles v. Brookville Area Sch. Dist., 669 A.2d 1079 [106 EDUC. L. REP. 712] (Pa. Commw. Ct. 1995).

appellate court in Pennsylvania affirmed.[110] It indicated that the trial court had not abused its discretion in upholding the principal's disciplinary action where it was supported by substantial evidence.

A school district in Texas challenged the reinstatement of a student that it expelled for assaulting a teacher. Prior to the school board reaching a final decision on whether to expel the student, it recessed into executive session. Upon returning to an open session, the board upheld the expulsion but shortened it to the remainder of the semester. After a trial court declared the expulsion void, the district sought further review. In reversing, an appellate court found the expulsion was appropriate, the student received due process, and the board did not violate the state's Open Meetings Law.[111]

In Wisconsin, a seventh-grade student who was expelled for bringing an unloaded BB pistol to school was placed on homebound instruction as a condition of his expulsion. After the State Superintendent of Public Instruction reversed the expulsion, the school district alleged that he had exceeded his authority. An appellate court reversed in favor of the district.[112] The court agreed that insofar as the legislature had not implicitly granted the superintendent the power to review a student's suspension, his decision was improper.

When a high school student was called into the principal's office on an anonymous tip, the administrator searched his coat pocket, found two cigarettes, and suspended him for five days. After the board of education and a trial court upheld the suspension, the student sought further review. An appellate court reversed in favor of the student.[113] The court pointed out that the board did not comply with the state statute that required it to adopt a policy identifying conduct for which a pupil may be excluded from school. The court asserted that the student could not be suspended because the board failed to specify possession of tobacco as grounds for suspension.

Desegregation

Desegregation Plan Oversight

The Second Circuit vacated and remanded a case reviewing the liability of the state of New York, various public agencies, and officials

---

[110] Burns v. Hitchcock, 683 A.2d 1322 [113 EDUC. L. REP. 1265] (Pa. Commw. Ct. 1996).

[111] United Indep. Sch. Dist. v. Gonzalez, 911 S. W.2d 118 [105 EDUC. L. REP. 341] (Tex. Ct. App. 1995).

[112] Madison Metropolitan Sch. Dist. v. Wisconsin Dep't of Pub. Instruction, 543 N.W.2d 843 [106 EDUC. L. REP. 1323] (Wis. Ct. App. 1995).

[113] Wilson v. South Cent. Local Sch. Dist. 669 N.E.2d 277 [111 EDUC. L. REP. 1345] (Ohio Ct. App. 1995).

in a long-running desegregation case from Yonkers.[114] After a trial court held that the city and board were liable for the vestiges of racial segregation, it precluded claims against state officials. On further review, the appellate tribunal found that state officials had full knowledge of the extent of de jure segregation and had legal authority to intervene to remedy unlawful segregation. The court decided that state officials were liable under section 1983 for injunctive relief. The court added that although the state, its department of education, and its board of regents could not be held liable under section 1983 because they were not persons within the meaning of the law, they could be found accountable pursuant to the Equal Educational Opportunities Act for failing to take appropriate steps to remedy segregation. The panel concluded that it would be appropriate for the district court to reconsider the liability of the Urban Development Corporation.

In a second case from New York, a federal district court ruled that despite noncompliance involving disabled and bilingual students, the city of Buffalo had reached its desegregation goals. Consequently, the court ended twenty years of judicial oversight and ordered the schools to be returned to the control of local officials.[115] The court stated that because the city had reached unitary status, it could relinquish supervision and control in incremental stages before compliance was achieved in every area.

When a district in South Carolina filed a cross claim against the state, a federal trial court ordered the state to pay fifteen percent of the costs of a desegregation remedy. On further review, the Fourth Circuit reversed.[116] The court noted that the government chose to sue the district alone for failure to follow the desegregation plan and also that the federal judiciary lacked the power to intervene in the internal affairs of state government.

In a related matter involving the same case from South Carolina, a federal trial court reviewed recommendations in a desegregation remedy involving school attendance zones.[117] The court rejected the revised recommendations to cover a new magnet school when it found that the original plan provided a better alternative.

News agencies in Louisiana challenged an order that prohibited a school board and others from commenting on drafts of a desegregation

---

[114] United States v. City of Yonkers, 96 F.3d 600 [112 EDUC. L. REP. 601] (2nd Cir. 1996).

[115] Arthur v. Nyquist, 904 F. Supp. 112 [105 EDUC. L. REP. 46] (W.D.N.Y. 1995).

[116] Stanley v. Darlington County Sch. Dist., 84 F.3d 707 [109 EDUC. L. REP. 1083] (4th Cir. 1996).

[117] Stanley v. Darlington County Sch. Dist., 915 F. Supp. 764 [107 EDUC. L. REP. 652] (D.S.C. 1996).

plan. The court also directed the parties to meet in private sessions. The Fifth Circuit vacated.[118] It agreed that the order was an unconstitutional prior restraint that violated the First Amendment rights of the news agencies to gather information since there was no compelling reason for the confidentiality requirement.

The Eighth Circuit upheld the denial of a motion by students and their parents in Kansas City to intervene in a school desegregation suit.[119] The court rebuffed the intervenors' contention that their concerns were not sufficiently protected. The court found that the plaintiff class adequately represented their interests.

A federal trial court in Alabama refused to order a board of education to undertake a comprehensive review of properties for new school construction.[120] The court observed that even though its job was not to substitute its judgment for that of the board, it could ensure the board considered the effect of the desegregation plan on minority students. The court decided that because the district had complied with its requirements, construction of new facilities could begin.

In Maryland, the federal district court granted a motion by a county board of education to modify racial admission guidelines governing entry into a magnet school.[121] The court permitted the board to revise the guidelines and remove approximately 330 black students from the magnet school waiting list and offer enrollment in available slots, regardless of race.

The federal district court in Massachusetts addressed attorney fees in a desegregation suit.[122] The court ruled that attorneys were entitled to compensation for their participation in the development of a new student assignment plan as well as their unsuccessful efforts to delay its implementation.

On remand from the Eleventh Circuit, a federal trial court in Florida rejected allegations that a board obstructed the goal of unitary status by using discriminatory busing, manipulating school capacity, and maintaining inadequate facilities in integrated neighborhoods.[123] Therefore, the court refused to permit intervenors to enter the case.

---

[118] Davis v. East Baton Rouge Parish Sch. Bd., 78 F.3d 920 [107 Educ. L. Rep. 540] (5th Cir. 1996).
[119] Jenkins v. State of Mo., 78 F.3d 1270 [107 Educ. L. Rep. 598] (8th Cir. 1996).
[120] Lee v. United States, 914 F. Supp. 489 [107 Educ. L. Rep. 127] (N.D. Ala. 1996).
[121] Vaughns v. Board of Educ. of Prince George's County, 941 F. Supp. 579 [113 Educ. L. Rep. 1231] (D. Md. 1996).
[122] Morgan v. Gittens, 915 F. Supp 457 [107 Educ. L. Rep. 613] (D. Mass. 1996).
[123] Bradley v. Pinellas County Sch. Bd., 165 F.R.D. 676 [108 Educ. L. Rep. 1177] (M.D. Fla. 1994).

Cross-district Remedies

The Third Circuit affirmed that school districts in Delaware achieved unitary status.[124] The court held that insofar as performance disparities in the schools were caused by socioeconomic factors, not de jure segregation, it was appropriate to end four decades of judicial supervision in this long-running desegregation suit.

The first of four cases involving the Eighth Circuit arose as part of ongoing litigation from Kansas City. The court affirmed an award of attorney fees after the plaintiff class opposed the Desegregation Monitoring Committee's use of ShareNet, an interactive electronic communication system.[125] The court found that the class opposed the use of the communication system because it was not part of the original voluntary interdistrict transfer plan. The court maintained that the state had to pay attorney fees for defending the desegregation remedy even though it, too, had disagreed with the use of ShareNet.

A mother in Arkansas appealed the denial of her claim that school districts and state officials intentionally caused segregation. The Eighth Circuit affirmed that since the policies of the districts did not produce any current segregative effect, there was no reason to consolidate systems or to create magnet schools to improve racial balance and eliminate disparities.[126]

In an action where school districts sued Arkansas and its Department of Education for funding practices that allegedly violated a desegregation settlement agreement, the Eighth Circuit affirmed that there were violations in the way the state disbursed workers' compensation money to school districts.[127] However, the court reversed in deciding that the state used appropriate procedures in excluding students who voluntarily transferred from districts where they were in the majority race for the purposes of calculating Minimum Foundation Program Aid funds.

On remand from the Eighth Circuit, a federal trial court in Arkansas examined a different aspect of the same desegregation case. This suit concerned a motion to enforce a settlement agreement between districts that was established to ensure equalization of funds after a majority-to-minority transfer of students in interdistrict schools. The court contended that while the agreement was designed to ensure equalization of funds, it

---

[124] Coalition To Save Our Children v. Board of Educ., 90 F.3d 752 [111 EDUC. L. REP. 132] (3rd Cir. 1996).

[125] Agyei *ex rel.* Jenkins v. State of Mo., 73 F.3d 201 [106 EDUC. L. REP. 80] (8th Cir. 1996).

[126] Edgerson *ex rel.* Edgerson v. Clinton, 86 F.3d 833 [110 EDUC. L. REP. 47] (8th Cir. 1996).

[127] Little Rock Sch. Dist. v. Pulaski County Special Sch. Dist. #1, 83 F.3d 1013 [109 EDUC. L. REP. 590] (8th Cir. 1996).

did not mean that the same amount had to be spent for instruction for each student who transferred from one school district to another.[128]

When the judge who had presided over a desegregation case in Cleveland for twenty-one years died, the plaintiffs sought to disqualify his replacement.[129] A federal district court in Ohio rejected the motion after finding that it was based on extrajudicial, rather than judicial, action.

State Court Cases

Students brought a declaratory judgment action against state officials to determine whether they had failed to provide all pupils with substantially equal educational opportunities in light of alleged racial and ethnic segregation in a metropolitan area. After a trial court entered judgment in favor of the officials, the students appealed. The Supreme Court of Connecticut reversed.[130] It held that since extreme racial and ethnic isolation deprived minority children of substantially equal educational opportunities, the state was required to enact remedial measures to address these inequities. In remanding, the court ordered the legislature to remedy both de jure and de facto segregation in public schools in light of the unconstitutional districting scheme of the state.

Following the entry of an order to remedy racial disparities and unequal educational opportunities in Philadelphia, a court in Pennsylvania determined funding liability. The court ruled that the Pennsylvania had to fund the order to the extent that the school district lacked power to raise the money to carry out the earlier mandate. The court directed the state and the governor to provide additional funds to ensure that the district would have sufficient financial resources to educate its students.[131]

Conclusion

Litigation continues to address a wide array of concerns relating to students in American public and private schools. This chapter addressed both constitutional and statutory concerns including attendance, freedom of religion and speech, discipline, and desegregation. It appears likely that several issues, including sexual abuse and harassment, discipline,

---

[128] Little Rock Sch. Dist. v. Pulaski County Special Sch. Dist. # 1, 934 F. Supp. 299 [112 EDUC. L. REP. 218] (E.D. Ark 1996).

[129] Reed v. Rhodes, 934 F. Supp. 1459 [112 EDUC. L. REP. 705] (N.D. Ohio 1996).

[130] Sheff v. O'Neill, 678 A.2d 1267 [111 EDUC. L. REP. 360] (Conn. 1996).

[131] Pennsylvania Human Relations Comm'n v. School Dist. of Phila., 681 A.2d 1366 [112 EDUC. L. REP. 957] (Pa. Commw. Ct. 1996). For the case joining the Commonwealth and Governor, *see* Pennsylvania Human Relations Comm'n v. School Dist. of Phila., 667 A.2d 1173 [105 EDUC. L. REP. 598] (Pa. Commw. Ct. 1995).

and searches will continue to grow and be defined by the courts. The combination of social issues and the increasingly litigious nature of American society seems to ensure that there will be a steady flow of cases concerning the rights of students.

4
BARGAINING

Julie F. Mead

Introduction

This chapter reviews judicial activity related to collective bargaining and labor relations in elementary and secondary schools. Although the Supreme Court did not consider a case dealing with bargaining in a school context, other courts heard a variety of bargaining disputes. Predictably, the majority of decisions considered the application of existing precedents to new disputes. The issues addressed in this chapter range from constitutional questions to the scope of arbitration to the consequences of adverse employment decisions. What follows is a review of 1996 rulings grouped according to topic.

Constitutional Issues

Four cases considered constitutional issues related to labor relations. One examined rights to the free exercise of religion under the First Amendment. Three opinions reviewed equal protection and due process under the Fourteenth Amendment, with the third action also considering the Contract Clause of Article 1 of the Constitution.

First Amendment

Lay teachers and Catholic elementary schools in the Diocese of Camden entered into a disagreement over the schools' unwillingness to allow a teachers' association to serve as a representative and bargaining agent for the teachers. The teachers contended that language in the state constitution granted individuals in the private sector the right to bargain collectively. The schools believed that they had an absolute right to refuse to recognize or bargain with the teachers because of the protection afforded them under the First Amendment. An appellate court in New Jersey reversed a grant of summary judgment that had been entered on behalf of the schools.[1] The court held that the compelling governmental interest expressed in the fundamental right to organize and bargain collectively under the state constitution prevailed over the claim that this burdened the free exercise of religion. The court reasoned that, like the collective bargaining pact that the Diocese crafted with the lay teachers in its high schools, any agreement with the elementary teachers union could be written to protect the religious autonomy and character of the schools. In addition, the court noted that any disputes arising from the bargaining still would have to be settled in court.

Fourteenth Amendment

In Pennsylvania, an appellate court reviewed an arbitration award after a bus driver was inappropriately denied an advancement to a bus mechanic position. The school district awarded the promotion to another employee with less seniority because he was a veteran. The court affirmed that special treatment in promotions under a veteran's preference act violated equal protection.[2] The court pointed out that giving another preference to an individual who already had received one during the initial hiring process was unreasonable and unconstitutional.

---

[1] South Jersey Catholic Sch. Teachers Ass'n v. St. Teresa of the Infant Jesus Church Elementary Sch., 675 A.2d 1155 [109 Educ. L. Rep. 822] (N.J. Super Ct. App. Div. 1996).

[2] Belle Vernon Sch. Dist. v. Teamsters Local Union 782, 670 A.2d 1201 [106 Educ. L. Rep. 1203] (Pa. Commw. Ct. 1996).

An Indiana teachers' association challenged the refusal of a school board to conduct a unit election for its nonteaching employees. Even though there never was an election, the board recognized and bargained with a local affiliate of the American Federation of State County and Municipal Employees (AFSCME). A federal district court rejected the association's contention that the board's failure to conduct an election violated the Equal Protection Clause of the Fourteenth Amendment. On further review, the Seventh Circuit affirmed.[3] The court maintained that the teachers' union and the municipal employees' union were not similarly situated since the board had a long-standing relationship with the AFSCME and was bound by an existing contract with the AFSCME that might have been violated by calling for the requested election.

Unions challenged the constitutionality of a new statute that terminated their status as the exclusive bargaining representative of nonteaching employees in the Chicago public schools.[4] A federal district court in Illinois rejected the argument proffered by the unions that the law violated the Due Process Clause of the Fourteenth Amendment based on the notion that any property interest that the employees had ceased when their contracts expired. In addition, the court determined that the Due Process Clause was satisfied when the normal legislative process was followed and the enactment of the statute was not arbitrary or irrational. Likewise, the court decided that the Equal Protection Clause was inapplicable because just as teachers and other school employees are not equally situated, neither are unions and third parties entering into contracts with the district. Turning to the Contract Clause claim, the court rebuffed the argument advanced by the unions that the law was unenforceable as it had unconstitutionally impaired their contractual relationships with the district. The court pointed out that the claim lacked merit because the contracts had expired and the law was rationally related to the legislature's goal of rectifying the problems in the school system.

Recognition and Representational Issues

Tutors of students with learning disabilities charged that a union unfairly represented them by negotiating terms and conditions of employment that were significantly less favorable than those of other instructional personnel. More specifically, the tutors' contract precluded continuing contracts yet included the tutors in the same bargaining unit

---

[3] Indiana State Teachers Ass'n v. Board of Sch. Comm'r of Indianapolis, 101 F.3d 1179 [114 EDUC. L. REP. 766] (7th Cir. 1996).
[4] Bricklayers Union Local 21 v. Edgar, 922 F. Supp. 100 [109 EDUC. L. REP. 148] (E.D. Ill. 1996).

as the teachers. The Supreme Court of Ohio upheld the dismissal of the complaint by the State Employment Relations Board because the tutors failed to provide evidence that they were unlawfully included in the same bargaining unit as the teachers.[5]

The first of two cases from New York involved a union's challenge of a board's refusal to appropriate funds for a collective bargaining agreement. The board argued that the contract did not go into effect until the board specifically acted to authorize funding. An appellate court affirmed that neither the language of the agreement nor past practice supported the board's contention.[6] The court also noted that a newly elected board could not repudiate the lawful acts of its predecessor.

After an organization that represented teaching assistants and school nurses was disbanded, a district challenged a decision by the Public Employment Relations Board (PERB) allowing the teaching assistants and nurses to join the same bargaining unit as the teachers. An appellate court affirmed.[7] It ruled that the determination by the PERB was valid because there was a sufficient community of interest permitting the teaching assistants and nurses to be included in the same unit as the teachers.

Similarly, an appellate court affirmed the certification by the Nebraska Commission of Industrial Relations of a bargaining unit comprised of principals and supervisors.[8] A district had questioned the certification on the ground that allowing supervisors and the employees they oversee to be in the same bargaining unit was contrary to law. The court stated that the certification was proper and consistent in light of state statutes and precedent that disfavor the fragmentation of bargaining units in the public sector.

Rights and Obligations of
Exclusive Bargaining Representatives

The Supreme Court of Indiana reviewed the allegations of a teachers' association that a board of education committed an unfair labor practice by appointing some of its board members to a textbook advisory

---

[5] State *ex rel.* Allen v. State Employment Relations Bd., 666 N.E.2d 1119 [110 Educ. L. Rep. 803] (Ohio 1996).

[6] Middle Country Adm'rs Ass'n v. Board of Educ. of the Middle Country Cent. Sch. Dist., 640 N.Y.S.2d 52 (N.Y. App. Div. 1996).

[7] Board of Educ. of the Union-Endicott Cent. Sch. Dist. v. New York State Pub. Employment Relations Bd., 649 N.Y.S.2d 523 [114 Educ. L. Rep. 278] (N.Y. App. Div. 1996).

[8] Papillion/LaVista Sch. Principals and Supervisors Org. v. Papillion/ LaVista Sch. Dist., 555 N.W.2d 563 [114 Educ. L. Rep. 307] (Neb. Ct. App. 1996).

committee. The court affirmed in favor of the union.[9] The court concluded that when a board uses its advisory committee as the sole vehicle for discussing textbooks with the union representing its educators, the bargaining agent is entitled to select all teacher members of the group.

When the routes of a bus driver who transported special education students to school were reduced, she claimed that her union failed to represent her adequately in enforcing a collective bargaining agreement. The driver also charged that the union president's sexual harassment of her amounted to discrimination as well as tortious interference with and breach of contract. The Supreme Court of Minnesota affirmed that the driver failed to substantiate her claims.[10] It found that the driver did not make a prima facie claim of inadequate representation because she failed to allege any violations of her bargaining agreement. The court posited that her claims of discrimination, tortious interference, and breach of contract failed because the alleged misconduct did not implicate union activity.

A black teacher successfully sought further review of the dismissal of his allegation that his union knew of past racial discrimination by the board of education and failed to represent him in the second stage of his grievance. The teacher asserted that the union's conduct constituted acquiescence in the racial discrimination. Although an appellate court in Florida did not address the merits of the teacher's claims, it remanded for further proceedings in holding that the dismissal of his petition was improper.[11]

Scope of Bargaining

Five cases examined the scope of bargaining between school systems and the unions of their employees. Three decisions concerned mandatory topics of negotiations. Two actions considered whether disputed matters were permissible topics of bargaining.

Mandatory Topics Of Bargaining

In Pennsylvania, a school district that was engaged in negotiations with the representative of its secretarial, custodial, and maintenance staff informed the union that it was considering subcontracting in order to save money. The union challenged the board's action on the basis that

---

[9] Marion Teachers Ass'n v. Board of Sch. Trustees of Marion Community Sch. Corp., 672 N.E.2d 1363 [114 Educ. L. Rep. 625] (Ind. 1996).

[10] Lipka v. Minnesota Sch. Employees Ass'n, Local 1980, 550 N.W.2d 618 (Minn. 1996).

[11] Weaver v. Leon Classroom Teachers Ass'n, 680 So. 2d 478 [113 Educ. L. Rep. 995](Fla. Dist. Ct. App. 1996).

state law prohibits such a practice unless the parties have bargained to impasse. Moreover, even though the union continued to articulate a desire to negotiate, as evidenced by its making two salary and benefit proposals that went unanswered, the board declared an impasse and voted to subcontract union services to private contractors. An appellate court ruled that the district's failure to make a counterproposal did not, by itself, constitute an unfair labor practice.[12] However, the court affirmed that the board's failure to continue bargaining when the union expressed a willingness to do so was an unfair labor practice.

At issue in Illinois were so called zipper clauses that close bargaining during the term of an agreement and make a written contract the exclusive statement of the rights and obligations of the parties. Narrow zipper clauses are a mandatory topic of bargaining under state law and waive the right to bargain over issues already addressed in negotiations between parties. Broad zipper clauses are nonmandatory and preclude bargaining on any issue not included in the contract, even if the issue was not a topic of bargaining that was contemplated at the time of bargaining. In the case at bar, an education association contested a board's definition of a clause as broad. The association contended that a board of education had inappropriately created an impasse by insisting on a broad zipper clause. An appellate court decreed that broad zipper clauses are a permissive topic of bargaining, otherwise employees would be denied their statutory right to midterm bargaining.[13] The court then examined the language of the clause and determined that the zipper clause was actually a narrow clause. Accordingly, the court upheld the decision of the Educational Labor Relations Board that the district had not violated state law by declaring an impasse over the contested zipper clause.

A midterm increase in health insurance benefits led to a disagreement between a school district and its teachers' association. The Michigan Education Special Services Association (MESSA) is a subsidiary of the Michigan Education Association (MEA) that administers insurance plans for MEA members and provides health care benefits to employees in bargaining units represented by the MEA. Even though MESSA did not negotiate with the district, it increased lifetime maximum health insurance benefits. An appellate court agreed that such a unilateral change was a bargaining violation.[14] The court rejected the argument that the board

---

[12] Morrisville Sch. Dist. v. Pennsylvania Labor Relations Bd., 687 A.2d 5 [115 EDUC. L. REP. 29](Pa. Commw. Ct. 1996).

[13] Mt. Vernon Educ. Ass'n v. Illinois Educ. Labor Relations Bd., 663 N.E. 2d 1067 [109 EDUC. L. REP. 305] (Ill App. Ct. 1996).

[14] St. Clair Intermediate Sch. Dist. v. Intermediate Educ. Ass'n/ Michigan Educ. Ass'n, 555 N.W.2d 267 [114 EDUC. L. REP. 302] (Mich. Ct. App. 1996).

waived its right to bargain when it accepted a contract with services from MESSA since internal MESSA documents reserved the right to modify its policies unilaterally. The court explained that since bargaining rights could be waived only by explicit language, none of which was in the contract between the board and MESSA, there could not be a unilateral change in the benefits.

Permissive Topics Of Bargaining

The union representing a school bus driver appealed the dismissal of its claim. The union maintained that the driver was entitled to arbitration and that the district was required to provide just cause for the nonrenewal of the driver's one-year contract. The board argued that since such an interpretation would have conflicted with state law, it was outside the scope of bargaining. The board also responded that the driver's contract was not renewed at the end of its term, not discharged during the term of his employment. The Supreme Court of Washington reversed in favor of the union.[15] The court acknowledged that insofar as state law does not preclude the board from bargaining additional just cause provisions in a contract, the meaning of the clause was properly subject to arbitration.

A taxpayer unsuccessfully challenged a school board's negotiated agreement with its superintendent and the unions representing its teachers and administrators. The contract provided that any unused sick leave could be converted into cash upon retirement or dismissal. An appellate court in New York affirmed that the board had the statutory authority to negotiate the contested provisions as reasonable consideration for the services performed by their employees.[16] The court found that just as the treatment of unused sick days was proper in the union contracts, so too, it was appropriate in the agreement between the board and superintendent.

Grievability and Arbitrability

Decisions reported in this section demonstrate the continuing legal presumption that employer-employee controversies should be settled by grievances and arbitration. Six cases considered issues related to arbitrability. Five rulings examined procedural aspects of arbitration.

---

[15] Peninsula Sch. Dist. No. 401 v. Public Sch. Employees of Peninsula, 924 P.2d 13 [113 EDUC. L. REP. 477](Wash. 1996).

[16] Perrenod v. Liberty Bd. of Educ., 636 N.Y.S.2d 210 [106 EDUC. L. REP. 302] (N.Y. App. Div. 1996).

Presumption and Arbitrability

The first five of the six cases in this section reflect judicial support for arbitration as the appropriate vehicle to resolve labor disputes. A janitor who was charged with criminal misconduct for making sexual comments to and inappropriately touching two female baby sitters in his home denied that the incidents occurred. Even so, the janitor entered a plea to two counts of simple assault and was fined. Subsequently, the school district discharged the janitor for violating its policy against sexual harassment. When the district succeeded in having an arbitration award ordering the janitor's reinstatement overturned, he appealed. The Supreme Court of Iowa reversed in favor of the janitor.[17] The court rejected the district's argument that the dispute was not abritrable, because the janitor was charged with misconduct rather than incompetence. The court reasoned that the district's decision to fire the janitor necessarily involved an evaluative process. The court added that since contract language specifically granted employees the right to challenge evaluations, the board's action was subject to arbitration. Finally, the court ruled that the district's claim that forcing it to rehire the janitor would impair its statutory duty to provide a safe environment for students went to the merits of the arbitrator's decision and was beyond the scope of judicial review.

At issue in Pennsylvania was whether a school board's determination that course enrollments had declined was subject to arbitration. A union charged that a teacher was improperly furloughed because there was no evidence of a substantial decrease in student numbers. An appellate court, in upholding an award to the union, found that the union contract expressly incorporated the statutory requirement that a district demonstrate the existence of a substantial decrease in registrations before furloughing an employee. The court held that the question of substantiality was arbitrable.[18]

The authority of a school district to set course enrollments also was litigated in New York. A teachers' union successfully challenged a board's decision to increase class size beyond the limit specified in its own policies. An appellate court affirmed that an arbitrator should decide whether the change in class size fell within the scope of a contractual prohibition against modifying rules that substantially affect working conditions.[19]

The union again prevailed in a second case involving the same parties. An appellate court in New York affirmed that the district's failure to

---

[17] Postville Community Sch. Dist. v. Billmeyer, 548 N.W.2d 558 [109 Educ. L. Rep. 1368](Iowa 1996).

[18] Ambridge Area Sch. Dist. v. Ambridge Area Educ. Ass'n, PSEA/NEA, 670 A.2d 1207 [106 Educ. L. Rep. 1208] (Pa. Commw. Ct. 1996).

[19] Board of Educ. of Plainedge Union Free Sch. Dist. #9 v. Plainedge Fed'n of Teachers, 645 N.Y.S.2d 489 [111 Educ. L. Rep. 934](N.Y. App. Div. 1996).

maintain a public address and intercom system violated its collective bargaining agreement.[20] As such, the court held that an arbitration hearing was the proper forum for dispute resolution.

A school board sought further review of a finding that it committed an unfair labor practice by refusing to arbitrate a grievance related to a one-day suspension of a teacher who called her principal a "wimp." The board contended that discipline was solely within its discretion since the suspension was unrelated to any plans to dismiss the teacher. An appellate court affirmed that the board violated the Illinois Educational Labor Relations Act.[21] The court noted that simply because a board has the authority to act does not mean that the exercise of its power cannot be subject to review by an arbitrator.

In the only case not to support arbitration, a union unsuccessfully appealed the denial of its request for arbitration when a baseball coach's stipendiary contract was not renewed for a third season. The superintendent chose not to renew the coach's contract not only because the coach had two consecutive unimpressive seasons but also because the coach had expressed a negative attitude in the school yearbook. The union claimed that since the nonrenewal was disciplinary, it was arbitrable under the bargaining agreement between the parties. The Supreme Judicial Court of Massachusetts disagreed.[22] It held that statutes governing the employment contracts of coaches do not require the district to demonstrate just cause for nonrenewal. Also, the court indicated that state law limits coaching contracts to three years. Accordingly, the court ruled that the nonrenewal of the stipendiary contract was not subject to arbitration since the coach could not receive any lawful relief.

Procedural Issues

The Supreme Court of Kansas dismissed a school board's appeal of an order compelling it to submit to arbitration.[23] The panel ruled that the trial court's decision was not subject to appeal because it was not the final order. The court reasoned that when arbitration is compelled, further judicial relief may not be pursued until an award is rendered since it constitutes the final appeal order.

---

[20] Board of Educ. of Plainedge Union Free Sch. Dist. v. Plainedge Fed'n of Teachers, 645 N.Y.S.2d 491 [111 Educ. L. Rep. 936](N.Y. App. Div. 1996).

[21] Granite City Community Unit Sch. Dist. v. Illinois Educ. Labor Relations Bd., 664 N.E.2d 1060 [109 Educ. L. Rep. 1343] (Ill. App. Ct. 1996).

[22] School Comm. of Natick v. Education Ass'n of Natick, 666 N.E.2d 486 [110 Educ. L. Rep. 784](Mass. 1996).

[23] National Educ. Ass'n-Topeka v. Unified Sch. Dist. No. 501, 925 P.2d 835 [113 Educ. L. Rep. 1310](Kan. 1996).

After a teacher was disciplined for improper sexual conduct with students, a school district refused the teacher's request to disclose the students' names as part of the grievance process. The district asserted that it had an obligation to protect the students and their confidentiality. In this case of first impression, the Supreme Court of Delaware affirmed that the district committed an unfair labor practice by unconditionally refusing to disclose the students' names without even attempting to consult with the parents of the students.[24] The court also held that the parents had the right to voice an objection to the release of the names of their children or to request limitations on disclosures. The court did not address whether the parents had the right to prevent disclosure completely because it pointed out that this would have been beyond the scope of the controversy before the court and would have required the court to render an impermissible advisory opinion.

Two former school board employees sought further review of the dismissal of their claim for compensation for accrued, but unused, vacation days. The former career service employees maintained that since their jobs had been terminated, they had no ability to file a grievance over lost compensation. An appellate court in Illinois reversed in favor of the employees.[25] The court indicated that although the bargaining agreement contained provisions for calculating vacation pay for full-time employees, it did not address remuneration for individuals whose jobs had been terminated. As such, the court remanded in concluding that the employees were not required to exhaust administrative remedies under the bargaining agreement before seeking judicial relief.

In the first of two cases from New York, a board of education sought further review when one of its employees individually sued for damages over an alleged breach of their collective bargaining agreement. An appellate court reversed in favor of the board when it determined that the employee lacked standing.[26] The court was of the opinion that such a suit would only be proper if the bargaining agreement specifically granted the employee the right or if he charged that the union failed to represent his interests properly.

The second case from New York considered the timeliness of a grievance and a request for arbitration where a custodian was reassigned to the night shift. After an arbitrator ruled in favor of the janitor, the

---

[24] Colonial Educ. Ass'n v. Board of Educ. of Colonial Sch. Dist., 685 A.2d 361 [114 EDUC. L. REP. 873] (Del. 1996).
[25] Daniels v. Board of Educ. of Chicago, 661 N.E.2d 468 [107 EDUC. L. REP. 246](Ill. App. Ct. 1996).
[26] Tomlinson v. Board of Educ. of Lakeland Cent. Sch. Dist. of Shrub Oak, 636 N.Y.S.2d 855 [106 EDUC. L. REP. 855] (N.Y. App. Div. 1996).

district claimed that the grievance should have been time barred since the janitor failed to file his complaint within thirty days of learning of the transfer, as required. An appellate court affirmed in favor of the janitor.[27] The court agreed with the arbitrator in noting that the janitor's complaint was filed twenty-eight days after he reported for his new assignment, but the court concluded that filing a grievance prior to that date would have been premature since informal processes might have caused the district to change its intention to reassign.

Judicial Review

Consistent with a trend in recent years, a significant number of cases dealt with the judicial review of arbitration awards. These decisions fell into four categories: seven considered salary and benefits; two reviewed issues around working conditions; five examined questions related to dismissal and nonrenewal; and four addressed disputes surrounding reduction-in-force.

Salary and Benefits

A special education tutor tried to compel her district to pay her according to the teacher's salary schedule in a collective bargaining agreement. The tutor maintained that her pay should have been based on the minimum pay scale specified in state law rather than on the hourly basis outlined in her bargaining agreement. The tutor further argued that since the board improperly reduced the hours of her employment, she was entitled to additional compensation. After a lower court granted the district's motions for summary judgment, the tutor appealed. The Supreme Court of Ohio affirmed in favor of the district.[28] The court contended that since the legislature intended collective bargaining agreements to prevail over conflicting statutes, the contract's differential treatment of teachers and tutors did not violate state law. The court added that rather than specify a minimum number of hours, the contract for tutoring services simply established a level of compensation for each hour served. As such, the court observed that the district did not unlawfully reduce the tutor's compensation.

The Supreme Court of New Jersey examined whether state law prohibits a board of education from paying salary increments to teachers

---

[27] *In re* Board of Educ. of Oneonta City Sch. Dist., 646 N.Y.S.2d 202 (N.Y. App. Div. 1996).

[28] State *ex rel.* Burch v. Sheffield-Sheffield Lake City Sch. Dist. Bd. of Educ., 661 N.E.2d 1086 [107 Educ. L. Rep. 965](Ohio 1996).

following the expiration of a three-year collective bargaining agreement.[29] It held that payment for a fourth year violated the state education code as the legislature specifically limited a board's authority to a maximum of three years. In addition, the court found that the prohibition applied only to increments for teachers and that the contracts of other staff members were governed by general state labor laws that did not contain such restrictions.

Advancement on an agreed upon salary schedule was in dispute in a case from New York that looked at whether teachers could move up two steps in a year. An arbitrator judged that teachers could not advance more than one position even though they would have been placed at levels that did not accurately reflect the number of years of service they completed with the district. An appellate court affirmed that the arbitrator exceeded the scope of his authority by improperly basing his ruling on past practices that negated the express language of the contract.[30]

In Maryland, a union negotiated an agreement with a city for wage increases to bring the pay of its teachers in parity with their colleagues in suburban districts. After the city failed to pay the increases due to a series of shortfalls, the union filed a complaint that eventually led to arbitration. The arbitrator decided that the city had breached its wage agreement but refused to grant any remedy to the teachers. On further review, an appellate court offered that although the arbitrator's failure to fashion a remedy for an identified breach was an abdication of his duties, his initial determination was flawed.[31] The court observed that since the wage agreement would have been valid and binding only with the approval of the Board of Estimates, the city's failure to acquiesce to the contract meant that there was no wage agreement to breach.

A school district that had not invoked a proration of benefits clause in five years notified new teachers that it would prorate benefits and therefore would no longer provide coverage for the month of August. When the union made a demand to bargain over the clause, the board responded that it had no duty to do so because the clause already was agreed to in the contract. A hearing officer ruled in favor of the district but the state Employment Relations Commission and an appellate court found in favor of the union. However, on further review, the Supreme Court of Michigan reversed in favor of the district on the ground that the unambiguous language in the collective bargaining contract was

---

[29] Board of Educ. of Neptune v. Neptune Township Educ. Ass'n, 675 A. 2d 611 [115 EDUC. L. REP. 372] (N.J. 1996).

[30] Sachem Cent. Teachers Ass'n v. Board of Educ. of Sachem Cent. Sch. Dist., 642 N.Y.S.2d 969 [109 EDUC. L. REP. 1365](N.Y. App. Div. 1996).

[31] Baltimore Teachers Union v. Mayor and City Council of Baltimore, 671 A.2d 80 [106 EDUC. L. REP. 1214](Md. Spec. Ct. App. 1996).

controlling.[32] The court noted that past practice only controls when it is widely acknowledged and mutually accepted by both parties to the contract. Further, the court maintained that since the union, as the party asserting that past practice replaced contract language, failed to demonstrate that there was a meeting of the minds with respect to the new terms and conditions, the district acted properly.

Insurance benefits were at the center of the dispute after a school district unilaterally changed the deductible in a health insurance plan. Under the change, employees would have had to submit claims both to the insurer and the district for a determination of eligibility. After an arbitrator decided that the district violated the terms of its bargaining contract and ordered a return to the original plan, the district sought judicial review. An appellate court in Pennsylvania upheld the arbitration award.[33] The court reasoned that the arbitrator's decision should be left in place since it properly drew its essence from the collective bargaining contract.

A second case from Pennsylvania involved a controversy where teachers had health and life insurance premiums deducted from their pay following a strike. An appellate court affirmed that the school district had violated the agreement that it entered into with the union in order to end the work stoppage.[34] The agreement specifically stated that the teachers would not suffer the loss of work days or other reprisals for engaging in the strike. Even so, the district deducted health and life insurance premiums from teachers' checks for the period of time in which the strike occurred. The court ordered the district not only to stop making the deductions because they were reprisals contrary to the language of the bargaining agreement but also to return monies subtracted from the teachers' salaries.

A teacher who was wrongfully discharged then reinstated with back pay and full benefits subsequently took an early retirement. Even so, the board of education refused to compensate the teacher for all of his sick days. A trial court ordered the district to pay the teacher for some, but not all, of the days awarded him as compensation for his wrongful discharge. At the same time, the court denied the teacher's motion for relief with respect to the time that accumulated prior to his being fired on the basis that such a payment was contrary to public policy. On further review, an appellate court in Illinois reversed in favor of the teacher.[35] The court

---

[32] Port Huron Educ. Ass'n v. Port Huron Area Sch. Dist., 550 N.W.2d 228 [110 EDUC. L. REP. 1230] (Mich. 1996).

[33] Susquenita Sch. Dist. v. Susquenita Educ. Ass'n, 676 A.2d 706 [109 EDUC. L. REP. 1319](Pa. Commw. Ct. 1996).

[34] Burrell Educ. Ass'n v. Burrell Sch. Dist., 674 A.2d 348 [108 EDUC. L. REP. 792] (Pa. Commw. Ct. 1996).

[35] Grant v. Board of Educ. of Chicago, 668 N.E.2d 1188 [112 EDUC. L. REP. 390] (Ill. App. Ct. 1996).

stated that public policy did not preclude payment for accumulated sick leave, even when the number of days is large. Yet, although the court found that the teacher was entitled to credit for the unused days, it did not permit him to accept a payment since he did not qualify for it under the terms of his collective bargaining agreement. Finally, the court determined that since the language of the settlement agreement between the parties was ambiguous over what the district may have owed the teacher, it remanded for consideration of the system's obligation and whether the district satisfied its duty.

Working Conditions

A union alleged that a school district committed an unfair labor practice by not presenting the union's proposal to a board-appointed teacher preparation time study committee. Subsequently, the Employment Relations Board dismissed the union's complaint over the district's refusal to comply with an arbitration award ordering the district to incorporate the union's proposal on preparation time into their collective bargaining agreement. An appellate court in Oregon affirmed.[36] The court pointed out that since the board-appointed committee had not reached an agreement on teacher preparation time, the arbitrator exceeded his authority by ordering a remedy that improperly modified the contract.

In Pennsylvania, a union sought further review of an order vacating an arbitration award where a school district chose not to replace two retiring itinerant art teachers. A board of arbitrators found that the district violated the contract's maintenance of standards clause by unilaterally increasing the class assignments of the remaining art teachers. After a trial court vacated the award, an appellate court reversed in favor of the union.[37] The panel reflected that since the arbitration award was drawn from the essence of the collective bargaining agreement, it should not have been disturbed.

Dismissal And Nonrenewal

A board of education appealed a ruling that ordered it to comply with a provision in a bargaining agreement over the nonrenewal of a probationary teacher's contract. Language in the agreement provided that a nontenured teacher was entitled to a thirty-day notice before the board decided not to renew a contract and established a just cause requirement to justify any such action. The Supreme Court of California reversed in

[36] Chenowith Educ. Ass'n v. Chenowith Sch. Dist. 9, 918 P.2d 854 [110 Educ. L. Rep. 872] (Or. Ct. App. 1996).
[37] Williamsport Area Sch. Dist. v. Williamsport Educ. Ass'n, 686 A.2d 885 [115 Educ. L. Rep. 24] (Pa. Commw. Ct. 1996).

favor of the district.[38] The court held that state law granted districts the absolute right to decide not to re-elect probationary teachers without providing cause or other procedural protection and without regard to contrary provisions in a collective bargaining agreement.

The Supreme Court of Alaska partially reversed in favor of a former Reserve Officer Training Corps instructor who was dismissed for the alleged sexual abuse of students even though the instructor had not exhausted contractual remedies.[39] The court reasoned that because the board not only suspended the teacher without pay but was also the body to whom an appeal of last resort would have been made, the grievance process was rendered futile.

A nontenured teacher who learned that she would not be re-employed despite receiving a satisfactory performance evaluation reviewed her file and uncovered derogatory information. An arbitrator declared that the rating was false in light of the administrator's true appraisal of the teacher's skills. Not providing her with accurate information, even if motivated by kindness, deprived her of an opportunity to take remedial measures that may have saved her job. The arbitrator also ordered the derogatory material removed from the teacher's file. Finally, the arbitrator awarded the teacher an amount equal to one year's salary. After a trial court reversed the arbitration award, the teacher's union sought further review. An appellate court in Massachusetts reinstated those parts of the award that decreed that the misleading job evaluation was a procedural violation of the collective bargaining agreement and that the salary award was within the scope of the arbitrator's authority.[40] However, the court concluded that the arbitrator exceeded his authority in ordering the district to remove the derogatory material from the teacher's file because the information had little impact on the decision not to renew her contract.

A custodian challenged his dismissal for engaging in sexual relations with his girlfriend on school premises during evening working hours. A hearing officer observed that the custodian had not violated any of the school board's rules. The board accepted the hearing officer's findings of fact but posited that the officer misinterpreted board policies and dismissed the custodian for conduct unbecoming one of its employees. An appellate court in Florida affirmed the school board's judgment that

[38] Board of Educ. of the Round Valley Unified Sch. Dist. v. Round Valley Teachers Ass'n, 52 Cal. Rptr.2d 115 [108 Educ. L. Rep. 947] (Cal. 1996).
[39] Romulus v. Anchorage Sch. Dist., 910 P.2d 610 [106 Educ. L. Rep. 1332] (Alaska 1996).
[40] School Comm. of Boston v. Boston Teachers Union, Local 66, 664 N.E.2d 478 [109 Educ. L. Rep. 374 (Mass. App. Ct. 1996).

the custodian violated board rules.[41] Yet, the court ruled that the dismissal was unwarranted since the custodian, who had been employed for eleven years, had not previously been sanctioned for violating rules and his bargaining agreement contained provisions calling for progressive discipline. Accordingly, the court remanded for a determination of an appropriate penalty.

A city board of education sought further review of an arbitration award that excluded evidence of a warehouse supervisor's conviction for embezzling union funds. An appellate court in Connecticut reversed in favor of the board.[42] The court indicated that the award violated public policy since the supervisor's conviction demonstrated a history of a disregard for public trust and his reinstatement would have restored an admitted thief to his former position.

Reduction-in-force

A tenured teacher asserted that her school district had to allow her to supervise additional study hall periods before it could place her on unrequested leave. The teacher also argued that her bargaining contract required the district to reassign less senior colleagues who supervised study halls in order to satisfy its obligations with respect to seniority under the mandatory bumping rights provisions of state law. An appellate court in Minnesota affirmed that the seniority provisions only applied to classes for which a teacher is licensed.[43] The court concluded that since supervising study hall did not require a license, the statute did not obligate the district to bump junior faculty to accommodate the tenured teacher.

In the first of two cases from New York, a school district challenged an arbitration award that ordered it to grant back pay to teachers whose contracts had been terminated and entitled the teachers to be recalled to their former positions. The district argued that the arbitrator usurped his power in attempting to determine the number of teachers it had to employ. An appellate court upheld the arbitration award.[44] The court offered that the order was within the bounds of public policy and the arbitrator's authority.

A high school technology teacher whose employment was terminated due to curricular changes was considered for an opening in an elementary

---

[41] Bell v. School Bd. of Dade County, 681 So. 2d 843 [113 EDUC. L. REP. 1351] (Fla. Dist. Ct. App. 1996).

[42] Board of Educ. of the City of Hartford v. Local 566, Council 4, AFSCME, 683 A.2d 1036 [113 EDUC. L. REP. 1260] (Conn. App. Ct. 1996).

[43] Kvernmo v. Independent Sch. Dist. No. 403, 541 N.W.2d 620 [105 EDUC. LAW REP. 1231](Minn. Ct. App. 1996).

[44] Board of Educ. v. Port Jefferson Station Teachers Ass'n, 642 N.Y.S.2d 954 [109 EDUC. L. REP. 1360](N.Y. App. Div. 1996).

school. However, the district offered the job to someone else because the former technology teacher was the weakest candidate for the job. After an arbitrator ordered the teacher appointed to the position in the elementary school, the district sought further review. An appellate court in New York affirmed.[45] In rejecting the district's argument that the award violated public policy, the court reasoned that the arbitrator merely gave effect to the provision in the bargaining agreement that gave preference to certified members of the unit who lost their jobs due to a reduction-in-force.

A teacher's union for a special education district filed an unfair labor complaint alleging that a participating school system refused to comply with a binding arbitration award. The arbitrator determined that the school system violated provisions of its bargaining agreement by failing to provide a list of vacant positions for tenured teachers after taking back programs from a special education district. The Illinois Education Labor Relations Board dismissed the union's complaint and an appellate court affirmed.[46] The court maintained that the award was unenforceable since it exceeded the arbitrator's authority. Further, the court was of the opinion that the special education district had neither the actual nor apparent authority to agree on behalf of the participating local school systems to post notices of vacant positions for the benefit of the special education teachers.

Miscellaneous

Five cases did not appear to fit any of the categories above and are reported in this section. A union representing bus drivers sought further review of the state Employment Relations Commission's dismissal of its charge that a board of education committed an unfair labor practice by terminating the contracts of several of its members. The board notified the union that it would terminate the expired contracts following unsuccessful attempts to reach a successor agreement through bargaining. An appellate court in Michigan affirmed.[47] The court acknowledged that the district did not commit an unfair labor practice by giving notice of its intent to terminate the contracts under the old agreement and by setting an effective date for its action. The court pointed out that just because the district honored the old contracts for more than six months before providing notice of their termination, this did not alter the fact that the agreement had expired.

---

[45] Middle Country Teachers Ass'n v. Middle Country Cent. Sch. Dist., 647 N.Y.S.2d 286 [113 EDUC. L. REP. 348](N.Y. App. Div. 1996).

[46] SEDOL Teachers Union, Lake County Fed'n of Teachers v. Illinois Educ. Labor Relations Bd., 668 N.E.2d 1117 [112 EDUC. LAW REP. 380] (Ill. App. Ct. 1996).

[47] Pinckney Community Sch. Bus Drivers Ass'n v. Pinckney Community Sch. Bd. of Educ., 548 N.W.2d 713 [109 EDUC. L. REP. 1373](Mich. Ct. App. 1996).

In the first of two cases from New York, a union challenged an order compelling several of its members and officers to respond to a deposition on the basis that the dispute was more properly subject to the authority of the PERB. An appellate panel affirmed that a trial court had the jurisdiction to order the union members to respond.[48] The court observed that permitting the questioning to proceed would not interfere with the rights of union members to organize and consult with their officials on matters affecting their employment.

A year after a district unilaterally eliminated the jobs of elementary school media specialists, it hired lower paid librarians who were not represented by a union. As such, the union charged that the district had improperly subcontracted for services since the responsibilities of the media specialists and librarians were essentially identical. After the PERB found that the district committed an unfair labor practice, an appellate court in New York affirmed.[49] The court rejected the district's argument that the union could not file a complaint against it until after negotiations on the matter had taken place. The court held not only that there was no requirement for the union to begin negotiations before filing a complaint but also that the determination by PERB was supported by substantial evidence.

In Pennsylvania, an arbitrator ordered the reinstatement of a teacher whose employment was terminated without just cause. At the same time, the arbitrator penalized the teacher a year's pay while reducing his seniority and pension credit. The arbitrator reasoned that something had to be done about the teacher's giving false testimony about the attendance records of students who had complained that the teacher engaged in inappropriate physical contact. On further review, an appellate court reversed in favor of the teacher.[50] The court decreed that the arbitrator exceeded the scope of his authority in imposing such penalties against the teacher.

In a second case from Pennsylvania, an appellate court upheld a school board's determination that a teacher who replaced a permanent science teacher who later resigned was not a temporary professional employee but a substitute teacher.[51] Insofar as the substitute teacher had not taught for two years, the court decided that he was not a temporary professional employee. As such, the court found that the collective bargaining agreement did not entitle him to an available permanent position.

---

[48] Children's Village v. Greenburgh Eleven Teachers' Union Fed'n of Teachers, 648 N.Y.S.2d 152 [113 Educ. L. Rep. 886](N.Y. App. Div. 1996).

[49] Hewlett-Woodmere Union Free Sch. Dist. v. New York State Pub. Employment Relations Bd., 648 N.Y.S.2d 673 [113 Educ. L. Rep. 1272](N.Y. App. Div. 1996).

[50] Philadelphia Fed'n of Teachers v. School Dist. of Phila., 684 A.2d 671 [114 Educ. L. Rep. 220](Pa. Commw. Ct. 1996).

[51] Kielbowick v. Ambridge Area Sch. Bd., 668 A.2d 1228 [106 Educ. L. Rep. 227] (Pa. Commw. Ct. 1995).

Conclusion

Although there were fewer cases this year than in the recent past, litigation on issues related to collective bargaining continue to occupy significant space on court calendars across the country. As this review indicates, judicial deference toward administrative remedies continues. Accordingly, the role of bargaining remains central to defining the relationship between school districts and their employees.

5
STUDENTS WITH DISABILITIES

Allan G. Osborne, Jr.

Introduction

During 1996, litigation over the rights of students with disabilities continued at as significant a pace as it has in previous years. As in the past, many suits involved procedural issues and contested placement decisions under the Individuals with Disabilities Education Act (IDEA).[1] Several actions dealt with procedural rights dispute resolution. Many claims evolved around the basic issue of whether a school district had offered the student a free appropriate public education (FAPE). In many cases, parents sought compensation for alleged denials of the rights guaranteed by the IDEA.

Consistent with the trend in recent years, suits also have been filed on behalf of students with disabilities under section 504 of the Rehabilitation Act[2] and the Americans with Disabilities Act (ADA)[3] as well as the IDEA. In most of these actions, parents claimed that their children were discriminated against based on their disabilities.

In previous editions of the *Yearbook*, suits filed on behalf of employees who charged discrimination under either section 504 or the ADA were reported in this chapter. However, in order to avoid duplication with other chapters of this *Yearbook*, employees' cases are no longer reported here. In addition, the title of this chapter has been revised to reflect this change.

Entitlement to Services

The IDEA requires school districts to provide a FAPE consisting of special education and related services to students with disabilities.[4] Yet,

---

[1] 20 U.S.C. § 1400 *et seq.*
[2] 29 U.S.C. § 794.
[3] 42 U.S.C. §§ 12101 - 12213.
[4] 20 U.S.C. § 1401(18).

the IDEA does not establish substantive standards by which to judge the adequacy of FAPE services. The IDEA mandates that students must be afforded specially designed instruction[5] in conformance with their Individualized Education Programs (IEP).[6] In *Board of Education of Hendrick Hudson Central School District v. Rowley,*[7] the Supreme Court reasoned that students with disabilities are entitled to personalized instruction with support services sufficient to permit them to benefit from the education they receive. Even though *Rowley* cautioned lower courts not to impose their views of preferable educational methods on school districts, the lower courts frequently are asked to determine what level of services is required to meet the minimum standards of the IDEA.

Students attending private schools also filed suit to ensure their rights under the IDEA.[8] Some of these actions were decided on the basis of the Education Department General Administrative Regulations (EDGAR)[9] as well as the IDEA. Under EDGAR, a district is required to provide comparable benefits to students enrolled in private schools.[10] For example, a federal trial court in Louisiana decreed that EDGAR required a district to provide a sign language interpreter to a hearing-impaired student who attended a parochial school.[11] Further, a district court in Mississippi declared that a student in a private religious school was entitled to receive related services such as speech, occupational, and physical therapy under EDGAR.[12] However, the Louisiana and Mississippi courts favorably cited a ruling by a district court in Indiana that was later overturned by the Seventh Circuit.[13] The Seventh Circuit held that EDGAR did not entitle a student in a parochial school to the on-site delivery of the services of an instructional assistant at her private school. The appellate court ruled that the district discharged its obligation by making the necessary services available at a public school. A district court in Missouri issued a similar judgment involving a student with Down's Syndrome whose parents had asked the public schools to provide a special education teacher to

---

[5] 20 U.S.C. § 1401(16).
[6] 20 U.S.C. § 1401(18)(d).
[7] 458 U.S. 176 [5 Educ. L. Rep. 34] (1982).
[8] 34 C.F.R. § 300.452.
[9] 34 C.F.R. §§ 76.651-76.662.
[10] 34 C.F.R. § 76.654(a).
[11] Cefalu v. East Baton Rouge Parish Sch. Bd., 907 F. Supp. 966 [105 Educ. L. Rep. 979] (M.D. La. 1995).
[12] Natchez-Adams Sch. Dist. v. Searing, 918 F. Supp. 1028 [108 Educ. L. Rep. 174] (S.D. Miss. 1996).
[13] K.R. v. Anderson, 887 F. Supp. 1217 [101 Educ. L. Rep. 213] (S.D. Ind. 1995), *rev'd* 81 F.3d 673 [108 Educ. L. Rep. 533] (7th Cir. 1996).

coordinate her IEP, speech and occupational therapy, and the services of an instructional aide, all on the premises of the parochial school.[14]

According to a district court in Illinois, a student who had a speech impairment caused by nodules on his vocal chords was entitled to receive special education services.[15] Even though the student was performing at an age-appropriate academic level, his overall ability to communicate was impaired. The court interpreted educational performance to mean more than a student's ability to meet academic criteria and included the development of communication skills.

In a suit from South Dakota, the Eighth Circuit affirmed a ruling that a student who had cerebral palsy was entitled to services under the IDEA even though she was enrolled in college preparatory courses.[16] The court stated that if it were not for the specialized instruction and services that she received, her ability to learn and do the required class work would have been adversely affected by her disability.

The Sixth Circuit reversed a district court's decision that students who resided in a residential facility in Ohio, but whose parents lived in other states, were not, as nonresidents, entitled to a FAPE in Ohio.[17] The court posited that the students should have received special education services in the states where their parents resided. The court found that if the parents were dissatisfied with their children's education, they should have followed the dispute resolution process of the IDEA instead of unilaterally enrolling their children in the Ohio facility.

The IDEA does not apply solely to school districts. It also covers state agencies that may be involved in the education of children. Therefore, students under the auspices of state agencies are entitled to the benefits of the IDEA. A federal district court in New York decided that, as a political subdivision of the state that is involved in providing education to disabled students, the Department of Social Services was subject to the requirements of the IDEA.[18] As such, the court refused to dismiss the Department from a lawsuit seeking a publicly paid residential placement for a student with multiple disabilities. Similarly, a school district may still be required to provide special education services to children who

---

[14] Foley v. Special Sch. Dist. of St. Louis County, 927 F. Supp. 1214 [110 EDUC. L. REP. 630] (E.D. Mo. 1996).

[15] Mary P. v. Illinois State Bd. of Educ., 919 F. Supp. 1173 [108 EDUC. L. REP. 609] (N.D. Ill. 1996), *amended by* 934 F. Supp. 989 [112 EDUC. L. REP. 248] (N.D. Ill. 1996).

[16] Yankton Sch. Dist. v. Schramm, 93 F.3d 1369 [111 EDUC. L. REP. 1143] (8th Cir. 1996), *aff'g* 900 F. Supp. 1182 [104 EDUC. L. REP. 645] (D.S.D. 1995).

[17] Wise v. Ohio Dep't of Educ., 80 F.3d 177 [108 EDUC. L. REP. 82] (6th Cir. 1996), *rev'g* 863 F. Supp. 570 [94 EDUC. L. REP. 1286] (N.D. Ohio 1994).

[18] King v. Pine Plains Cent. Sch. Dist., 918 F. Supp. 772 [108 EDUC. L. REP. 161] (S.D.N.Y. 1996).

come under the auspices of other state agencies. The Supreme Court of New Hampshire decided that a district was required to pay for a student's special education services while he was remanded to a residential facility by a juvenile court.[19]

Procedural Safeguards

The IDEA contains an elaborate system of due process safeguards to ensure that a student with disabilities is properly identified, evaluated, and placed.[20] The IDEA regulations state that the parents or guardians of a child with disabilities must be provided with the opportunity to participate in the development of their child's IEP.[21] The IDEA also requires a school district to obtain parental consent prior to evaluating a child or making an initial placement.[22] Once a student has been placed in special education, a district must provide parents or guardians with proper notice before initiating a change in placement.[23] Once placed, a student's situation must be reviewed at least annually[24] and the student must be re-evaluated at least every three years.[25]

Under the IDEA, the parents of a student with disabilities may be entitled to an independent evaluation at public expense if they disagree with the school district's evaluation.[26] However, a district may challenge the request for an independent evaluation in an administrative hearing. If the district's evaluation is found to be appropriate, the parents are not entitled to have an independent evaluation at public expense.[27] Moreover, the IDEA stipulates that an IEP must contain statements of the student's current educational performance, the annual goals and short term objectives, the specific educational services to be provided, the extent to which the child can participate in general education, the date of initiation and duration of services, and the evaluation criteria used to determine whether objectives are being met.[28]

---

[19] Ashland Sch. Dist. v. New Hampshire Div. for Children, Youth, and Families, 681 A.2d 71 [112 EDUC. L. REP. 284] (N.H. 1996).
[20] 20 U.S.C. § 1415.
[21] 34 C.F.R. § 300.345.
[22] 34 C.F.R. § 300.504(b).
[23] 20 U.S.C. § 1415(b)(1)(C).
[24] 34 C.F.R. § 300.343(d).
[25] 34 C.F.R. § 300.534(b).
[26] 20 U.S.C. § 1415(b)(1)(A) and 34 C.F.R. § 300.503.
[27] 34 C.F.R. § 300.503(b).
[28] 20 U.S.C. § 1401(20).

Evaluation

The Circuit Court for the District of Columbia reasoned that a school system does not have an absolute right to conduct its own testing of a student who has been evaluated independently. The court observed that under some circumstances a district may be required to rely on an independent evaluation rather than submit a student to excessive duplicative testing.[29] The court added that the parents' contention that the district did not have any right to test their daughter since she already had been evaluated independently was without merit. As such, the court remanded for further findings of fact. However, the Seventh Circuit affirmed that a district in Indiana could not be forced to rely solely on an independent evaluation conducted at the parents' behest.[30]

Parents seeking an independent evaluation are not specifically required to notify a school district of their intent. Therefore, after indicating that parents were not obligated to notify their district before obtaining an independent evaluation, a federal trial court in Iowa ordered the district to reimburse the parents for the costs of testing.[31]

The Ninth Circuit affirmed that an evaluation performed at the request of a school district in Washington was deficient because it failed to include anyone with knowledge of the disorders known to cause the student's problems on the assessment team.[32] The court pointed out that this omission violated the IDEA mandate that an evaluation be completed by a multidisciplinary team with at least one teacher or specialist who has knowledge of the suspected disability.[33]

Rights of Parents or Guardians

In a suit where the parents of a student with disabilities refused to consent to a school district's evaluation, the Circuit Court for the District of Columbia concluded that the parents were entitled to an answer to their questions about the nature of the testing.[34] The parents withheld consent for the testing because they were not satisfied with the school district's response to their questions. The court remanded for a determination of whether the district properly responded to the parents' inquiry.

---

[29] Holland v. District of Columbia, 71 F.3d 417 [105 EDUC. L. REP. 397] (D.C. Cir. 1995).

[30] Johnson v. Duneland Sch. Corp., 92 F.3d 554 [111 EDUC. L. REP. 756] (7th Cir. 1996).

[31] Raymond S. v. Ramirez, 918 F. Supp. 1280 [108 EDUC. L. REP. 196] (N.D. Iowa 1996).

[32] Seattle Sch. Dist., No. 1 v. B.S., 82 F.3d 1493 [109 EDUC. L. REP. 55] (9th Cir. 1996).

[33] 34 C.F.R. § 300.532(e).

[34] Holland v. District of Columbia, 71 F.3d 417 [105 EDUC. L. REP. 397] (D.C. Cir. 1995).

The Sixth Circuit remanded a suit from Tennessee to determine whether a school district provided a parent with a clear understanding of its placement recommendation.[35] The court ordered a further determination of facts after the father claimed that his rights had been violated by a state agency that allegedly had failed to inform him of the status quo provision of the IDEA.

Development of Individualized Education Programs

A federal trial court in New York ruled that a school district did not follow proper procedures when it placed a student in a special education program in a public school prior to developing the student's IEP.[36] The court added that even after the IEP was developed, it did not establish the student's needs with the requisite precision because it was based on a broad test score that masked specific areas of deficit. The court found that the student's IEP failed to identify where his deficit was most profoundly manifested, that it was based on outdated data, and that it failed to set forth measurable criteria to assess progress. Similarly, the Supreme Court of Idaho decided that an IEP was defective because it lacked goals, objectives, and information about how a student would be incorporated into a classroom setting.[37]

Change in Placement

The Third Circuit agreed with a lower court ruling that a school district in Pennsylvania was required to maintain a student's placement in a school outside the district pending all appeals under the IDEA.[38] Similarly, a federal trial court in New York granted a preliminary injunction requiring a school district to maintain a child's placement in a private school pending the completion of all proceedings under the IDEA.[39] An interesting aspect of the case was that an IEP calling for the student's placement in the private school had not been executed even though the district had funded the private school. At the same time, the court stated that there was no authority to support the proposition that a current educational placement must be reflected in an IEP.

---

[35] Tennessee Dep't of Mental Health and Mental Retardation v. Paul B., 88 F.3d 1466 [110 EDUC. L. REP. 1009] (6th Cir. 1996).
[36] Evans v. Board of Educ. of the Rhinebeck Cent. Sch. Dist., 930 F. Supp. 83 [111 EDUC. L. REP. 200] (S.D.N.Y. 1996).
[37] Doolittle v. Meridian Joint Sch. Dist. No. 2, Ada County, 919 P.2d 334 [110 EDUC. L. REP. 1282] (Idaho 1996).
[38] Drinker v. Colonial Sch. Dist., 78 F.3d 859 [107 EDUC. L. REP. 530] (3d Cir. 1996), *aff'g* 888 F. Supp. 674 [101 EDUC. L. REP. 782] (E.D. Pa. 1995).
[39] Evans v. Board of Educ. of the Rhinebeck Cent. Sch. Dist., 921 F. Supp. 1184 [109 EDUC. L. REP. 113] (S.D.N.Y. 1996).

Administrative and judicial proceedings can be lengthy as decisions at various stages in the process may reverse previous rulings. Parents seeking changes in placements often are left wondering when they may initiate requests without incurring personal financial risks. In a dispute that arose in Pennsylvania, the Third Circuit affirmed that financial responsibility for a placement is imposed on a school district as soon as an administrative or judicial decision has established the pendent placement.[40]

In a case from Tennessee, the Sixth Circuit held that the status quo provision of the IDEA is activated only when a parent alleges that there has been a substantive violation of the statute and has initiated administrative review to challenge the IEP.[41] According to the court, the status quo provision is not designed to prolong a current educational placement unless there is a genuine appealable issue regarding its appropriateness.

When a school district makes an interim educational placement in a private institution, its intention to do so for a limited duration must be clearly enunciated. As such, a district court in Oklahoma ruled that a private school setting was a child's current placement under the status quo provision of the IDEA since her parents had not been notified that another option would be considered when the interim placement expired.[42] The court found that the child was placed in the private school pursuant to a settlement agreement that was silent on any plans for her beyond the interim setting. Thus, the court was of the opinion that the student's parents were entitled to assume that the private school placement would be funded until another setting was either agreed upon by the parties or dictated by administrative or judicial proceedings.

The Seventh Circuit decreed that a school district did not violate the status quo provision of the IDEA even though a due process hearing was pending when the district stopped funding the student's program upon his reaching the age of twenty-one.[43] The court maintained that except for claims for compensatory education, entitlements created by the IDEA expire when a pupil turns twenty-one and cannot be extended by parents simply filing suit on the eve of a student's twenty-first birthday.

---

[40] Susquenita Sch. Dist. v. Raelee S., 96 F.3d 78 [112 EDUC. L. REP. 590] (3d Cir. 1996).
[41] Tennessee Dep't of Mental Health and Mental Retardation v. Paul B., 88 F.3d 1466 [110 EDUC. L. REP. 1009] (6th Cir. 1996).
[42] Doe v. Independent Sch. Dist. No. 9 of Tulsa County, Okla., 938 F. Supp. 758 [113 EDUC. L. REP. 286] (N.D. Okla. 1996).
[43] Board of Educ. of Oak Park & River Forest High Sch. Dist. 200 v. Illinois State Bd. of Educ., 79 F.3d 654 [108 EDUC. L. REP. 32] (7th Cir. 1996), *rev'g* 886 F. Supp. 1417 [101 EDUC. L. REP. 142] (N.D. Ill. 1995).

According to a federal district court in New York, the Department of Social Services did not change the placement of a child in a residential facility when it obtained an order from the Family Court requiring his parents to pay for part of his education costs.[44] The court observed that since the support order did not modify the student's program, it did not constitute a change in placement.

Insofar as the administrative proceedings of the IDEA may be used to contest whether a student is disabled, the question sometimes arises as to the applicability of the status quo provision when a child's parents challenge such a finding. In a case from Illinois, the Seventh Circuit suggested that a flexible approach is needed when applying the status quo provision to students who have not yet been identified as disabled.[45] The court ascertained that before placement protection is invoked, students and their parents must reasonably demonstrate that school officials knew or should have known of the students' disabilities.

Dispute Resolution

If parents disagree with a school district's decisions regarding a proposed IEP or any aspect of a FAPE, they may request an impartial due process hearing.[46] Any party not satisfied with the final decision of an administrative proceeding may appeal to a state or federal court.[47] Yet, administrative remedies must be exhausted prior to resorting to the courts unless it is futile to do so. During the pendency of an administrative or judicial action, a school district may not change a student's placement absent parental consent[48] or a court order.[49]

The IDEA empowers the judiciary to review the record of administrative proceedings, to hear additional evidence, and to "grant such relief as the court determines is appropriate" based on the preponderance of evidence standard.[50] However, the Supreme Court has cautioned judges not to substitute their views of proper educational methodology for those of competent school authorities.[51] The IDEA does

---

[44] King v. Pine Plains Cent. Sch. Dist., 918 F. Supp. 772 [108 EDUC. L. REP. 161] (S.D.N.Y. 1996).

[45] Rodiriecus L. v. Waukegan Sch. Dist. No. 60, 90 F.3d 249 [111 EDUC. L. REP. 94] (7th Cir. 1996).

[46] 20 U.S.C. § 1415(b)(2).

[47] 20 U.S.C. § 1415(e)(2).

[48] 20 U.S.C. § 1415(e)(3).

[49] Honig v. Doe, 484 U.S. 305 [43 EDUC. L. REP. 857] (1988).

[50] 20 U.S.C. § 1415(e)(2)(C).

[51] Board of Educ. of Hendrick Hudson Cent. Sch. Dist. v. Rowley, 458 U.S. 176 [5 EDUC. L. REP. 34] (1982).

not contain a statute of limitations for filing a lawsuit; as such, courts must borrow one from analogous state laws.

The IDEA is not the exclusive avenue through which parents may enforce the rights of children with disabilities. The IDEA specifically stipulates that none of its provisions can be interpreted to restrict or limit rights, procedures, and/or remedies available under the Constitution, section 504, or other federal statutes protecting the rights of students with disabilities.[52] Consequently, suits frequently are filed under section 504, the ADA, and section 1983 of the Civil Rights Act of 1871[53] in addition to the IDEA.

Administrative Hearings

A number of suits dealt with whether parents had properly exhausted administrative remedies prior to seeking judicial intervention. Several courts dismissed actions because parents previously had not submitted claims to a hearing officer. In the first of two cases from Pennsylvania, the Third Circuit indicated that the state, through its administrative process, should be allowed to address all claims before they are presented to the courts.[54] The same court affirmed that issues over the student's placement could not be litigated because his parents had not presented them to an administrative appeals panel.[55] Similarly, a federal district court in Louisiana decided that administrative review could obviate the need for judicial intervention or streamline the facts and issues if an appeal is required.[56]

In New York, a federal district court dismissed a suit for failure to exhaust administrative remedies. The court reasoned that the parents deprived state authorities of an opportunity to make and review a determination as to the most appropriate placement and deprived the court of a factual record.[57]

A question sometimes arises as to whether parents must exhaust administrative remedies on an IEP that was proposed while proceedings regarding a previous IEP are still pending. For example, a federal district court in New York dismissed a claim for tuition reimbursement after the

---

[52] 20 U.S.C. § 1415(f).

[53] 42 U.S.C. § 1983.

[54] Jeremy H. v. Mount Lebanon Sch. Dist., 95 F.3d 272 [112 Educ. L. Rep. 70] (3d Cir. 1996).

[55] Drinker v. Colonial Sch. Dist., 888 F. Supp. 674 [101 Educ. L. Rep. 782] (E.D. Pa. 1995), aff'd 78 F.3d 859 [107 Educ. L. Rep. 530] (3d Cir. 1996).

[56] Doe v. Vernon Parish Sch. Bd., 928 F. Supp. 663 [110 Educ. L. Rep. 687] (W.D. La. 1996).

[57] Mr. and Mrs. R. ex rel. D.R. v. Bedford Bd. of Educ., 926 F. Supp. 47 [110 Educ. L. Rep. 129] (S.D.N.Y. 1996); see also Bruschini v. Board of Educ. of the Arlington Cent. Sch. Dist., 911 F. Supp. 104 [106 Educ. L. Rep. 615] (S.D.N.Y. 1995).

same request was denied by a hearing officer because the parents had not exhausted administrative remedies.[58] Similarly, the Tenth Circuit affirmed that parents in Colorado had to exhaust administrative remedies for a subsequent IEP even if their claims were the same as those regarding the first IEP.[59] However, a federal district court in Pennsylvania posited that requiring a parent to begin the administrative process anew in order to seek reimbursement for a student's tenth-grade year, where remuneration for the ninth-grade had yet to be settled, would have been an exercise in futility.[60]

If parents bring claims against two agencies that share responsibility for educating their child, they must exhaust administrative remedies against both organizations. In a suit from Florida, parents who succeeded in administrative proceedings against a school district alleged that the state failed to prevent the district from denying their son a FAPE. A federal district court dismissed the action because the parents had not exhausted administrative remedies regarding their allegations against the state.[61]

A federal district court in Indiana held that evidence did not support a parent's contention that pursuing administrative remedies would have been futile. The court found that the mother's claim that she was not fully informed of her rights by the school district was without merit.[62] Similarly, a federal district court in Maryland dismissed a suit after concluding that the parent had not alleged any facts to demonstrate that administrative action would have been futile.[63]

The Supreme Court of North Dakota affirmed that parents had to exhaust administrative remedies on their claim that an award of reimbursement for boarding care was not sufficient. The court observed that this issue was uniquely amenable to the administrative process.[64]

In the District of Columbia, the federal trial court denied a petition to join a class action suit, ruling that the parents first had to exhaust

[58] Bruschini v. Board of Educ. of the Arlington Cent. Sch. Dist., 911 F. Supp. 104 [106 EDUC. L. REP. 615] (S.D.N.Y. 1995).
[59] Urban v. Jefferson County Sch. Dist. R-1, 89 F.3d 720 [110 EDUC. L. REP. 1069] (10th Cir. 1996), *aff'g* 870 F. Supp. 1558 [96 EDUC. L. REP. 952] (D. Colo. 1994).
[60] Christen G. v. Lower Merion Sch. Dist., 919 F. Supp. 793 [108 EDUC. L. REP. 553] (E.D. Pa. 1996).
[61] Whitehead v. School Bd. for Hillsborough County, Fla., 932 F. Supp. 1393 [111 EDUC. L. REP. 1212] (M.D. Fla. 1996).
[62] Smith v. Indianapolis Pub. Sch., 916 F. Supp. 872 [107 EDUC. L. REP. 772] (S.D. Ind. 1995).
[63] Koster v. Frederick County Bd. of Educ., 921 F. Supp. 1453 [109 EDUC. L. REP. 126] (D. Md. 1996).
[64] Lapp v. Reeder Pub. Sch. Dist. No. 3, 544 N.W.2d 164 [107 EDUC. L. REP. 296] (N.D. 1996).

administrative remedies.[65] The court was of the opinion that without an administrative record, it was not equipped to pass judgment on claims that the school district failed to meet the needs of its students.

According to the federal district court in West Virginia, parents must exhaust administrative remedies if relief is available under the IDEA, even when they attempt to circumvent the dispute resolution process by filing suit under other statutes or the constitution.[66] On the other hand, in a case from Pennsylvania, the Third Circuit stated that when parents exhaust administrative remedies under the IDEA, they also have met any exhaustion requirements for claims under other statutes.[67]

Courts decided that parents were not required to exhaust administrative remedies when their claims raised issues that were beyond the authority of hearing officers. For example, a federal district court in Pennsylvania noted that whether the First Amendment prohibits tuition reimbursement for a sectarian school was entirely a legal issue that did not require exhaustion.[68] Similarly, a district court in New York ruled that a challenge to a generally applicable policy or procedure would have been futile since hearing officers do not have the authority to alter existing policies.[69] At the same time, the district court in Vermont pointed out that claims regarding a state's complaint resolution procedure did not require exhaustion since a hearing officer lacked the authority to grant relief.[70] Further, the Supreme Court of New Hampshire reversed in concluding that the administrative process was neither designed nor intended to provide a forum for districts to resolve disputes with state agencies over funding obligations for the special education component of a judicially ordered placement.[71]

After determining that a student was not entitled to a hearing, the federal district court in Minnesota maintained that it would have been futile to require exhaustion of his disability discrimination claim because he would have been denied a hearing.[72] The court posited that the student's

---

[65] Lemon v. District of Columbia, 920 F. Supp. 8 [108 Educ. L. Rep. 647] (D.D.C. 1996).

[66] Doe v. Alfred, 906 F. Supp. 1092 [105 Educ. L. Rep. 534] (S.D. W. Va. 1995).

[67] Jeremy H. v. Mount Lebanon Sch. Dist., 95 F.3d 272 [112 Educ. L. Rep. 70] (3d Cir. 1996).

[68] Christen G. v. Lower Merion Sch. Dist., 919 F. Supp. 793 [108 Educ. L. Rep. 553] (E.D. Pa. 1996).

[69] King v. Pine Plains Cent. Sch. Dist., 918 F. Supp. 772 [108 Educ. L. Rep. 161] (S.D.N.Y. 1996).

[70] Upper Valley Ass'n for Handicapped Citizens v. Mills, 928 F. Supp. 429 [110 Educ. L. Rep. 647] (D. Vt. 1996).

[71] Ashland Sch. Dist. v. New Hampshire Div. for Children, Youth, and Families, 681 A.2d 71 [112 Educ. L. Rep. 284] (N.H. 1996).

[72] Thompson v. Board of the Special Sch. Dist. No. 1, 936 F. Supp. 644 [112 Educ. L. Rep. 888] (D. Minn. 1996).

present school district was not required to provide him with a hearing on claims contesting a former system's evaluation and IEP.

A federal trial court in New York held that a school district violated a parent's right to a prompt hearing. The court contended that the district violated the IDEA, which requires a final decision to be reached within forty-five days of the request for a hearing, because the hearing was not even scheduled until seventy-one days after the mother requested it.[73]

Court Proceedings

Two appeals were dismissed on technical grounds. The Seventh Circuit decided that a case from Illinois was moot insofar as it could not grant relief to parents in a dispute over their son's fifth-grade IEP because he was already in the eighth-grade.[74] The court stated that not only was the student unlikely to face the same situation in the school again but also that the student's parents had received the relief they sought because their son's former IEP remained in force during the pendency of the proceedings. The second suit was dismissed based on res judicata after an appellate court in New York decreed that the gravamen of the action was the same as in a federal case between the parties.[75] The court refused to hear the appeal after the parents elected to have the federal action dismissed.

Stipulations made at an administrative proceeding are binding in court according to a federal trial court in New York.[76] The court ruled that the stipulations were valid and remained in force during the pendency of the subsequent trial.

A district court in Illinois concluded that the IDEA does not confer original jurisdiction over parties who did not participate in administrative hearings. Rather, the court maintained that it had supplemental jurisdiction over a school district's claim for an order requiring a state agency to pay for a student's residential placement.[77] The dispute arose when the parents of a child with disabilities succeeded in obtaining the placement in administrative hearings and the district filed suit against two state agencies

---

[73] Evans v. Board of Educ. of the Rhinebeck Cent. Sch. Dist., 930 F. Supp. 83 [111 Educ. L. Rep. 200] (S.D.N.Y. 1996).
[74] Board of Educ. of Downers Grove Grade Sch. Dist. No. 58 v. Steven L., 89 F.3d 464 [110 Educ. L. Rep. 1057] (7th Cir. 1996), *vacating and remanding* 898 F. Supp. 1252 [104 Educ. L. Rep. 139] (N.D. Ill. 1995).
[75] Frutiger v. Hamilton Cent. Sch. Dist., 644 N.Y.S.2d 582 [110 Educ. L. Rep. 1172] (N.Y. App. Div. 1996).
[76] Bruschini v. Board of Educ. of the Arlington Cent. Sch. Dist., 911 F. Supp. 104 [106 Educ. L. Rep. 615] (S.D.N.Y. 1995).
[77] Board of Educ. of Community High Sch. Dist No. 218, Cook, County, Ill. v. Illinois State Bd. of Educ., 940 F. Supp. 1321 [113 Educ. L. Rep. 1171] (N.D. Ill. 1996).

seeking an order that would have required them to pay for the cost of housing the student.

Standing to Sue

A federal district court in New York held that parents who sought reimbursement for private school tuition lacked standing to challenge an allegedly unlawful state policy because the denial of their claim was not based on the disputed policy.[78] The court stated that the parents failed to show that their injury was traceable to the state's allegedly unlawful conduct.

In Pennsylvania, the Third Circuit contended that students, parents, and a public advocacy group had standing to challenge state procedures for receiving and resolving complaints.[79] The court found that the attempt to seek redress by filing suit under the IDEA was allowable because it arose out of the inability of the students to secure a satisfactory education.

A federal trial court in Illinois determined that a school district had standing to sue a state agency over payment for a residential placement.[80] The court reasoned that since it had the power to reverse an administrative order requiring the district to pay for the placement, the district had standing to present a claim against the agency.

Statute of Limitations

A federal trial court in Alabama noted that a school district's appeal of an administrative decision and the parents' request for attorney fees were both time barred.[81] The court based its judgment on a finding that the appropriate statute of limitations for such an action was the thirty days period prescribed by the state administrative code. The court added that the code applied to requests for attorney fees since the fees were inextricably connected to the administrative proceedings. Similarly, the Ninth Circuit indicated that the state administrative procedures statute applied to a civil action in Montana under the IDEA.[82] In addition, the court decided that the statute also granted a thirty days limitations period.

In a case from Pennsylvania, the Third Circuit posited that the limitations period for a suit over an administrative action began when

---

[78] Yamen v. Board of Educ. of the Arlington Cent. Sch. Dist., 909 F. Supp. 207 [106 EDUC. L. REP. 153] (S.D.N.Y. 1996).

[79] Beth V. v. Carroll, 87 F.3d 80 [110 EDUC. L. REP. 585] (3d Cir. 1996).

[80] Board of Educ. of Community High Sch. Dist No. 218, Cook, County, Ill. v. Illinois State Bd. of Educ., 940 F. Supp. 1321 [113 EDUC. L. REP. 1171] (N.D. Ill. 1996).

[81] Andalusia City Bd. of Educ. v. Andress, 916 F. Supp. 1179 [107 EDUC. L. REP. 800] (M.D. Ala. 1996).

[82] Livingston Sch. Dist. Nos. 4 and 1 v. Keenan, 82 F.3d 912 [109 EDUC. L. REP. 38] (9th Cir. 1996).

the appellate panel issued its decision.[83] The lower court had stated that the clock on the two-year statute of limitations started when the parents rejected the IEP. The appellate court concluded that since the IDEA requires exhaustion, this was inappropriate.

A district court in New York followed precedent from the Third Circuit in ruling that a four-month statute of limitations applies to lawsuits involving the IDEA.[84] The court maintained that the suit was untimely since it was filed seven months after the state review officer's final decision was issued.

Actions Under Other Statutes

Courts have held that if relief is available under the IDEA, parents must file suit under the IDEA before seeking redress under another law or the constitution. Moreover, whether a court requires exhaustion of remedies often depends on its interpretation of whether the IDEA can provide relief.

In a case from Illinois, the Seventh Circuit was of the opinion that a student who sought relief under section 1983, section 504, and the ADA had to exhaust remedies under the IDEA even though the IDEA does not authorize damages because the complaint dealt with actions that had both an educational source and an adverse educational consequence.[85] The court concluded that a nondamages remedy in the form of compensatory services might be available even though the student was not seeking such redress. On the other hand, a district court in Ohio offered that where a student athlete with a disability who attended a nonpublic school sought relief under section 504 and the ADA, he was not required to exhaust remedies under the IDEA since he did not have an IEP from which to appeal.[86]

A federal district court in West Virginia decreed that prior to filing suit under section 1983 alleging violations of the IDEA, a parent was required to exhaust administrative remedies pursuant to the IDEA since it made relief available.[87] Similarly, the federal district court in Minnesota decided that if relief sought under the ADA is available under the IDEA, administrative remedies pursuant to the IDEA must first be exhausted

---

[83] Jeremy H. v. Mount Lebanon Sch. Dist., 95 F.3d 272 [112 EDUC. L. REP. 70] (3d Cir. 1996).

[84] Berkowitz v. New York City Bd. of Educ., 921 F. Supp. 963 [109 EDUC. L. REP. 105] (E.D.N.Y. 1996).

[85] Charlie F. v. Board of Educ. of Skokie Sch. Dist. 68, 98 F.3d 989 [113 EDUC. L. REP. 559] (7th Cir. 1996).

[86] Rhodes v. Ohio High Sch. Athletic Ass'n, 939 F. Supp. 584 [113 EDUC. L. REP. 716] (N.D. Ohio 1996).

[87] Doe v. Alfred, 906 F. Supp. 1092 [105 EDUC. L. REP. 534] (S.D. W. Va. 1995).

before a claim under the ADA can proceed.[88] The court observed that the only way to avoid having to exhaust remedies was to articulate a distinction between the ADA and IDEA claims.

The Supreme Court of Wyoming affirmed that parties cannot circumvent IDEA procedures by asserting claims under other laws.[89] The court reasoned that a claimant cannot deliberately avoid cognizable claims under the IDEA.

In Connecticut, a district court held that although there is no constitutional right to participate in sports, the inclusion of a sports activity in a student's IEP transformed it into a federally protected right.[90] As such, the court found that the student's section 1983 claim was viable where he was deemed ineligible to participate on the swimming team because he was too old under an athletic association's eligibility rules. However, the Second Circuit subsequently dismissed the claim as moot in light of the fact that the student would not seek a waiver of the age rule for future seasons.

A guardian ad litem unsuccessfully sought attorney fees under section 1983 in an action challenging the failure of the New Mexico Children, Youth, and Families Department to appoint a surrogate parent.[91] A state court affirmed that claims over the student's right to special education were not cognizable against the Department under section 1983 because the IDEA and Rehabilitation Act did not create a cause of action against the Department for the appointment of a surrogate parent or for providing a FAPE.

The federal district court in Minnesota mandated that a section 1983 claim can be brought on the basis of violations of IDEA regulations.[92] Yet, the same court rejected a section 1983 claim after determining that parents had not presented any evidence that a school district was indifferent to their daughter's rights under the IDEA.[93] The court concluded that the district advanced reasonable explanations for its delay in providing services to the student and that her parents had not shown

---

[88] Hoekstra v. Independent Sch. Dist. No. 283, St. Louis Park, Minn., 916 F. Supp. 941 [107 EDUC. L. REP. 779] (D. Minn. 1996). *See also* Jeremy H. v. Mount Lebanon Sch. Dist., 95 F.3d 272 [112 EDUC. L. REP. 70] (3d Cir. 1996).

[89] Koopman v. Fremont County Sch. Dist., 911 P.2d 1049 [107 EDUC. L. REP. 310] (Wyo. 1996).

[90] Dennin v. Connecticut Interscholastic Athletic Conference, 913 F. Supp. 663 [106 EDUC. L. REP. 1130] (D. Conn. 1996), *appeal dismissed as moot* 94 F.3d 96 [111 EDUC. L. REP. 1154] (2d Cir. 1996).

[91] *In re* T.B., 913 P.2d 272 [108 EDUC. L. REP. 389] (N.M. Ct. App. 1996).

[92] Brantley v. Independent Sch. Dist. No. 625, St. Paul Pub. Sch., 936 F. Supp. 649 [112 EDUC. L. REP. 893] (D. Minn. 1996).

[93] Hoekstra v. Independent Sch. Dist. No. 283, St. Louis Park, Minn., 916 F. Supp. 941 [107 EDUC. L. REP. 779] (D. Minn. 1996).

that the district's failure to train its employees to write IEPs was related to the alleged injury.

According to the Eighth Circuit, claims for damages based on the IDEA cannot be pursued in section 1983 actions. The court contended that general and punitive damages for the types of injuries alleged by the parent of a student with disabilities were not available under the IDEA.[94]

In a section 1983 action, the federal district court in Vermont certified a class that included all individuals or organizations within the state who are or will be eligible to file a complaint under the IDEA.[95] The suit alleged that the state failed to comply with the requirements of the IDEA. However, the district court in Minnesota held that the Eleventh Amendment protects unconsenting states from lawsuits for damages brought pursuant to section 1983.[96]

In two similar cases, a federal trial court in Illinois ruled that school districts could not bring section 1983 suits for damages against a state agency because school districts are not persons for the purposes of section 1983.[97] In the second case, the court added that the Eleventh Amendment gave the state immunity from claims for monetary relief.

Placement

IDEA regulations require school districts to ensure that a continuum of alternative placements exists to meet the needs of students with disabilities for special education and related services.[98] The continuum must range from placement in general education to private residential facilities and must include homebound services. However, the placement chosen for any given student must be in the least restrictive environment (LRE) and removal from general education can occur only to the extent necessary to provide special education and related services.[99] All placements must be made at public expense and must meet state education standards.[100] Each placement must be reviewed at least annually and

---

[94] Heidemann v. Rother, 84 F.3d 1021 (8th Cir. 1996).
[95] Upper Valley Ass'n for Handicapped Citizens v. Mills, 168 F.R.D. 167 [112 Educ. L. Rep. 943] (D. Vt. 1996); *see also* 928 F. Supp. 429 [110 Educ. L. Rep. 647] (D. Vt. 1996).
[96] Thompson v. Board of the Special Sch. Dist. No. 1, 936 F. Supp. 644 [112 Educ. L. Rep. 888] (D. Minn. 1996).
[97] Barbara Z. v. Obradovich, 937 F. Supp. 710 [113 Educ. L. Rep. 159] (N.D. Ill. 1996); Board of Educ. of Community High Sch. Dist. No. 218, Cook, County, Ill. v. Illinois State Bd. of Educ., 940 F. Supp. 1321 [113 Educ. L. Rep. 1171] (N.D. Ill. 1996).
[98] 34 C.F.R. § 300.551.
[99] 34 C.F.R. § 300.550.
[100] 20 U.S.C. § 1401(18).

revised if necessary.[101] The Supreme Court has held that an appropriate education is one that is developed in compliance with IDEA procedures and is reasonably calculated to enable a child to receive educational benefits.[102] Although states must adopt policies and procedures that are consistent with the IDEA, states may provide greater benefits than those required by federal law. If a state does establish higher standards, courts will consider those requirements when evaluating the appropriateness of an IEP.[103]

Appropriate Educational Placement

The federal district court in Massachusetts upheld a hearing officer's interim order to place a student in a public special education program after determining that not a single clinician, expert, or person familiar with the child suggested that the private setting desired by the parents was appropriate.[104] The court added that most of the elements sought by the parents in the private facility were included in the public school program.

The federal district court in Maryland upheld a community-based residential placement recommended by a school district. The court found that the placement would enable the student to receive educational benefits.[105] Although the district's offer was slow in coming, the court determined that this was because the parents had declined several opportunities to meet with educators to develop an IEP and that their actions had the effect of frustrating and deferring pursuit of the school district's plan.

In Pennsylvania, a federal trial court decided that a district's proposed IEP for a student's ninth-grade year that called for her to be educated in a private school was appropriate. However, the court indicated that the district's suggested plan for her tenth-grade year was not.[106] The court observed that the mother rejected all three choices presented by the school district because each contained an emotional support component that she believed was not needed. After the mother enrolled her daughter in a

---

[101] 34 C.F.R. § 300.552(a)(1).
[102] Board of Educ. of Hendrick Hudson Cent. Sch. Dist. v. Rowley, 458 U.S. 176 [5 Educ. L. Rep. 34] (1982).
[103] *See* David D. v. Dartmouth Sch. Comm., 775 F.2d 411 [28 Educ. L. Rep. 70] (1st Cir. 1985); Geis v. Board of Educ. of Parsippany-Troy Hills, Morris County, 774 F.2d 575 [27 Educ. L. Rep. 1093] (3d Cir. 1985).
[104] Andrew S. v. Massachusetts Dep't of Educ., 917 F. Supp. 70 [107 Educ. L. Rep. 814] (D. Mass. 1995).
[105] Sanger v. Montgomery County Bd. of Educ., 916 F. Supp. 518 [107 Educ. L. Rep. 754] (D. Md. 1996).
[106] Christen G. v. Lower Merion Sch. Dist., 919 F. Supp. 793 [108 Educ. L. Rep. 553] (E.D. Pa. 1996).

sectarian school for children with learning differences, a hearing officer concluded that the district's proposed IEP was appropriate and that inclusion of the emotional support component was proper. Yet, since the tenth-grade IEP called for the student's return to the public schools, the hearing officer was of the opinion that it was inappropriate and, after a lengthy delay, the district developed another IEP calling for placement in a private setting. The court ruled that the delay in developing the IEP was inexcusable.

The federal trial court in Vermont found that a district offered an appropriate education after a school committed substantial resources to develop an IEP that met the student's needs.[107] The court stated that there are many criteria by which to judge educational benefits in addition to grade level scores on standardized tests. Specifically, the court indicated that grades, socialization skills, level of participation, consistency of effort, and commitment to studies are all relevant in determining whether a student has progressed educationally.

Based on the testimony of expert witnesses, a district court in Wisconsin left a proposed IEP in place noting that it was unable to conclude that a student would not benefit from a proposed plan.[108] A district court in Texas also judged that a proposed IEP was appropriate since it was similar to a previous plan that had produced positive benefits.[109] The court determined that the IEP was individualized to address the student's needs in the LRE and was developed to be implemented by the school's staff in a collaborative manner.

In a case from Minnesota, the Eighth Circuit affirmed that an IEP was appropriate even though it contained several procedural and technical deficiencies.[110] The court posited that since the deficiencies neither compromised the student's right to an appropriate education nor the parents' opportunity to participate in the formulation of the IEP, it did not cause a deprivation of educational benefit.

The Third Circuit, in a case from New Jersey, held that receiving trivial benefits from an educational placement is not sufficient.[111] The appellate panel agreed that an educational program wherein the student's

[107] Mather v. Hartford Sch. Dist., 928 F. Supp. 437 [110 EDUC. L. REP. 655] (D. Vt. 1996).
[108] Heather S. v. State of Wis., 937 F. Supp. 824 [113 EDUC. L. REP. 173] (E.D. Wis. 1996).
[109] Cypress-Fairbanks Indep. Sch. Dist. v. Michael F., 931 F. Supp. 474 (S.D. Tex. 1995).
[110] Independent Sch. Dist. No. 283 v. J.D. *ex rel.* S.D., 88 F.3d 556 [110 EDUC. L. REP. 987] (8th Cir. 1996).
[111] M.C. *ex rel.* J.C. v. Central Regional Sch. Dist., 81 F.3d 389 [108 EDUC. L. REP. 522] (3d Cir. 1996).

achievements were minimal, inconsistent, and scattered was inappropriate. Similarly, a district court in New York stated that a proposed IEP was inappropriate after finding that the student's academic performance had not improved under a similar IEP and that an instructor hired to tutor him was not qualified.[112]

Least Restrictive Environment

Courts have consistently ruled that the IDEA does not require a placement in a student's neighborhood school. The Fifth and Tenth Circuits, as well as district courts in Michigan and Indiana,[113] observed that placements in neighborhood settings are preferable unless a student's needs must be met elsewhere. Even so, the courts agreed that nothing in the IDEA or its regulations requires children to be placed in local schools in every instance. In fact, the Fifth Circuit specifically pointed out that placements in regional schools are authorized by the IDEA.

In Illinois, a federal district court held that private or segregated placements are reserved for exceptional instances.[114] The court observed that since a student, who had Attention Deficit Hyperactivity Disorder, was not severely disabled, his situation did not fit into the narrow exceptions to the IDEA in favor of mainstreaming. The court denied the private school placement that his parents preferred.

A federal district court in Indiana ruled that a student who had an IQ rating of 32 and functioned at a level less than that of a two-year-old should not have been assigned to a regular fourth-grade class.[115] The court determined that the curriculum in the class would have to be adapted beyond recognition to fit the student's needs and that he required a great deal of one-to-one attention. The court concluded that such efforts were not required by the IDEA especially when there was little evidence that the child would derive any benefit from being placed in a regular classroom.

---

[112] Evans v. Board of Educ. of the Rhinebeck Cent. Sch. Dist., 930 F. Supp. 83 [111 EDUC. L. REP. 200] (S.D.N.Y. 1996).
[113] Flour Bluff Indep. Sch. Dist. v. Katherine M., 91 F.3d 689 [111 EDUC. L. REP. 637] (5th Cir. 1996); Urban v. Jefferson County Sch. Dist. R-1, 89 F.3d 720 [110 EDUC. L. REP. 1069] (10th Cir. 1996); Hudson v. Bloomfield Hills Pub. Sch., 910 F. Supp. 1291 [106 EDUC. L. REP. 593] (E.D. Mich. 1995); D.F. v. Western Sch. Corp., 921 F. Supp. 559 [109 EDUC. L. REP. 74] (S.D. Ind. 1996).
[114] Monticello Sch. Dist. No. 25 v. Illinois State Bd. of Educ., 910 F. Supp. 446 [106 EDUC. L. REP. 555] (C.D. Ill. 1995).
[115] D.F. v. Western Sch. Corp., 921 F. Supp. 559 [109 EDUC. L. REP. 74] (S.D. Ind. 1996).

Private Facilities

In a case from Washington, the Ninth Circuit approved a residential placement for a student with an attachment, oppositional defiant, and conduct disorders, as well as a histrionic personality after finding that she had deteriorated in placement in a mainstream classroom and had disrupted the class to the point where she had been expelled.[116] The court pointed out that the residential setting was not a medical facility even though it addressed disabilities stemming from medical or psychiatric disorders since it was an accredited educational institution under state law.

The Third Circuit affirmed that a student who was severely mentally retarded required a residential placement.[117] The trial court decreed that the student, who lived in New Jersey, needed intensive, around the clock instruction. The appellate panel agreed noting that an IEP calling for placement in a public school neither addressed the student's self-stimulatory behaviors nor allowed him to practice skills after the school day ended.

A district court in New York denied a motion for a preliminary injunction to block an order of the Family Court requiring parents to pay a portion of their child's expenses at a residential school.[118] After the Family Court ordered the student to be placed in the residential facility, his parents claimed that it was necessary for educational purposes but the Department of Social Services disagreed. In denying the injunction, the court indicated that the parents failed to present evidence that they were likely to suffer harm that could not be fully compensated.

Related Services

The IDEA requires school districts to provide related or supportive services to students with disabilities if they are needed to help children benefit from their special education programs.[119] The IDEA specifically mentions such developmental, supportive, and corrective services as transportation, speech pathology, audiology, psychological services, physical therapy, occupational therapy, recreation (including therapeutic recreation and social work services), counseling services (including

---

[116] Seattle Sch. Dist., No. 1 v. B.S., 82 F.3d 1493 [109 EDUC. L. REP. 55] (9th Cir. 1996).
[117] M.C. *ex rel.* J.C. v. Central Regional Sch. Dist., 81 F.3d 389 [108 EDUC. L. REP. 522] (3d Cir. 1996).
[118] King v. Pine Plains Cent. Sch. Dist., 923 F. Supp. 541 [109 EDUC. L. REP. 659] (S.D.N.Y. 1996), *see also* 918 F. Supp. 772 [108 EDUC. L. REP. 161] (S.D.N.Y. 1996) for previous action in the same case.
[119] 20 U.S.C. § 1401(a)(17).

rehabilitation counseling), medical services (for diagnostic or evaluative purposes only), and early identification and assessment as related services.

According to the Supreme Court, related services must be provided only to students receiving special education. Moreover, services that are necessary to help students benefit from special education must be incorporated into their IEPs.[120] The only limitation placed on what can be considered a related service is that medical services are exempted unless they are specifically for diagnostic or evaluative purposes.

In New Jersey, the federal trial court contended that a child with severe multiple disabilities who required constant supervision by a full-time nurse or other specially trained person to monitor her tracheostomy tube and provide suctioning when needed was not entitled to have these services provided at school district expense.[121] The court decided that since these were medical services, the district was not obligated to provide the requested assistance.

Discipline

There are no provisions in the IDEA that specifically refer to discipline. Even so, disciplinary sanctions that are applied to students with disabilities are sometimes the source of litigation. Courts have held that the change in placement and status quo provisions of the IDEA apply to the disciplinary process. The Supreme Court, in *Honig v. Doe*,[122] ruled that students in special education cannot be expelled for disciplinary reasons if their misconduct is a manifestation of their disabilities. However, *Honig* has not left school districts without recourse. Special education students may be suspended temporarily and are subject to other normal disciplinary sanctions. When necessary, a school district may seek judicial intervention pending completion of administrative due process hearings if educators believe that a student is dangerous and they cannot reach an agreement with the child's parents concerning a proper placement. *Honig* also allows schools to use ordinary disciplinary sanctions, such as suspensions of ten days or less, that do not result in changes of placements for students in special education.

In a case from Virginia, the Fourth Circuit upheld a determination by the Secretary of Education that school districts must provide educational services during expulsion periods to students whose

---

[120] Irving Indep. Sch. Dist. v. Tatro, 468 U.S. 883 [18 Educ. L. Rep. 138] (1984).
[121] Fulginiti v. Roxbury Township Pub. Sch., 921 F. Supp. 1320 [109 Educ. L. Rep. 119] (D.N.J. 1996).
[122] 484 U.S. 305 [43 Educ. L. Rep. 857] (1988).

misbehavior is unrelated to their disabilities.[123] The court stated that when a state refuses to offer educational services to students based on their misconduct, regardless of whether their misbehavior is a manifestation of their disabilities, it has ceased to assure pupils' rights to a FAPE. The court emphasized that students do not forfeit their rights when they misbehave in a manner unrelated to their disabilities.

The Seventh Circuit, in a suit from Illinois, found that a flexible approach to applying the status quo provision of the IDEA is needed when students face disciplinary action but have requested evaluations for special education.[124] The court stated that before the placement protection provision of the IDEA is invoked, students must demonstrate that educators reasonably knew, or should have known, of their disabilities. The court added that the IDEA was not designed to protect disruptive children from routine and appropriate school discipline.

In a 1994 case that only recently was reported, a federal trial court in Tennessee was of the opinion that a school district's filing of an unruly petition after a student vandalized a lavatory amounted to a change in placement.[125] In reasoning that juvenile court proceedings have the potential to change a student's placement in a significant manner, it noted that nothing in the record indicated that the child presented a risk of injury to anyone.

A district court in Mississippi approved the transfer of a student, who had remained defiant and aggressive even after implementation of a behavioral management plan at an alternative school, to a self-contained classroom located in a courtroom at the sheriff's office.[126] A hearing officer had permitted the transfer for a maximum of forty-five days and the court denied the parents' motion to block the switch. The court concluded that the district's finding that the student was potentially dangerous was reasonable in light of evidence that he had been disruptive, was often violent, and had demonstrated the ability to threaten and harm others.

The federal district court in Massachusetts refused to reissue a preliminary injunction that would have allowed a student to return to school after he had been suspended indefinitely.[127] The court initially

---

[123] Commonwealth of Va. Dep't of Educ. v. Riley, 86 F.3d 1337 [110 Educ. L. Rep. 552] (4th Cir. 1996). However, on October 11, 1996 the court vacated this decision and granted a rehearing *en banc*.
[124] Rodiriecus L. v. Waukegan Sch. Dist. No. 60, 90 F.3d 249 [111 Educ. L. Rep. 94] (7th Cir. 1996).
[125] Morgan v. Chris L., 927 F. Supp. 267 [110 Educ. L. Rep. 190] (E.D. Tenn. 1996).
[126] Taylor v. Corinth Pub. Sch. Dist., 917 F. Supp. 464 [107 Educ. L. Rep. 830] (N.D. Miss. 1996).
[127] Richard V. v. City of Medford, 924 F. Supp. 320 [109 Educ. L. Rep. 1181] (D. Mass. 1996).

granted an injunction to return the student to school after an evaluation determined that he was disabled. Subsequently, the court vacated the injunction as moot when the student enrolled in a parochial school. However, when the parochial school placement did not work out, the student attempted to re-enter the public system. The court ruled that because there were no exceptional circumstances warranting the reissuance of the injunction, the student and his parents would have to file a new complaint under the IDEA.

Remedies

If a school district fails to provide an appropriate placement for a student with disabilities, the courts are empowered to grant such relief as they deem appropriate.[128] The relief frequently involves reimbursement of costs borne by the parents in unilaterally obtaining appropriate services for their child. The Supreme Court has stated that school districts may be required to reimburse parents for costs incurred in providing their children with special education and related services if these placements are found to be appropriate.[129] In *Florence County School District Four v. Carter*,[130] the Supreme Court decreed that reimbursement is allowed even if the facility chosen by the parents is not state-approved as long as it offers an otherwise appropriate education. Compensatory education has been awarded where parents did not have the financial means to obtain private services while litigation was pending.

Congress passed the Handicapped Children's Protection Act in 1986 to allow parents who prevail in IDEA suits to recover their legal expenses.[131] In 1990, Congress enacted legislation specifically to abrogate states' Eleventh Amendment immunity to lawsuits in federal courts for any actions that occurred after October 30, 1990.[132] These amendments were adopted in response to Supreme Court rulings that the original IDEA did not allow for recovery of attorney fees by prevailing parents[133] and did not specifically abrogate the states' sovereign immunity.[134]

---

[128] 20 U.S.C. § 1415(e)(2).
[129] Burlington Sch. Comm. v. Department of Educ., Commonwealth of Mass., 471 U.S. 359 [23 EDUC. L. REP. 1189] (1985).
[130] 114 S. Ct. 361 [86 EDUC. L. REP. 41] (1993).
[131] 20 U.S.C. § 1414(e)(4)(B) *et seq.*
[132] 20 U.S.C. § 1403.
[133] Smith v. Robinson, 468 U.S. 992 [18 EDUC. L. REP. 148] (1984).
[134] Dellmuth v. Muth, 491 U.S. 223 [53 EDUC. L. REP. 792](1989).

Damages

According to three courts, general or punitive damages are not available under the IDEA as a matter of law.[135] Along these lines, the federal district court in Minnesota held that a claim for monetary relief to compensate a student for past deprivation of a FAPE was inappropriate as it would have constituted damages.[136]

A district court in Florida agreed that while parents are not entitled to punitive damages under the IDEA, such relief may be available under section 504 if intentional discrimination or retaliatory conduct can be shown.[137] The court added that the only appropriate remedies for violations of the IDEA are reimbursement awards to compensate parents for services that the school district should have provided.

The Supreme Court of Nebraska decided that when a school district contracts with a private service provider, the district cannot be held liable for damages resulting from the contractor's negligence.[138] After the medical center that a district contracted with failed to provide services during a seven month period, a student allegedly developed dislocated hips. The court reasoned that the district did not have any duty to monitor the care of a physical therapy patient or report changes in her care to her parents. The court concluded that the district was entitled to rely on the competence of the professional therapist and medical center to properly treat patients under their care.

A federal trial court in Illinois characterized a school district's claim against two state agencies to recover reimbursements that it made to a prevailing parent for attorney fees as a claim for damages.[139] In the original suit, the parents sought a residential placement for their child. Following extensive appeals, the case was resolved when the state Board of Education agreed to fund the residential placement. The district claimed that the failure of the agencies to develop an interagency agreement specifying financial responsibility for residential placements, as required by the IDEA, caused the district to engage in costly administrative and judicial proceedings. However, the court found that the district's position that a residential placement was inappropriate was a contributing cause of the litigation along with the lack of an interagency agreement. The

---

[135] Brantley v. Independent Sch. Dist. No. 625, St. Paul Pub. Sch., 936 F. Supp. 649 [112 EDUC. L. REP. 893] (D. Minn. 1996); Charlie F. v. Board of Educ. of Skokie Sch. Dist. 68, 98 F.3d 989 [113 EDUC. L. REP. 559] (7th Cir. 1996); Heidemann v. Rother, 84 F.3d 1022 (8th Cir. 1996).

[136] *Id.* Brantley.

[137] Whitehead v. School Bd. for Hillsborough County, Fla., 918 F. Supp. 1515 [108 EDUC. L. REP. 239] (M.D. Fla. 1996).

[138] Crider v. Bayard City Sch., 553 N.W.2d 147 [112 EDUC. L. REP. 1023] (Neb. 1996).

[139] Barbara Z. v. Obradovich, 937 F. Supp. 710 [113 EDUC. L. REP. 159] (N.D. Ill. 1996).

court maintained that each of the agencies should reimburse the district for one-third of the parent's attorney fees.

Tuition Reimbursement

In a suit where a hearing officer contended that a school district failed to offer an appropriate IEP for a child's fourth-grade year but did so in October of his fifth-grade year, a district court in Missouri held that the parents were entitled to private school tuition reimbursement for both years.[140] The court pointed out that the parents were required to sign a contract with the private school in September obligating them to pay tuition for the full fifth-grade year. However, since the court found that the district's IEP for the fifth-grade was inappropriate, it awarded reimbursement on that basis as well. The court rejected the parents' request for reimbursement for interest on a loan they had taken out to pay the private school, noting that the IDEA does not permit this kind of remedy.

In a dispute where parents withheld their consent for an evaluation and enrolled their child in a private school, the Circuit Court for the District of Columbia remanded for further findings of fact.[141] The court indicated that the parents would be entitled to tuition reimbursement if the school district could not show that it provided a reasonably informative answer to their request for clarification about the proposed evaluation.

Courts continue to rely upon *Florence County* in granting reimbursement for services that were deemed appropriate even though they were not state approved. The Supreme Court of Idaho awarded tuition reimbursement to the parents of a hearing-impaired student who had been enrolled in a parochial school after deciding that the district failed to develop an appropriate IEP.[142] Similarly, a district court in New York permitted reimbursement for applied behavioral analysis that was provided by trained, but uncertified, personnel in adjudicating that an autistic infant was entitled to those services under Part H of the IDEA.[143]

After determining that a student was entitled to speech therapy under the IDEA because his communication skills were impaired, a district court in Illinois granted reimbursement to parents who had obtained speech

---

[140] Fort Zumwalt Sch. Dist. v. Missouri State Bd. of Educ., 923 F. Supp. 1216 [109 EDUC. L. REP. 721] (E.D. Mo. 1996).
[141] Holland v. District of Columbia, 71 F.3d 417 [105 EDUC. L. REP. 397] (D.C. Cir. 1995).
[142] Doolittle v. Meridian Joint Sch. Dist. No. 2, Ada County, 919 P.2d 334 [110 EDUC. L. REP. 1282] (Idaho 1996).
[143] Malkentzos v. DeBuono, 923 F. Supp. 505 [109 EDUC. L. REP. 646] (S.D.N.Y. 1996) (*citing* 20 U.S.C. § 1471 *et seq.*); *see also* Still v. DeBuono, 927 F. Supp. 125 [110 EDUC. L. REP. 183] (S.D.N.Y. 1996).

therapy services privately.[144] However, the court later amended the award, stating that the parents were not entitled to reimbursement for services obtained prior to the time they first registered their dissatisfaction with the district.

A district court in Pennsylvania reimbursed a mother for her daughter's second, but not first, year in a religious institution for students with learning differences after holding that the public school district failed to offer an appropriate IEP.[145] Even though the parochial school was not state-certified for serving students with disabilities and most of its teachers were not certificated in special education, the court posited that the parochial school provided an appropriate education. The court further stated that the First Amendment did not bar such an award because the IDEA had a secular purpose, reimbursement went to the child's mother and not to the school, and the parent had not been offered a financial incentive to enroll her daughter in the sectarian school. In denying payment for the first year's tuition, the court observed that the district offered an appropriate IEP for that year.

As noted in part in the previous case and at least four other rulings, courts denied reimbursement when they found that public school districts offered and had the capacity to implement appropriate IEPs.[146] Further, a district court in Tennessee denied a request for reimbursement in finding that a child's parents unilaterally enrolled him in a private residential school without contacting the district and affording it the opportunity to develop an IEP.[147] Prior to enrolling in the residential facility, the student had attended another private school at his parents' expense. The court examined a hypothetical situation in which the parents unilaterally enrolled their son in a private facility after they attempted to negotiate an appropriate placement with the school district. According to the court, the fact that the district was not given the opportunity to develop an appropriate educational placement precluded reimbursement.

---

[144] Mary P. v. Illinois State Bd. of Educ., 919 F. Supp. 1173 [108 Educ. L. Rep. 609] (N.D. Ill. 1996), *amended by* 934 F. Supp. 989 [112 Educ. L. Rep. 248] (N.D. Ill. 1996).
[145] Christen G. v. Lower Merion Sch. Dist., 919 F. Supp. 793 [108 Educ. L. Rep. 553] (E.D. Pa. 1996).
[146] Independent Sch. Dist. No. 283 v. J.D. *ex rel.* S.D., 88 F.3d 556 [110 Educ. L. Rep. 987] (8th Cir. 1996); Sanger v. Montgomery County Bd. of Educ., 916 F. Supp. 518 [107 Educ. L. Rep. 754] (D. Md. 1996); Mather v. Hartford Sch. Dist., 928 F. Supp. 437 [110 Educ. L. Rep. 655] (D. Vt. 1996); Cypress-Fairbanks Indep. Sch. Dist. v. Michael F., 931 F. Supp. 474 (S.D. Tex. 1995).
[147] Doe v. Metropolitan Nashville Pub. Sch., 931 F. Supp. 551 [111 Educ. L. Rep. 788] (M.D. Tenn. 1996).

Compensatory Services

In a case from New Jersey, the Third Circuit overturned the denial of compensatory services to a student who had been in a program where he made little progress, positing that compensation accrues from the point that a school district knows, or should know, of the failure of an IEP.[148] In remanding, the court stated that the student was entitled to compensatory services for the period of deprivation minus an amount of time reasonably required for the district to have rectified the problem.

Attorney Fees

Courts routinely award attorney fees to parents who are the prevailing party.[149] For example, in a suit from South Dakota, the Eighth Circuit held that parents were entitled to attorney fees even though they had been represented by a publicly funded counsel.[150]

A district court in Tennessee judged that a parent was the prevailing party since her lawsuit was the catalyst for the school district's decision to alter its placement recommendation.[151] After a hearing officer upheld the district's choice of transferring a child to the public schools, the mother sought further review. While court action was pending, the district agreed that the child should remain at the state school he had been attending. The court was of the opinion that absent the proceedings instigated by the parent, the child would have been transferred to the public schools.

In Texas, a district court ordered reimbursement for one-fourth of the counsel fees accrued by parents in connection with administrative hearings because the parents prevailed on only one of four issues.[152] In addition, the court determined that the school district's offer to meet to consider the parents' complaints about their daughter's IEP did not constitute a settlement offer that was comparable to a hearing officer's order to incorporate measurable goals and objectives into the IEP.

The federal trial court for the District of Columbia granted reimbursement to prevailing plaintiffs in a suit filed on behalf of several students but reduced the requested award after finding it excessive in

---

[148] M.C. *ex rel.* J.C. v. Central Regional Sch. Dist., 81 F.3d 389 [108 Educ. L. Rep. 522] (3d Cir. 1996).

[149] Mary P. v. Illinois State Bd. of Educ., 919 F. Supp. 1173 [108 Educ. L. Rep. 609] (N.D. Ill. 1996), *amended* 934 F. Supp. 989 [112 Educ. L. Rep. 248] (N.D. Ill. 1996); Morgan v. Chris L., 927 F. Supp. 267 [110 Educ. L. Rep. 190] (E.D. Tenn. 1994).

[150] Yankton Sch. Dist. v. Schramm, 93 F.3d 1369 [111 Educ. L. Rep. 1143] (8th Cir. 1996), *aff'g* 900 F. Supp. 1182 [104 Educ. L. Rep. 645] (D.S.D. 1995).

[151] Rynes v. Knox County Bd. of Educ., 907 F. Supp. 1169 [105 Educ. L. Rep. 996] (E.D. Tenn. 1995).

[152] Virginia McC. v. Corrigan-Camden Indep. Sch. Dist., 909 F. Supp. 1023 [106 Educ. L. Rep. 508] (E.D. Tex. 1996).

relation to the nature of the litigation.[153] Upon closer inspection, the court discovered that attorney fees were almost identical for all of the plaintiffs even though each one submitted virtually the same documents. The court cited not only numerous examples of identical charges being made for the preparation of documents that varied only in the name of the plaintiff but also an example whereby one attorney billed a cumulative total of thirty hours all on the same day.

On remand from the Seventh Circuit, a federal trial court in Illinois denied a request for attorney fees in noting that a school district had tendered a written settlement offer to the parents that was more favorable than the relief the parents obtained from a hearing officer.[154] The appellate court remanded after indicating that the dispute was not time barred.

The Eighth Circuit, in a case from Minnesota, upheld a denial of attorney fees, agreeing that a student was not the prevailing party because the revisions to her IEP were de minimis and the school district had agreed to provide more than she was entitled to under the IDEA.[155] Similarly, the Tenth Circuit, in a suit from Colorado, affirmed a denial of fees, declaring that the parents did not succeed to the degree necessary for an award.[156]

In a decision that seems self-evident, the Supreme Court of North Dakota affirmed that parents were not the prevailing party after a lower court dismissed their lawsuit for failure to exhaust administrative remedies.[157] Further, the Seventh Circuit denied attorney fees in a case from Illinois after finding that the suit was moot on its merits.[158]

The Sixth Circuit upheld a denial of attorney fees in concluding that a parent in Ohio prematurely requested a due process hearing.[159] The court maintained that when the parent requested the hearing, the IEP process was well underway and there was no underlying dispute. The hearing had been dismissed before reaching the merits of the claims because the parent and district had agreed on an IEP.

---

[153] Bridgeforth v. District of Columbia, 933 F. Supp. 7 [112 EDUC. L. REP. 107] (D.D.C. 1996).

[154] Dell v. Board of Educ., Township High Sch. Dist. 113, 918 F. Supp. 212 [108 EDUC. L. REP. 139] (N.D. Ill. 1995) *on remand from* 32 F.3d 1053 [93 EDUC. L. REP. 1143] (7th Cir. 1994).

[155] Schmidt v. Special Sch. Dist. No. 1, 77 F.3d 1084 [107 EDUC. L. REP. 476] (8th Cir. 1996).

[156] Urban v. Jefferson County Sch. Dist. R-1, 89 F.3d 720 [110 EDUC. L. REP. 1069] (10th Cir. 1996), *aff'g* 870 F. Supp. 1558 [96 EDUC. L. REP. 952] (D. Colo. 1994).

[157] Lapp v. Reeder Pub. Sch. Dist. No. 3, 544 N.W.2d [107 EDUC. L. REP. 296] (N.D. 1996).

[158] Board of Educ. of Downers Grove Grade Sch. Dist. No. 58 v. Steven L., 89 F.3d 464 [110 EDUC. L. REP. 1057] (7th Cir. 1996).

[159] Payne v. Board of Educ., Cleveland City Sch., 88 F.3d 392 [110 EDUC. L. REP. 968] (6th Cir. 1996).

In a similar case from California, the Ninth Circuit offered that the parents of a student with disabilities, who retained an attorney shortly after making an initial request for an evaluation of their child, failed to establish that a dispute existed between the parties before the school district agreed to the placement requested by the parents.[160] The court also rejected the parents' request for attorney fees.

The Supreme Court of Indiana denied fees to a prevailing parent-attorney who represented his son in due process proceedings.[161] The court based its decision on the fact that fee-shifting terms in other federal legislation similar to the attorney fees provision of the IDEA do not allow for pro se attorneys to collect reimbursement.

A district court in Florida denied a request by the state Department of Education for a fee award made in adjudicating that it was not a party to the original dispute and that the hearing officer had clearly identified a school district as the sole defendant.[162] The court ruled that attorney fees cannot be obtained from a nondefendant.

In Illinois, a federal trial court held that a school district could not recover legal expenses from state agencies because the IDEA does not allow courts to award attorney fees to a prevailing party that is not a parent.[163] The court noted that the dispute began when a school district refused to place a student in a private residential facility. When the child's parents filed suit, the district counterclaimed, alleging that the Board of Education and Department of Mental Health and Developmental Disabilities failed to develop interagency agreements as required by the IDEA, thus forcing the district to incur unnecessary litigation expenses.

Other IDEA Issues

Parents cannot be required to use their insurance coverage if doing so would incur a financial loss, even indirectly. In a suit where the parents' health insurance carrier had partially paid for an independent evaluation, a federal trial court in Iowa ordered the school district to reimburse the insurance company since payment for the evaluation decreased the available lifetime coverage under the policy.[164]

---

[160] Kletzelman v. Capistrano Unified Sch. Dist., 91 F.3d 68 (9th Cir. 1996).
[161] Miller v. West Lafayette Community Sch. Corp., 665 N.E.2d 905 [110 EDUC. L. REP. 370] (Ind. 1996).
[162] Whitehead v. School Bd. for Hillsborough County, Fla., 932 F. Supp. 1393 [111 EDUC. L. REP. 1212] (M.D. Fla. 1996).
[163] Board of Educ. of Community High Sch. Dist No. 218, Cook, County, Ill. v. Illinois State Bd. of Educ., 940 F. Supp. 1321 [113 EDUC. L. REP. 1171] (N.D. Ill. 1996).
[164] Raymond S. v. Ramirez, 918 F. Supp. 1280 [108 EDUC. L. REP. 196] (N.D. Iowa 1996).

In Connecticut, Medicaid recipients challenged agencies that refused to pay for home health nursing services outside the home. The federal district court decreed that state regulations restricting the provision of home health services to those in the home itself were an impermissible construction of the Medicaid Act.[165]

A district court in New York, in one of the first claims filed under Part H of the IDEA,[166] found that early intervention services are the equivalent of a FAPE and must meet the unique needs of a child and his or her family.[167] As such, the court relied upon *Rowley* in determining that the services offered the child were insufficient.

School districts must include transition plans in the IEPs of students who are sixteen years of age or older.[168] The Eighth Circuit affirmed that a South Dakota school district's minimal approach to transition planning that left most of the responsibility on the parents was insufficient.[169] Yet the Tenth Circuit agreed that the failure of a district in Colorado to include transition services in an IEP did not amount to a denial of an appropriate education.[170] The court emphasized that it is important to distinguish between a statement of transition services in an IEP and the actual delivery of the services. It added that there was substantial evidence in the record to conclude that the student had benefitted from actual transition services.

The Fourth Circuit, in a suit from Virginia, ruled that the Department of Education was not required to abide by the notice and comment provisions of the Administrative Procedures Act[171] before implementing its disciplinary interpretations.[172] The court stated that the Department simply issued an interpretive rule stating what it thought the IDEA meant.

In the same cse, the Fourth Circuit upheld a decision by the U.S. Department of Education to withhold funds from the Commonwealth of Virginia for discontinuing educational services to students who had been expelled for misbehavior that was not a manifestation of their disability.[173] The court interpreted the plain language of the IDEA as allowing the

---

[165] Skubel v. Sullivan, 925 F. Supp. 930 [110 Educ. L. Rep. 53] (D. Conn. 1996) *citing* 42 U.S.C. § 1396 *et seq.*
[166] 20 U.S.C. § 1471 *et seq.*
[167] Malkentzos v. DeBuono, 923 F. Supp. 505 [109 Educ. L. Rep. 646] (S.D.N.Y. 1996).
[168] 20 U.S.C. § 1401(a)(20).
[169] Yankton Sch. Dist. v. Schramm, 93 F.3d 1369 [111 Educ. L. Rep. 1143] (8th Cir. 1996), *aff'g* 900 F. Supp. 1182 [104 Educ. L. Rep. 645] (D.S.D. 1995).
[170] Urban v. Jefferson County Sch. Dist. R-1, 89 F.3d 720 [110 Educ. L. Rep. 1069] (10th Cir. 1996).
[171] 5 U.S.C. § 553.
[172] Commonwealth of Va. Dep't of Educ. v. Riley, 86 F.3d 1337 [110 Educ. L. Rep. 552] (4th Cir. 1996). However, on October 11, 1996 the court vacated this decision and granted a rehearing *en banc*.
[173] *Id.*

Department to withhold a state's entire allotment of funds under the Act if it substantially failed to comply with any provision of the statute.

Parents in Vermont filed suit claiming that the state failed both to develop and implement procedures to ensure a timely investigation of complaints regarding noncompliance with the IDEA and to correct instances of the same. The federal district court was of the opinion that there is a private remedy for the enforcement of claims seeking compliance with the IDEA complaint resolution procedures.[174] Similarly, the Third Circuit noted that there is a private right of action under the IDEA to enforce compliance with its complaint resolution procedures.[175]

A teacher in California who complained to her superiors that the school district was failing to comply with federal and state special education laws later reported the matter to the state. The teacher subsequently filed suit under the False Claims Act charging that the district retaliated against her when she was disciplined for using improper corporal punishment and for permitting a student to arrive late for school without proper authority. The Ninth Circuit held that the district's actions did not violate the False Claims Act.[176]

State Laws

Special education is governed by state as well as federal law. Each state's special education statutes must be consistent with the IDEA; however, differences do exist. Most states have legislation similar in scope to the IDEA, but several states have requirements that go beyond the provisions of federal law. Some states have higher standards of what constitutes an appropriate education and/or stricter procedural requirements. In other instances, state laws establish procedures for the implementation of special education programs that are not explicitly covered by federal statutes. Federal and state courts are frequently called upon to interpret those provisions.

Indiana

A federal trial court in Indiana ruled that where the divorced parents of a child with a disability had joint custody, and each resided in a different school system, the district of the father's residence had some responsibility

---

[174] Upper Valley Ass'n for Handicapped Citizens v. Mills, 928 F. Supp. 429 [110 Educ. L. Rep. 647] (D. Vt. 1996).

[175] Beth V. v. Carroll, 87 F.3d 80 [110 Educ. L. Rep. 585] (3d Cir. 1996).

[176] United States *ex rel.* Hopper v. Anton, 91 F.3d 1261 [111 Educ. L. Rep. 676] (9th Cir. 1996) *citing* 31 U.S.C. § 3730.

for the student's education.[177] The parents had filed suit over the proper placement of their son. The district in which the father resided moved to dismiss claiming that it did not owe the child a duty since he did not reside within its boundaries. The court rejected the district's motion to dismiss.

New Hampshire

According to the Supreme Court of New Hampshire, evaluating individuals who are incarcerated in correctional institutions is the responsibility of the inmate's home school district.[178] The court affirmed that when an educationally disabled person between the ages of eighteen and twenty-one is incarcerated, the district that bears financial responsibility for the student's education must enter the state prison to perform the evaluations and develop the IEP.

New York

Under state law, a federal trial court in New York declared that a school district is no longer responsible for paying a student's tuition or developing his IEP once a Family Court has issued an order placing the child in a residential facility.[179] The court reasoned that a district is obliged only to provide information about the student, make recommendations regarding his education, and pay a specified sum to the state for partial reimbursement of the child's placement expenses.

In a second case from New York, an appellate court issued yet another decision in the long-running dispute regarding the constitutionality of a state law that allows a village inhabited by a sect of Satmar Hasidic Jews to form their own school district. Following the Supreme Court's decision in *Board of Education of Kiryas Joel Village School District v. Grumet*[180] striking down the statute that created a special school system whose boundaries were coterminous with the village, the state assembly passed a new law that expanded the authority to organize a new district to other municipalities. However, upon closer scrutiny, the court found that the conditions established in the new law for the formation of a district effectively excluded all municipalities except the village of Kiryas Joel.[181] The court, in positing that the new law was little more than the prior

---

[177] Linda W. v. Indiana Dep't of Educ., 927 F. Supp. 303 [110 EDUC. L. REP. 196] (N.D. Ind. 1996).

[178] Nashua Sch. Dist. v. State of N.H., 667 A.2d 1036 [105 EDUC. L. REP. 578] (N.H. 1995).

[179] King v. Pine Plains Cent. Sch. Dist., 918 F. Supp. 772 [108 EDUC. L. REP. 161] (S.D.N.Y. 1996).

[180] 114 S. Ct. 2481 [91 EDUC. L. REP. 810] (1994).

[181] Grumet v. Cuomo, 647 N.Y.S.2d 565 [113 EDUC. L. REP. 362] (N.Y. App. Div. 1996), rev'g 625 N.Y.S.2d 1000 [100 EDUC. L. REP. 252] (N.Y. Sup. Ct. 1995).

statute resurrected, held that the new law also violated the Establishment Clause of the First Amendment.

In another long standing dispute from New York, the Second Circuit decided that the state's residency statute was not so arbitrary and unreasonable that it deprived parents of substantive due process.[182] The court found that the statute, which presumed that children resided with their parents in the absence of parental abandonment, was not unreasonable. As such, it concluded that the district where the natural parents resided was responsible for a student's special education costs, regardless of where the child actually lived.

North Carolina

In a suit involving the residency of a special education student, an appellate court in North Carolina ruled that since the child actually resided with his grandmother, the county in which she resided had to admit him into its school system.[183] The student went to live with his grandmother in order to receive all necessary care but the district had rejected his application for admittance, claiming that he was not a resident or domiciliary of the state.

Discrimination Under the Rehabilitation Act, Section 504

Section 504 of the Rehabilitation Act of 1973, as amended, provides that "[n]o otherwise qualified individual with a disability . . . shall, solely by reason of her or his disability be excluded from participation in, be denied the benefits of, or be subjected to discrimination under any program or activity receiving [f]ederal financial assistance . . . ."[184] This Act effectively prohibits any recipient of federal funds from discriminating against individuals with disabilities in the provision of services or employment. Section 504 applies to any agency that receives federal funds, not just the schools.

A person is considered to have a disability under section 504 if he or she has a physical or mental impairment that substantially limits one or more of life's major activities, has a record of such an impairment, or is regarded as having such an impairment.[185] Major life activities are

---

[182] Catlin v. Sobol, 93 F.3d 1112 [111 Educ. L. Rep. 1114] (2d Cir. 1996).
[183] Craven County Bd. of Educ. v. Willoughby, 466 S.E.2d 334 [106 Educ. L. Rep. 930] (N.C. Ct. App. 1996).
[184] 29 U.S.C. § 794.
[185] 29 U.S.C. § 706(7)(B).

"functions such as caring for oneself, performing manual tasks, walking, seeing, hearing, speaking, breathing, learning, and working."[186] The Supreme Court has held that a person is otherwise qualified to participate in a program for purposes of section 504 if the person is capable of meeting all of the requirements of a program in spite of the disability.[187] If a person is otherwise qualified, a recipient of federal funds is expected to make reasonable accommodations for the individual's disabilities unless doing so would create an undue hardship.[188]

Students

Elementary and Secondary

Students with disabilities at the elementary and secondary level have rights under section 504 as well as the IDEA. Often, children and their parents can file suits that present claims under both statutes. Frequently, the claims stated under one statute are identical or similar to those made under the other law; however, sometimes distinct claims are brought under section 504.

In Minnesota, the federal district court held that an incorrect evaluation or a substantively faulty IEP cannot, by itself, sustain a discrimination claim under section 504.[189] The court stated that either bad faith or gross misjudgment must be shown before a violation can be found. In the absence of bad faith, inappropriate decisions are, at most, errors in professional judgment, according to the court.

The issue of whether age eligibility rules for participation in athletics can be applied to students with disabilities who are overage because they have repeated grades has been controversial for several years. A new twist to the dilemma arose in a case from Connecticut where athletic competition was specified in the IEP of a nineteen-year-old student as a means of fostering his self-esteem, self-confidence, and social skills. The federal district court issued a preliminary injunction allowing the student to participate, stating that section 504 requires an individual analysis of the purpose behind the age eligibility rule. The Second Circuit dismissed an appeal by the athletic conference as moot.[190]

---

[186] 34 C.F.R. § 104.3(j)(2)(ii).
[187] School Bd. of Nassau County v. Arline, 480 U.S. 273 [37 Educ. L. Rep. 448] (1987); Southeastern Community College v. Davis, 442 U.S. 397 (1979).
[188] 34 C.F.R. § 104.12(a).
[189] Brantley v. Independent Sch. Dist. No. 625, St. Paul Pub. Sch., 936 F. Supp. 649 [112 Educ. L. Rep. 893] (D. Minn. 1996).
[190] Dennin v. Connecticut Interscholastic Athletic Conference, 913 F. Supp. 663 [106 Educ. L. Rep. 1130] (D. Conn. 1996), *appeal dismissed as moot* 94 F.3d 96 [111 Educ. L. Rep. 1154] (2d Cir. 1996).

In Ohio, a district court decided that an eight semester rule that prohibited a student with a disability, who had repeated his freshman year, from competing as a senior did not violate section 504.[191] The court reasoned that the student was ineligible because of the passage of time measured in semesters, not because of his disability.

A district court in Indiana found that section 504 was not violated when a school district met the LRE requirements of the IDEA.[192] The parents of a student with moderate to severe disabilities contended that the district's refusal to place their son in a regular fourth-grade classroom in his neighborhood school violated section 504.

In Alabama, a district court declared that a teacher's physical discipline of a hearing-impaired student was not discriminatory as his actions were not based on the child's disability.[193] The teacher head-butted the student when he failed to respond to a verbal command. The court ruled that although the situation may have been aggravated by the student's disability, there was an insufficient factual basis to sustain a discrimination claim.

Higher Education

Students who were unable to meet academic requirements for a degree or admission into a program of study did not fare well in claims brought under section 504. A district court in Texas held that the inability to conceptually organize the material on a doctoral comprehensive examination is not a disability within the meaning of section 504.[194]

A district court in Georgia entered judgment in favor of a medical school that dismissed a student due to his unsatisfactory academic performance.[195] The student failed courses due to his inability to integrate and process information promptly and accurately. The court, noting that the student would not be given extra time to diagnose medical problems in emergency situations, concluded that there was no accommodation that would enable him to meet the essential requirements of the program. Similarly, a district court in Virginia maintained that a student with a learning disability who applied to medical school but did not meet the academic requirements for admission was not otherwise qualified.[196]

---

[191] Rhodes v. Ohio High Sch. Athletic Ass'n, 939 F. Supp. 584 [113 EDUC. L. REP. 716] (N.D. Ohio 1996).
[192] D.F. v. Western Sch. Corp., 921 F. Supp. 559 [109 EDUC. L. REP. 74] (S.D. Ind. 1996).
[193] Gaither v. Barron, 924 F. Supp. 134 [109 EDUC. L. REP. 754] (M.D. Ala. 1996).
[194] Tips v. Regents of Texas Tech Univ., 921 F. Supp. 1515 [109 EDUC. L. REP. 131] (N.D. Tex. 1996).
[195] Ellis v. Morehouse Sch. of Med., 925 F. Supp. 1529 [1,10 EDUC. L. REP. 106] (N.D. Ga. 1996).
[196] Betts v. Rector and Visitors of the Univ. of Virginia, 939 F. Supp. 461 [113 EDUC. L. REP. 705] (W.D. Va. 1996).

In New York, a district court ruled in favor of a college that dismissed an occupational therapy student who had not met the criteria of passing two graded field placements.[197] The court posited that since the college had no knowledge of the student's disability at the time of her dismissal, charges of discrimination could not be supported.

An athlete who suffered an attack of ventricular fibrillation and was not allowed to participate in intercollegiate basketball unsuccessfully sought reinstatement on his team.[198] Following an episode of syncope, the student had an automatic cardioverter defibrillator implanted in his abdomen. A district court had ruled in his favor, but the Seventh Circuit reversed and remanded. It held that playing college basketball is not, in and of itself, a major life activity as it is not a basic function of life on par with walking, breathing, and speaking. The court added that an impairment that interfered with the student's ability to perform a particular function but did not significantly decrease his ability to acquire a satisfactory education did not substantially limit the major life activity of learning as it only foreclosed a small portion of his collegiate opportunities.

A district court in Pennsylvania stated that a student who had been dismissed from a municipal police training program following the discovery that he had undergone psychiatric treatment failed to show that he was disabled.[199] The court was of the opinion that the student had not asserted a factual basis that could lead to the determination that he was substantially limited in any major life activity. In a subsequent suit, the court pointed out that since it already had ruled that the student was not disabled, the law of the case doctrine dictated that an action could not be maintained against a different defendant.[200]

Other Section 504 Issues

Insofar as section 504 does not contain a statute of limitations for filing suit, one must be borrowed from analogous state law. As such, a district court in Alabama noted that the state's two-year statute of limitations for personal injuries applied to a claim for damages brought under section 504.[201]

---

[197] Goodwin v. Keuka College, 929 F. Supp. 90 [110 Educ. L. Rep. 1084] (W.D.N.Y. 1995).

[198] Knapp v. Northwestern Univ., 101 F.3d 473 [114 Educ. L. Rep. 460] (7th Cir. 1996), rev'g 938 F. Supp. 508 [113 Educ. L. Rep. 269] (N.D. Ill. 1996) and 942 F. Supp. 1191 [114 Educ. L. Rep. 169] (N.D. Ill. 1996).

[199] Gardiner v. Mercyhurst College, 942 F. Supp. 1050 [114 Educ. L. Rep. 157] (W.D. Pa. 1995).

[200] Gardiner v. Mercyhurst College, 942 F. Supp. 1055 [114 Educ. L. Rep. 162] (W.D. Pa. 1996).

[201] Andalusia City Bd. of Educ., v. Andress, 916 F. Supp. 1179 [107 Educ. L. Rep. 800] (M.D. Ala. 1996).

According to a federal district court in Florida, parents of students with disabilities may be able to sue under section 504 to recover compensatory and punitive damages if they successfully can show intentional discrimination.[202] The court added that damages also are available for retaliatory conduct when parents attempt to assert their rights under the Rehabilitation Act. The court rounded out its opinion by indicating that parties seeking damages under section 504 are entitled to a jury trial.

The Third Circuit held that parents in Pennsylvania who exhausted administrative remedies under the IDEA were not required to do the same under section 504.[203] The court offered that by following the due process procedures of the IDEA, the parents met any exhaustion requirements pursuant to section 504.

Americans with Disabilities Act

The ADA,[204] which was enacted in 1990, is designed to prohibit discrimination against persons with disabilities in a wide range of activities sponsored by private as well as public entities. The greatest impact of the ADA is on the private sector. Generally, compliance with section 504 satisfies the dictates of the ADA; however, several provisions of the ADA addressed loopholes in section 504 and codified judicial interpretations of the Rehabilitation Act. Many suits that arise in the public sector are now brought on the basis of the ADA as well as section 504. In most instances, the disposition is identical under both laws. Decisions that previously were discussed in the section 504 part of this chapter and resulted in identical decisions under the ADA are not repeated here.[205]

---

[202] Whitehead v. School Bd. for Hillsborough County, Fla., 918 F. Supp. 1515 [108 EDUC. L. REP. 239] (M.D. Fla. 1996).

[203] Jeremy H. v. Mount Lebanon Sch. Dist., 95 F.3d 272 [112 EDUC. L. REP. 70] (3d Cir. 1996).

[204] 42 U.S.C. § 12101 *et seq.*

[205] Tips v. Regents of Texas Tech Univ., 921 F. Supp. 1515 [109 EDUC. L. REP. 131] (N.D. Tex. 1996); Dennin v. Connecticut Interscholastic Athletic Conference, 913 F. Supp. 663 [106 EDUC. L. REP. 1130] (D. Conn. 1996), *appeal dismissed as moot* 94 F.3d 96 [111 EDUC. L. REP. 1154] (2d Cir. 1996); D.F. v. Western Sch. Corp., 921 F. Supp. 559 [109 EDUC. L. REP. 74] (S.D. Ind. 1996); Gaither v. Barron, 924 F. Supp. 134 [109 EDUC. L. REP. 754] (M.D. Ala. 1996); Jeremy H. v. Mount Lebanon Sch. Dist., 95 F.3d 272 [112 EDUC. L. REP. 70] (3d Cir. 1996); Brantley v. Independent Sch. Dist. No. 625, St. Paul Pub. Sch., 936 F. Supp. 649 [112 EDUC. L. REP. 893] (D. Minn. 1996); Ellis v. Morehouse Sch. of Med., 925 F. Supp. 1529 [110 EDUC. L. REP. 106] (N.D. Ga. 1996); Goodwin v. Keuka College, 929 F. Supp. 90 [110 EDUC. L. REP. 1084] (W.D.N.Y. 1995); Rhodes v. Ohio High Sch. Athletic Ass'n, 939 F. Supp. 584 [113 EDUC. L. REP. 716] (N.D. Ohio 1996); Betts v. Rector and Visitors of the Univ. of Virginia, 939 F. Supp. 461 [113 EDUC. L. REP. 705] (W.D. Va. 1996); Gardiner v. Mercyhurst College, 942 F. Supp. 1050 [114 EDUC. L. REP. 157] (W.D. Pa. 1995), 942 F. Supp. 1055 [114 EDUC. L. REP. 162] (W.D. Pa. 1996).

In Minnesota, the federal trial court ascertained that a school district did not violate the ADA by refusing to provide a physically disabled student with an elevator key.[206] It found that school officials did not furnish a key when requested because they wanted both to verify that the independent use of the elevator by the student was safe and to develop criteria for the issuance of keys to pupils. The court agreed that this explanation was legitimate and nondiscriminatory.

The Tenth Circuit affirmed that the ADA did not confer the right to attend a neighborhood school upon a student with a disability in Colorado.[207] The court stated that since the student was not entitled to a placement in the neighborhood school under the IDEA, he could not obtain one under the ADA.

Conclusion

As in previous years, litigation in special education continued at a rapid pace in 1996. Once again, most of the suits dealt with placement and procedural issues and the majority of decisions relied on precedent.

The issue of providing services to students in parochial schools continued to be controversial and courts were split on the requirements of the EDGAR regulations. Several federal district courts held that EDGAR mandates the provision of services on-site while one appeals court ruled that EDGAR did not require the on-site delivery of instructional assistance.

Another controversial issue is whether students who are undergoing evaluations but have not yet been classified as disabled are entitled to the protections of the IDEA when facing disciplinary actions. Although this question remains controversial, it most likely will be settled by legislative, rather than judicial, decree.

A number of cases involving students with disabilities were filed under both section 504 and the ADA. As in previous years, plaintiffs gained nothing under the ADA that they were not already entitled to under section 504.

---

[206] Hoekstra v. Independent Sch. Dist. No. 283, St. Louis Park, Minn., 916 F. Supp. 941 [107 EDUC. L. REP. 779] (D. Minn. 1996).

[207] Urban v. Jefferson County Sch. Dist. R-1, 89 F.3d. 720 [110 Educ. L. Rep. 1069] (10th Cir. 1996).

6
TORTS

William J. Evans, Jr.

Introduction

Tort law offers remedies to individuals for harm caused by the unreasonable conduct of others. This chapter examines cases brought by or on behalf of students, school employees and, in some instances, visitors on school grounds. Tort actions arising out of interscholastic sports are discussed in Chapter 7, *Sports*

Negligence

Negligence is the most common tort committed by school personnel. A tort can arise when an improper act, or failure to act, causes injury to another. In addition, an individual cannot be liable for a tort unless there is a causal relationship between the alleged conduct and the injury. When an injured party claims that a tort has occurred, the behavior of school personnel is measured against what a reasonable and prudent professional of similar training and experience would, or should, have done in the same or similar circumstances.

Injuries

Schools are responsible for maintaining a safe and healthy environment in which learning can take place. The following cases are divided into categories according to where or how an injury was sustained and when the defense was not sovereign or statutory immunity.

Off School Property and After School Hours

Parents of a fifth-grade student brought an action for damages based on injuries the student suffered when, on the way home from school, he walked off of a sidewalk and into the rear wheels of a tractor trailer. The Supreme Court of Idaho affirmed that the district was not liable for negligent highway maintenance or design.[1] The court also agreed that the district did not assume a duty to provide crossing guards, safety patrols, or busing.

The passenger in a car that was struck by a school bus sued the bus driver for alleged injuries to his neck and foot. The Supreme Court of Arkansas affirmed that the accident was not the proximate cause of the injuries.[2] The court pointed out that the passenger's medical expert could not say that the injuries were caused by the accident.

When the negligent driving of a teacher who was transporting a child to a school function caused the student to be injured, the student settled the claim by granting the teacher a general release. A trial court dismissed the student's later action against the school district. On further review, an appellate court in Michigan affirmed that the release of the teacher discharged the district from any possible liability.[3]

Three students violated school rules by not taking a shuttle bus and instead taking a car. When the car they were riding in was involved in an

---

[1] Rife v. Long, 908 P.2d 143 [105 EDUC. L. REP. 1256] (Idaho 1995).
[2] Anselmo v. Turk, 924 S.W.2d 798 [114 EDUC. L. REP. 1293] (Ark. 1996).
[3] Penrod v. Branson R-IV Pub. Sch. Dist., 916 S.W.2d 866 [107 EDUC. L. REP. 1051] (Mo. Ct. App. 1996).

accident, two of the students were killed and the third student was severely brain damaged. A trial court dismissed the action brought by the parents of the surviving student alleging that the district failed to enforce its regulations regarding transportation. An appellate panel in Ohio affirmed that there was no evidence of bad faith or reckless exercise of a discretionary function by the district or its employees.[4]

In a second case from Ohio, a homeowner's estate sought further review of the dismissal of their wrongful death action against a school board and a vocational construction teacher who worked on the decedent's house as part of a class project. Even though the teacher had moved furniture to serve as a barrier to the exposed sides of the opening in the room that was being worked on and warned the decedent that the insulation covering it would not support any weight, the homeowner died after falling through the opening. An appellate court affirmed.[5] The court indicated that while the teacher had not complied with applicable building codes, his action did not rise to the level of recklessness or bad faith that could make him liable.

After a twelve-year-old student and her classmates attended a special drug awareness program in a local park, she did not return from the lunch break. Following a thirty minute search that included a visit to the student's home, the teacher and other children returned to school. The student, who was late in returning to the park, was raped by two acquaintances. A trial court in New York dismissed the student's claim against the school district and an appellate tribunal affirmed.[6] The court found it unnecessary to examine the student's allegation of negligent supervision where the unforeseeable criminal conduct of the rapists absolved the board of any culpability.

Parents of a student in Connecticut sued a board of education, school officials, and teachers claiming that failure to address their son's academic deficiencies caused him great emotional distress that led to his suicide. An appellate court affirmed that actions by the town police force were an intervening cause that relieved the defendants of liability.[7] The court ruled that the police had responded to warnings about a suicide at the student's address, but the student took his life an hour after the police left.

---

[4] Steele v. Auburn Vocational Sch. Dist., 661 N.E.2d 767 [107 EDUC. L. REP. 273] (Ohio Ct. App. 1996).
[5] Hackathorn v. Preisse, 663 N.E.2d 384 [108 EDUC. L. REP. 863] (Ohio Ct. App. 1996).
[6] Bell v. Board of Educ. of the City of N.Y., 646 N.Y.S.2d 499 [112 EDUC. L. REP. 401] (N.Y. App. Div. 1996). *See also* Farrukh v. Board of Educ. of the City of N.Y., 643 N.Y.S.2d 118 [110 EDUC. L. REP. 323] (N.Y. App. Div. 1996) (holding that a trial court erred in dismissing an action where a school had not exercised reasonable care in supervision of a young student with a disability).
[7] Brown v. Board of Educ. of Milford, 681 A.2d 996 [112 EDUC. L. REP. 953] (Conn. Ct. App. 1996).

School Settings During School Hours

A high school student unsuccessfully sued the female teacher with whom he had sexual relations, his principal, and his school district. The Supreme Court of Minnesota held that since sexual relations between a teacher and student are not a well known hazard, the district and principal could not have foreseen such a possibility.[8] The court added that even though the sexual activity took place during school hours, insofar as the teacher's actions could not be viewed as directly related to her duties, liability could not be imputed to the district or principal.

In a second case from Minnesota, the parents of a preschool student who broke her arm when she fell from a monkey bar after leaving a line of students returning from recess sought further review of a judgment in favor of the school. An appellate court affirmed that the jury had been properly instructed that the school was not required to provide constant supervision of all children at all times.[9] Moreover, the court was of the opinion that there was no evidence that additional oversight could have prevented the accident because it occurred in the presence of two supervisors.

A former student and his parent sued for the loss of parental consortium after he was physically and sexually abused by other pupils at his boarding school. The federal district court in Connecticut dismissed in observing that the state does not recognize such a cause of action.[10]

In California, a student who alleged that she had been sexually abused sought further review of the dismissal of her claim against a principal and the district where the principal formerly had been employed. An appellate court reversed in favor of the student.[11] The court stated that the district could be liable for the student's abuse under misrepresentation, fraud, and negligence since the district failed to disclose known or reasonably suspected acts of sexual molestation that the principal had committed.

In the first of three cases from New York, a school challenged the denial of its motion for summary judgment in a suit filed by a student who was injured when she struck her head on the bottom of the shallow end of its swimming pool. An appellate panel reversed and dismissed in

---

[8] P.L. v. Aubert, 545 N.W.2d 666 [108 Educ. L. Rep. 887] (Minn. 1996).
[9] Hernandez v. Renville Pub. Sch. Dist.No. 654, 542 N.W.2d 671 [106 Educ. L. Rep.. 886] (Minn. Ct. App. 1996).
[10] Hyun v. South Kent Sch., 166 F.R.D. 272 [110 Educ. L. Rep.. 705] (D. Conn. 1996).
[11] Randi W. v. Livingston Union Sch. Dist., 49 Cal. Rptr.2d 471 [106 Educ. L. Rep.. 772] (Cal. Ct. App. 1995).

favor of the school.[12] The court noted that the student's negligence was the sole cause of the accident as she was an experienced swimmer and diver who was familiar with the depth of the pool.

Following the sexual assault of her five-year-old daughter, a mother successfully sued a city and its board of education. On further review, an appellate court in New York affirmed.[13] The court determined that by allowing a kindergarten student to go to a bathroom unattended, the school did not act with prudence consistent with its responsibility under the doctrine of in loco parentis.

Parents sued a school alleging that a teacher failed to report that their daughter had been sexually abused by one of her relatives. An appellate court in New York reversed a verdict in favor of the school and reinstated the complaint.[14] Even though the court refused to recognize a common law duty to report abuse, it held that the teacher could be held liable if it were found that she breached her statutory duty to report child abuse.

In the first of two cases from Tennessee, the mother of a middle school student who was injured during a fight in the girl's locker room sought further review of the dismissal of her claim. An appellate court affirmed.[15] It reasoned that even if the physical education teacher acted negligently by allowing students to enter the locker room ahead of schedule, the injuries that the child sustained were not reasonably foreseeable. The court also contended that the principal's discretionary judgment in assigning one teacher to supervise both boys and girls was a judgment for which he could not be found negligent.

Parents unsuccessfully alleged negligent supervision and hiring after their children were sexually assaulted by a teacher. An appellate court in Tennessee affirmed that the school did not breach its duty to provide a safe environment by allowing the teacher to change the lock to his office without maintaining a duplicate key.[16] Further, the court declared that the school's alleged failure to supervise the teacher was not the proximate cause of the students' injuries.

---

[12] Aronson v. Horace Mann-Barnard Sch., 637 N.Y.S.2d 410 [106 EDUC. L. REP. 1281] (N.Y. App. Div. 1996).

[13] Garcia v. City of N.Y., 646 N.Y.S.2d 508 [112 EDUC. L. REP. 409] (N.Y. App. Div. 1996).

[14] Kimberly S.M. v. Bradford Cent. Sch., 649 N.Y.S.2d 588 [114 EDUC. L. REP. 284] (N.Y. App. Div. 1996).

[15] Chudasama v. Metropolitan Gov't of Nashville and Davidson County, 914 S.W.2d 922 [107 EDUC. L. REP. 347] (Tenn. Ct. App. 1996).

[16] Doe v. Coffee County Bd. of Educ., 925 S.W.2d 534 [111 EDUC. L. REP. 569] (Tenn. Ct. App. 1996).

A student was hurt when he slipped and fell while running laps in the school gym. Following the dismissal of the student's complaint in favor of the board of education, an appellate court in Illinois reversed and remanded for a determination of whether the gym could be used for recreational purposes.[17] However, the court also affirmed that the student failed to prove that the district willfully and wantonly contributed to his injury.

In the first of two cases from Ohio, the parents of an elementary school student sought further review of a grant of summary judgment in favor of the system after their daughter was injured when she fell from monkey bars during recess. An appellate court affirmed.[18] The court posited that the parents were unable to raise any genuine issues of negligence by the school system despite testimony that it was lightly raining during the recess.

The parents of a middle school student, who was assaulted by classmates after the teacher left the room to attend a faculty meeting, sought further review after a trial court granted the district's motion for summary judgment. On further review, an appellate court in Ohio affirmed.[19] The court found that the teacher's decision to leave the students alone was within the scope of her discretionary authority. In addition, the court pointed out that the students previously had worked on their own and had behaved responsibly.

An appellate court in Florida reversed in favor of a school when a mother filed suit after a teacher accidentally shut a door on her one-year-old son's finger.[20] Despite testimony that the teacher could have prevented the accident had she looked for the child, evidence indicated that the student came up behind the teacher. Moreover, the court acknowledged that there were no allegations that the teacher had ignored the child, allowed him to wander from his designated play area, or had neglected him in any way.

En Route to and from School

Passengers in a car sued a district to recover for injuries they sustained in an accident involving their vehicle and a school bus. An appellate court in Texas affirmed that since the bus driver was not acting as an employee of her school district at the time of the accident, the system

---

[17] Ozuk v. River Grove Bd. of Educ., 666 N.E.2d 687 [111 EDUC. L. REP. 1290] (Ill. App. Ct. 1996).
[18] Ratliff v. Oberlin City Sch., 669 N.E.2d 89 [111 EDUC. L. REP. 1342] (Ohio Ct. App. 1996).
[19] Marcum v. Talawanda City Sch., 670 N.E.2d 1067 [113 EDUC. L. REP. 401] (Ohio Ct. App. 1996).
[20] La Petite Academy v. Nassef *ex rel.* Kniffel, 674 So. 2d 181 [110 EDUC. L. REP. 497] (Fla. Dist. Ct. App. 1996).

was not liable.[21] The court maintained that the driver worked for the transportation department of the county schools, which involved a consortium of thirteen districts. The driver also worked as a teacher for the school system that owned the bus. Yet, in the face of conflicting evidence, the court contended that the jury could reasonably have concluded that the driver was not under the control and direction of her district while on her regular bus route.

The parents of a six-year-old student filed suit after their child crossed the street, dropped her belongings, and was struck by a school bus as she attempted to board it. An appellate court in Pennsylvania affirmed a grant of summary judgment in favor of the district.[22] The court offered that since the district had neither statutory nor common law duties with respect to an off-roadway loading zone, it could not be held accountable under state law.

In Illinois, a student who was sexually abused by a school bus driver sued the district and the company that employed the driver. Following a jury verdict that the defendants were not liable for negligent supervision and hiring, the student sought further review. An appellate court affirmed.[23] The court reasoned that the only thing the district and bus company could have known was that the driver had a tendency to be late and that there was neither a factual nor a logical relationship between this information and the attack on the student.

A child who was hit by a car as he stepped off of a school bus challenged a grant of summary judgment on behalf of the district. An appellate court in New York affirmed.[24] The court indicated that the district's obligation to provide bus stops did not extend beyond the location of the stop. At the same time, the court affirmed the denial of the bus company's motion to dismiss because there were material questions of fact as to whether the driver violated vehicle and traffic laws.

In a second case from New York, an appellate court affirmed the denial of a transportation company's motion for summary judgment after a student was assaulted while riding on a school bus.[25] The court reached

---

[21] White v. Liberty Eylau Sch. Dist., 920 S.W.2d 809 [109 EDUC. L. REP. 464] (Tex. Ct. App. 1996).

[22] Dunaway v. Southeastern Sch. Dist., 676 A.2d 1281 [110 EDUC. L. REP. 214 (Pa. Commw. Ct. 1996). *See also* Chainani v. Board of Educ. of the City of N.Y., 639 N.Y.S.2d 971 [108 EDUC. L. REP. 828] (N.Y. 1996) (holding that if a district contracts out for transportation, it cannot be held liable for injuries to students that occur between their homes and bus stops).

[23] Giraldi v. Community Consol. Sch. Dist. #62, 665 N.E.2d 332 [110 EDUC. L. REP. 269] (Ill. App. Ct. 1996).

[24] Womack v. Duvernay, 645 N.Y.S.2d 831 [111 EDUC. L. REP. 950 (N.Y. App. Div. 1996).

its decision based on the fact that the bus driver, who was the only competent adult on the bus at the time of the assault, had not yet been deposed.

In School Buildings and on School Grounds

A police officer was injured when he slipped and fell on an exterior stairway while responding to a burglar alarm at a school. After a trial court entered a judgment in favor of the district even though the jury ruled in favor of the officer, an appellate tribunal reversed. On further review, the Supreme Court of North Carolina affirmed.[26] The court stated that the district owed the officer the same duty of care as an invitee, namely to keep the property safe and to warn of hidden perils or unsafe conditions that could be ascertained by reasonable inspection. The court concluded that since the evidence raised a jury question that the district had constructive, if not actual, knowledge, but failed to correct the dangerous condition of the stairs, its negligence was the proximate cause of the officer's injuries.

In Pennsylvania, a woman unsuccessfully sued a school district for injuries that she sustained when she slipped and fell on a patch of ice in one of its parking areas. An appellate court affirmed.[27] The court observed that the real property exception to governmental immunity was inapplicable as the icy condition was not caused by improper design, construction, deterioration, or inherent defects of the real estate.

Landowners sued a board of education, architect, contractor, and city alleging that the improper siting and construction of a school caused flooding that damaged crops and farmland. After an intermediate appellate panel ruled in favor of the landowners, the defendants sought further review. The Supreme Court of New Jersey affirmed in noting that the continuing nuisance was one that could be physically removed or legally abated.[28] The court held that the claims against the city and board could be pursued to the extent that injuries were suffered within the relevant statute of limitation.

---

[25] Levy v. Board of Educ. of City of Yonkers, 648 N.Y.S.2d 141 [113 Educ. L. Rep. 884](N.Y. App. Div. 1996).

[26] Newton v. New Hanover County Bd. of Educ., 467 S.E.2d 58 [106 Educ. L. Rep. 1392] (N.C. 1996).

[27] Metkus v. Pennsbury Sch. Dist., 674 A.2d 355 [108 Educ. L. Rep. 797] (Pa. Commw. Ct. 1996). *See also* Leonard v. Fox Chapel Sch. Dist., 674 A.2d 767 [108 Educ. L. Rep. 1217] (Pa. Commw. Ct. 1996) (holding that a student on crutches who slipped on a accumulation of water was unable to establish a real property exception to governmental immunity).

[28] Russo Farms v. Vineland Bd. of Educ., 675 A.2d 1077 [109 Educ. L. Rep. 800] (N.J. 1996).

The federal trial court in Kansas granted a district's motion for summary judgment in an action by a vocational student who was injured after falling in a school welding area.[29] The court posited that the student had not given educators notice of a dangerous condition, and there was no evidence that there were concealed risks present. In addition, the court pointed out that the school had neither created nor maintained a dangerous condition that was an exception to the rule requiring proof that it was on notice.

Where a fifteen-year-old student was injured when he fell through a school's skylight while attempting to retrieve a handball, an appellate court in New York affirmed a grant of summary judgment in favor of the district.[30] The court found that since the student was aware of the skylight's location, the district did not have a duty to warn him about the readily observable condition.

The estate of a pedestrian challenged a ruling in favor of a school in a suit relating to injuries that the decedent suffered in a slip and fall on its sidewalk. An appellate court in New York reversed in favor of the estate.[31] The panel held that the trial court was obliged to consider whether the estate presented a prima facie case that there was sufficient credible evidence that the school had actual and constructive notice of the unsafe condition of the icy sidewalk.

Corporal Punishment

A teacher who was convicted of assault after paddling a fourth-grade student for failing to complete an in-class assignment sought further review. An appellate court in Kentucky reversed in favor of the teacher, since it judged that she had not used excessive force.[32] The court concluded that the teacher had not been wanton or reckless in her use of force and that the student was not at risk of death, physical injury, disfigurement, extreme pain, or mental distress.

---

[29] Kimes v. Unified Sch. Dist. No. 480, 934 F. Supp. 1275 [112 Educ. L. Rep. 252] (D. Kan. 1996).

[30] Kurshals v. Connetquot Cent. Sch. Dist., 643 N.Y.S.2d 622 [110 Educ. L. Rep. 342] (N.Y. App. Div. 1996).

[31] Keeton v. Cardinal O'Hara High Sch., 649 N.Y.S.2d 627 [114 Educ. L. Rep. 289] (N.Y. App. Div. 1996). For a case with similar facts and outcome, *see* Zima v. North Colonie Cent. Sch. Dist., 639 N.Y.S.2d 558 [108 Educ. L. Rep. 363] (N.Y. App. Div. 1996).

[32] Holbrook v. Commonwealth of Ky., 925 S.W.2d 191 [111 Educ. L. Rep. 557] (Ky. Ct. App. 1996).

Negligence Defenses

School districts, administrators, and/or teachers involved in negligence actions have a number of defenses available. These protections range from common law sovereign immunity to more affirmative defenses. The motivation behind common law immunity is to limit the flow of public money to private citizens because such payments detract from the educational functions of the schools. Affirmative defenses bar recovery by parties whose behavior in some way caused their injuries.

Immunity
Common Law (Governmental Immunity)

Insofar as school districts are agencies created to perform the governmental function of education, courts traditionally are reluctant to disturb their immunity. Injured parties had partial success in challenging this form of immunity in only the first two of the four reported cases.

After a woman on an escalator was injured by the jostling of a large group of improperly supervised students who were on a field trip, she unsuccessfully sued the city. An appellate court in Massachusetts agreed that the city was immune from the claim that the school district was negligent in deciding how many chaperones to send on the trip.[33] However, the court reversed in finding that it was a question of fact as to whether the chaperones negligently supervised the students.

The mother of a student who was injured when he was assaulted by a classmate challenged the dismissal of her action against the school district and teacher. An appellate court affirmed that administrators did not have a duty to create a campus discipline management plan.[34] At the same time, the court reversed with regard to the teacher, since there was a question of fact as to whether her failure to create a plan was the proximate cause of the student's injuries.

After a student committed suicide, her parents unsuccessfully filed a wrongful death action against the school district and a guidance counselor. An appellate court in Minnesota agreed that discretionary function immunity protected the district's failure to adopt a suicide prevention policy.[35] Further, the court was of the opinion that official immunity protected the counselor's decision on whether to inform the student's parents immediately about her statements contemplating suicide.

---

[33] Alake v. City of Boston, 666 N.E.2d 1022 [110 EDUC. L. REP. 794] (Mass. Ct. App. 1996).

[34] Downing v. Brown, 925 S.W.2d 316 [111 EDUC. L. REP. 560] (Tex. Ct. App. 1996).

[35] Killen v. Independent Sch. Dist. No. 706, 547 N.W.2d 113 [109 EDUC. L. REP. 387] (Minn. Ct. App. 1996).

Foreseeability was the primary issue in a case from Georgia where a student was attacked by a classmate who wielded a hammer. In fact, the injured student and his sister had been threatened by the assailant following an earlier altercation on their school bus. An appellate court upheld a grant of summary judgment on behalf of the district based on sovereign immunity.[36] The court also indicated that since the threats had not been reported to school officials, a finding of negligence was precluded because the attack was not reasonably foreseeable.

Statutory Immunity

As with common law immunity, injured parties had limited success against school districts insofar as they prevailed in only the first three of the eight reported decisions.

A system appealed a ruling in favor of a worker who brought a premises liability claim against his school. The worker alleged that the school did not properly control dust levels in a woodworking classroom even though it had actual and constructive notice of his problem. The Supreme Court of Rhode Island affirmed in favor of the teacher.[37] The court reasoned that since the school system knew that the worker had difficulty with the wood dust, it owed him a special duty. The court added that since the operation of the school was a governmental, rather than proprietary, function, damages were capped under the state's Tort Claims Act.

The Supreme Judicial Court of Maine agreed with a student who claimed that locking the doors to his high school constituted the operation of a public building within the exception to governmental immunity under the state Tort Claims Act.[38] As such, the court declared that a town was responsible for the injuries that the student sustained when he was assaulted by unauthorized visitors who allegedly entered through doors that were left unlocked in violation of the school's operating procedures.

Parents sought further review of the dismissal of their suit against a district to recover for injuries that their son received when he fell from a swing in a playground at school. An appellate court in Arizona reversed in favor of the parents when it rejected the district's assertion of immunity for not providing sufficient cushioning material under the swing set.[39] The court contended that once the district erected the playground, it was

---

[36] Rawls v. Bulloch County Sch. Dist., 477 S.E.2d 383 [113 EDUC. L. REP. 1328] (Ga. Ct. App. 1996).
[37] Chakuroff v. Boyle, 667 A.2d 1256 [105 EDUC. L. REP. 620] (R.I. 1995).
[38] Lynch v. Town of Kittery, 677 A.2d 524 [110 EDUC. L. REP. 720] (Me. 1996).
[39] Schabel v. Deer Valley Unified Sch., 920 P.2d 41 [111 EDUC. L. REP. 545 (Ariz. Ct. App. 1996).

obliged to implement its decision in a manner consistent with the duty of care that it owed to its students.

A district appealed a ruling in favor of the parents of a student who was injured during a scuffle in a school restroom. On further review, the Supreme Court of Utah reversed in favor of the district.[40] The court determined that the district was immune under an exception to the waiver of immunity for injuries arising from the assault.

Eight months after receiving a rubella vaccination at her high school, a student gave birth to a child with congenital rubella syndrome. Subsequently, the student alleged that the district negligently conducted an initial screening that failed to disclose her pregnancy. Reversing in favor of the district, an appellate court in New Jersey found that the school system was immune under a statute that protected public entities conducting examinations designed to diagnose diseases or physical or mental illness.[41]

The mother of a student who was fatally shot while at his high school unsuccessfully brought a wrongful death action against the city and board of education. An appellate court in Illinois affirmed that the mother failed to state a cause of action for premises liability since she was unable to allege that the board created or facilitated the condition that caused her son's death or that the board had actual or constructive knowledge of criminal conduct.[42] The court added that the board did not owe the deceased student a special duty because his mother had not alleged the board's awareness of a particular threat or specific danger.

A mother unsuccessfully filed suit against two teachers and their principal claiming negligent and excessive discipline for their failure to allow an injured first-grade student to go to the nurse. An appellate court in Texas affirmed a grant of summary judgment in favor of the educators.[43] According to the court, the educators were entitled to immunity since they exercised judgment and discretion within the scope of their employment.

After a woman injured her ankle while walking on the grounds of an elementary school and prevailed in her personal injury suit, a school board sought further review. An appellate court in North Carolina reversed.[44]

---

[40] Taylor v. Ogden City Sch. Dist., 927 P.2d 159 [114 EDUC. L. REP. 641] (Utah 1996).

[41] Kemp v. State of N.J., 670 A.2d 31 [106 EDUC. L. REP. 741] (N.J. Super. Ct. App. Div. 1996).

[42] Lawson v. City of Chicago, 662 N.E.2d 1377 [108 EDUC. L. REP. 814] (Ill. App. Ct. 1996).

[43] Davis v. Gonzales, 931 S.W.2d 15 [113 EDUC. L. REP. 984] (Tex. Ct. App. 1996).

[44] Hallman v. Charlotte-Mecklenburg Bd. of Educ., 477 S.E.2d 179 [113 EDUC. L. REP. 1321] (N.C. Ct. App. 1996).

The court maintained that the board did not waive statutory immunity by participating in a city risk management agreement where there was no insurance coverage for claims under $1,000,000.

Other Defenses

Comparative Negligence

Parents of a child who was injured on a school playground challenged a jury verdict that found the youngster fifty percent at fault. An appellate court in New York affirmed.[45] The court held that since testimony regarding proper supervision and inspection of the playground did not require special training or intelligence, the parents' proposed expert witness was properly excluded.

The mother and estate of two children who were killed when they drove their car into an intersection sought further review of a grant of summary judgment to the school district. An appellate court in Illinois reversed.[46] The court ruled that summary judgment was precluded where there were questions of fact as to whether a school bus contributed to the accident by improperly blocking the roadway.

In the first of two cases from Louisiana, a teenager and her mother alleged that a teacher/coach had enticed the girl into a homosexual relationship. They also claimed that the teacher/coach aided and abetted such a relationship between the girl and a school bus driver. On further review, an appellate court reversed a judgment that the girl was ten percent at fault because the relationships were consensual.[47] In relying on expert opinion that it is not possible for a child to give consent, the court concluded that the teacher/coach and bus driver were each fifty percent at fault.

After the mother of a six-year-old child who was rendered a paraplegic after falling from playground equipment during recess obtained a judgment in her favor, the defendants sought further review. An appellate court in Louisiana affirmed that the contractor and architects were equally at fault as they were solely responsible for the improper installation of the equipment.[48] Likewise, the court agreed that the board was also fifty percent at fault based on its failure to maintain the equipment in a safe manner.

---

[45] Fortunato v. Dover Union Free Sch. Dist., 638 N.Y.S.2d 727 [107 EDUC. L. REP. 930] (N.Y. App. Div. 1996).

[46] Watkins v. Schmitt, 665 N.E.2d 1379 [110 EDUC. L. REP. 307] (Ill. 1996).

[47] Landreneau v. Fruge, 676 So. 2d 701 [111 EDUC. L. REP. 582] (La. Ct. App. 1996). *See also* Clanton v. Gwinnett County Sch. Dist., 464 S.E.2d 918 [105 EDUC. L. REP. 1289] (Ga. Ct. App. 1995) (holding that the plaintiffs were not entitled to instruction that a child under six years of age is presumed incapable of contributory negligence).

[48] Cooper v. City of New Orleans, 680 So. 2d 1259 [113 EDUC. L. REP. 1009] (La. Ct. App. 1996).

Notice of Claim

The requirement that an injured party file a timely notice of claim is designed to provide a defendant with the opportunity to investigate a complaint while the facts surrounding it still are recent. Even so, courts granted injured parties extensions to file late notices in the first five of the ten reported cases.

A high school cheerleader who was injured at a game appealed the denial of her application to serve late notice of claim. The Supreme Court of New Hampshire reversed.[49] The court pointed out that the action commenced when the cheerleader's attorney prepared the writ with the intention of serving it on the school district.

Guardians who had been awarded permanent custody of, but had not adopted, the child who lived with them for nine years filed suit against the school district that owned the swimming pool in which she drowned. The child's natural mother moved to intervene as a third party plaintiff. The district argued that the guardians should not have been permitted to recover for the wrongful death of a ward because such an appointment terminates upon the death of the child. In addition, it claimed that the mother's suit should have been barred for failure to file a timely notice of claim. The Supreme Court of Utah agreed that the guardians could not sue since their personal rights did not continue after the child's death.[50] At the same time, the court noted that the notice of claim filed by the guardians was legally sufficient to support the mother's wrongful death action.

The first of three cases from New York granting requests to file late notices of claim involved a child who was injured while participating in a swimming program sponsored by a school district. An appellate court in New York affirmed in favor of the student.[51] The court acknowledged that since the school employees who were present when the child was injured repeatedly contacted his family to check on his recovery, the delay in filing did not cause the district undue prejudice.

Where a student received a gunshot wound while at his high school, an appellate court in New York upheld his request to file a late notice of claim.[52] The court found that the board of education was not prejudiced by filing a late claim because it acquired actual knowledge of the facts on the day of the shooting.

---

[49] Desaulnier v. Manchester Sch. Dist., 667 A.2d 1380 [105 Educ. L. Rep. 624] (N.H. 1995).

[50] Moreno v. Board of Educ. of the Jordan Sch. Dist., 926 P.2d 886 [114 Educ. L. Rep. 326] (Utah 1996).

[51] Cure v. City of Hudson Sch. Dist., 634 N.Y.S.2d 884 [105 Educ. L. Rep. 678] (N.Y. App. Div. 1995).

[52] Artis v. Board of Educ. of Amityville Union Free Sch. Dist., 638 N.Y.S.2d 99 [107 Educ. L. Rep. 251] (N. Y. App. Div. 1996).

A student who was injured between classes was promptly examined by the school nurse who called an ambulance and completed an accident report. Subsequently, the child's parents sought further review of the dismissal of their application to file a late notice of claim. An appellate court in New York reversed in favor of the student and her parents.[53] The court declared that the report should have alerted the school to the necessity of completing a thorough investigation of the incident.

The first case denying an application for a late notice of claim was an appeal by a high school student who was injured when a bus ran over his foot. The Supreme Court of Utah affirmed.[54] The court decreed that even though the student filed a timely notice of claim with the state's Attorney General, he failed to comply with the Governmental Immunity Act by not informing the school board of his suit.

Where a student was stabbed while in a rest room in his high school, his mother brought suit against the other pupil and his parent. However, the mother voluntarily dismissed her state court action and filed a suit in federal court while adding a civil rights claim to her petition. When the court dismissed both the federal cause of action and the supplemental state claim, a trial court denied the mother's request to serve a late notice of claim. On further review, the Supreme Court of Oklahoma affirmed.[55] It observed that neither state nor federal law allowed a new filing in state court following a voluntary dismissal where the statute of limitations had expired and the action being refiled had been dismissed in federal court.

The first of three cases from New York denying requests to file late notices of claim involved a student who was injured during a volleyball practice. After a trial court ruled that a student incident report prepared by a school nurse was sufficient, the district sought further review. An appellate court reversed.[56] The court found that since the report did not provide the district with the essential facts constituting the student's charge of negligence, she should not have been granted the extension to serve the late notice of claim.

Even though a student was sexually abused by a teacher in August 1992, her father did not file a notice of claim until March 1995. Following a meeting with the school psychologist and the teacher a month after the incident occurred, the student's father asked district employees not to question his daughter or to pursue the matter further. The father

---

[53] Bird v. Port Byron Cent. Sch. Dist., 647 N.Y.S.2d 627 [114 Educ. L. Rep. 250] (N.Y. App. Div. 1996).
[54] Shunk v. State of Utah, 924 P.2d 879 [113 Educ. L. Rep. 957] (Utah 1996).
[55] Pointer v. Western Heights Indep. Sch. Dist., 919 P.2d 5 [110 Educ. L. Rep. 1279] (Okla. 1996).
[56] Rusiecki v. Clarkstown Cent. Sch. Dist., 643 N.Y.S.2d 132 [110 Educ. L. Rep. 328] (N.Y. App. Div. 1996).

subsequently claimed he did not learn about the seriousness of the incident until May 1994, but did not offer a reasonable excuse for the delay in filing the claim. An appellate court upheld the denial of the claim.[57] The court reasoned that the delay would have seriously prejudiced the district's ability to defend itself against the claim that it improperly handled the allegation of sexual abuse.

A student was injured in a violent altercation with a peer as they were leaving school, but the three- and one-half-year delay in filing her claim was unrelated to her injury. As such, an appellate court in New York reversed a decision that permitted her to file a late notice of claim.[58] It stated that the principal's filing of an incident report did not sufficiently inform the district of the student's claim of negligent supervision.

Liability Insurance

The mother of an elementary school student who had brittle bones appealed a jury verdict in favor of a school district's insurer. The Supreme Court of Arkansas reversed and ordered a new trial.[59] The court found that the trial judge erred by not instructing the jury that the student qualified as an "eggshell plaintiff" who was susceptible to enhanced injury by virtue of his existing condition.

A district's general liability insurer appealed the judgment that it, rather than the company that provided its automobile policy, had primary coverage after a kindergarten student was injured as she stepped off a school bus. The Supreme Court of Michigan reversed in favor of the general liability insurer.[60] The court determined that since the child's injuries were a foreseeable consequence of the bus driver's negligence in dropping her off at the wrong stop, coverage should have been provided under the automobile liability policy.

In New Hampshire, a school district appealed a grant of summary judgment in favor of its errors and omissions insurer. The dispute arose over the district's coverage for claims of negligent hiring and supervision

---

[57] Bordan v. Mamaroneck Sch. Dist., 646 N.Y.S.2d 373 [111 EDUC. L. REP. 1325] (N.Y. App. Div. 1996). *See also* Blackowiak v. Kemp, 546 N.W.2d 1 [108 EDUC. L. REP. 899] (Minn. 1996) (holding that late notice of claim was impermissible where the alleged sexual abuse occurred twenty-two years earlier).

[58] Dunlea v. Mahopac Cent. Sch. Dist., 648 N.Y.S.2d 673 [113 EDUC. L. REP. 1273] (N.Y. App. Div. 1996).

[59] Primm v. United States Fidelity &. Guar. Ins., 922 S.W.2d 319 [110 EDUC. L. REP. 460] (Ark. 1996).

[60] Pacific Employers Ins. v. Michigan Mut. Ins., 549 N.W.2d 872 [110 EDUC. L. REP. 840] (Mich. 1996). *See also* Board of Educ. of Rockcastle County v. Kirby, 926 S.W.2d 455 [111 EDUC. L. REP. 1046] (Ky. 1996) (holding that immunity was waived to the extent of insurance coverage).

brought by parents and students against a teacher who plotted with her students and subsequently killed her husband. The First Circuit affirmed in favor of the insurer.[61] The court contended that the policy's assault and battery and bodily injury exclusions precluded coverage.

An errors and omissions insurer appealed a ruling that it had the duty to defend and indemnify a school district in Texas against claims arising out of a teacher's abuse of second-grade students. The Fifth Circuit reversed in favor of the insurer.[62] The court indicated that coverage was explicitly precluded by exclusions of claims which would not have existed "but for" the misconduct of the teacher. The court added that the policy did not cover liability under title IX since it was related to and dependent upon the teacher's criminal assault.

School districts unsuccessfully sought a declaratory judgment that their insurers were responsible for asbestos-related property damages. An appellate court in Illinois affirmed in favor of the insurers based on the failure of the districts to comply with the limitations provisions of their policies.[63] The court concluded that the doctrine of nullum tempus (time does not run against the government) was inapplicable to the notice and suit limitation provisions of insurance policies.

A kindergarten teacher challenged a decision of the New Jersey State Board of Education to deny his request for attorney's fees that he incurred in successfully defending himself against charges of sexual assault and endangering the welfare of children. An appellate court reversed in favor of the teacher.[64] According to the court, indemnification was appropriate since the charges arose out of the teacher's employment.

Where a teacher tried to have his homeowners' insurer defend and indemnify him against charges that he had sexual intercourse with a sixteen-year-old student, a federal trial court in Pennsylvania found that the coverage was void and unenforceable.[65] The court noted that the

[61] Winnacunnet v. National Union Fire Ins., 84 F.3d 32 [109 Educ. L. Rep. 607] (1st Cir. 1996).
[62] Canutillo Indep. Sch. Dist. v. National Union Fire Ins., 99 F.3d 695 [113 Educ. L. Rep. 1108] (5th Cir. 1996). *See also* Erie Ins. Exchange v. Claypoole, 673 A.2d. 348 [108 Educ. L. Rep. 302] (Pa. Super. Ct. 1996) (holding that polices did not provide coverage for a driver's sexual molestation of students).
[63] Evergreen Park Sch. Dist. No 124 v. Federal Ins. Co., 658 N.E.2d 1235 [105 Educ. L. Rep. 1140] (Ill. App. Ct. 1995). *See also* White Plains City Sch. Dist. Bd. of Educ. v. Merchants Mut. Ins., 639 N.Y.S.2d 431 [108 Educ. L. Rep. 356] (N.Y. App. Div. 1996) (holding that employee exclusions barred coverage for injury from alleged exposure to asbestos).
[64] Bower v. Board of Educ. of the City of East Orange, 670 A.2d 106 [106 Educ. L. Rep. 760] (N.J. Super. Ct. App. Div. 1996).
[65] Teti v. Huron Ins., 914 F. Supp. 1132 [107 Educ. L. Rep. 173] (E.D. Pa. 1996).

doctrine of inferred intent was inapplicable to the intentional injury exclusion since the student was legally capable of consent.

In Louisiana, a school district's insurer established that a policy's abuse or molestation exclusion precluded coverage for alleged negligence in connection with the rape of a kindergarten student. An appellate court affirmed that the intentional act exception did not apply.[66] The court offered that the exception operates only when an intentional tort is committed by the insured, not by a third party.

The insurer of a school district was successful in its action against its comprehensive general liability insurer. An appellate court in Indiana affirmed that personal injury coverage extended to the publication of or utterance of defamatory or disparaging material.[67] The court pointed out that the policy applied even though educators and board members intentionally, rather than negligently, made remarks about a teacher.

Employee Injuries

Injured school employees enjoyed at least partial success in the first four of the seven cases in this section. In the first of two actions from Ohio, a teacher's assistant sued a city school system and several administrators alleging that their intentional conduct caused her physical injury and emotional distress. She challenged the summary dismissal of her claim and an appellate court reversed.[68] The court found that since there were genuine issues of material fact as to whether the administrators had actual knowledge of how violent the student with a disability that the assistant worked with was and if there had been a substantial certainty that he might cause her an injury, summary judgment in favor of the board was inappropriate.

A librarian sought further review of her unsuccessful suit that alleged her school district knew that materials being used for construction work in her office were potentially toxic. An appellate court in Ohio reversed a grant of summary judgment that had been entered in favor of the district.[69] The court maintained that such a ruling was improper where

[66] Jones v. Doe, 673 So. 2d 1163 [109 EDUC. L. REP. 1411] (La. Ct. App. 1996). But *see* Vester v. Nash/Rocky Mount Bd. of Educ., 477 S.E.2d 246 [113 EDUC. L. REP. 1324] (N.C. Ct. App. 1996) (holding that the purchase of liability insurance did not waive a board's sovereign immunity against charges of negligent supervision of a school bus).
[67] Indiana Ins. v. North Vermillion Community Sch. Corp., 665 N.E.2d 630 [110 EDUC. L. REP. 362] (Ind. Ct. App. 1996).
[68] Ross v. Maumee City Sch., 658 N.E.2d 800 [105 EDUC. L. REP. 689] (Ohio Ct. App. 1996).
[69] Peaspanen v. Board of Educ. of Ashtabula Area City Sch. Dist., 669 N.E.2d 284 [111 EDUC. L. REP. 1349] (Ohio Ct. App. 1996).

there were material questions of fact as to what district officials actually knew about the materials in question.

In New York, a teacher and her husband brought a personal injury and loss of consortium action against a school board after she was struck in the eye by a ball. Following a judgment in favor of the teacher, the board sought further review. An appellate court affirmed that there was an adequate basis to find that the board did not have an appropriate supervision plan for 500 students participating in unrestricted, unsupervised, and uncontrolled free play during recess.[70] However, the court also reversed and ordered a new trial, stating that the amount of damages awarded to the teacher and her husband was excessive.

An injured employee prevailed in only the first of three cases from New York involving scaffolding. A worker who was hurt when he fell from a permanently affixed ladder while carrying a vacuum from one roof level to another sued his district. A trial court partially granted the worker's motion for summary judgment.[71] The court declared that the worker came within the protection of the scaffolding law since his actions were an integral part of the removal and replacement of the roof.

After a worker who fell while attaching plywood to a wall unsuccessfully sued his school district, an appellate court affirmed a ruling in favor of the district.[72] The court acknowledged that there was evidence that the worker was recalcitrant because he acted contrary to his supervisor's direct order and refused to use scaffolding.

An employee who was injured when the scaffolding he was working on collapsed sought further review of a ruling in favor of a board of education. An appellate panel affirmed.[73] The court observed that since the employee was replacing a light bulb, he could not base his negligence claims on the statutes relating to scaffolding or construction.

In Ohio, a board employee who injured his ankle in a school gymnasium had to have the lower portion of his leg amputated. The employee's estate unsuccessfully claimed that the chain of events caused him to miss a follow up appointment with his doctor and contributed to his death from lung cancer. An appellate court upheld a grant of summary

---

[70] Meyers v. City of N.Y., 646 N.Y.S.2d 685 [112 EDUC. L. REP. 414] (N.Y. App. Div. 1996).

[71] Shaver v. Kenmore Town of Tonawanda Union Free Sch. Dist., 644 N.Y.S.2d 885 [110 EDUC. L. REP. 1191] (N.Y. Sup. Ct. 1996).

[72] Jastrzebski v. North Shore Sch. Dist., 637 N.Y.S.2d 439 [106 EDUC. L. REP. 1283] (N.Y. App. Div. 1996).

[73] Bermel v. Board of Educ. of the City of N.Y., 647 N.Y.S.2d 548 [113 EDUC. L. REP. 359] (N.Y. App. Div. 1996).

judgment in favor of the board.[74] The court pointed out that the accident at school was a remote rather than a proximate cause of the employee's failure to make the follow-up visit to the doctor.

Workers' Compensation

School systems prevailed in all five of the cases involving the calculation or modification of workers' compensation benefits. A teacher's assistant appealed the Workers' Compensation Board's denial of her request for additional physical therapy treatments for an injury that she received at work. The Supreme Court of Alaska affirmed in favor of the Board.[75] The court decided that the Board properly limited the number of visits that the teaching assistant could make to a physical therapist since the service provider failed to file a timely treatment plan.

In Florida, a school board sought further review of a ruling that adjusted a staff member's workers' compensation award to take into account the concurrent wages that she earned from her son's dry cleaning business. An appellate court reversed in favor of the board.[76] The court found that the staff member could not include the outside income in the calculation of her average weekly wage because the business did not meet the definition of employment as she and her son were the only employees.

After a former teacher's aide was awarded temporary disability benefits due to an injury that she sustained while placing a wheelchair-bound student on a bus, a school board sought further review. An appellate court in Louisiana reversed.[77] The court remanded for a better determination of the cause of the disability and to consider whether the aide would be able to continue working if her duties were modified.

In Washington, a board challenged an award of temporary total disability benefits to a school bus driver. An appellate court reversed.[78] It determined that the state Board of Industrial Insurance Appeals erred in calculating the driver's wages as an intermittent worker and in attempting to treat her as a nonintermittent worker when computing disability benefits.

A woman challenged an order that permitted a school district to offset her widow's benefits against future workers' compensation death benefits.

---

[74] Kemerer v. Antwerp Bd. of Educ., 664 N.E.2d 1380 [109 EDUC. L. REP. 926] (Ohio Ct. App. 1995).
[75] Hale v. Anchorage Sch. Dist., 922 P.2d 268 [112 EDUC. L. REP. 461] (Alaska 1996).
[76] Putnam County Sch. Bd. v. DeBose, 667 So. 2d 447 [107 EDUC. L. REP. 406] (Fla. Dist. Ct. App. 1996).
[77] Perrodin v. St. Landry Parish Sch. Bd., 676 So. 2d 612 [111 EDUC. L. REP. 574] (La. Ct. App. 1996).
[78] School Dist. No. 401 Pierce County v. Minturn, 920 P.2d 601 [111 EDUC. L. REP. 973] (Wash. Ct. App. 1996).

An appellate court in Colorado affirmed.[79] The court reasoned that an administrative law judge acted within his discretion in permitting the offset.

School employees had either full or partial success in the first four of eight cases where they requested benefits. A teacher who was injured in a work-related traffic accident successfully made a claim for benefits. An appellate court in Louisiana affirmed that requiring the teacher to take sabbatical leave in lieu of compensation benefits violated the state's workers' compensations statutes.[80]

Workers' compensation claimants brought a section 1983 action against a school district and private insurers alleging that their due process rights were violated when their medical benefits were discontinued without prior notice. A federal trial court in Pennsylvania dismissed the action against the insurers on the basis that they are not private actors for the purposes of section 1983.[81] However, the court was of the opinion that issues of fact as to whether the district was a state actor precluded summary judgment in its favor.

An elementary school music instructor was reassigned to a position teaching social studies after his job was eliminated. The Workers' Compensation Board denied his request for stress-related disorder compensation. On further review, an appellate court in Oregon reversed in favor of the teacher.[82] The court held that the Board erred in failing to articulate a rational connection between the facts and its legal conclusion that the preparation associated with the teacher's social studies position was of a sort generally inherent in every working situation, thus concluding that his stress-related disorder was not compensable.

In a case from Louisiana with mixed results, a board disagreed with a ruling that granted an injured school bus driver's request for temporary total disability benefits. An appellate court partially reversed in favor of the board.[83] The court found that the board's reliance upon a doctor's report as a basis for terminating the driver's benefits was not so arbitrary and capricious as to be subject to penalties and attorney's fees. In addition, the court remanded for further consideration when it noted that the driver's decision to attend retraining classes did not affect her entitlement to supplemental benefits.

---

[79] Renz v. Larimer County Sch. Dist., 924 P.2d 1177 [113 EDUC. L. REP. 968] (Colo. Ct. App. 1996).]

[80] Hollingsworth v. East Baton Rouge Parish Sch. Bd., 666 So. 2d 376 [106 EDUC. L. REP. 444](La. Ct. App. 1995).

[81] Sullivan v. Barnett, 913 F. Supp. 895 [106 EDUC. L. REP. 1164] (E.D. Pa. 1996).

[82] Whitlock v. Klamath County Sch. Dist., 920 P.2d 175 [111 EDUC. L. REP. 552] (Or. Ct. App. 1996).

[83] Rochon v. Iberia Parish Sch. Bd., 673 So. 2d 239 [109 EDUC. L. REP. 1015] (La. Ct. App. 1996).

The first of four cases won by boards was filed by a teacher who broke his hip when he fell while returning from his car in the school parking lot. Reversing in favor of the board, an appellate court in Florida indicated that a Judge of Compensation Claims improperly applied the positional risk test rather than determining whether the teacher's job created an increased hazard of injury due to his preexisting osteoporosis.[84]

A teacher who was injured while intervening in a fight between students disputed the dismissal of his personal injury suit against the board of education. An appellate court in New York affirmed.[85] The court reasoned that the teacher's personal injury suit was barred by the state's Workers' Compensation Law because his claim related to an injury that he sustained while at work.

In the first of two cases from New Jersey, an appellate court reversed in favor of a board of education that had been sued by its former superintendent.[86] The court concluded that the superintendent's request for disability benefits was not supported by credible evidence that his heart and psychiatric conditions were significantly aggravated by the nature of his employment.

Where a teacher who received temporary disability benefits was awarded additional assistance during the summer recess period, the school system sought further review. An appellate court in New Jersey overturned the award on the basis that the teacher, who received her full annual salary, was injured in the course of her job and that her duties ended with the close of the school year.[87]

Defamation/Intentional Infliction of Emotional Distress

In the first of three cases from New York, an appellate court viewed a trustee's remarks that the transfer of two six-year-old students from one school to another without first contacting their mother was a cruel and inhumane act as personal opinion and rhetorical hyperbole rather than objective fact. As such, the court affirmed a grant of summary

---

[84] Hernando County Sch. Bd. v. Dokoupil, 667 So. 2d 275 [107 EDUC. L. REP. 393] (Fla. Dist. Ct. App. 1995).
[85] Scionti v. Board of Educ. of Middle Country Sch. Dist., 638 N.Y.S.2d 748 [107 EDUC. L. REP. 933] (N.Y. App. Div. 1996).
[86] Dietrich v. Toms River Bd. of Educ., 683 A.2d 212 [113 EDUC. L. REP. 833] (N.J. Super. Ct. App. Div. 1996).
[87] Outland v. Monmouth-Ocean Educ. Serv. Comm'n, 685 A.2d 68 [114 EDUC. L. REP. 552] (N.J. Super. Ct. App. Div. 1996).

judgment in an action by the principal of the school that the children attended.[88]

Similarly, a school board employee unsuccessfully alleged that she was defamed by the contents of a letter that an interviewer sent to her supervisor. An appellate panel agreed.[89] The court observed that the claim was not actionable since the interviewer's statements about the employee's inappropriate behavior while on the job interview were opinions, not facts.

Conversely, an appellate court in New York refused to dismiss a defamation action that a teacher brought against a school district and one of its board members. The court agreed that the board member's statement that the teacher had struck a student was reasonably susceptible of a defamatory connotation.[90]

School board trustees sued a superintendent for slander and defamation after the superintendent claimed that they authorized him to procure a credit card in the district's name during his tenure on the job. Based on a sworn affidavit, the superintendent asserted immunity on the basis that he made the statement in the course of his job. After a trial court denied the superintendent's motion for summary judgment, an appellate tribunal in Texas affirmed.[91] The court viewed the affidavit as a conclusory and self-serving statement that did not conclusively establish whether the superintendent's statements were made within the scope of his employment.

A treasurer sued his former school district for defamation and intentional infliction of emotional distress based on a remark by the superintendent concerning an alleged error in his budget. An appellate court in Ohio affirmed a grant of summary judgment in favor of the district.[92] The court held the treasurer failed to demonstrate that the remark was made with a high degree of awareness of its probable falsity so as to show actual malice.

In Texas, a vice principal sued teachers and their state association for defamation and negligent infliction of emotional distress over remarks that they made about her in a grievance hearing before the school board. After a trial court granted summary judgment in favor of the teachers and their association, the administrator requested further review. An

---

[88] Albano v. Sylvester, 635 N.Y.S.2d 55 [105 EDUC. L. REP. 687] (N.Y. App. Div. 1995).

[89] Morrison v. Poullet, 643 N.Y.S.2d 185 [110 EDUC. L. REP. 331] (N.Y. App. Div. 1996).

[90] McCormack v. Port Washington Union Free Sch. Dist., 638 N.Y.S.2d 488 [107 EDUC. L. REP. 924] (N.Y. App. Div. 1996).

[91] Gallegos v. Escalon, 918 S.W.2d 62 [108 EDUC. L. REP. 452] (Tex. Ct. App. 1996).

[92] Lakota Local Sch. Dist. v. Brickner, 671 N.E.2d 578 [113 EDUC. L. REP. 1277] (Ohio Ct. App. 1996).

appellate panel affirmed.[93] The court pointed out that since the grievance hearing was quasi-judicial, the witnesses were entitled to absolute immunity.

Constitutional Torts

As has been the trend in recent years, there were a significant number of sexual abuse actions initiated on behalf of students. In fact, ten of the twenty-one cases in this section involve sexual abuse or misconduct by school personnel while an additional five concern sexual harassment. The remaining six decisions address a variety of civil rights claims.

Student Initiated Cases

Students prevailed in whole or in part in the first four of the ten cases litigating sexual misconduct. Administrators in Texas appealed the denial of their motion to dismiss a section 1983 claim where a thirteen-year-old student was raped by a school custodian. The Fifth Circuit affirmed.[94] It ruled that the section 1983 claim was appropriate based on allegations of the district's inadequate hiring policies and its failure to investigate or take action on reports that staff members were sexually abusing children. According to the court, the educators violated the student's right to bodily integrity by instituting a process that placed her in harm's way.

In Massachusetts, a former student brought civil rights charges against a teacher stemming from sexual abuse that had taken place more than twenty years earlier. The federal district court deemed the federal cause of action timely on the basis that discovery rules under section 1983 claims accrue when an injured party knows or has reason to know of the harm.[95] Yet, the court stated that school officials were not liable under either the state Civil Rights Act or Tort Claims Act because there was no evidence that the officials improperly supervised the teacher, particularly since most of the sexual contact took place off school property.

Parents brought a civil rights action against a district, instructor, and school counselor alleging that their son was a victim of a criminal sexual assault by an elementary school teacher. The federal district court in Nevada partially granted the defendants' motion for summary judgment.[96] The court found that there was no evidence either that the school counselor

---

[93] Hernandez v. Hayes, 931 S.W.2d 648 [113 Educ. L. Rep. 1343] (Tex. Ct. App. 1996).

[94] John Doe v. Hillsboro Indep. Sch. Dist., 81 F.3d 1395 [108 Educ L. Rep. 1088] (5th Cir. 1996).

[95] Armstrong v. Lamy, 938 F. Supp. 1018 [113 Educ. L. Rep. 641] (D. Mass. 1996).

[96] Knackert *ex. rel.* Doe v. Estes, 926 F. Supp. 979 [110 Educ. L. Rep. 171] (D. Nev. 1996).

refused to terminate the teacher's sexual predations or that there was a policy in effect repudiating the student's rights. However, the court rejected the district's motion to dismiss since there was a legitimate question as to whether it had developed a policy for which it could be held accountable.

A principal, superintendent, and school board in Missouri unsuccessfully sought summary judgment after a sixteen-year-old student accused her teacher of sexual misconduct. When the teacher reached a settlement with the student, all of the claims against him were dropped. Other than a state law negligence charge against a board member, a federal trial court denied the motions to dismiss. The court held that the board was subject to strict liability under title IX for the teacher's intentional act of sexual misconduct.[97] The court also permitted the section 1983 claim to proceed under the theory that the board had implied notice that its failure to educate teachers about the need to safeguard the constitutional rights of students to be free from sexual abuse and other violations of bodily integrity would be likely to result in its liability.

Parents in Rhode Island appealed the dismissal of their section 1983 and state tort claims derived from reports of possible abuse of their child that were filed by a teacher and a crisis center. The First Circuit agreed that school officials did not violate the Fourth Amendment prohibition against unreasonable seizure after one child was transported to another building so that siblings could be interviewed together.[98] The court added that since there was no evidence that the teacher or crisis center acted with malice in filing the reports of abuse, they were entitled to immunity under state law.

In Texas, a school district appealed a jury verdict in favor of parents whose daughter was sexually abused by her teacher. The Fifth Circuit reversed in favor of the district.[99] The court ruled that since title IX was enacted pursuant to Congress' spending clause power, the law did not warn that districts could be strictly liable for such conduct.

Fourteen years after a school district allegedly covered-up allegations of sexual misconduct by a music teacher, he assaulted another student in a neighboring system where he worked. The child and his parents brought a section 1983 action against the teacher and both school districts. A federal trial court in Pennsylvania granted the defendants' motions for

---

[97] Bolon v. Rolla Pub. Sch., 917 F. Supp. 1423 [108 Educ. L. Rep. 101] (E.D. Mo. 1996).

[98] Wojcik v. Town of N. Smithfield, 76 F.3d 1 [108 Educ. L. Rep. 1065] (1st Cir. 1996).

[99] Canutillo Indep. Sch. Dist. v. Leija, 101 F.3d 393 [114 Educ. L. Rep. 439] (5th Cir. 1996.).

summary judgment.[100] The court found not only that the alleged cover-up did not amount to "but for" causation under section 1983, but also that the termination procedures followed by the first district, even if constitutionally inadequate, did not encourage the teacher's further abuse of children.

The mother of a child who had been sexually molested by a teacher unsuccessfully filed a section 1983 action against the teacher, school district, and its officials.[101] A federal trial court in Texas explained that even though the teacher had been employed by the district at the time of the assaults, the student's withdrawal from school five months before they took place precluded its responsibility. Moreover, the court observed that even if the state-created danger theory of liability had been accepted, it was inapplicable since the teacher committed the molestation in the student's home.

Parents of an eight-year-old child who was sexually molested while participating in a swimming program sponsored by a school board challenged the dismissal of their section 1983 action against the system and the coach who allegedly touched their daughter. An appellate court in New Jersey affirmed that while the student's right to personal body integrity had been violated, the board was not liable because there was no evidence that it acted with deliberate indifference that led to the violation of her right.[102]

In Michigan, parents brought a section 1983 suit against a gym teacher in an elementary school for allegedly exposing himself to their children. The parents claimed a deprivation of their liberty interest in the creation and maintenance of the parent-child relationship arising out of the teacher's behavior. A federal district court granted the teacher's motion to dismiss.[103] The court was of the opinion that the parents failed to state a claim for such a deprivation because they did not prove that governmental action was directed toward a protected aspect of the relationship and that any injury was not merely incidental.

Students had at least partial success in the first four of the five cases addressing sexual harassment. A former student and her parents sued a district and administrators for failing to prevent her from being sexually harassed while she was in high school. After the young woman informed

---

[100] Doe v. Methacton Sch. Dist., 914 F. Supp. 101 [107 EDUC. L. REP. 117] (E.D. Pa. 1996).

[101] Becerra v. Asher, 921 F. Supp. 1538 [109 EDUC. L. REP. 135] (S.D. Tex. 1996).

[102] C.P. v. Piscataway Bd. of Educ., 681 A.2d 105 [112 EDUC. L. REP. 293] (N.J. Super. Ct. App. Div. 1996). *See* Does v. Covington County Sch. Bd. of Educ., 930 F. Supp. 554 [111 EDUC. L. REP. 265] (M.D. Ala. 1996) (holding that school officials were entitled to qualified immunity from student's section 1983 action).

[103] Divergilio v. Skiba, 919 F. Supp. 265 [108 EDUC. L. REP. 273] (E.D. Mich. 1996).

her parents of the names of students who damaged their home while attending a party there, they retaliated against her over a two-year period. Even though the girl and her parents reported the attacks regularly, administrators offered little protection. A federal trial court in Iowa concluded that the student could raise a title IX claim over the district's failure to act on the hostile sexual environment and whether she suffered physical harm due to their inability to prevent the physical assaults by peers.[104] Further, the court denied the defendants' motion for summary judgment on the negligent infliction of emotional distress claim but granted one for the charges of intentional infliction of emotional distress and violations of section 1983.

A high school student and his parents filed title IX and state charges against a district, principal, and teacher alleging that he was sexually harassed by his teacher. The relationship between the two did not involve sexual intercourse but lasted for six months and ended with the student's attempted suicide. A federal district court in Michigan dismissed negligence claims against the district and principal based on governmental immunity.[105]

In Georgia, a mother filed suit on behalf of her daughter who, over a six month period, was sexually harassed and abused by a classmate. The mother asserted that even though she reported that a male student fondled her daughter and directed offensive language at her while in school, administrators did not take corrective steps. After a federal district court dismissed the mother's claim, the Eleventh Circuit affirmed that educators did not violate the girl's due process and equal protection rights.[106] At the same time, the court added that the mother had established a valid title IX claim since the board knowingly permitted a hostile environment to be created by the classmate's sexual harassment of her daughter.

A student in Nebraska alleged that the hostile environment that existed in his high school allowed him to develop a homosexual relationship with one of his teachers. The federal trial court in Nebraska granted a motion for summary judgment in favor of the district, several administrators, and the teacher. On further review, the Eighth Circuit affirmed that the district and its officials were not liable under section 1983 as there was no pattern of unconstitutional acts by subordinates

---

[104] Burrow v. Postville Community Sch. Dist., 929 F. Supp. 1193 [110 EDUC. L. REP. 1102] (N.D. Iowa 1996).

[105] Nelson v. Almont Community Sch., 931 F. Supp. 1345 [111 EDUC. L. REP. 799] (E.D. Mich. 1996).

[106] Davis v. Monroe County Bd. of Educ., 74 F.3d 1186 [106 EDUC. L. REP. 486] (11th Cir. 1996).

that showed deliberate indifference.[107] However, the court reversed on the title IX claim when it decided that there were genuine issues of material fact as to whether the student voluntarily participated in the sexual relationship with his teacher and whether the teacher's advances were unwelcome.

In Iowa, a federal trial court granted a school district's motion for judgment as a matter of law after a jury returned a verdict in favor of a student who had been raped by a former boyfriend.[108] The student had requested damages under title IX for peer-to-peer sexual harassment. The court acknowledged that the district had made efforts to separate the students by sending the boy to an alternative school and made special arrangements for the girl's instruction. The court reasoned that the student and her parents failed to establish the district's intentional inability to take proper remedial steps.

School districts prevailed in all but the first of the six remaining cases in this section. A principal appealed the denial of his motion for qualified immunity in a section 1983 suit where three students in Idaho alleged that he used excessive force in slapping, punching, and choking them and throwing one of them head first into a locker. On one occasion the police even charged the principal with assault and battery for his use of excessive force. The Ninth Circuit affirmed.[109] The court offered that the students had a constitutional right to be free from the use of force and that a reasonable principal would not have engaged in such conduct.

Two high school students in Georgia brought section 1983 actions against the district after they were suspended from school in separate incidents. The Eleventh Circuit affirmed in favor of the board and administrators.[110] The court indicated that the student who was suspended for fighting, screaming obscenities, and refusing to cooperate with and assaulting administrators had been provided with sufficient procedural due process under the Fourteenth Amendment. Turning to the second student, who was excluded for possessing a look-alike illegal substance, the court

---

[107] Kinman v. Omaha Pub. Sch. Dist., 94 F.3d 463 [112 EDUC. L. REP. 583] (8th Cir. 1996). *See also* Shepard v. Kemp, 912 F. Supp. 120 [106 EDUC. L. REP. 689] (M.D. Pa. 1995) and Larson v. Miller, 76 F.3d 1446 [107 EDUC. L. REP. 84] (8th Cir. 1996) for cases holding that there was not a pattern of unconstitutional behavior under section 1983.

[108] Wright v. Mason City Community Sch. Dist., 940 F. Supp. 1412 [113 EDUC. L. REP. 1182] (N.D. Iowa 1996). *See also* Garza v. Galena Park Indep. Sch. Dist., 914 F. Supp. 1437 [107 EDUC. L. REP. 193] (S.D. Tex. 1994) and Rowinsky v. Bryan Indep. Sch. Dist., 80 F.3d 1006 [108 EDUC. L. REP. 502] (5th Cir. 1996) (denying section 1983 and Title IX claims).

[109] P.B. v. Koch, 96 F.3d 1298 [112 EDUC. L. REP. 687] (9th Cir. 1996).

[110] C.B. v. Driscoll, 82 F.3d 383 [108 EDUC. L. REP. 1126] (11th Cir. 1996).

ruled not only that he had been afforded due process but also that his rights were not violated when he was transferred to an alternative school.

Parents and a student in Texas sued a band director, school district, and others for emotional distress. The plaintiffs claimed that the educators violated his rights under the First and Fourteenth Amendments to be free from emotional harassment, punishment absent personal guilt, and retaliation for exercising free speech. After a federal district court granted the defendants' motion to dismiss, the parents and student appealed. The Fifth Circuit affirmed that the case had been dismissed properly because it was frivolous.[111]

A student who misbehaved while on a tour of a detention center as part of a field trip was placed in a holding cell for seven minutes. The student subsequently asserted that school and jail officials violated her federal and state constitutional rights. A federal district court in North Carolina dismissed.[112] The court pointed out that the detention was a de minimis deprivation of the student's liberty and violated neither her procedural nor substantive due process rights. The court reiterated that the Eighth Amendment's prohibition of cruel and unusual punishment did not apply to the disciplining of students. Finally, the court stated that the student failed to provide sufficient evidence to support her claims of negligent and intentional infliction of emotional distress.

In Pennsylvania, a student unsuccessfully filed federal civil rights and state law claims against a teacher who attempted to discipline him by grabbing his arm and pulling him across a desk. A federal district court granted the teacher's motion for summary judgment on the civil rights charge when it found that the punishment did not rise to the level of a constitutional claim because it would have had to involve more than an ordinary tort.[113] The court dismissed the state law claims without prejudice.

A high school student challenged his ten-day suspension for leaving class without permission. The student maintained that he was not allowed to go to the restroom even though he was suffering from diarrhea. The teacher responded that the child simply misbehaved. An appellate court in Alabama affirmed a grant of summary judgment in favor of the educators.[114] The court ruled that the teacher and principal were immune

[111] Shinn v. College Station Indep. Sch. Dist., 96 F.3d 783 [112 EDUC. L. REP. 646] (5th Cir. 1996).
[112] Harris v. County of Forsyth, 921 F. Supp. 325 [108 EDUC. L. REP. 1139] (M.D.N.C. 1996).
[113] Jones v. Witinski, 931 F. Supp. 364 [111 EDUC. L. REP. 775] (M.D. Pa. 1996).
[114] Boyett v. Tomberlin, 678 So. 2d 124 [112 EDUC. L. REP. 547] (Ala. Civ. Ct. App. 1995).

from state tort claims because they acted within their discretionary authority. The court added that the student failed to show that he was deprived of constitutional rights or that the educators demonstrated bad faith or deliberate indifference to his needs.

Conclusion

A review of this year's litigation reveals the variety of unique factual settings from which tort actions arise. While school districts generally continue to be shielded from liability by virtue of common law and statutory immunity, injured parties are increasingly successful in notice of claim and workers' compensation actions. The disturbing trend toward cases involving sexual abuse and assault continues — these cases make up roughly twenty percent of all of the torts cases reported in this chapter.

7
SPORTS

Linda A. Sharp

Introduction

This chapter includes cases in K-12 and higher education dealing with student-athletes and coaches as well as athletic directors, facilities, and associations. The chapter does not discuss litigation pertaining to the instruction of physical education.

Eligibility

This section reviews seventeen cases: three challenged longevity rules; one concerned age; five dealt with transfers; two related to disciplinary sanctions; two questioned a rule of the National Collegiate Athletic Association (NCAA) which set a salary cap for coaches; one addressed the classification of a parochial school for athletic competition; one concerned a rule that prohibited outside participation in a sport; one examined the discontinuance of a sport program; and one dealt with the procedures delineated in a student handbook for choosing cheerleaders.

Longevity

In Indiana, a star high school baseball player challenged a declaration that he was ineligible for his senior year because of an "eight-semester" rule. According to the rule, once students enter ninth-grade, they have a maximum of four fall and four spring semesters of athletic eligibility. The student was unable to complete high school within four years because he repeated ninth-grade due to poor academic performance stemming from depression and psychological problems. The athletic association denied the student's request for an extra year of eligibility pursuant to its hardship rule. After a trial court enjoined the association from enforcing the rule, it sought further review. An appellate court reversed.[1] The court held that the rule was constitutional because the association had not acted in an arbitrary or capricious manner in denying the student's request for an exception.

The first of two cases in higher education that dealt with the applicability of the five-year rule of the NCAA was brought by a football player in Louisiana who challenged the rule in federal district court. The court dismissed the claim on the basis that the NCAA is not a state actor. Returning to a state venue, lower courts enjoined the enforcement of the rule. The Supreme Court of Louisiana, however, reversed and vacated.[2] The court noted that the judiciary should not interfere with the internal affairs of a private association except when its actions are capricious, arbitrary, or unjustly discriminatory. The court concluded that since the player failed to show that the NCAA acted in such a manner, the injunction had to be vacated.

In a case from Florida, a student-athlete questioned the NCAA's declaration that he was ineligible under the five-year rule. The player's five-year time clock began in 1991 and he was red-shirted for that season. He participated in 1992, 1993, and 1994, but suffered a season-ending ankle injury in the first game of 1995. Under the five-year rule, 1995 should have been the player's final year. The NCAA rejected the student's petition to permit him to play for another season. After the student obtained a preliminary injunction, the NCAA sought further review. An appellate court reversed.[3] It stated that the judiciary may intervene in the internal affairs of a private association only in exceptional circumstances that were not present in the case at bar since the NCAA's procedures were both adequate and fair.

Age

After a nineteen-year-old student with Downs Syndrome was not permitted to join his school swimming team, an athletic conference allowed him to participate as a nonscoring exhibition swimmer. The federal trial court in Connecticut enjoined the application of the rule. On appeal, the Second Circuit dismissed the case as moot.[4] The court pointed

---

[1] Indiana High Sch. Athletic Ass'n v. Reyes, 659 N.E.2d 158 [105 Educ. L. Rep. 1200] (Ind. Ct. App. 1995).
[2] Jones v. National Collegiate Athletic Ass'n, 679 So. 2d 381 [112 Educ. L. Rep. 1112] (La. 1996).
[3] National Collegiate Athletic Ass'n v. Brinkworth, 680 So. 2d 1081 [113 Educ. L. Rep. 1004] (Fla. Dist. Ct. App. 1996).
[4] Dennin v. Connecticut Interscholastic Athletic Conference, 94 F.3d 96 [111 Educ. L. Rep. 1154] (2nd Cir. 1996).

out that the swimming season had been completed with the student as a participant and that the matter did not fall within the exception to the mootness doctrine as being capable of repetition, yet evading review.

Transfer

The first of five cases dealing with transfer rules to prevent or delay participation was filed by black high school athletes in Alabama. The pupils challenged a county board's policy that required student-athletes who switched schools under a Majority to Minority Transfer Program to forego a year of eligibility. The program, which was designed to help eliminate racial segregation, allowed students who lived in school attendance zones where their race was in the majority to transfer to one where their race was in the minority. The district adopted the eligibility policy because it was concerned that the program could be used to facilitate athletic recruiting to the detriment of Black schools. Even so, the students alleged that the policy violated title VI and their rights to equal protection. A federal district court ruled in favor of the board.[5] It found that the policy did not have a disproportionate adverse impact on Black students. In fact, the court contended that there was evidence suggesting a beneficial impact on Black students. The court further reasoned that even if the students had been able to show that the policy had a racially disproportionate adverse effect, the school system still would have prevailed. The court observed that the district established a legitimate justification for the policy since it attempted to prevent athletic recruiting and to help revitalize predominantly Black high schools.

A high school student enjoined the Pennsylvania Interscholastic Athletic Association (PIAA) from denying his request for eligibility to play basketball. The PIAA had invoked the rule that denied student-athletes the right to compete in a sport that they played at another school one year after transfer. On further review, an appellate court affirmed.[6] The court acknowledged that even though the student had no property right that would have entitled him to due process under the Fourteenth Amendment, the PIAA acted arbitrarily and capriciously since its procedure allowed a decision to be made simply on rumors and hearsay.

A student-athlete who was suspended for disciplinary reasons transferred to another high school. Subsequently, the state athletic association certified the student's eligibility since the transfer form, which

---

[5] Young v. Montgomery County Bd. of Educ., 922 F. Supp. 544 [109 EDUC. L. REP. 202] (M.D. Ala. 1996).
[6] Boyle v. Pennsylvania Interscholastic Athletic Ass'n, 676 A.2d 695 [109 EDUC. L. REP. 1310] (Pa. Commw. Ct. 1996).

was signed by both principals, asserted that his change of residence was bona fide. However, when the association ascertained that the change of residence was not bona fide, it declared the student ineligible. After the student enjoined the enforcement of the association's action, the Supreme Court of Kentucky dismissed the case as moot.[7] The court observed that once the baseball season was over, there was no question about the student's eligibility.

In the first of two cases relating to Indiana High School Athletic Association (IHSAA) transfer rules, a varsity swimmer challenged a transfer rule that prohibited him from joining the swimming team for one year after transferring from a private to a public school. The student changed schools for academic and financial reasons. An appellate court affirmed an injunction against the enforcement of the rule.[8] The court indicated that the rule was overbroad when applied to deny the student's eligibility to swim since he transferred for reasons unrelated to athletics.

In the second case, a high school volleyball player who transferred from a public to a parochial school after converting to Catholicism tried to enjoin the applicability of the transfer rule. A federal trial court denied injunctive relief.[9] The court noted that the ISHAA was a state actor and that the student had a protected interest, but that she was unable to demonstrate how the notice and hearing she received were inadequate under the Fourteenth Amendment. The court added that there was no evidence in the record that the transfer rule, which is neutral on its face, burdened her First Amendment free exercise rights.

Discipline

A high school wrestler who was disqualified for misbehavior in a match and barred from participating in the remainder of the tournament enjoined the PIAA from taking such an action. On further review, an appellate court in Pennsylvania dismissed the PIAA's action as moot.[10] The court rejected the PIAA's request to not declare the matter moot because it was convinced that the association failed to present a record that permitted meaningful review.

---

[7] Kentucky High Sch. Athletic Ass'n v. Runyon, 920 S.W.2d 525 [109 EDUC. L. REP. 462] (Ky. 1996).

[8] Indiana High Sch. Athletic Ass'n v. Carlberg, 661 N.E.2d 833 [107 EDUC. L. REP. 961] (Ind. Ct. App. 1996).

[9] Robbins v. Indiana High Sch. Athletic Ass'n, 941 F. Supp. 786 [113 EDUC. L. REP. 1240] (S.D. Ind. 1996).

[10] Pagnotta v. Pennsylvania Interscholastic Athletic Ass'n, 681 A.2d 235 [112 EDUC. L. REP. 289] (Pa. Commw. Ct. 1996).

In Illinois, a high school enjoined its athletic association from banning its wrestling team from a meet due to violations of one of its bylaws. The bylaw prohibited wrestling teams from participating in more than four meets exclusive of those sponsored by the association. On further review, an appellate panel dismissed the case as moot when it disagreed with the school's claim that the case should have been heard under the "public interest" exception to the mootness doctrine.[11] The court stated that there was simply no question of a public nature requiring its consideration.

Salary Cap for Coaches

Basketball coaches and universities prevailed in their challenge to a NCAA rule that set a salary cap for entry level positions. The action was based on antitrust grounds as the plaintiffs alleged that the rule violated the Sherman Act as a restraint of trade. The federal district court in Kansas granted summary judgment in favor of the coaches and universities when it found that the NCAA failed to establish that the rule enhanced competition or promoted a legitimate, competitive goal. Thereafter, the plaintiffs filed a motion for sanctions based on the NCAA's failure to answer interrogatories that were relevant to the question of relief. The court ordered the NCAA to comply with the discovery requests and awarded sanctions for not doing so in a timely manner.[12] The court reasoned that the NCAA was not excused from disclosing information on the basis that it lacked the legal authority to require its constituents to provide data since the NCAA helped create the situation by discouraging member schools from assisting in this endeavor.

In a companion case, men's baseball coaches with restricted earnings sought certification as a class in their antitrust action against the NCAA based on the salary cap rule. The court granted the motion of class certification for the injunctive and declaratory aspects of the claim but refused to do so for damages claims.[13]

Classifications of Parochial Schools

In New York, public and nonpublic high schools must meet different eligibility standards and classifications before joining athletic associations. Accordingly, a Catholic high school appealed a grant of summary judgment in favor of the state public athletic association. The school

---

[11] Mt. Carmel High Sch. v. Illinois High Sch. Ass'n, 664 N.E.2d 252 [109 EDUC. L. REP. 877] (Ill. App. Ct. 1996).
[12] Law v. National Collegiate Athletic Ass'n, 167 F.R.D. 464 [111 EDUC. L. REP. 822] (D. Kan. 1996).
[13] Schreiber v. National Collegiate Athletic Ass'n, 167 F.R.D. 169 [110 EDUC. L. REP. 710] (D. Kan. 1996).

argued that its exclusion would have violated its right to equal protection since the referendum that it faced before becoming eligible for membership did not apply to applicants from public schools. The Court of Appeals of New York affirmed a grant of summary judgment in favor of the association.[14] The court held that since the association had a rational basis for distinctions in membership requirements, its action was appropriate. The court stated that the membership qualifications were consistent with and furthered the association's identified purposes by reasonably assuring that member schools would have the opportunity to compete on a relatively level playing field.

Outside Participation

Fathers sued a high school activities association over its "anti-competitive camp rule" that prohibited interscholastic basketball players from attending competitive team camps in the summer or school-organized practices during the spring or summer. The fathers asserted that they had the right to send their sons to such summer camps to play with their teammates, receive instruction from their coaches, and otherwise have the freedom to decide what activities to engage in without being penalized by the association. The fathers also questioned the "three players to a squad," "outside team," and the "anti-clinic and private instruction" rules. After a trial court enjoined the enforcement of these rules, the association appealed. The Supreme Court of Kansas reversed.[15] The court noted that, contrary to the claims of the fathers, the rules were not the result of the unconstitutional delegation of legislative authority. In remanding, the panel directed the lower court to address whether the association lacked jurisdiction to regulate nonschool activities and if the rules were arbitrary, capricious, and unreasonable.

Discontinuance of Sport

Student-athletes challenged the state university's elimination of four varsity intercollegiate teams in an effort to achieve a more gender-equitable program. The athletes' primary contention was that the determination was not made in accord with proper university procedures since the intercollegiate athletic board, which made the recommendation to drop the sports, was improperly constituted. An appellate court in New

---

[14] Archbishop Walsh High Sch. v. Section VI of the N.Y. State Pub. High Sch. Athletic Ass'n, 643 N.Y.S.2d 928 [110 Educ. L. Rep. 350] (N.Y. 1996).
[15] Robinson v. Kansas State High Sch. Activities Ass'n, 917 P.2d 836 [110 Educ. L. Rep. 435] (Kan. 1996).

York affirmed the dismissal of the action.[16] The court held that since the board's role was only advisory to the university president, who made the final decision, its improper constitution did not affect the validity of the determination to drop the sports.

Student Handbook Procedures

In a case from Alabama, a cheerleader sued her high school and the board of education. The young woman alleged that the decision of the cheerleading squad's sponsor to choose the head cheerleaders herself rather than follow the procedures in the student handbook violated her rights to due process and equal protection. A federal district court granted the defendants' motion to dismiss.[17] In regard to the due process claim, the court stated that the student had no property interest where she had only a mere expectation of being chosen as a head cheerleader. Turning to the equal protection claim, the court reasoned that the student failed to demonstrate that she was treated differently than others who were similarly situated.

Equality of Programs

Gender

Female students brought a title IX class action suit seeking to force a state university to field fast pitch softball and soccer teams. A federal district court in Louisiana held that the university violated title IX by not providing a fast pitch softball team.[18] It chose not to join the majority of courts which have found numerical proportionality to be a "safe harbor." Under this theory, courts have held that as long as male and female athletes are represented in the same proportion as in the general student population, then a university has complied with the "opportunity" aspect of title IX. The court posited that there was no evidence to support the underlying assumption that interest and ability to participate in sports is equal between all men and women on campuses. Even so, the court ruled in favor of the women when it pointed out that the university did not present any credible evidence to establish what the interests and abilities of the student population are or have been. In contrast, the court acknowledged that the students presented credible evidence of their interest in and substantial

---

[16] Lichten v. State Univ. of N.Y. at Albany, 646 N.Y.S.2d 402 [111 Educ. L. Rep. 1333] (N.Y. App. Div. 1996).

[17] James v. Tallassee High Sch., 907 F. Supp. 364 [105 Educ. L. Rep. 559] (M.D. Ala. 1995).

[18] Pederson v. Louisiana State Univ., 912 F. Supp. 892 [106 Educ. L. Rep. 1060] (M.D. La. 1996).

ability to play softball. The court added that the women lacked standing to pursue the claim about the soccer team.

After obtaining a preliminary injunction, student-athletes in Rhode Island prevailed in a trial on the merits challenging a university's decision to change the women's gymnastics and volleyball teams from varsity to club status. The First Circuit affirmed in part and reversed in part.[19] The court viewed with suspicion the university's claim that its relative interests approach fully and effectively accommodated the concerns and abilities of the under-represented gender. The court responded that the university's assertion that females are less interested in participating in intercollegiate athletics than males ignores the fact that title IX was enacted to remedy discrimination resulting from stereotypical notions of women's pursuits and abilities. The court further indicated that the tremendous growth in women's participation in sports since the enactment of title IX disproved the university's argument that females are less interested in sports for reasons unrelated to lack of opportunity. Yet, even though the appellate tribunal found that the university violated title IX, it held that the district court erred in rejecting out-of-hand the alternative plan to comply with title IX by reducing the number of men's varsity teams. The court concluded that the university should have been given the opportunity to submit another plan in an attempt to comply with title IX.

A fifteen-year-old high school student was denied permission to try out for the wrestling team because of her gender even though she participated in the sport when she was in eighth-grade. Therefore, the student filed suit based on title IX and equal protection. The federal district court in Kansas granted the student's request for a preliminary injunction on the basis that she had shown the substantial likelihood of success on the merits of her equal protection claim.[20] The court observed that while safety is an important governmental objective, the district's policy of prohibiting females from wrestling was not related to this goal where it was unable to provide any evidence that young women were at a greater risk. Further, the court maintained that despite the district's interest in avoiding sexual harassment, forbidding females from wrestling was not substantially related to this goal. The court reasoned that since wrestling is an athletic, rather than a sexual, activity, there is no reason to suspect that girls who seek to join the team would be likely to mistake the contact which is inherent in the sport for sexual misconduct.

---

[19] Cohen v. Brown Univ., 101 F.3d 155 [114 Educ. L. Rep. 394] (1st Cir. 1996).
[20] Adams v. Baker, 919 F. Supp. 1496 [108 Educ. L. Rep. 637] (D. Kan. 1996).

Race

An African-American student unsuccessfully sued a state university and coach, alleging that he was subject to disparate treatment, including the loss of his scholarship and demotion from the gymnastics team, due to his race. A federal district court in Ohio dismissed the student's complaint.[21] The court held that the civil rights causes of action against the university and the coach in his official capacity were barred by the Eleventh Amendment.

Disability

A student in Illinois filed suit under the Rehabilitation Act when his university prevented him from playing intercollegiate basketball because he suffered from ventricular fibrillation. After a federal district court issued an order that allowed the student to play, the Seventh Circuit reversed in ruling, as a matter of law, that he was not disabled within the meaning of the Act.[22] The court stated that the student's frustration in not being able to achieve his goal of playing college basketball notwithstanding, the university's decision did not substantially limit his pursuit of an education since the Act does not guarantee an individual the exact experience that he may desire, just a fair one. The court added that the student was not "otherwise qualified" to play basketball. On this issue, the court was of the opinion that its place in cases where conflicting medical opinions exist is to make sure that the decision-maker has reasonably considered and relied upon sufficient evidence specific to the individual and the potential injury, not to determine on its own which evidence it believes is more persuasive. The court declined to say that the university's decision was correct, but emphasized that it was not illegal under the Rehabilitation Act.

Tort

In 1996, thirty-seven tort cases involved sports. The first eight dealt with intentional torts. Of the remaining negligence cases, twenty-six concerned participants and three dealt with spectators.

---

[21] Davis v. Kent State Univ., 928 F. Supp. 729 [110 EDUC. L. REP. 689] (N.D. Ohio 1996).
[22] Knapp v. Northwestern Univ., 101 F.3d 473 [114 EDUC. L. REP. 460] (7th Cir. 1996). For the proceedings in trial court, *see* 938 F. Supp. 508 [113 EDUC. L. REP. 269] (N.D. Ill. 1996), 942 F. Supp. 1191 [114 EDUC. L. REP. 169] (N.D. Ill. 1996).

Intentional

Assault and Battery

The first of two cases from Texas dealing with excessive force by coaches was filed on behalf of a fourteen-year-old junior high school student who alleged that his rights to equal protection and due process were violated. The incident began when two coaches called the student into an office to talk with him about improving his grades so that he could participate in high school sports. The student further claimed that the coaches threatened him with bodily harm and one of them placed a handgun against his head and threatened to kill him if he did not raise his grades. An appellate court affirmed the denial of the coaches' motion for summary judgment.[23] The court noted that since the coaches did not engage in paddling or other physical force typically associated with corporal punishment, their behavior raised a question of fact as to whether they used excessive force in disciplining the student. As such, the court agreed that the coaches failed to demonstrate that they were entitled to qualified immunity.

After a student-athlete brought a section 1983 claim against his coach and high school, the suit was removed to a federal district court that remanded back to a state venue. The student asserted that he had been restrained in a locker room against his will, that he was constantly berated by members of the athletic department, that he was disciplined differently from his teammates, and that he was harassed and intimidated. A trial court granted the district's, but not the coach's, motion for summary judgment. On further review, an appellate court in Texas affirmed.[24] According to the court, the coach was not entitled to immunity because there was a question of fact as to whether he acted within the scope of his employment.

In New York, a student unsuccessfully alleged that his university was vicariously liable for an assault by his karate instructor who struck him during a class when he refused to perform a reverse push-up because he thought that it was an unsafe activity. A court dismissed in acknowledging that even if the instructor were an employee, his acts were beyond the scope of his job.[25] The court decided that the university could not be vicariously liable.

A fifteen-year-old student and her parents filed section 1983 and state law claims against a high school principal and athletic director after

---

[23] Spacek v. Charles, 928 S.W.2d 88 [112 Educ. L. Rep. 525] (Tex. Ct. App. 1996).
[24] Newman v. Obersteller, 915 S.W.2d 198 [107 Educ. L. Rep. 352] (Tex. Ct. App. 1996).
[25] Forester v. State of N.Y., 645 N.Y.S.2d 971 [111 Educ. L. Rep. 956] (N.Y. Ct. Cl. 1996).

the student allegedly had a sexual affair with a coach. The student and her parents argued that, as the coach's supervisor, the principal owed a constitutional duty not to act with deliberate indifference toward the evidence of possible sexual molestation. They also charged that the educators failed to report the coach promptly to governmental authorities under Texas law. A federal trial court denied the defendants' motion for summary judgment, but the Fifth Circuit reversed in holding that they enjoyed qualified immunity.[26] Regarding the section 1983 claim, the court indicated that nothing in the record suggested that the principal had any inkling of the coach's propensity to approach young women. Turning to the state law claim, the court noted that there was no evidence to support the allegation that the athletic director was aware of any facts triggering his duty to report and that, even so, he did so promptly when the principal had actual cause to believe that abuse was taking place.

Three students and their parents in Tennessee filed a section 1983 suit action against a high school soccer coach, principal, board of education, and superintendent claiming that the students had been sexually harassed and physically abused. The Sixth Circuit affirmed the dismissal of most of the plaintiffs' claims but remanded on the title IX charge for an additional hearing.[27] It agreed that a single slap did not violate a student's substantive due process rights. The court added that the other defendants were not liable under section 1983 for the coach's constitutional torts.

Defamation

A women's college basketball coach appealed a grant of summary judgment in favor of the publishers of a pre-season publication where she filed a defamation suit based on an author's comment that she "usually finds a way to screw things up." The Circuit Court for the District of Columbia affirmed.[28] The court held that the statements were not actionable since the coach was unable to show that they were objectively verifiable and false. The court added that ambiguity in the facts surrounding the coach's performance was fatal to her claim.

In California, a former university basketball coach alleged that statements an administrator made about him after he was fired were defamatory. The complaint charged that the vice chancellor said that the father of one of the team's star players felt that the coach put so much

---

[26] John Doe v. Rains County Indep. Sch. Dist., 76 F.3d 666 [107 EDUC. L. REP. 44] (5th Cir. 1996).
[27] Lillard v. Shelby County Bd. of Educ., 76 F.3d 716 [107 EDUC. L. REP. 49] (6th Cir. 1996).
[28] Washington v. Smith, 80 F.3d 555 [108 EDUC. L. REP. 499] (D.C. Cir. 1996).

pressure on his son that he became physically ill. In addition, the athletic director told the media that the players were beaten down and in trouble psychologically. An appellate panel ruled that the trial court was correct in sustaining a demurrer to the complaint since the comments were not actionable factual assertions.[29] Turning to the athletic director's statement, the court posited that the coach's admissions that he was a strict disciplinarian who exhibited emotional outbursts in which he leveled sharp criticisms at the players established the defense of truth.

Hazing

A high school football player in Utah was hazed by four teammates who taped him to a towel rack in the shower area and brought a young woman he had dated into the room. Subsequently, the federal district court dismissed the civil rights claims that the student filed against the coach, principal, and school district. The Tenth Circuit partially affirmed and partially reversed.[30] The court upheld the dismissal of the harassment claim under title IX on the ground that the student could not establish that the hostility was sexual in nature. However, the court reasoned that the student had stated a First Amendment claim since he alleged that he was denied the benefit of participating on the football team after he told his parents and school officials about the hazing. The court added that school officials were not entitled to a dismissal based on qualified immunity since the complaint stated a claim that they violated clearly established law.

Negligence
Participants

The first of three cases dealing with procedural matters was a wrongful death action brought against a school district by the guardians of a child who drowned in a pool owned by the district. The guardians had been awarded permanent custody of, but had not adopted, the child who lived with them for nine years. The child's natural mother moved to intervene as a third party plaintiff. The district argued that the guardians should not have been permitted to recover for the wrongful death of a ward because such an appointment terminates upon the demise of the child. Also, it responded that the mother's suit should have been barred for failure to file a timely notice of claim. The Supreme Court of Utah agreed that the guardians could not bring suit since none of their personal

---

[29] Campanelli v. Regents of Univ. of Cal., 51 Cal. Rptr.2d 891 [108 Educ. L. Rep. 801] (Cal. Ct. App. 1996).
[30] Seamons v. Snow, 84 F.3d 1226 [109 Educ. L. Rep. 1103] (10th Cir. 1996).

rights or responsibilities continued after the child's death.[31] However, the court concluded that the notice of claim filed by the guardians was legally sufficient to support the mother's wrongful death action.

A cheerleader appealed after her personal injury suit against a school district was dismissed on the basis that it was barred by the statute of limitations. The Supreme Court of New Hampshire reversed.[32] The court decided that the action was timely because it was considered to be commenced when the attorney for the student prepared a writ with the intention of having it served upon the district. The applicable rule, stated the court, is that there is a rebuttable presumption, which the district had not overcome, that the date of the writ is the true time when the action was brought.

A hockey player for a university in North Dakota commenced an action in Minnesota alleging that he was injured due to the negligence of his coaches. The athlete was hurt when he took part in a ten kilometer race as part of pre-season conditioning and suffered extensive internal damage due to dehydration. An appellate court affirmed the dismissal on jurisdictional grounds.[33] The court concluded that since the claims arose in North Dakota, its law applied and the Minnesota courts should not have exercised jurisdiction as a matter of comity.

In the only case dealing with immunity, a student who injured her foot in a physical education class when a volleyball standard separated from a pole appealed a ruling in favor of her professor and the university's safety officer. The Supreme Court of Wisconsin affirmed that both defendants were immune.[34] In regard to the professor, the court noted that a jury finding that certain conduct was negligent did not equate to a breach of a ministerial duty. As to the safety officer, the court maintained that the time, mode, and occasion for performing an investigation of an accident and the appropriate corrective action to be taken were totally within his judgment and discretion.

The first of five cases on the question of the duty of care was brought by a high school student who eventually lost his vision in an eye that was injured during his team's basketball practice. The student alleged that the district breached its duties to warn players of the dangers of basketball and to allow the players to wear protective gear such as goggles. The

---

[31] Moreno v. Board of Educ. of the Jordan Sch. Dist., 926 P.2d 886 [114 Educ. L. Rep. 326] (Utah 1996).

[32] Desaulnier v. Manchester Sch. Dist., 667 A.2d 1380 [105 Educ. L. Rep. 624] (N.H. 1995).

[33] Reed v. University of N.D., 543 N.W.2d 106 [106 Educ. L. Rep. 891] (Minn. Ct. App. 1996).

[34] Kimps v. Hill, 546 N.W.2d 151 [108 Educ. L. Rep. 930] (Wis. 1996).

Supreme Court of Illinois affirmed a jury verdict in favor of the district.[35] The court stated that a district has an obligation to provide all players with safety equipment that is necessary to protect them from reasonably foreseeable serious injury. Yet, the jury found that the district had not breached this duty. Therefore, reasoned the court, to impose a duty to warn the athletes would relieve the district of its obligation to purchase and provide such equipment and would unfairly place the burden of providing this gear upon the students.

After a university student was paralyzed in a sledding accident in which he hit a light pole in a parking lot at the bottom of a hill on campus, an appellate court pointed out that the institution had a duty to protect him from or warn him of the risk of injury. On remand, a trial court disregarded the directions of the appellate tribunal and held that the university did not owe the injured student a duty. On further review, an appellate panel again reversed on the basis that the lower court should not have revisited the question of duty, under the law of the case doctrine, and concluded that the student was entitled to damages. The Supreme Court of Louisiana reversed in holding that the university had no duty of care.[36] Using a duty-risk analysis, the court noted that the light pole was of great social utility as it served important safety interests by providing light to pedestrians and users of the parking lot. Further, it observed that the likelihood of the harm was minimal since the pole was obvious to those sledding on the hill and the risks of colliding with it were well-known. Consequently, the court was of the opinion that insofar as the condition was not unreasonably dangerous, the university had no duty to the injured student.

In another case from Louisiana, an injured football player sued the state high school association after he became a quadriplegic because of an improper and illegal tackle during a game. An appellate court decided that the association had no duty to regulate the conduct of all athletes in the games or to warn the player that he could have been injured.[37] The court posited that the association has no involvement in the selection, training, supervision, or payment of teachers, coaches, referees, or other officials. As to the duty to warn, the court reasoned that the association's function is to provide a framework for interscholastic competitions, not to ensure the safety of those who participate in various sports. Any duty

---

[35] Palmer v. Mt. Vernon Township High Sch., 662 N.E.2d 1260 [108 EDUC. L. REP. 808] (Ill. 1996).
[36] Pitre v. Louisiana Tech Univ., 673 So. 2d 585 [109 EDUC. L. REP. 1398] (La. 1996).
[37] Edwards v. Doug Ruedlinger, Inc., 669 So. 2d 541 [107 EDUC. L. REP. 1070] (La. Ct. App. 1996).

to warn of risks, stated the court, is better left to those who instruct and guide the players.

A third case from Louisiana dealt with a high school football coach's duty of care after a player with a history of neck injuries suffered a ruptured cervical disc when he was tackled. The athlete, a star who was heavily recruited, entered a state university on a football scholarship but had to end his playing career due to problems related to his high school injury. The player alleged negligence because the coach did not require him to wear a neck roll in the game in which he was injured, despite his history of neck problems. An appellate court affirmed a judgment in favor of the player in pointing out that the record supported the finding that the coach was eighty percent at fault.[38] The court indicated that a coach's reasonable duty to protect players from injury includes providing, and requiring, athletes to wear protective equipment. In light of evidence which showed that the coach had a very lax attitude toward safety, the court decided that he breached his duty of care by allowing the player to play without a neck roll.

In another football case, a player brought a negligence action against a physical therapy company that encouraged its employees to provide volunteer services to local high schools. One of the company's employees, a certified athletic trainer, treated the player for pain in his right foot, an injury that the trainer attributed to an ingrown toenail. However, when the condition worsened, the player followed the trainer's advice and consulted with his family physician. After suffering complications with his toe, the student sued for malpractice and negligent hiring or supervision. A trial court in Georgia, in rejecting the company's motion to dismiss, ruled that it breached a statutory duty by failing to have a physician on staff who was available to the trainers. On further review, an appellate court reversed in finding that the company did not breach its statutory duty.[39] However, the panel acknowledged that the statute relied upon was inapplicable to athletic trainers for a high school. In regard to the allegations of negligent hiring and supervision, the court stated that the claim had to be dismissed since the student failed to file the expert affidavit that is required in malpractice claims.

The first three of four cases from New York focused on the assumption of risk defense. A college baseball player who was hit in the eye while pitching batting practice for a high school team unsuccessfully sued the

---

[38] Harvey v. Ouachita Parish Sch. Bd., 674 So. 2d 372 [110 EDUC. L. REP. 507] (La. Ct. App. 1996).

[39] Georgia Physical Therapy, Inc. v. McCullough, 466 S.E.2d 635 [106 EDUC. L. REP. 1383] (Ga. Ct. App. 1996).

district for negligence. An appellate court affirmed.[40] It held that the plaintiff, an experienced player, was well aware of the risks of the game, including a ball hit directly at the pitcher. There was no evidence, concluded the court, that the risk of injury was concealed or unreasonably increased or that the coach directed the player to disregard a chance that he would not have otherwise assumed.

A football player who broke his leg while participating in full contact drills alleged that the coach was negligent in failing to have the athletes wear "pinnies" to distinguish between members of the offensive and defensive units. After a trial court ruled in favor of the student, an appellate panel in New York reversed and dismissed.[41] The court reasoned that regardless of whether pinnies are protective equipment, the coach's alleged failure to require the players to wear them in a practice drill did not expose the student to unassumed, concealed, or unreasonably increased risks. The court held that the player assumed the risk of injury since he knew that being tackled in a violent manner is an inherent risk of football.

A varsity swimmer who was injured while performing a racing start at the shallow end of a pool unsuccessfully alleged that his high school created a dangerous condition by permitting him to do so. The swimmer also claimed that the slope of the blocks exceeded the angle permitted by industry rules and regulations, thereby contributing substantially to his loss of balance that caused him to strike his head against the bottom of the pool. An appellate court in New York affirmed a grant of summary judgment in favor of the district.[42] The court stated that information in the record showed that the experienced swimmer voluntarily assumed, and was fully aware of, the risks inherent in diving off of the starting blocks into the shallow end of the pool. The court decided that even if the slope of the blocks exceeded regulations, they neither constituted a hidden danger nor contributed to the accident.

In the fourth case from New York, a school sought further review of a judgment in favor of one of its student-athletes, an experienced swimmer who was injured while diving in its swimming pool. The student, who was familiar with the depth of the water at the shallow end, had performed a number of racing dives without incident before she misexecuted one and struck her head on the bottom of the pool. An appellate court dismissed and granted summary judgment for the school when it held that the

---

[40] Esposito v. Carmel Cent. Sch. Dist., 640 N.Y.S.2d 606 [108 Educ. L. Rep. 852] (N.Y. App. Div. 1996).

[41] Hunt v. Skaneateles Cent. Sch. Dist., 643 N.Y.S.2d 252 [110 Educ. L. Rep. 336] (N.Y. App. Div. 1996).

[42] Clark v. Sachem Sch. Dist. at Holbrook, 641 N.Y.S.2d 890 [109 Educ. L. Rep. 338] (N.Y. App. Div. 1996).

230 / Yearbook of Education Law 1997

swimmer's negligence in performing the dive was the sole cause of her injury.[43] The court concluded that the record eliminated any legal cause of the swimmer's injuries other than her own negligence.

Three of the six cases on the question of supervision were set on school playgrounds. The parents of a student who was injured in a fall from the monkey bars in her elementary school's playground alleged that the children should not have been allowed on the equipment since it had just rained and the metal was slippery. The parents further stated that there was not enough mulch beneath the equipment to break a child's fall. An appellate court in Ohio affirmed a grant of summary judgment in favor of the school system.[44] The court declared that there is no general duty to watch over each child at all times and that educators are bound only by the common law duty to exercise care that is reasonably necessary to avoid foreseeable injuries.

After a seven-year-old girl was injured when her foot became caught in a merry-go-round on the school playground, a trial court entered judgment on a jury verdict that found the district and the child each fifty percent at fault. On further review, an appellate court in New York affirmed as it rejected the argument that the exclusion of expert testimony was improper.[45] The court reasoned that there was no need for professional or scientific knowledge or skill that was outside the range of ordinary training or intelligence.

A child who was enrolled in a preschool summer program was hurt in a fall from the monkey bars on a school playground. The preschoolers had been told not to use the monkey bars, but the child was injured when she climbed on them as she waited with other students before entering school. A trial court entered judgment for the school. On further review, an appellate court in Minnesota affirmed.[46] The court noted that the record did not contain any evidence that supervision probably would have prevented the accident. To the contrary, it acknowledged that the record indicated that the accident occurred despite the presence of two supervisors on the playground. The court concluded that the evidence showed that the accident resulted from the type of unexpected student act that teachers are not required to anticipate.

---

[43] Aronson v. Horace Mann-Barnard Sch., 637 N.Y.S.2d 410 [106 EDUC. L. REP. 1281] (N.Y. App. Div. 1996).
[44] Ratliff v. Oberlin City Sch., 669 N.E.2d 89 [111 EDUC. L. REP. 1342] (Ohio Ct. App. 1995).
[45] Fortunato v. Dover Union Free Sch. Dist., 638 N.Y.S.2d 727 [107 EDUC. L. REP. 930] (N.Y. App. Div. 1996).
[46] Hernandez v. Renville Pub. Sch. Dist. No. 654, 542 N.W.2d 671 [106 EDUC. L. REP. 886] (Minn. Ct. App. 1996).

The first of three cases from New York involved a student in special education who was injured while playing with classmates and two teachers in front of the school gymnasium. The student walked after a ball that rolled away and was injured when an unsecured wooden platform that had been resting against the gym fell over. The student, through his mother, alleged that inadequate supervision and negligence led to his injury. Following a jury verdict on behalf of the board of education, the mother sought further review. An appellate court reversed in favor of the mother.[47] Regarding the verdict, the court was of the opinion that the jury's finding that the board was not negligent was against the weight of the evidence. On the issue of inadequate supervision, the court decided that the claim should not have been dismissed since the record revealed that the mother had established a prima facie case of negligent supervision.

In the first of two cases dealing with cheerleaders, a high school student was injured when two teammates attempted to lift her into the air and she fell backwards. The cheerleader, who had performed the maneuver with the aid of a spotter, was denied such assistance because there was not enough help present. The student's suit against her school district claimed that the teacher in charge of the cheerleading squad failed to provide proper supervision by allowing her to perform without a spotter and that her injury would have been prevented if one had been present. An appellate court in New York affirmed the denial of the district's motion for summary judgment.[48] The court stated that there were issues of fact as to whether the teacher failed to provide proper supervision by permitting the cheerleader to perform without a spotter.

A cheerleader who was hurt when she fell on a gym floor sued her own district and the school system that hosted the basketball game. An appellate court in New York agreed that the host school was not liable for the young woman's injuries because it had no control over the cheerleading activities and it did not conceal or unreasonably increase the risks assumed by the student.[49] According to the court, summary judgment was properly denied where there was a question of fact as to whether the student's own coach provided proper supervision of the cheerleading activities.

The first of six cases on premises liability turned on whether a student was an invitee or a licensee. An eighth-grade student hurt his leg while participating in a two-week spring football clinic operated by varsity

---

[47] Farrukh v. Board of Educ. of the City of N.Y., 643 N.Y.S.2d 118 [110 Educ. L. Rep. 323] (N.Y. App. Div. 1996).

[48] Cody v. Massapequa Union Free Sch. Dist. No. 23, 642 N.Y.S.2d 329 [109 Educ. L. Rep. 893] (N.Y. App. Div. 1996).

[49] Sheehan v. Hicksville Union Free Sch. Dist., 645 N.Y.S.2d 181 [114 Educ. L. Rep. 248] (N.Y. App. Div. 1996).

coaches that served to familiarize future high school football players with the team. Although the clinics were designated as voluntary, and participants neither paid a fee to attend nor used school equipment, a player had no hope of making the team unless he attended. The student appealed a judgment that his suit was barred because he was a licensee who was unable to show that the district was willfully or wantonly negligent. The Supreme Court of Nebraska reversed when it found that the student was an invitee, not a licensee, who was injured when he was on campus for a school function.[50] The court added that the student had accepted an invitation to attend the clinic that was being conducted for the mutual advantage of both parties.

While competing in the state tournament, a high school tennis player was injured by a defect in the playing surface of a court owned by the town. An appellate court not only affirmed the dismissal but also held that imposing a supplemental duty of care on the secondary school association that ran the tournament would have effectively circumvented the provisions of the recreational use statute. The Supreme Court of Connecticut reversed.[51] After an extensive review of the statute's legislative history, the court ruled that allowing the municipality to have immunity under this law would have been anomalous because public entities essentially pass on the costs for recreational facilities or services to the citizenry in the form of taxes. The court concluded that since the municipality is not an owner within the meaning of the act, it was not entitled to immunity.

In a case from Louisiana, the mother of a six-year-old child who became a paraplegic after falling from playground equipment sued the board of education, contractor, architect, and manufacturer of equipment. The mother alleged that the height of the equipment was unsafe and that the surface below it was improper. After the mother settled with all of the defendants except the board, a trial court decided that the board was fifty percent liable. On further review, an appellate court affirmed.[52] It stated that there was no error in the allocation of fault.

In a Kansas case on the applicability of a recreational use statute, a student-athlete who was injured when he was hit by a discus as he crossed a playground during track practice sued the board of education. At the time of the student's injury, the track coach was working with the girls' relay team. When a trial court entered judgment on a verdict in favor of

---

[50] McIntosh v. Omaha Public Sch., 544 N.W.2d 502 [107 EDUC. L. REP. 995] (Neb. 1996).

[51] Conway v. Town of Wilton, 680 A.2d 242 [111 EDUC. L. REP. 1219] (Conn. 1996).

[52] Cooper v. City of New Orleans, 680 So. 2d 1259 [113 EDUC. L. REP. 1009] (La. Ct. App. 1996).

the student, the board sought further review. An appellate court reversed.[53] It ruled that the recreational use exception to the Tort Claims Act applied where the injury resulted from a school sponsored, supervised activity on a playground since it is a public recreational area. Under the statutory provisions, the court noted, an employee is not liable for any injury on public property used for recreation unless gross and wanton negligence can be shown. As such, the court maintained that even though the coach may have been at fault, the evidence did not support a judgment of gross or wanton negligence since there was no indication that he knew of the dangerous condition and was indifferent to the consequences.

The first of two cases from New York was filed by a baseball player who sued his district after he was injured when he tripped due to a concealed hole or drain while running after a fly ball in the outfield behind his junior high school. At the time he was injured, the player was competing on district-owned property in a nonschool-sponsored competition. Both the student and district sued the team sponsor. After a trial court granted summary judgment for both the district and the sponsor, the sponsor sought further review. An appellate court affirmed in favor of the sponsor.[54] However, it added that the district was not entitled to such a ruling since there were genuine issues of material fact regarding the exact location of the accident and whether the risk was concealed.

A fifteen-year-old student who fell through the skylight of his junior high school when he climbed onto the roof to retrieve a ball unsuccessfully sued the district. An appellate court in New York affirmed a grant of summary judgment in favor of the district.[55] The court observed that a landowner does not have a duty to warn against a condition that is readily observable. The court reasoned that the skylight was neither defective nor an unobservable dangerous condition. The court concluded that the accident clearly happened because of the student's misuse of the skylight, an extraordinary occurrence that the district did not have to guard against.

One case dealt with injuries sustained by a former university football player during team practice. The student alleged that by requiring him to practice with the team despite his academic ineligibility, the board of regents and coach violated his rights under the Fourteenth Amendment, breached a contract with him, and were negligent. A federal district court in Missouri dismissed the section 1983 claim in which the student asserted that he had a protected liberty interest in refusing to practice football

---

[53] Lanning v. Anderson, 921 P.2d 813 [111 EDUC. L. REP. 1361] (Kan. Ct. App. 1996).

[54] Zayas v. Half Hollow Hills Sch. Dist., 641 N.Y.S.2d 701 [109 EDUC. L. REP. 329] (N.Y. App. Div. 1996).

[55] Kurshals v. Connequot Cent. Sch. Dist., 643 N.Y.S.2d 622 [110 EDUC. L. REP. 342] (N.Y. App. Div. 1996).

while he was academically ineligible.[56] It noted that the history of the due process clause did not support the student's claim. Further, the court declined to exercise supplemental jurisdiction over the state law claims.

In Ohio, an intercollegiate basketball player who was injured in a weight-lifting program claimed that a person who ran the university's program failed to spot the lift as he had promised. As such, the student alleged that a substantial weight fell on him and caused a pectoral muscle to rupture. After a trial court granted summary judgment in favor of the university and its employee, the student sought further review. An appellate court reversed and remanded.[57] Using the standard of recklessness, the court held that summary judgment was precluded where there was an issue of fact as to whether the supervisor had been reckless in failing to perform as a spotter after agreeing to do so.

Spectators

Liability by a public entity for the criminal act of a third party was at issue after a woman was injured by a ricocheting bullet as she left the public school where her daughter had competed in a cheerleading event. The woman alleged that the school district was not only negligent but also breached its duty by failing to provide sufficient security at the competition. An appellate court in the District of Columbia affirmed a grant of summary judgment in favor of the school system.[58] It ruled that where an injury is caused by the intervening act of a third party, foreseeability of the risk must be more precisely shown because of the extraordinary nature of the criminal conduct. The court decided that although there had been previous shootings in the vicinity of the school, such generic information by itself does not create a duty to protect against the use of firearms. It maintained that the woman was unable to show that the district should have anticipated the prospect of violent criminal conduct. The court offered that since the record was insufficient to establish that the criminal act was reasonably foreseeable, summary judgment in favor of the district was appropriate.

In the first of two cases from New York, a spectator who was hit by a baseball while attending a high school game alleged that her injuries were caused by the negligence of school personnel. The woman claimed that school employees failed to supervise the players properly during warm-up exercises and did not provide protection to spectators from balls

---

[56] Canada v. Thomas, 915 F. Supp. 145 [107 EDUC. L. REP. 209] (W.D. Mo. 1996).

[57] Sicard v. University of Dayton, 660 N.E.2d 1241 [106 EDUC. L. REP. 1305] (Ohio Ct. App. 1995).

[58] Bailey v. District of Columbia, 668 A.2d 817 [106 EDUC. L. REP. 215] (D.C. App. 1995).

thrown outside of the field of play. An appellate court affirmed a judgment against the spectator.[59] The court determined that the board of education met the duty of care imposed by law by screening the area of the field behind home plate and by having a large enough area to protect as many spectators as may reasonably have been expected to desire such seating. The court concluded that lack of supervision was not a proximate cause of the accident.

The mother of a child who participated in a swimming activity at a high school filed suit against the district and town that sponsored the program after she fell in the parking lot while accompanying her child to the pool. According to an appellate court in New York, the town was entitled to summary judgment because it was not responsible for maintaining the parking lot.[60]

Employment

Ten cases dealt with employment issues. Two involved adverse employment decisions; two concerned contract disputes; one dealt with collective bargaining; four examined discrimination; and one presented a First Amendment concern.

Adverse Employment Decisions
Refusal to Renew Coaching Contract
A teacher appealed the denial of his request for a writ of mandamus to compel a school board to issue him another supplemental contract as a girls' basketball coach. The Supreme Court of Ohio affirmed.[61] It noted that the teacher could not establish either a clear legal right to the supplemental contract or a corresponding legal duty on the part of the board to provide the same. The court indicated that even if it accepted the teacher's contention that the board did not comply with the proper statutory procedure in adopting the resolution not to offer him a contract, he still would not have been entitled to employment under a supplemental agreement.

Where a teacher who also served as a seventh-grade football coach for many years was reassigned away from his athletic duties without being given a reason for the change, he alleged that it was disciplinary

[59] Lynch v. Board of Educ. for Oceanside Sch. Dist., 640 N.Y.S.2d 142 [108 Educ. L. Rep. 845] (N.Y. App. Div. 1996).
[60] Lugo v. Town of Irondequoit, 649 N.Y.S.2d 277 [114 Educ. L. Rep. 273] (N.Y. App. Div. 1996).
[61] State *ex rel.* Savarese v. Buckeye Local Sch. Dist. Bd. of Educ., 660 N.E.2d 463 [106 Educ. L. Rep. 871] (Ohio 1996).

because he attended an unrelated school board meeting. The educator unsuccessfully asserted that his reassignment violated the State Teacher Fair Dismissal Act. On appeal, the Supreme Court of Arkansas affirmed a grant of summary judgment in favor of the district.[62] The court observed that the district was relieved of complying with the Act because the teacher had signed a superseding contract following the decision not to offer him a coaching position.

Contract Disputes

A former head football coach unsuccessfully brought suit for breach of contract, intentional interference with employment relations, and intentional infliction of emotional distress against a college, its administrators, and three players who sent a letter of complaint to the college's vice president. An appellate court in Pennsylvania affirmed a grant of summary judgment in favor of the defendants.[63] The court reasoned that there was no breach of contract because the coach was hired under consecutive one-year contracts and he was simply not offered another pact when the last one expired. It pointed out that the students' sharing their criticisms of the coach with administrators did not constitute intentional interference with an employment relationship. The court concluded that the coach did not demonstrate the outrageous conduct necessary to make out a prima facie case of intentional infliction of emotional distress.

A teacher-football coach alleged a breach of contract by the board of education after the superintendent hired him as head basketball coach at another high school. Based on this information, the coach quit his previous position and conducted a variety of fund-raising events for the team on his own time during the summer before the start of the season. Yet, after he completed two weeks of practice with the team, the teacher was notified that he was being replaced by the former basketball coach who had prevailed in his grievance against the board. A trial court granted the board's motion for judgment on the pleadings. On further review, the Supreme Court of Appeals of West Virginia affirmed in part and reversed in part.[64] The court posited that the coach could not prevail on a breach of contract claim because the board was required to follow the grievance decision. However, it remanded on the issue of whether the coach should

---

[62] McCaskill v. Fort Smith Pub. Sch., 921 S.W.2d 945 [109 Educ. L. Rep. 1392] (Ark. 1996).

[63] Small v. Juniata College, 682 A.2d 350 [112 Educ. L. Rep. 1006] (Pa. Super. Ct. 1996).

[64] Copley v. Mingo County Bd. of Educ., 466 S.E.2d 139 [106 Educ. L. Rep. 915] (W. Va. 1995).

be compensated for services he performed under the contract prior to learning about the grievance decision.

Collective Bargaining

After a teacher's stipendiary baseball coaching contract was not renewed, his union filed a grievance on his behalf. A trial court granted summary judgment in favor of the school committee when it agreed that such a contract was not subject to arbitration under the terms of the collective bargaining agreement between the parties. On appeal, the Supreme Judicial Court of Massachusetts affirmed.[65] It rejected the union's argument that although the initial decision to appoint a person to a coaching position was nonarbitrable, an incumbent was entitled to remain on the job subject to dismissal or nonrenewal only for just cause. The court reasoned that a just cause provision would have been contrary to legislative intent insofar as it would have rendered a coach capable of getting tenure.

Discrimination

Gender

A former female head coach of a women's softball team brought an action against the university alleging violations of the Equal Pay Act, title VII, section 1983, and state law. A federal district court in North Carolina granted the university's motion for summary judgment.[66] On the Equal Pay Act claim, the court noted that the coach failed to show that males who were paid more than her did substantially equal work under essentially the same conditions. The court further stated that the woman's qualifications were not comparable to her male peers in terms of background or experience. As to the title VII claim, it ruled that the woman was unable to make out a prima facie case where there was no genuine dispute of material fact as to whether her salary was determined by factors other than sex. The court added that the female coach failed to produce evidence from which a reasonable person could conclude that the university's stated reasons for the decision that she challenged were unworthy of credence and, as such, were a pretext for sex discrimination.

A male who formerly coached a women's basketball team alleged retaliatory discharge in violation of title IX, breach of contract, violations of his First Amendment rights, and wrongful discharge when he sued the

---

[65] School Comm. of Natick v. Education Ass'n of Natick, 666 N.E.2d 486 [110 Educ. L. Rep. 784] (Mass. 1996).

[66] Bartges v. University of N.C. at Charlotte, 908 F. Supp. 1312 [106 Educ. L. Rep. 124] (W.D.N.C. 1995).

college and its athletic director. The coach claimed that his contract was not renewed because he made several inquiries and complaints about the apparent inequities in how resources were allocated for the women's and men's teams. The federal district court in Kansas rejected the college's motion for summary judgment on the title IX charge when it held that the coach could maintain his retaliation claim.[67] However, the court granted the athletic director's motion for summary judgment on the title IX allegation as it pointed out that such a suit may only be brought against institutions, not individuals. Turning to the First Amendment claim, the court reasoned that since the coach's comments about gender inequity touched upon matters of public concern, he should have an opportunity to proceed with this allegation.

Civil Rights

An African-American who was an assistant men's basketball coach sued a state university and its white head coach alleging employment discrimination as well as violations of his First Amendment rights of free speech and association. More specifically, he claimed that he was mistreated for exercising his First Amendment rights to speech by advising players of their eligibility for financial assistance and association rights by having close, personal relationships with several members of the team. In addition, the coach argued that his contract was not renewed because of his race. A federal district court in Texas granted summary judgment in favor of the defendants and the Fifth Circuit affirmed.[68] The court agreed that there was an absence of evidence to support the coach's discrimination claim. On the First Amendment claim, the court was of the opinion that the coach's comments were not on matters of public concern for the purposes of speech and that the association claim, based on his social relationships with players, were not entitled to constitutional protection.

A former head basketball coach in California alleged that comments by university officials following his firing deprived him of his liberty interests without due process. He argued that his liberty interests were violated because the derogatory comments made about him at the time of the termination of his employment made it impossible for him to secure a new job. The coach added that comments by the athletic director and a university vice chancellor placed a stigma upon his good name, reputation, honor, and integrity that foreclosed his freedom to take advantage of

---

[67] Clay v. Board of Trustees of Neosho County Community College, 905 F. Supp. 1488 [105 EDUC. L. REP. 439] (D. Kan. 1995).

[68] Wallace v. Texas Tech Univ., 80 F.3d 1042 [108 EDUC. L. REP. 1069] (5th Cir. 1996).

other employment opportunities. After a federal district court in California dismissed the coach's complaint for failure to state a claim, the Ninth Circuit reversed.[69] It held that the coach stated facts sufficient to establish that the officials imposed a stigma upon him. The court noted that a finder of fact could construe the administrators' statements as accusing the coach not just of yelling and cursing at his players, but of engaging in a campaign of abuse designed to inflict harm.

First Amendment

A teacher alleged that he was relieved of his supplemental duties as assistant football coach in retaliation for derogatory comments he made about the athletic director and his deceased wife. The teacher also made disapproving remarks about certain financial expenditures by the athletic department and other coaches' abuses of the district's tobacco use policy. The coach's suit against the district and superintendent claimed that his removal violated his First Amendment free speech and due process rights. A federal district court in Texas granted the defendants' motion for summary judgment.[70] The court stated that even if it found that the comments related to matters of public concern, there was no evidence to support the coach's allegation that he was reassigned because of the statements. On the due process charge, the court concluded that since the teacher did not have a property interest in his coaching duties, their loss was insufficient to trigger a constitutional deprivation of liberty claim.

Miscellaneous

Criminal

A criminal indictment for mail fraud charged members of a basketball coaching staff in Texas with executing a fraudulent scheme to establish academic eligibility that would have permitted five transfer students to play for the university. The coaches helped the players, who were recruited from two-year colleges, obtain the necessary credits for eligibility by providing them with written coursework or answers to correspondence exams, which were then sent to the sponsoring schools as the players' work. The coaches' convictions in federal district court were affirmed by the Fifth Circuit.[71] The court agreed that the coaches deprived the university of its intangible right to the honest services of its employees.

---

[69] Campanelli v. Bockrath, 100 F.3d 1476 [114 Educ. L. Rep. 385] (9th Cir. 1996).

[70] Hill v. Silsbee Indep. Sch. Dist., 933 F. Supp. 616 [112 Educ. L. Rep. 150] (E.D. Tex. 1996).

[71] United States v. Gray, 96 F.3d 769 [112 Educ. L. Rep. 637] (5th Cir. 1996).

In Ohio, an individual was convicted of breaking and entering as well as vandalism after he ransacked the concession stand at a high school football field. In addition, he broke a window in the school building. An appellate court modified the vandalism conviction because the state had not shown the element of physical harm to property. However, the court affirmed the breaking and entering conviction.[72]

Contracts

Football fans who contracted with tour operators for packages to the Rose Bowl only to learn that their tickets were unavailable when they reached Pasadena, sued a state university, whose team was playing in the game, for breach of contract, conspiracy, and negligence. A trial court dismissed the complaint for failure to state a claim. On further review, an appellate court in Wisconsin affirmed.[73] The court ruled that although the university was a party to the conference and football tournament association, the fans were not third-party beneficiaries who could sue for a breach of the agreement. Based on state public policy, the court held that the fans could not recover against the university in negligence. Turning to the conspiracy claim, the court decided that since the fans did not allege any concerted action on the part of the university, the claim that it put tickets into the hands of scalpers did not establish that they acted together.

A university sued a broker for breach of contract and negligence over the procurement of insurance to cover nonperformance by the promoter of an athletic event. The event, which did not take place as planned, was a football game that the university's team was scheduled to play in Ireland. The university alleged that it believed that the broker had obtained insurance to cover funds it spent preparing for the game. After a jury verdict in favor of the university, an appellate court in Indiana affirmed.[74] As to the insurance company's contention that the university should not have recovered because it could have reviewed the policy at any time, the court acknowledged that the duty of an insured to acquaint itself with a policy may be excused when the strength of the agent's oral assurances lulled the customer into not reading, or reading inattentively, dense and rebarbative language. The evidence, stated the court, supported

---

[72] State of Ohio v. Levingston, 666 N.E.2d 312 [110 Educ. L. Rep. 397] (Ohio Ct. App. 1995).
[73] Anderson v. Regents of the Univ. of Cal., 554 N.W.2d 509 [113 Educ. L. Rep. 904] (Wis. Ct. App. 1996).
[74] Rollins Burdick Hunter of Utah v. Board of Trustees of Ball State Univ., 665 N.E.2d 914 [110 Educ. L. Rep. 373] (Ind. Ct. App. 1996).

the finding that the insurance agent had assured the university that the policy had the nonperformance clause that it had requested.

Workers' Compensation

A sport management student at a university in Florida was injured during his internship with a professional basketball team when he struck his head against an antenna that was protruding from a radio mounted on the wall of a supply and copy room. A trial court granted the team's motion for summary judgment on the student's negligence claim on the basis that workers' compensation was the exclusive remedy in this situation. An appellate court agreed.[75] The court maintained that the student was not a volunteer so as to be excluded from the definition of employee for the purposes of workers' compensation since he received twenty-five dollars on each occasion that he attended ten required home games. The court pointed out that even if the student had not received any monetary remuneration, he still would have been subject to workers' compensation law because his participation in the internship program constituted valuable consideration where it was necessary to satisfy his degree requirements.

Trademark Infringement

A state high school athletic association sought a preliminary injunction to protect its trademark "March Madness" from infringement by a company that owns a license for the same from the NCAA. Even though the association had used the trademark since the early 1940s to designate its annual March tournament, the NCAA began licensing the use of the term "March Madness" in 1993 or 1994 to producers of goods and services related to its post-season event. A federal district court in Illinois denied the association's motion for a preliminary injunction and the Seventh Circuit affirmed.[76] The court reasoned that whether "March Madness" was referred to as quasi-generic, on its way to becoming generic, or a dual-use term, it is a name that the public has affixed to something other than the Illinois high school basketball tournament. A trademark owner, said the court, is not allowed to withdraw a name from the public domain if it is being used to denote someone else's good or service, leaving that organization and its customers speechless.

---

[75] Hallal v. RDV Sports, 682 So. 2d 1235 [114 EDUC. L. REP. 718] (Fla. Dist. Ct. App. 1996).

[76] Illinois High Sch. Ass'n v. GTE Vantage, 99 F.3d 244 [113 EDUC. L. REP. 1103] (7th Cir. 1996).

Fraudulent Conveyance

A judgment creditor sued a judgment debtor after the debtor assigned part of his rights in a private sports box at a university to a friend for money and the remainder of these rights to his children for little or no money. The creditor asserted that the conveyance to the children was a fraudulent transfer. A trial court entered judgment for the debtor, but the Supreme Court of Nevada reversed in holding that the interest in the sports box was subject to execution and capable of fraudulent transfer.[77] In remanding, the lower court was instructed to determine whether fair consideration was received for the transfer.

Real Property

The Supreme Court of North Carolina affirmed that a county board of education was statutorily authorized to condemn land for use as wetlands mitigation and a source of fill.[78] The court reasoned that the board had the discretion to determine whether the use of the property was necessary for the construction of proposed athletic facilities even though the facilities would not sit on the condemned land.

Data Practices Act

The head coach of a women's gymnastics team who was fired later sued the university for a violation of the Data Practices Act in making statements to the media concerning information in her personnel file. The Act protects personnel information as private but allows a government entity to make investigative data public to dispel widespread rumor. The coach also based her claim on breach of contract, unjust enrichment, and promissory estoppel. After a trial court entered summary judgment for the university, the coach sought further review. An appellate court in Minnesota reversed in favor of the coach.[79] Faced with an issue of first impression as to which section of the Act should prevail, the panel found that the lower court erred in granting summary judgment over two statements made to a radio station and a newspaper regarding the university's disciplinary action against the coach. The court determined that, as a policy matter, the section of the Act dealing with the protection of personnel data must prevail over the part that permits the release of information to dispel rumor.

---

[77] Sportsco Enterprises v. Morris, 917 P.2d 934 [110 EDUC. L. REP. 448] (Nev. 1996).
[78] Dare County Bd. of Educ. v. Sakaria, 466 S.E.2d 717 [108 EDUC. L. REP. 406] (N.C. 1996).
[79] Deli v. Hasselmo, 542 N.W.2d 649 [106 EDUC. L. REP. 876] (Minn. Ct. App. 1996),

Administrative Law

An association of chiropractors sought further review of an order of the State Board of Education that declined the opportunity to amend a rule to allow chiropractors to perform required physicals for prospective interscholastic athletes. An appellate court in North Carolina affirmed.[80] The court held that since the board's decision not to act was rule-making, it was not subject to judicial review.

Conclusion

The rate of litigation involving sports in educational settings has remained fairly constant in recent years. Perhaps the most significant trend is the increase in title IX suits. In light of the litigiousness of American society, it is likely that there will be a steady flow of suits involving sports law for many years to come.

---

[80] North Carolina Chiropractic Ass'n v. North Carolina State Bd. of Educ., 468 S.E.2d 539 [108 EDUC. L. REP. 972] (N.C. App. 1996).

8
HIGHER EDUCATION

Robert M. Hendrickson*

M. Christopher Brown, a doctoral student and graduate assistant in the Higher Education Program, Pennsylvania State University, assisted in the preparation of this chapter.

Introduction

A wide variety of issues were litigated in higher education over the past year. A Supreme Court case on tribal gaming operations could limit litigation in states that claim Eleventh Amendment Immunity. In its ruling, the Court abandoned a previous decision that stated that the Commerce Clause was an exception to a state's sovereign immunity claims. The Court also addressed the admissions policies of a military academy in South Carolina that excluded women while refusing to hear a notorious affirmative action case from a law school in Texas.

Lower courts examined questions over the selection of boards of trustees and the scope of their institutional control. One of the cases involving sunshine laws dealt with the release of FBI records from a 1930 investigation that were at the heart of a student's dissertation. A title VI case on a dual system of higher education evaluated the appropriateness of court ordered compliance plans. Actions under title VII alleging discrimination based on gender, race, religion, and national origin were again numerous. Litigation under title IX has evolved from procedural and jurisdictional issues to disputes on the merits. Further, a unique Americans with Disabilities Act claim was brought by a doctoral student who alleged that her "inability to conceptually organize material" was a handicap. Sexual harassment cases involved faculty and students inside and outside of the classroom and student-to-student situations as well.

Student issues dealing with financial aid were again heavily litigated as cases challenged regulations aimed primarily at proprietary schools that were designed to make institutions more accountable for financial aid. Suits on discipline continue to raise issues about due process and liberty interests. Similarly, disagreements over academic dismissals present questions of a like nature but are concentrated in the professional and graduate levels. Organizational access to university facilities and funds along with violations of federal constitutional and statutory provisions round out this section of the chapter.

Liability issues including bodily injury, negligence, contract disputes, and deceptive practices continue to move through the courts. Copyright and patent issues were again active. The American Bar Association's accreditation of law schools was challenged as an antitrust violation as were salary policies of the National Collegiate Athletic Association.

This year's case law reflects the continuing propensity to seek judicial relief regardless of the severity of the harm as some actions sought to expand the scope of the law beyond its original intent. Finally, a number of this year's actions bordered on being frivolous; if this develops into a trend, it could diminish the seriousness of public support for the ongoing protection of the rights of all those associated with American higher education.

Intergovernmental Relations

The lead case in this section involves a decision by the Supreme Court that may increase the scope of sovereign immunity for public institutions of higher learning. *Seminole Tribe of Florida v. Florida*[1] sought to compel the state to negotiate the creation of a casino on a reservation under the Indian Gaming Regulatory Act (IGRA). The IGRA, enacted pursuant to the Indian Commerce Clause, allows tribes to conduct gaming activities as long as they establish a valid compact with the state within which their reservations are located. When the Governor of Florida refused to comply with the statutory obligation to negotiate in good faith, the Seminoles brought suit to compel him to do so. A federal district court in Florida refused the Governor's motion to dismiss under the Eleventh Amendment.[2] However, the Eleventh Circuit reversed and dismissed in finding that the Indian Commerce Clause did not give Congress the power to abrogate a state's immunity.[3]

On further review, the Supreme Court affirmed that the only two circumstances where Congress has the power to abrogate a state's immunity, under the Fourteenth Amendment and the Interstate Commerce Clause, are indistinguishable from the Indian Commerce Clause. Even so, the court abandoned its Commerce Clause ruling of *Pennsylvania v. Union Gas Company*[4] on the basis that it was of questionable precedency value. In holding that the judiciary cannot use Articles I and III of the Constitution to circumvent the Eleventh Amendment, the Court was of the opinion that the Commerce Clause cannot abrogate a state's immunity. The full implications for sovereign immunity in higher education remain to be seen.

---

[1] 116 S. Ct. 1114 (1996).
[2] Seminole Tribe of Fla. v. Florida, 801 F. Supp. 655 (S.D. Fla. 1992).
[3] Florida v. Seminole Tribe of Fla., 11 F.3d 1016 (11th Cir. 1994).
[4] 491 U.S. 1 (1991).

Legislative Authority

A statute in Kentucky required all state agencies to use blind vendors under the federal Randolph-Sheppard Vending Stand Act. When negotiations over the university's commission from a blind vendor's sales broke down, the vendor sought declaratory and injunctive relief to prevent the university from entering into a contract with a private dealer. An appellate tribunal, affirming in part, declared that the university could not restrict the blind vendor's product selection.[5] The court added that the Department for the Blind did not have the right of first refusal when the university chose to expand its food services. However, the court decreed that the university was required to negotiate a fair agreement with the blind vendor that would not subject him to unreasonable competition.

Board Authority

The authority of boards of trustees to control institutions of higher learning was before the courts in a number of ways. When the Board of Trustees of the University of Bridgeport, which was faced with financial difficulties, decided to merge with the Professors' World Peace Academy, it was challenged by a number of individuals including one of its "life trustees." The Supreme Court of Connecticut affirmed that the trustee had neither standing to question the agreement as ultra vires nor could she do so under common law.[6] The court indicated that since being a life trustee is an honorary position that is not accorded the full management responsibilities and privileges of a regular trustee, she could not claim that her presence was required before the Board could act.

The Supreme Court of New Mexico reasoned that the terms of two trustees appointed by the previous governor expired at the time designated by statute, not when the former chief executive said that they did.[7] At the same time, the court acknowledged that the trustees could remain in office until the state senate ratified the new appointees of the incoming governor.

Elected members of boards of trustees challenged legislation that would have cost them their positions before the completion of their current terms of office. The Supreme Court of Illinois pointed out that since the legislation did not allow the trustees to finish their terms, it violated the

---

[5] Kentucky State Univ. v. Kentucky Dep't for the Blind, 923 S.W.2d 296 [110 EDUC. L. REP. 484] (Ky. Ct. App. 1996).

[6] Steeneck v. University of Bridgeport, 668 A.2d 688 [106 EDUC. L. REP. 203] (Conn. 1995).

[7] Denish v. Johnson, 910 P.2d 914 [106 EDUC. L. REP. 1349] (N.M. 1996).

right to vote guarantees under the state constitution.[8] However, the court also stated that the unconstitutional provision was severable from the remainder of the statute's reorganization provisions.

Students in New York unsuccessfully disputed a board's authority to close down four intercollegiate athletic programs in order to bring the university into compliance with title IX and conference requirements. An appellate court affirmed that because the Intercollegiate Athletics Board's recommendations were only advisory, the suit was properly dismissed.[9]

When the board of trustees of a community college elected to discontinue its management of the school bookstore and entered into a contract with a private company, a labor union and classified employees unsuccessfully questioned its action. An appellate court in California affirmed a grant of summary judgment in favor of the college.[10] The court observed that nothing in the state's Education Code prohibited the college from entering into a special services contract with a private firm.

The regents of a public university in Colorado disagreed with a determination by the Secretary of State that its employee publication advocating voting on two referenda violated the state law against using public funds for political activities. The court affirmed that the publication constituted the misuse of public funds only as it applied to the paragraphs that commented on the referenda.[11]

In a long-running class action suit opposing discriminatory practices in the state's post secondary system, voters in Alabama sued the Governor, Chancellor, and State Board of Education when they attempted to change the terms of board members from staggered to concurrent. A federal district court noted that the Voting Rights Act required the state to obtain pre-clearance, either from the federal trial court for the District of Columbia or from the United States Attorney General, to determine whether the change denied or abridged the rights of voters on the basis of race or color.[12] Even though the court found that state officials failed to procure clearance, it gave them ninety days to do so.

Students in Ohio unsuccessfully alleged that a university president violated their rights under the First and Fourteenth Amendment by blatantly disregarding Robert's Rules of Order and Senate bylaws during a discussion

---

[8] Tully v. Edgar, 664 N.E.2d 43 [109 EDUC. L. REP. 315] (Ill. 1996).
[9] *In re* Lichten, 646 N.Y.S.2d 402 [111 EDUC. L. REP. 1333] (N.Y. App. Div. 1996).
[10] Service Employees Int'l Union, Local 715 v. Board of Trustees of the W. Valley/ Mission Comm., 55 Cal. Rptr.2d 44 [111 EDUC. L. REP. 431] (Cal. Ct. App. 1996).
[11] Regents of the Univ. of Colo. v. Meyer, 899 P.2d 316 [102 EDUC. L. REP. 345] (Colo. Ct. App. 1995).
[12] Shuford v. Alabama State Bd. of Educ., 920 F. Supp. 1233 [108 EDUC. L. REP. 705] (M.D. Ala. 1996).

of the university's policy on sexual harassment. An appellate court affirmed the dismissal of these claims for lack of subject matter jurisdiction.[13]

Two different states considered the authority of agencies over matters involving colleges and universities. A student in New York sought judicial review of an adjudication by a deputy commissioner of Vocational and Educational Services for the Disabled. An appellate court confirmed that a hearing officer's placement of a student in an independent out-of-state learning program was inappropriate since it was inadequately designed to meet her needs.[14]

A board in Louisiana challenged a determination of the Commission on Ethics of Public Employees that prevented faculty members at a medical school from entering into a contract in their private capacities with a nonprofit corporation. The faculty members had set up a corporation to deliver private practice services in the university's medical center. An appellate court posited that the board had standing to question the commission's action.[15] The court remanded for a new hearing because the board presented insufficient evidence to the commission.

Accreditation

The first of three cases in an ongoing dispute between a law school that was denied accreditation and the American Bar Association (ABA) involved disclosure. A federal district court in Massachusetts permitted the ABA to depose the attorney who had written the school's accreditation report but never represented the school.[16] The court stated that the school waived the attorney-client privilege by its disclosure of and reliance upon the accreditation report. In a second matter, the same court decreed that the school should bear the ABA's costs on reconsideration of its second order to comply with discovery.[17]

In the third case, the law school brought allegations of unfair competition, fraud, deceit, tortuous misrepresentation, and breach of contract against the ABA. The federal district court in Massachusetts posited that it had the authority to assert jurisdiction over the controversy under the Higher Education Act.[18] The court contended that even though

---

[13] Lucas v. Gee, 662 N.E.2d 382 [107 EDUC. L. REP. 990] (Ohio Ct. App. 1995).

[14] *In re* Singer, 643 N.Y.S.2d 752 [110 EDUC. L. REP. 346] (N.Y. App. Div. 1996).

[15] *In re* Board of Supervisors of La. State Univ. and Agric. and Mechanical College, 669 So. 2d 593 [107 EDUC. L. REP. 1075] (La. Ct. App. 1996).

[16] Massachusetts Sch. of Law at Andover v. American Bar Ass'n, 895 F. Supp. 88 [103 EDUC. L. REP. 123] (E.D. Pa. 1995).

[17] Massachusetts Sch. of Law at Andover v. American Bar Ass'n, 914 F. Supp. 1172 [107 EDUC. L. REP. 184] (E.D. Pa. 1996).

[18] Massachusetts Sch. of Law at Andover v. American Bar Ass'n, 914 F. Supp. 688 [107 EDUC. L. REP. 144] (D. Mass. 1996).

the law school neither sought nor received federal funds, it was not outside of the Act's reach.

Sunshine Laws

Parties continue to litigate access to official records based on open-meeting or sunshine laws. Under the Freedom of Information Act (FOIA), a graduate student in Pennsylvania sought records from the Federal Bureau of Investigation (FBI) pertaining to an organization that it investigated during the 1930s. The student, who used the records as part of a doctoral thesis on David Lasser and The Workers Alliance of America, had obtained a release from Mr. Lasser. However, after the FBI relied upon the Vaughn index to block disclosure of substantial portions of the information, the student appealed. The Third Circuit reversed.[19] The court held that the FBI failed to describe adequately the information that could be withheld or to link it to exemptions within the FOIA.

Citizens unsuccessfully sought access to records pertaining to animals that were used in research under Indiana's Public Records Act. An appellate court affirmed a grant of summary judgment in favor of the university.[20] The court ascertained that the Act clearly exempted research protocols and applications from public disclosure to private citizens.

In Louisiana, a citizen was denied access to a university's Animal Care and Use Committee records. On further review, an appellate court affirmed that since federal law governed the committee's meetings and records, they were not subject to access through either the state's Public Records or Open Meeting Laws.[21]

Conversely, in the first of two cases from New York, a trial court offered that even though records were kept pursuant to federal law, they were still subject to disclosure under the state's Freedom of Information Law (FOIL).[22] As such, the court stated that the sources of information relating to how cats and dogs were obtained for university health science research could not be withheld from the public. However, the court denied the animal rights group's request for attorney fees under the FOIL.

The Court of Appeals of New York maintained that records of a subcontracting bookstore concerning required texts for courses at a

---

[19] Davin v. United States Dep't of Justice, 60 F.3d 1043 [102 EDUC. L. REP. 35] (3rd Cir. 1995).

[20] Robinson v. Indiana Univ., 659 N.E.2d 153 [105 EDUC. L. REP. 1195] (Ind. Ct. App. 1995).

[21] Dorson v. Louisiana, 657 So. 2d 755 [102 EDUC. L. REP. 381] (La. Ct. App. 1995).

[22] *In re* Citizens for Alternatives to Animal Labs, 643 N.Y.S.2d 323 [110 EDUC. L. REP. 338] (N.Y. Sup. Ct. 1996).

university were exempt from the state's FOIL.[23] The court concluded that the information was not subject to disclosure just because it dealt with course offerings at a public university.

In Michigan, a citizen sought further review of the denial of his request to gain access to meeting records and the financial condition of a public university's foundation. In reversing, an appellate court granted access under both the state's Open Meeting Act and the FOIA.[24]

However, the Supreme Court of Pennsylvania quashed a request from a student newspaper to review the public safety records of a community college.[25] The court was of the opinion that the college was not a public agency within the meaning of the state's Right to Know Act.

Where a college board granted a housing allowance to two of its vice presidents in a closed session, a union challenged its action. An appellate court in New Jersey decreed that the board violated the state's Open Meeting Act.[26] However, the court entered judgment in favor of the board since its rectified the error by subsequently ratifying its vote at an open meeting for which notice had been duly provided.

An appellate court in Illinois reversed in favor of a housing provider in a dispute over information relating to students.[27] The court indicated that the disclosure of the names, addresses, and telephone numbers of incoming first-year students at a public university to an off-campus housing owner was not an invasion of privacy under the state's FOIA.

Taxation

At issue in one case was whether a community college could charge a county commission out-of-district tuition for students who attended its classes. After a lower court found that the statute authorizing the assessment was constitutional, the parties announced that they had reached a settlement. Even so, the court denied a motion to convert the settlement into a declaratory judgment. The Supreme Court of Kansas affirmed.[28] The panel agreed that the lower court did not abuse its discretion by

---

[23] *In re* Encore College Bookstores, 639 N.Y.S.2d 990 [108 Educ. L. Rep. 834] (N.Y. 1995).

[24] Jackson v. Eastern Mich. Univ. Found., 544 N.W.2d 737 [107 Educ. L. Rep. 1002] (Mich. Ct. App. 1996).

[25] Community College of Phila. v. Brown, 674 A.2d 670 [108 Educ. L. Rep. 1205] (Pa. 1996).

[26] Council of N.J. State College Locals v. Trenton State College Bd. of Trustees, 663 A.2d 664 [103 Educ. L. Rep. 277] (N.J. Super. Ct. Law Div. 1995).

[27] Lieber v. Southern Ill. Univ., 664 N.E.2d 1155 [109 Educ. L. Rep. 1350] (Ill. Ct. App. 1996).

[28] Labette Community College v. Board of County Comm'rs, 907 P.2d 127 [105 Educ. L. Rep. 760] (Kan. 1995).

refusing to recognize the settlement and that the county waived its right to appeal by entering into the agreement.

A private university appealed the denial of its challenge to its tax assessment. The Supreme Judicial Court of Massachusetts affirmed the denial of a request for a tax abatement on land owned by the university.[29] The court noted that since the property was already tax exempt, it was not subject to the three year averaging provisions of the tax code.

In Illinois, a media corporation that was formed to operate the student newspaper at a state university disputed the denial of its request for a real property exemption. An appellate court reversed on the ground that since the nonprofit corporation was formed for educational purposes, it was entitled to an exemption.[30]

Zoning

After a private college challenged an order that prevented it from razing a newly acquired building that was accorded landmark status, a city sought further review. An appellate court in New York reversed.[31] The court ruled that designating the building a historical landmark did not amount to a taking.

Residents of a neighborhood adjacent to a private university unsuccessfully sought to prevent the institution from building a new law school near their homes on the basis that the university previously had agreed not to do so. An appellate court in the District of Columbia upheld a grant of summary judgment in favor of the university.[32] It found that the university had not made such an agreement and that the residents could not rely on promissory and equitable estoppel since they had not been raised at trial.

In Louisiana, a resident sued a public university when his property was damaged by the university's unauthorized use of land adjacent to campus as an unimproved parking lot for students. An appellate court agreed that the university was liable.[33] The court stated that the university violated a zoning law by allowing its property to be used as a parking area for students where the only access to the facility was by way of the landowner's driveway.

---

[29] Massachusetts Inst. of Tech. v. Board of Assessors of Cambridge, 663 N.E.2d 567 [108 EDUC. L. REP. 872] (Mass. 1996).
[30] Illini Media Co. v. Department of Revenue, 216 Ill. 69 [109 EDUC. L. REP. 882] (Ill. App. Ct. 1996).
[31] Canisius College v. City of Buffalo, 629 N.Y.S.2d 886 [102 EDUC. L. REP. 733] (N.Y. App. Div. 1995).
[32] Duke v. American Univ., 675 A.2d 26 [109 EDUC. L. REP. 275] (D.C. Ct. App. 1996).
[33] Varnado v. Southern Univ. at New Orleans, 673 So. 2d 1289 [109 EDUC. L. REP. 1421] (La. Ct. App. 1996).

A district sued a public university claiming that its failure to develop long range plans to accommodate increases in elementary school enrollments violated the California Environmental Quality Act (CEQA). An appellate court affirmed that classroom overcrowding per se did not have a significant effect on the environment under CEQA.[34] The court added that while the plan had to, and did, include information on the effect of the development on school enrollment, it was neither required to solve the attendance problem nor provide money for new classrooms.

In a second case in California, a district filed suit against a private college in connection with its request to erect a new building for its business school. The college obtained a writ of mandate exempting it from a city law that required new construction projects to pay a fee to the local district. On further review, an appellate court reversed.[35] The court observed that tax exempt status does not extend to school development fees since the new building constituted commercial or industrial construction under the law that imposed the fee.

Land use involving hazardous waste was litigated once again this year when the Environmental Protection Agency (EPA) was part of a controversy over a landfill that was placed on the National Priority List. A university objected to the designation as unacceptable based on the use of unfiltered water, the locations where the samples were drawn, the flawed procedures used to process them, and contamination of the site. The Circuit Court for the District of Columbia rejected the university's arguments.[36] The court pointed out that the EPA provided a valid scientific rationale for conducting the sampling and analysis since it had not acted arbitrarily or capriciously.

The federal district court in New Jersey held that a state college and a public hospital using the same hazardous waste site could be joined to a complaint as third parties.[37] However, the court asserted that the hospital, but not the college, was an alter ego of the state for the purposes of immunity. The court added that the state, through previous litigation under its Environmental Protection Act, waived Eleventh Amendment immunity in third party claims.

---

[34] Goleta Union Sch. Dist. v. Regents of the Univ. of Cal., 44 Cal. Rptr.2d 110 [102 EDUC. L. REP. 688] (Cal. Ct. App. 1995).
[35] Loyola Marymount Univ. v. Los Angeles Unified Sch. Dist., 53 Cal. Rptr.2d 424 [109 EDUC. L. REP. 1323] (Cal. Ct. App. 1996).
[36] Board of Regents of Univ. of Wash. v. Environmental Protection Agency, 86 F.3d 1214 [110 EDUC. L. REP. 543] (D.C. Cir. 1996).
[37] New Jersey Dep't of Environmental Protection v. Gloucester Environmental Management Servs., 923 F. Supp. 651 [109 EDUC. L. REP. 666] (D.N.J. 1995).

Jurisdiction

The Supreme Court of North Dakota affirmed that a nonstudent who voluntarily went to a campus police station for questioning, but was not arrested, was unable to bring false arrest charges against an officer and the editor of the student newspaper.[38] The court judged that a false arrest had not taken place when the editor called the police because the nonstudent refused to leave the newspaper office after an argument over an advertisement.

The state sought further review after a motorist who was arrested by a campus police officer and charged with driving while intoxicated on a public roadway adjacent to the college was able to suppress the evidence. An appellate court in Massachusetts affirmed.[39] The court acknowledged that although college police have the power to apprehend individuals who violate the law on campus, this arrest was invalid because it was made on a public roadway.

In California, an appellate panel affirmed a guilty verdict in a case involving the possession of firearms.[40] The court agreed that the statute prohibiting firearms on the grounds of a state university applied to an apartment complex that was owned and operated by the institution even though it was on land adjacent to campus that was separated from it by a public roadway.

Ownership

An international fraternity's alumni association that was incorporated to own, maintain, and manage a chapter house transferred ownership to a local corporation after the college required all such organizations on campus to disaffiliate or lose official recognition. Subsequently, a trial court ruled in favor of the association when it was challenged by the international fraternity and the undergraduate members of the local chapter. The Supreme Judicial Court of Maine affirmed that the association had the authority to transfer ownership of the house to the new corporation.[41]

An individual who held a lease on box seats at a university sports arena assigned part of his rights to a friend six months after he executed a confession of judgment in an unrelated matter. The Supreme Court of Nevada offered that the debtor had a property interest in the box and the

---

[38] Wishnatsky v. Bergquist, 550 N.W.2d 394 [110 EDUC. L. REP. 1246] (N.D. 1996).
[39] Commonwealth v. Mullen, 664 N.E.2d 854 [109 EDUC. L. REP. 915] (Mass. App. Ct. 1996).
[40] People v. Anaim, 54 Cal. Rptr.2d 876 [110 EDUC. L. REP. 1161] (Cal. Ct. App. 1996).
[41] Delta Kappa Epsilon Theta Chapter v. Theta Chapter House Corp., 661 A.2d 1152 [102 EDUC. L. REP. 218] (Me. 1995).

transfer could be fraudulent.[42] As such, the court remanded for a determination of whether the debtor received fair consideration for the transfer.

In Illinois, a citizen filed suit against former faculty members at a state university who allegedly took equipment without permission when they accepted positions at another school. The university recovered money for work performed while one of the faculty members was in its employ through a settlement agreement, but released two others. The citizen sought further review of the dismissal of his claim. An appellate court reversed in deciding that since the university's board was a nominal defendant, the case was not precluded on the basis of sovereign immunity.[43] Further, the court was of the opinion that the settlement agreement that violated state law by allowing the transfer of public property without compensation did not deprive the citizen of standing under the state's Recovery Act.

University Hospitals

Five cases examined reimbursements made by the federal government to university hospitals that serve as Medicare providers. A teaching hospital in Minnesota challenged the rules covering re-examining and re-auditing of graduate medical education (GME) costs used to calculate its Medicare reimbursement. The Eighth Circuit affirmed that the regulations were reasonable and valid.[44]

Three university medical centers in California sought reimbursement for interest expenses on working capital loans granted by the state Board of Regents. The loans had been used for patient care necessitated by a decline in state funding due to a budget shortfall. After the Provider Reimbursement Review Board (PRRB) rejected the university's request for interest reimbursement, a federal district court granted the government's motion for summary judgment. On appeal, the Ninth Circuit agreed that the interest on loans was not reimbursable and the regulation did not present an irrebuttable presumption violating the regents' rights to due process.[45]

A faculty member alleged that his medical college acted fraudulently when it requested reimbursement for two radiology residents whose funding was assumed to have been approved by the Veterans

[42] Sportsco Enterprises v. Morris, 917 P.2d 934 [110 EDUC. L. REP. 448] (Nev. 1996).
[43] People v. Bosmann, 664 N.E.2d 119 [109 EDUC. L. REP. 869] (Ill. App. Ct. 1996).
[44] St. Paul-Ramsey Medical Ctr. v. Shalala, 91 F.3d 57 [111 EDUC. L. REP. 189] (8th Cir. 1996).
[45] Regents of the Univ. of Cal. v. Shalala, 82 F.3d 291 [108 EDUC. L. REP. 1118] (9th Cir. 1996).

Administration (VA). The college, which operated a VA facility, indicated that the positions for the residents would probably have been funded but had to commit to them before a final decision could be rendered. A federal trial court in Illinois ruled in favor of the medical school on the False Claims Act charge and the Seventh Circuit affirmed.[46] The court held that sending an invoice that included the two positions which the school thought had been funded was not fraud.

In Ohio, a public university challenged the PRRB's denial of jurisdiction dealing with the readjustment of indirect medical education (IME) costs over several years. The intermediary, an insurance company, reopened the cost reports submitted by the university's hospital and approved changes in the reimbursement amounts for GME and the diagnostic related group (DRG) but failed to adjust the IME payment. In response to the university's suit over whether the PRRB has jurisdiction, the court stated that the PRRB lacked authority to order the reopening of the cost report by the intermediary.[47]

Federal Statutory and Constitutional Issues
First Amendment
A university unsuccessfully brought a libel suit against a newspaper that reported on a controversy involving homeless people on campus and the resultant increase in crime in the neighborhood. Moreover, since the university advocated an alternative life style harkening back to the 1960s, the paper characterized it as a "sensuality school" offering a "unique course in carnal knowledge" and discussed the head and founders' history of drug prosecutions. An appellate court in California affirmed the dismissal of the university's claim.[48] It agreed that the university could not sustain its libel suit where the newspaper exercised its constitutional rights. The court reflected that the allegedly defamatory statements were either true, privileged, or incapable of being proven false.

Criminal Prosecutions
Owners of a proprietary school in Illinois appealed their convictions for mail and wire fraud and for making false statements to the Department of Education (DOE). The owners had uttered false statements about and backdated enrollments and had made personal purchases with money

---

[46] Hindo v. University Health Sciences/The Chicago Med. Sch., 65 F.3d 608 (103 EDUC. L. REP.) (7th Cir. 1995).

[47] University of Cincinnati v. Shalala, 891 F. Supp. 1262 [102 EDUC. L. REP. 529] (S.D. Ohio 1995).

[48] Lafayette Morehouse, Inc. v. Chronicle Publ'g, 44 Cal. Rptr.2d 46 [102 EDUC. L. REP. 678] (Cal. Ct. App. 1995).

drawn from the DOE's Pell Grant account. The Seventh Circuit affirmed.[49] The court found that the evidence, which was gathered legally, supported the charge of misapplication of federal financial aid funds, a scheme to defraud the DOE, bankruptcy fraud, statements over eligibility to participate based on accreditation, and obstructive conduct of the DOE's investigation.

Defendants in Tennessee who were observed setting fire to a campus dormitory after an altercation with college students appealed their convictions for conspiracy, arson, and perjury. The Sixth Circuit affirmed.[50] The panel agreed that the convictions were supported by the evidence and that the federal trial court had jurisdiction because the college was engaged in interstate commerce.

A state university moved to dismiss wrongful assault, arrest, and prosecution charges brought against its athletic and police departments over an incident that occurred at a football game on campus. A federal district court granted the motion to dismiss on the basis that the plaintiffs waived their right to file suit when they submitted their case to the Tennessee Claims Commission.[51]

University police officers observed a defendant carrying furniture across campus. He refused to identify himself and fled the scene. After a trial court dismissed the indictment, an appellate court reinstated the charge. On further review, the Court of Appeals of New York affirmed that the evidence was sufficient to sustain the indictment.[52]

A student sought further review of the dismissal of his conversion, false imprisonment, defamation, slander of title, and negligence charges against a university president, police chief, and investigator. The university police, suspecting that a drug deal was in progress on campus, detained the student, confiscated his car and money, and retained possession of those items for about a year. The Supreme Court of Alabama affirmed in favor of the university on all counts except for conversion.[53] The court observed that since the investigator could not claim immunity, the conversion claim was remanded for trial.

In North Carolina, a defendant challenged his conviction for burglary of a sorority house pursuant to the single dwelling provisions of state law. An appellate court upheld the conviction.[54] The court noted that jury

---

[49] United States v. Ross, 77 F.3d 1525 [107 Educ. L. Rep. 484] (7th Cir. 1996).
[50] United States v. Sherlin, 67 F.3d 1208 [104 Educ. L. Rep. 69] (6th Cir. 1995).
[51] Mirabella v. University of Tenn., 915 F. Supp. 925 [107 Educ. L. Rep. 674] (E.D. Tenn. 1994).
[52] People v. Jensen, 630 N.Y.S.2d 989 [103 Educ. L. Rep. 369] (N.Y. 1995).
[53] Lightfoot v. Floyd, 667 So. 2d 56 [107 Educ. L. Rep. 378] (Ala. 1995).
[54] North Carolina v. Merritt, 463 S.E.2d 590 [104 Educ. L. Rep. 1381] (N.C. Ct. App. 1995).

instructions defining the public area adjacent to the house director's apartment as a single dwelling unit under the statute was harmless error.

Privacy

Pursuant to a subpoena, a university released information concerning the poor academic record of an expert witness who was dropped from its medical school. Subsequently, the witness appealed the dismissal of his claim that the university violated the state statute governing the release of public records. The Supreme Court of Iowa affirmed in favor of the university.[55] The court pointed out that the witness failed to demonstrate that the legislature intended to create a private remedy.

A private college had a regulation requiring all students living in dormitories to consent to unannounced, unscheduled entries into their rooms. After being informed that contraband was located in a student's room, the director of housing knocked, did not receive an answer, used his master key to enter, and discovered drugs plus an electronic scale used to measure portions of the illegal substances. The contraband was turned over to local narcotics agents and was used as evidence in the student's criminal conviction. On appeal, the Supreme Court of Tennessee affirmed.[56] The court maintained that since the evidence was confiscated by an official of the private college, and not an agent of the state, the student could not suppress it on the basis that his Fourth Amendment rights had been violated.

In Minnesota, a physician who was affiliated with a medical school sought to suppress evidence that was seized in searches of the offices of his private practice that were located on university property and the home of his partner. The federal district court denied the doctor's motion to dismiss on the ground that he did not have standing to challenge the search of his partner's residence.[57] However, it added that the doctor could dispute the search and seizure of records in his office even though he shared the space with the university.

In a companion case involving the Food and Drug Administration (FDA), the same doctor was charged with violating various laws in connection with the experimental drug program that he administered. The federal district court in Minnesota rejected the doctor's motion to dismiss.[58] The court decided that the requirements of the Food, Drug,

---

[55] Marcus v. Young, 538 N.W.2d 285 [103 Educ. L. Rep. 1213] (Iowa 1995).
[56] State of Tenn. v. Burroughs, 926 S.W.2d 243 [111 Educ. L. Rep. 1027] (Tenn. 1996).
[57] United States v. Najarian, 915 F. Supp. 1441 [107 Educ. L. Rep. 705] (D. Minn. 1995).
[58] United States v. Najarian, 915 F. Supp. 1460 [107 Educ. L. Rep. 724] (D. Minn. 1995).

and Cosmetic Act calling for the reporting of adverse drug reactions to the FDA was not overly vague. In addition, the court refused to dismiss the charge of noncompliance based on estoppel and would not permit the gravity doctrine to preclude the use of statements that the doctor made to university officials.

When a college began videotaping locker rooms after several thefts occurred, security officers sued for invasion of privacy. The federal district court in Kansas granted the university's motion for summary judgment.[59] The court mandated that even where the employees had an expectation of privacy, the warrantless search was reasonable under the workplace search standards.

Discrimination in Employment

Title VI of the Civil Rights Act of 1964

As reflected by a case on remand in a federal district court in Alabama,[60] litigation under title VI against dual systems of higher education has continued for more than a decade. Using a panel of experts, the court attempted to find a strategy to achieve compliance within the Alabama system of higher education. Reviewing the complex situations of historically Black institutions (HBI) and predominantly White institutions (PWI) located in close proximity, and noting that the HBIs still have very low White enrollments, the court evaluated a number of remedies. It was especially critical of the management of both Alabama State University and Alabama A&M University because they continued to focus on traditional students while failing to cultivate adult education programs that could substantially have changed the populations on their campuses. The court recommended that the universities work cooperatively with institutions that were nearby to develop enrollments of nontraditional students. In rejecting the transfer of programs as a solution, the court called for the strengthening of existing offerings or the establishment of new ones at the HBIs. Further, the court held that a single land grant extension system was feasible and would be educationally sound as long as both the PWIs and HBIs participated as equal partners.

---

[59] Thompson v. Johnson County Community College, 930 F. Supp. 501 [111 Educ. L. Rep. 257] (D. Kan. 1996).

[60] Knight v. Alabama, 900 F. Supp. 272 [104 Educ. L. Rep. 310] (N.D. Ala. 1995). For a history of the case, *see* Knight v. Alabama, 787 F. Supp. 1030 (N.D. Ala. 1991), *rev'd in part and remanded*, 14 F.3d 1534 (11th Cir. 1994).

Title VII of the Civil Rights Act of 1964

Once again, significant litigation occurred over allegations involving discrimination based on gender, race, nationality, or religion in hiring, dismissal, pay, and other benefits. A professor at a state university filed suit against the Equal Employment Opportunities Commission (EEOC), its officials, the Attorney General, and the Department of Justice (DOJ). The professor alleged that the EEOC and others neither adequately investigated his claim of racial discrimination nor notified him about the lapsed one-hundred-eighty-day period during which he could have filed a private right of action. A federal district court in Pennsylvania ruled that sovereign immunity precluded jurisdiction over the title VII and Administrative Procedures Act claims for damages against the EEOC, DOJ, and federal officials who acted in their official capacities.[61] Further, the court dismissed the professor's federal torts claim based on his failure to seek administrative remedies.

In a long-standing suit, African-American employees alleged that Alabama's post-secondary system of education engaged in discriminatory behavior by refusing to hire or promote them to presidential, faculty, administrative, or supervisory positions. In addition, a subclass of women charged gender discrimination in employment and promotion. Although an earlier consent decree on discrimination had been approved,[62] this time the court considered a request for judgment by the women who alleged violations of title VII and title IX. The original order established that twenty-five percent of presidential and other employees should be African-American by the year 1999. In this decree, the court created annual targets requiring fifty percent of new presidential and other employees to be women by the year 2005.[63] The court determined that the provisions of its order, that called for nondiscrimination on the basis of gender, job reporting procedures, recruitment of qualified women, and employment goals were not illegal since they were based on a finding of past discrimination.

In a related case, a white female in Alabama argued that a technical college in Alabama violated her rights under title VII when she was not offered a job. A federal district court partially granted the woman's motion for summary judgment on the basis that race was a factor when the college

---

[61] Forbes v. Reno, 893 F. Supp. 476 [102 Educ. L. Rep. 1004] (W.D. Pa. 1995).
[62] Shuford v. Alabama State Bd. of Educ., 846 F. Supp. 1511 [90 Educ. L. Rep. 194] (M.D. Ala. 1994).
[63] Shuford v. Alabama State Bd. of Educ., 897 F. Supp. 1535 [103 Educ. L. Rep. 978] (M.D. Ala. 1995).

chose to not hire the applicant.[64] At the same time, the court found that summary judgment was precluded due to the existence of material issues of fact as to whether the college would have reached the same hiring decision absent the impermissible factor. The court added that a good faith attempt to rely on a consent agreement was not a defense for the college and the woman, who was not a party to the original action, lacked standing to rely upon the decree.

Procedures

A university appealed a ruling in favor of a professor who filed a title VII action claiming that she had been subjected to a hostile work environment. The Court of Appeals for the District of Columbia reversed.[65] The court stated that the professor's title VII claim was precluded since she failed to exhaust administrative remedies with the EEOC.

In Ohio, a federal district court granted a professor's motion to stay proceedings on his title VII and Equal Pay claims and to compel the university to use the grievance system in his collective bargaining agreement. On appeal, the Sixth Circuit reversed in asserting that the trial court should not have considered the legality of the bargaining agreement since the issue had not been before an arbitrator.[66]

An African-American employee brought a civil rights suit against his university after he was suspended due to publicity surrounding his acquittal on rape charges. A federal district court in Pennsylvania posited that the university had Eleventh Amendment immunity.[67] Further, the court judged that the employee failed to support a claim of intent to discriminate under section 1981 and did not demonstrate that he had a property or liberty interest under section 1983 based on his being disciplined for sexual harassment in connection with the incident. The court concluded that the investigation, suspension, and publicity did not give rise to a discrimination claim under title VII.

In Maryland, the federal trial court dismissed the race and age discrimination case filed by a university employee pursuant to title VII, section 1981, and section 1985. The court offered that the woman failed to state a claim under section 1981 and section 1985 and that her title VII charge was time barred because she did not act within statutory time

---

[64] Salter v. Douglas MacArthur State Technical College, 929 F. Supp. 1470 [110 EDUC. L. REP. 1132] (M.D. Ala. 1996).
[65] Park v. Howard Univ., 71 F.3d 904 [105 EDUC. L. REP. 412] (D.C. Cir. 1995).
[66] Wedding v. University of Toledo, 89 F.3d 316 [110 EDUC. L. REP. 1045] (6th Cir. 1996).
[67] Boykin v. Bloomsburg Univ. of Pa., 893 F. Supp. 378 [102 EDUC. L. REP. 981] (M.D. Pa. 1995).

limits after the EEOC issued a right to sue letter.[68] The court also ruled that Eleventh Amendment immunity barred claims against the college and various administrators in their official capacities.

According to a federal district court in Virginia, a female professor who encountered difficulty in the tenure and promotion process did not suffer adverse employment action under title VII.[69] A presidential report was commissioned after an article detailing the professor's problems with gender-based discrimination at the university appeared in the local newspaper. The court found that the university did not retaliate against the professor for exercising her First Amendment rights under section 1983 even though the report criticized the professor for unprofessional behavior surrounding her title VII claims.

In Massachusetts, a male admissions officer brought a title VII claim alleging that the college failed to promote him solely because of his race. The federal trial court refused to order the discovery of the personnel files of former deans of admission on the basis that the officer failed to demonstrate their relevancy to his claim.[70] Further, the court denied the officer's request to review memoranda prepared for the president by staff in the affirmative action office since they were not subject to the self-critical analysis privilege.

In New York, a federal district court rejected a community college's claim that a title VII action brought by one of its employees should have been dismissed because she failed to comply with the state's notice of a claim requirement.[71] The court declared that failure to serve notice of claim did not bar the action and that the woman could name specific administrators in her suit even though they were not identified in earlier administrative proceedings.

A placement coordinator in Missouri who lost her job during a reclassification scheme sued a university claiming discrimination and constructive discharge. A federal district court indicated that the woman's suit was time barred because she did not file her claim in a timely manner.[72]

---

[68] Roberson v. Bowie State Univ., 899 F. Supp. 235 [104 EDUC. L. REP. 173] (D. Md. 1995). *See* Taye v. Amundson, 908 F. Supp. 21 [105 EDUC. L. REP. 1030] (D.D.C. 1995) (where the title VII claim of a parking attendant was time barred for failing to file in a timely manner after the EEOC issued a right to sue letter).

[69] Howze v. Virginia Polytechnic, 901 F. Supp. 1091 [104 EDUC. L. REP. 757] (W.D. Va. 1995).

[70] Whittingham v. Amherst College, 164 FRD 124 [106 Educ. L. Rptr 173] (D. Mass. 1995).

[71] Tout v. Erie Community College, 923 F. Supp. 13 [109 EDUC. L. REP. 231] (W.D.N.Y. 1995).

[72] Hill v. St. Louis Univ., 923 F. Supp. 1199 [109 EDUC. L. REP. 704] (E.D. Mo. 1996).

Shifting Burden of Proof

At a private university in New York, an employee of eastern European descent unsuccessfully alleged national origin discrimination when a Hispanic applicant was named director of the Spanish program. A federal district court granted the university's motion for summary judgment based on the legitimate nondiscriminatory reason that the individual who was hired had better qualifications.[73]

In the District of Columbia, a Jewish applicant who was not hired for a teaching position brought a title VII case claiming religious discrimination. The federal trial court found that the applicant's case was without merit insofar as he was unable to establish a prima facie case of discrimination because he lacked practical and theoretical teaching experience.[74] Moreover, the court was of the opinion that the existence of anti-Semitic postings on the campus had no relationship to the institution's decision not to hire the applicant.

Another Jewish faculty member claimed religious discrimination and retaliation when the university failed to elevate him from a temporary to a permanent position.[75] A federal district court in New York decided that the university rebutted the professor's prima facie case of discrimination by showing he was unable to establish a viable experimental laboratory in solid mechanics. The court added that the professor failed to establish any evidence to substantiate his retaliation claim.

A female assistant professor from Israel unsuccessfully claimed that her denial of tenure for substandard teaching was a pretext for discrimination based on gender, national origin, and religion. A federal district court in Michigan disagreed.[76] The court reasoned that the faculty member had received several warnings that she needed to improve her teaching.

After a state college employed a male faculty member, it later hired his wife at a lower salary even though she had similar qualifications. Subsequently, the female appealed a grant of summary judgment in favor of the institution in her suit based on title VII and the Equal Pay Act. The Supreme Court of Montana revered in favor of the professor.[77] The court remanded in acknowledging that the professor had established a prima facie case of gender discrimination.

---

[73] Stern v. Trustees of Columbia Univ., 903 F. Supp. 601 [104 Educ. L. Rep. 1128] (S.D.N.Y. 1995).

[74] Shipkovitz v. Board of Trustees of Univ. of D.C., 914 F. Supp. 1 [107 Educ. L. Rep. 113] (D.D.C. 1996).

[75] Spencer v. City Univ. of N.Y./College of Staten Island, 932 F. Supp. 540 [111 Educ. L. Rep. 1168] (S.D.N.Y. 1996).

[76] Javetz v. Board of Control, Grand Valley State Univ., 903 F. Supp. 1181 [104 Educ. L. Rep. 1191] (W.D. Mich. 1995).

[77] Heiat v. Eastern Mont. College, 912 P.2d 787 [107 Educ. L. Rep. 1020] (Mont. 1996).

Class Action Suits

A class of female faculty members sued their university alleging that a salary schedule that set different pay schemes for various disciplines had a disparate impact on women. The women, most of whom were in the humanities, generally received salaries that were less than those of their predominantly male colleagues in the natural sciences. The federal district court in Rhode Island pointed out that the women failed to establish a prima facie case of disparate impact since the salary scheme was based on a business necessity that the university had substantiated.[78]

Retaliation

Two former employees of a college in Texas appealed a grant of summary judgment in favor of the institution in their title VII retaliation claim. One employee who filed a hostile work environment claim against her supervisor was fired after she misplaced a storeroom key and had a duplicate secretly made by the other employee. When both employees were dismissed, they filed their retaliation claim. The Fifth Circuit reversed in favor of the employees.[79] The court ascertained that the employees raised sufficient factual issues as to whether the supervisor's conduct violated title VII.

A female faculty member in Wisconsin who was on a yearly, fixed-term contract sued her university for pay discrimination based on gender and for retaliation under title IX over the nonrenewal of her contract. Even though the woman had more experience and a greater teaching load than a male colleague, both she and the male colleague received the same salary when the university went to a new base pay schedule. The federal district court granted the university's motion for summary judgment. On further review, the Seventh Circuit affirmed that the woman failed to establish a prima facie case under title VII.[80] The court found that the dean decided to rely more heavily on tenure track faculty to offer courses and thereby reduced the number of fixed term, yearly contract faculty.

After a woman unsuccessfully applied for a position as a tree surgeon within a university's maintenance department, she filed gender discrimination charges with the EEOC. Then, when the woman was placed in the training program, she filed a retaliation claim against the instructors and her supervisor. The woman alleged that she was treated differently than male trainees since she was not given a weight lifting belt, was made to use a chain saw with one hand, and received fewer hours of

---

[78] Donnelly v. Rhode Island Bd. of Governors for Higher Educ., 929 F. Supp. 583 [110 EDUC. L. REP. 1090] (D.R.I. 1996).

[79] Long v. Eastfield College, 88 F.3d 300 [110 EDUC. L. REP. 957] (5th Cir. 1996).

[80] Johnson v. University of Wisc., 70 F.3d 469 [104 EDUC. L. REP. 1046] (7th Cir. 1995).

instruction. A federal district court in Indiana granted the university's motion for summary judgment and the Seventh Circuit affirmed.[81] The appellate court agreed that the university demonstrated that male and female trainees were treated the same.

Four tenured faculty members sued when their university decided to phase out a dental hygiene program. The women alleged gender discrimination based on the First Amendment, Fourteenth Amendment, title VII and title IX, and state statutes as well as retaliation for bringing their claim. A federal district court in Iowa granted the university's motion for summary judgment on the gender claim but ruled in favor of the women on the retaliation charge. On appeal, the Eighth Circuit reversed on the retaliation claim.[82] The court concluded that the retaliation claim was baseless since the university chose to fold the dental hygiene program into another department before its final students graduated rather than allow it to remain as a stand-alone department until it was closed.

An affirmative action officer at a community college in California who was dismissed for attempting to expand her authority under a new chief executive appealed after a federal district court granted the school's motion for summary judgment in her title VII retaliation claim. The Ninth Circuit affirmed that the college acted properly since the officer unilaterally acted beyond the scope of her authority on several occasions.[83]

In New York, a federal trial court partially denied a university's motion for summary judgment after an executive secretary alleged that the dean had sexually harassed her during her employment and retaliated by dismissing her when she filed suit.[84] The court maintained that since the claim was filed within the appropriate statutory limits, it was necessary to consider whether the secretary was dismissed because she filed her claim or because she refused to accede to the alleged sexual advances. However, the court granted the university's motion as to the sexual harassment claim as it was not filed within the appropriate statutory time frame.

An African-American employee at a university hospital claimed that he was not promoted because of his race and that he was eventually dismissed in retaliation for bringing a claim before the EEOC. Moreover, three other employees claimed that they were dismissed in retaliation for participating in the employee's EEOC claim. A federal trial court in Illinois granted the hospital's motion for summary judgment when it found that

[81] Smart v. Ball State Univ., 89 F.3d 437 [110 Educ. L. Rep. 1050] (7th Cir. 1996).
[82] Brine v. University of Iowa, 90 F.3d 271 [111 Educ. L. Rep. 101] (8th Cir. 1996).
[83] Nelson v. Pima Community College, 83 F.3d 1075 [109 Educ. L. Rep. 598] (9th Cir. 1996).
[84] Burrell v. City Univ. of N.Y., 894 F. Supp. 750 [103 Educ. L. Rep. 105] (S.D.N.Y. 1995).

the worker had falsified employment records.[85] Further, the court was satisfied that the hospital demonstrated that its decision to dismiss the other employees as part of a legitimate reduction-in-force was made before their supervisor had any knowledge of their participation in the EEOC claim.

The Equal Pay Act

Male professors in Virginia appealed a grant of summary judgment in favor of their university in a title VII claim based on the Equal Pay Act where the institution gave raises to female faculty members in response to their salary equity study. The Fourth Circuit reversed in favor of the male professors.[86] The court determined that the existence of material questions of fact as to the appropriate performance factors for calculating salary increases precluded a ruling in favor of the university.

Two female African-American secretaries filed an Equal Pay Act claim when they discovered that a white male secretary, who had been hired into their unit at a later date, had a higher hourly salary. When this disparity was brought to the attention of university administrators, they explained that the higher salary had to do with the timing of the hire and the lack of a system to ensure that salaries for newer staff members would be comparable to those who were currently employed. Even so, the secretaries rejected the university's offer to award them back pay and to adjust their salaries. A federal district court in Alabama granted the university's motion for summary judgment and the Eleventh Circuit affirmed.[87] The court noted that the university had not only adequately demonstrated that nondiscriminatory factors resulted in the salary disparity but also that the secretaries failed to prove that the institution's intent to discriminate was the dominant factor in the dispute.

In North Carolina, a female coach who sued her university alleging that her pay was unequal to male colleagues added charges under title VII and title IX as well as section 1983. A federal district court granted the university's motion for summary judgment.[88] It reflected that the coach could not sustain her Equal Pay Act claim since her male replacement was hired at a lesser salary. The court concluded that the nonrenewal of the coach's contract, which gave rise to her other claims, was based on a

---

[85] Parks v. University of Chicago Hosp. and Clinics, 896 F. Supp. 775 [103 EDUC. L. REP. 704] (N.D. Ill. 1995).

[86] Smith v. Virginia Commonwealth Univ., 84 F.3d 672 [109 EDUC. L. REP. 1062] (4th Cir. 1996).

[87] Trotter v. Board of Trustees of the Univ. of Ala., 91 F.3d 1449 [111 EDUC. L. REP. 686] (11th Cir. 1996).

[88] Bartges v. University of N.C. at Charlotte, 908 F. Supp. 1312 [106 EDUC. L. REP. 124] (W.D.N.C. 1995).

controversy involving violations of the fund raising policies of both the team and the university.

Title IX of the Education Amendments of 1972

When the contract of a women's basketball coach was not renewed, he brought suit based on title IX, the First Amendment, wrongful discharge, and state law. Previously, the coach had publicly voiced concerns about the community college's failure to comply with title IX in the operation of its athletic programs, but never filed a claim with the Department of Education Office of Civil Rights. The federal district court in Kansas granted the college's motion for summary judgment on the coach's title IX claim against administrators in their individual capacities and for the state law charges against the board.[89] Yet, the court denied the motion with regard to the title IX allegation against the board and the section 1983 claim involving violations of the First Amendment. The court offered that title IX allows a private right of action for retaliation and does not require the exhaustion of administrative remedies before bringing suit. It added that public speech involving title IX gender discrimination in the athletic programs was protected by the First Amendment.

Two professors sued their university for allegedly violating the First Amendment and title IX as well as for breaching one of their contracts. The federal district court in Maine denied the university's motion for summary judgment on the title IX claim when it decided that the state's six-year statute of limitations was the appropriate time limit.[90] Moreover, the court indicated that the First Amendment claim was subsumed in the title IX charge. The court also observed that the professor who submitted his contractual dispute to arbitration pursuant to his collective bargaining agreement was precluded from bringing the breach of contract claim.

Age Discrimination In Employment

In Pennsylvania, a federal district court entered a grant of summary judgment in favor of a university in a dispute involving the Age Discrimination In Employment Act (ADEA) and the Americans with Disabilities Act (ADA) after a sixty-nine-year-old employee lost his job. The court posited that the university released the employee as part of a legitimate reduction-in-force. On appeal, the Third Circuit affirmed.[91]

---

[89] Clay v. Board of Trustees of Neosho County Community College, 905 F. Supp. 1488 [105 Educ. L. Rep. 439] (D. Kan. 1995).

[90] Nelson v. University of Me. Sys., 914 F. Supp. 643 [107 Educ. L. Rep. 135](D. Me. 1996).

[91] Kelly v. Drexel Univ., 94 F.3d 102 [111 Educ. L. Rep. 1160] (3rd Cir. 1996).

The court agreed that walking with a limp was not a disability within the meaning of the ADA since it did not limit a major life activity.

A professor in Indiana challenged a grant of summary judgment in favor of his university after he claimed that it failed to promote him because of his age. The Seventh Circuit affirmed.[92] The court stated that even though the professor had established a prima facie case of discrimination, he was unable to rebut the university's nonpretextual reasons that he had a less than superior record in teaching, service, and performance.

In the first of three cases from New York, two senior citizen golf course rangers argued that a university violated their rights under the ADEA when it chose not to renew their annual contracts. The university responded that the reorganization of the course made it impossible for the two employees to manage play. A federal district court denied the university's motion for summary judgment in reasoning that material issues existed as to whether its rationale was a pretext for age discrimination.[93]

A federal trial court in New York denied a university's motion for summary judgment where a job applicant filed an ADEA claim after rejecting a settlement offer.[94] The court found that the suit was not barred because the applicant refused the partial relief settlement.

The third case from New York involved a tenured female faculty member who filed suit under the ADEA along with title VII and Equal Pay Act claims of gender discrimination after she was forced to retire. A federal trial court granted the university's motion for summary judgment on the ADEA claim since its mandatory retirement policy was still in place.[95] At the same time, the court denied the university's motion for summary judgment on the professor's title VII and Equal Pay Act allegations.[96] After a jury rendered a verdict in favor of the professor on the title VII and Equal Pay Act claims, the court awarded attorney fees for those charges and for the ADEA claim in holding that even though her allegation was ultimately unsuccessful, it was not frivolous, unreasonable, or groundless.[97]

---

[92] Kuhn v. Ball State Univ., 78 F.3d 330 [107 Educ. L. Rep. 524] (7th Cir. 1996).
[93] Austin v. Cornell Univ., 891 F. Supp. 740 [102 Educ. L. Rep. 517] (N.D.N.Y. 1995).
[94] Gerardi v. Hofstra Univ., 897 F. Supp. 50 [103 Educ. L. Rep. 743] (E.D.N.Y. 1995).
[95] Pollis v. New Sch. for Soc. Research, 829 F. Supp. 584 [85 Educ. L. Rep. 825] (S.D.N.Y. 1993).
[96] Pollis v. New Sch. for Soc. Research, 913 F. Supp. 771 [106 Educ. L. Rep. 1139] (S.D.N.Y. 1996).
[97] Pollis v. New Sch. for Soc. Research, 930 F. Supp. 899 [111 Educ. L. Rep. 292] (S.D.N.Y. 1996).

Section 504 of the Rehabilitation Act of 1973 and the Americans with Disabilities Act

A former university employee brought suit under the Pregnancy Discrimination Act (PDA) and ADA when she was removed from her position for actions surrounding her taking sick leave because she sought medical treatment due to her infertility. A federal trial court in Illinois denied a motion to dismiss made by the Board of Governors of State Colleges and Universities.[98] The court pointed out that since infertility was pregnancy related, it was actionable under both the PDA and ADA.

A federal court in Texas ruled that " . . . the inability to conceptually organize material on a doctoral comprehensive exam,"[99] is not a disability under the ADA or the Rehabilitation Act. As such, the court was of the opinion a student failed to establish a prima facie case of discrimination against her university following her dismissal from a doctoral program due to her academic difficulties.

In New York, a law school professor who suffered a stroke that cost him the use of his left hand, arm, and leg, alleged salary discrimination based on his disability. A federal trial court granted the law school's motion for summary judgment.[100] The court observed that since the professor's physical impairment did not affect major life activities, it did not qualify as a disability.

Otherwise Qualified Individuals

A student-athlete on a scholarship was declared ineligible to participate in college football after the team doctor diagnosed him as having a congenitally narrow cervical canal that put him at risk of permanent severe neurological injury. Even when the player obtained evaluations that differed from those of the team doctor and agreed to indemnify the university, officials refused to declare him eligible. The federal trial court in Kansas denied the student's motion for a preliminary injunction based on the Rehabilitation Act.[101] The court asserted that a congenitally narrow cervical canal was not a disability within the meaning of the Act and, even if it were, the student-athlete was not otherwise qualified given the physician's diagnosis of high risk for serious injury.

---

[98] Erickson v. Board of Governors of State Colleges and Univ. for Northeastern Ill. Univ., 911 F. Supp. 316 [106 EDUC. L. REP. 621] (N.D. Ill. 1995).

[99] Tips v. Regents of Texas Tech. Univ., 921 F. Supp. 1515, 1516 [109 EDUC. L. REP. 131] (N.D. Tex. 1996).

[100] Redlich v. Albany Law Sch. of Union Univ., 899 F. Supp. 100 [104 EDUC. L. REP. 164] (N.D.N.Y. 1995).

[101] Pahulu v. University of Kan., 897 F. Supp. 1387 [103 EDUC. L. REP. 970] (D. Kan. 1995).

In Massachusetts, the federal district court rejected a university's motion for summary judgment in a suit by a student with severe depression who alleged that she was dismissed from a pastoral psychology program due to her disability.[102] The court stated that since the student presented material questions of fact as to whether she was otherwise qualified under Section 504, a trial was necessary to determine if the university's grounds for dismissing her were a pretext for discrimination.

A resident physician who was dismissed from a university hospital's anesthesiology program after becoming chemically dependent on narcotics sued under Section 504. A trial court granted the doctor's motion for summary judgment based on its contention that his rights to due process and his rights under the Administrative Procedures Act (APA) had been violated, On further review, the Supreme Court of Washington reversed on the basis that the doctor's due process rights were not violated and that the state Attorney General could represent the university in the APA claim.[103] The court added that material issues of fact as to whether he was otherwise qualified and whether his condition could be reasonably accommodated precluded summary judgment on the physician's claim pursuant to section 504.

Reasonable Accommodation

A former dean in Wisconsin who suffered from osteoarthritis and depression appealed a grant of summary judgment in favor of her university in a dispute over whether she had been provided with reasonable accommodations. The Seventh Circuit affirmed that the university did not violate the ADA since the dean refused its request to review her medical records.[104]

Decisions on the Merits

An assistant football coach in Tennessee who was dismissed following his arrest for driving while under the influence of alcohol sought further review of a grant of summary judgment in favor of the university.[105] The Sixth Circuit affirmed.[106] The court concluded that the university did not violate section 504 or the ADA because it fired the coach for his misconduct in being arrested rather than for his disability of alcoholism.

---

[102] Carlin v. Trustees of Boston Univ., 907 F. Supp. 509 [105 EDUC. L. REP. 940] (D. Mass. 1995).

[103] Sherman v. Washington, 905 P.2d 355 [104 EDUC. L. REP. 883] (Wash. 1995).

[104] Beck v. University of Wisc. Bd. of Regents, 75 F.3d 1130 [106 EDUC. L. REP. 1052] (7th Cir. 1996).

[105] Maddox v. University of Tenn., 907 F. Supp. 1144 [105 EDUC. L. REP. 986] (E.D. Tenn. 1994).

[106] Maddox v. University of Tenn., 62 F.2d 843 [102 EDUC. L. REP. 477] (6th Cir. 1995).

The federal district court in New Hampshire judged that a former faculty member's human relations problems and ineffective performance, not her alleged disability of morbid obesity, led to the nonrenewal of her contract.[107] The court decreed that since the professor's obesity did not limit her ability either to walk or to work and was not a disability under ADA, the college acted on the basis of a legitimate, nondiscriminatory business reasons.

Hiring Discrimination

An African-American applicant for a position at a private university in the District of Columbia sued under section 1981 and title VII when he was denied an interview.[108] The federal trial court granted the university's motion for summary judgment on the ground that the applicant could not base a prima facie case of discrimination on the premise that he met the minimum qualifications for the job.

In Indiana, a professor unsuccessfully brought a breach of contract claim in that state against a university in Colorado that made him a written offer of a job contingent upon the approval of its board of regents. When the board did not approve the offer, the professor filed his breach of contract claim. An appellate tribunal in Indiana affirmed a trial court ruling that it lacked jurisdiction over the out-of-state university.[109]

Faculty Employment

First Amendment Speech

In the first of two cases from Florida, three professors appealed a grant of summary judgment in favor of their community college. The faculty members alleged that their First Amendment rights to free speech were violated when they were fired in retaliation for union activities and for criticizing the college's administration. The Eleventh Circuit affirmed the denials with regard to two of the three professors when it found that there was insufficient admissible evidence to support their claims.[110] However, the court reversed and reinstated the third professor's allegations in ascertaining that there were sufficient issues of material fact as to whether the dissent policy violated the First Amendment.

Officials at a community college in Florida challenged the denial of their motion for summary judgment when they sought qualified immunity

---

[107] Nedder v. Rivier College, 908 F. Supp. 66 [105 EDUC. L. REP. 1033] (D.N.H. 1995).
[108] Bray v. Georgetown Univ., 917 F. Supp. 55 [107 EDUC. L. REP. 807] (D.D.C. 1996).
[109] Rosowsky v. University of Colo., 653 N.E.2d. 146 [102 EDUC. L. REP. 290] (Ind. Ct. App. 1995).
[110] Thornquest v. King, 61 F.3d 837 [102 EDUC. L. REP. 81] (11th Cir. 1995).

after being sued by a former faculty member. The professor alleged that he was dismissed because of his race and for exercising his right to protected speech based on his involvement with the NAACP. The Eleventh Circuit affirmed.[111] The court reasoned that since the professor submitted what it described as a shotgun pleading, it was impossible to determine which evidence went with which count.

A professor and former students brought a First Amendment claim against a university's chancellor for ordering the removal of photographs from a departmental display case. The federal trial court in Minnesota held that the chancellor was not entitled to qualified immunity.[112] The court added that the chancellor violated the First Amendment by removing the photographs of professors depicted as historical characters because they were carrying weapons .

In Nebraska, a professor sued his university and various officials for allegedly violating his First Amendment right to free speech in making salary determinations. The federal district court granted the university's motion for summary judgment.[113] The court observed that the professor's complaint about the university's salary guidelines that required him to list his affiliation with the university on his publications was not a matter of public concern protected by the First Amendment. The court also declared that the professor failed to establish any causal relationship between this dispute and the fact that he received a lower salary increase than he anticipated.

An instructor at a community college appealed a grant of summary judgment in favor of the school where he alleged that it violated his right to free speech under the First Amendment. The Supreme Court of Montana affirmed.[114] The court decided that the instructor who alleged that the college conditioned his rehiring upon his disavowal of his right to an expectation of continued employment did not establish a free speech claim because its failure to rehire him was not a matter of public debate.

Nontenured Faculty
Nonrenewal
In Nebraska, a former faculty member appealed a ruling in favor of her university after a grievance committee posited that her contract was

---

[111] Anderson v. District Bd. of Trustees of Cent. Fla. Community College, 77 F.3d 364 [107 EDUC. L. REP. 108] (11th Cir. 1996).
[112] Burnham v. Ianni, 899 F. Supp. 395 [104 EDUC. L. REP. 178] (D. Minn. 1995).
[113] Day v. Board of Regents of Univ. of Neb., 911 F. Supp. 1228 [106 EDUC. L. REP. 667] (D. Neb. 1995).
[114] Talley v. Flathead Valley Community College, 903 P.2d 789 [103 EDUC. L. REP. 1257] (Mont. 1995).

not renewed in retaliation for her filing a discrimination complaint. The Eighth Circuit affirmed that the university's reason for not renewing the faculty member's contract in light of her poor performance was not a pretext for employment discrimination.[115]

In New York, an assistant professor whose contract was not renewed unsuccessfully brought a section 1983 action against his university.[116] The court noted that the faculty member's critical speech about the appointment of an individual who lacked academic rank as chair of the department was not a matter of public concern that was protected by the First Amendment.

An instructor whose contract was not renewed filed a section 1983 suit claiming he was dismissed for exercising his right to protected speech under the First Amendment. The instructor's charge included speech in class, at faculty meetings, and through postings outside of his office concerning diversity on campus. Even though he spoke out on gender diversity, women thought that his classroom was an intimidating climate where his use of profanity interfered with their learning. A federal district court in Virginia granted the university's motion for summary judgment on the ground that since the instructor's in-class speech on diversity disrupted the college's pedagogical mission, it was not protected.[117] The court further indicated that even though the instructor's pronouncements at faculty meetings and the postings outside his office on diversity were protected speech, he was unable to demonstrate that it met the "but for" test as the sole justificationfor the nonrenewal of his contract.

Where a university dismissed a nontenured faculty member due to poor communication skills and his low level of productivity, he filed a section 1983 suit claiming violations of his federal and state civil rights. The federal district court in Puerto Rico ruled that the professor's claim failed because the university not only provided nonpretextual reasons for acting as it did but also afforded him the appropriate due process under its policy on nonrenewal.[118]

When a probationary assistant professor failed to make substantial progress toward tenure, he unsuccessfully sued after his contract was not renewed. The Supreme Court of North Dakota affirmed in favor of the university.[119] According to the court, the professor's suit was barred because he failed to exhaust the administrative remedies provided in his contract.

A university sought further review of an order calling for the reinstatement of a faculty member. An appellate court in North Carolina

---

[116] Harris v. Merwin, 901 F. Supp 509 [104 EDUC. L. REP. 689] (N.D.N.Y. 1995).
[117] Scallet v. Rosenblum, 911 F. Supp. 999 [106 EDUC. L. REP. 644] (W.D. Va. 1996).
[118] Ombe v. Fernandez, 914 F. Supp. 782 [107 EDUC. L. REP. 148] (D.P.R. 1996).
[119] Thompson v. Peterson, 546 N.W.2d 856 [108 EDUC. L. REP. 1273] (N.D. 1996).

affirmed.[120] The court maintained that the university's chancellor exceeded his authority in rejecting a grievance committee's report which concluded that his decision not to renew the faculty member's contract was based on impermissible considerations.

De Facto Tenure

An administrator on an annual contract who also filled a position as an adjunct associate professor sought further review of a ruling that he had not acquired de facto tenure. An appellate court in New Jersey affirmed that the administrator's letter of appointment clearly stated that he was in a nontenured position and that no one had ever acquired tenure at the university absent an affirmative action by its board of trustees.[121]

Breach of Contract

A faculty member whose contact was not renewed appealed a ruling in favor of the university in his breach of contract suit. The Supreme Court of Montana affirmed.[122] The court held that the college had no obligation to engage in arbitration where the faculty member was clearly employed under a one-year contract that did not contain any provisions for renewal.

In Minnesota, a fixed-term faculty member who lacked a Ph.D. claimed that the university breached her union contract when it reclassified her job as a tenure track position and looked to hire someone with a doctorate. An appellate court affirmed a grant of summary judgment in favor of the university.[123] The court offered that the university's broken promise to postpone reclassification was not a demonstrable injustice under promissory estoppel and that the faculty member was not injured by its failure to post notice of the vacancy as required by her union contact.

Denial of Tenure

The lead case in this section involves a dispute from Texas that could have profound effects on the way title IX employment discrimination suits can be litigated. A faculty member at a medical school alleged title IX sex discrimination when she was denied tenure. The university responded that it acted based on the faculty member's paucity of peer

---

[120] Simonel v. North Carolina Sch. of Arts, 460 S.E.2d 194 [102 EDUC. L. REP. 844] (N.C. Ct. App. 1995).
[121] Healy v. Farleigh Dickinson Univ., 671 A.2d 182 [106 EDUC. L. REP. 1234] (N.J. Super. Ct. App. Div. 1996).
[122] Schaal v. Flathead Valley Community College, 901 P.2d 541 [103 EDUC. L. REP. 438] (Mont. 1995).
[123] Faimon v. Winona State Univ., 540 N.W.2d 879 [105 EDUC. L. REP. 727] (Minn. Ct. App. 1995).

reviewed articles and her failure to sustain collegial relationships in her department. After a federal trial court ruled in favor of the professor, the Fifth Circuit reversed in favor of the university.[124] The court pointed out that title IX neither provided a direct private cause of action for an individual seeking monetary damages for alleged sexual discrimination by an educational institution that receives federal financial assistance nor did it do so indirectly through section 1983.

Professors in Nebraska who had been denied tenure unsuccessfully sued under section 1983 alleging that their rights to due process and equal protection were violated. The university's president sent the faculty members probationary one-year contracts rather than follow the recommendation of a grievance committee that their performances be reviewed in two years. On further review, the Eighth Circuit affirmed in favor of the university.[125] The court reasoned that the probationary contracts did not carry a presumption of renewal that entitled the faculty members to due process and that the professors could nor bring an equal protection claim since they were unable to demonstrate that they had been discriminated against.

After a federal district court granted a university's motion for summary judgment where a professor alleged that he had wrongfully been denied tenure, the Eighth Circuit reversed. On remand, the trial court certified the question to the Supreme Court of Oklahoma as to whether the professor had a legitimate claim to tenure pursuant to an informal, unwritten policy where a contrary, written plan was already in effect. The court judged that if a written tenure policy is an express contract, there can be no legitimate claim pursuant to an informal policy.[126]

A faculty member who was denied tenure unsuccessfully sued her university for breach of contract, her dean for intentional infliction of emotional distress, and her department chair for defamation. The Supreme Court of Iowa affirmed a grant of summary judgment in favor of the defendants.[127] The court contended that the university did not breach the faculty member's contract when it failed to adopt her proposed criteria to review her performance. The court added that the dean's angry outburst during a meeting with the professor did not rise to the level of outrageousness necessary to succeed on a claim of intentional infliction of emotional distress. Turning to the department chair, the court agreed

---

[124] Lakoski v. James, 66 F.3d 751 [103 EDUC. L. REP. 652] (5th Cir. 1995).

[125] Batra v. Board of Regents of the Univ. of Neb., 79 F.3d 717 [108 EDUC. L. REP. 48] (8th Cir. 1996).

[126] Jones v. University of Cent. Okla., 910 P.2d 987 [106 EDUC. L. REP. 1368] (Okla. 1995).

[127] Taggart v. Drake Univ., 549 N.W.2d 796 [110 EDUC. L. REP. 831] (Iowa 1996).

that the faculty member's defamation charge was without merit because his statements assessing her performance, which were entitled to qualified immunity, were not made with malice to harm through falsehood.

In the first of two cases from California, a faculty member with an international reputation as a probabilist in mathematics who was denied tenure obtained a writ of mandamus. As such, the court set aside the denial of his application for tenure, ordered the faculty member's reappointment, and called for a new review of his record. On further review, an appellate court reversed in favor of the university.[128] The court declared that the university's action, which was supported by the evidence in the record, should have been left undisturbed because it had not acted arbitrarily or capriciously.

The second of two cases from California was filed by a faculty member who claimed that he had been promised a continuing contract based on good performance. After a trial court rejected the college's demurrer that the faculty member's exclusive remedy was an administrative mandamus review under state law, an appellate panel granted a writ of mandate.[129] The court ruled that since judicial review of tenure decisions is limited to an evaluation of the fairness of the administrative hearings, the faculty member could not bypass those proceedings based on his allegation that there were deficiencies in the process.

In New York, a college sought further review of an order that required it to conduct a de novo review for a faculty member who was denied tenure. An appellate court affirmed in favor of the professor.[130] The court observed that a new review was appropriate since the college failed to follow its own rules both procedurally and in the application of its substantive criteria.

Allegations of Civil Rights Violations

A nun sought further review of the dismissal of her title VII sex discrimination suit in favor of the Catholic University of America when she was denied tenure in its Department of Canon Law. The Circuit Court for the District of Columbia affirmed in favor of the university.[131] The court stated that the ministerial exception precluded the application of title VII to the selection of tenured members in such a department.

---

[128] McGill v. Regents of the Univ. of Cal., 52 Cal. Rptr.2d 466 [108 EDUC. L. REP. 1228] (Cal. Ct. App. 1996).
[129] Pomona College v. Superior Ct. of Los Angeles County, 53 Cal. Rptr.2d 662 [110 EDUC. L. REP. 238] (Cal. Ct. App. 1996).
[130] Bennett v. Wells College, 641 N.Y.S.2d 929 [109 EDUC. L. REP. 341] (N.Y. App. Div. 1996).
[131] Equal Employment Opportunity Comm'n v. Catholic Univ. of Am., 83 F.3d 455 [109 EDUC. L. REP. 568] (D.C. Cir. 1996).

In Illinois, a faculty member who was denied promotion and tenure sued her university for sex discrimination. A federal district court granted the university's motion for summary judgment.[132] The court indicated that the faculty member's allegations of bias failed to prove that the university's proffered reason for denying her tenure, namely, her lack of scholarship, was a pretext for discrimination.

A federal district court in Virginia held that a faculty member of Puerto Rican descent failed to sustain her title VII discrimination claim when she was denied tenure.[133] The court reasoned that the university had a legitimate nondiscriminatory reason for denying tenure since the faculty member was unable to establish a prima facie case of discrimination because she could not show that she had a sustained record of scholarly productivity.

In New Jersey, an African-American faculty member filed a discrimination claim under section 1981 and section 1983 when, unlike two of her male colleagues, she did not receive tenure. The federal district court noted that the expiration of a two-year statute of limitations barred the claim.[134] The court added that the university's action was not a pretext for discrimination since the woman's scholarship did not measure up to its standards.

Dismissal During the Contract

A college appealed a directed verdict in favor of a faculty member who claimed that his one-year contract was unlawfully terminated prior to its expiration. The Supreme Court of Georgia reversed in favor of the college.[135] The court maintained that even though the college's procedures may have been flawed, it was up to a jury to determine whether the college had just cause for dismissal where the professor's contract was terminated due to his allegedly inadequate performance coupled with his poor treatment of female students.

Part-Time Faculty

A part-time faculty member at a community college filed suit after she was dismissed following the breakdown of negotiations over a one-year contract. A federal district court in North Carolina granted the

---

[132] Schneider v. Northwestern Univ., 925 F. Supp. 1347 [110 Educ. L. Rep. 79] (N.D. Ill. 1996).

[133] Rosado v. Virginia Commonwealth Univ., 927 F. Supp. 917 [110 Educ. L. Rep. 607] (E.D. Va. 1996).

[134] Stewart v. Rutgers, 930 F. Supp. 1034 [111 Educ. L. Rep. 303] (D.N.J. 1996).

[135] Savannah College of Art and Design v. Nulph, 460 S.E.2d 792 [102 Educ. L. Rep. 1230] (Ga. 1995).

college's motion for partial summary judgment.[136] The court ruled that the faculty member had not been subjected to false imprisonment when an administrator temporarily blocked the door as he asked her to return the keys to her office. In addition, the court was of the opinion that there was no contract since the professor refused to accept the college's performance criteria.

Tenured Faculty
Dismissal for Cause
In Wyoming, a tenured professor filed suit under section 1983 after his employment was terminated for cause based upon his communications with university donors concerning changes in his job responsibilities. The federal district court granted the motion to dismiss entered by the defendants.[137] According to the court, the professor failed to state a claim against the donors while Eleventh Amendment immunity barred the charges against the president and trustees. Further, the court posited that the professor's rights to due process were not violated since the university followed its procedures in terminating his employment.

A professor sought further review of the termination of his contract where he concealed his dual employment status with a university in North Carolina. An appellate court in Minnesota affirmed in favor of the university.[138] The court agreed that clear and convincing evidence supported the finding that the professor concealed his dual employment from the university. The court ascertained that the professor knew that officials would not have approved such an arrangement insofar as it violated the university's tenure regulations.

Denial of Employee Privileges
A Filipino priest who quit the faculty of a religiously affiliated college in South Dakota after he was denied a sabbatical unsuccessfully claimed that he had been discriminated against on the basis of his race, national origin, and gender. The Eighth Circuit affirmed.[139] The court agreed that the college had legitimate, nondiscriminatory reasons for rejecting the faculty member's unfocused application for a sabbatical.

In New Jersey, a university challenged an administrative determination that it retaliated against a librarian who alleged that he

---

[136] Caldwell v. Linker, 901 F. Supp. 1010 [104 Educ. L. Rep. 748] (M.D.N.C. 1995).
[137] Gressley v. Deutsch, 890 F. Supp. 1474 [102 Educ. L. Rep. 142] (D. Wyo. 1994).
[138] Zahavy v. University of Minn., 544 N.W.2d 32 [107 Educ. L. Rep. 285] (Minn. Ct. App. 1996).
[139] Roxas v. Presentation College, 90 F. 3d 310 [111 Educ. L. Rptr 107] (8th Cir. 1996).

was not promoted because he was of Chinese descent. An appellate court reversed in favor of the university.[140] The court concluded that sufficient evidence showed that the university based its judgment on legitimate reasons, namely the quality of his publications and research.

Dismissal for Financial Exigency

Tenured faculty members who rejected a two-year buyout when their contracts were terminated pursuant to an affiliation agreement between their college and a local university appealed a grant of summary judgment in favor of the institutions. An appellate court in Illinois reversed in favor of the faculty members.[141] The court acknowledged that the tenure agreement between the college and its faculty did not cease when the institutions affiliated since the college continued to exist independently. As such, the court decreed that it was a question of fact for a jury to determine whether the college was required to safeguard the tenure rights of the faculty under the affiliation agreement.

The first of two suits from Alabama involved an instructor at a community college who, after being informed that his position would be eliminated due to low enrollment, sought a writ of mandamus to compel his reinstatement. An appellate court affirmed that the state's Fair Dismissal Act was inapplicable to faculty members.[142]

A community college in Alabama challenged a decision in favor of an instructor whose contract was not renewed due to a decrease in the number of jobs at the school. An appellate court reversed in favor of the college on the basis that the instructor's suit was barred by sovereign immunity.[143]

In California, an instructor at a community college unsuccessfully brought a petition for a writ of mandate and declaratory relief based on his contention that his contract was terminated improperly due to financial exigencies. An appellate court affirmed in favor of the college.[144] The court agreed that even though the college terminated the instructor's contract before it conducted a hearing, it subsequently provided him with sufficient administrative due process.

---

[140] Chou v. Rutgers, 662 A.2d 986 [102 Educ. L. Rep. 656] (N.J. Super. Ct. App. Div. 1995).

[141] Gray v. Loyola Univ. of Chicago, 652 N.E.2d 1306 [102 Educ. L. Rep. 271] (Ill. App. Ct. 1995).

[142] Williams v. Ward, 667 So. 2d 1375 [107 Educ. L. Rep. 417] (Ala. Civ. App. 1994).

[143] Shoals Community College v. Colagross, 674 So. 2d 1311 [110 Educ. L. Rep. 877] (Ala. Civ. App. 1995).

[144] California Teachers Ass'n v. Butte Community College Dist., 56 Cal. Rptr.2d 269 [111 Educ. L. Rep. 1280] (Cal. Ct. App. 1996).

All Employees

Collective Bargaining

A community college district sought further review of a ruling in favor of the union that represented its employees in a dispute over whether the school could enter into a contract with a private company to maintain campus grounds. An appellate panel in California reversed in favor of the college.[145] The court judged that nothing in state law prohibited the college from entering into such a contract with a private company.

Bargaining Unit Membership

The first of three cases from Illinois on collective bargaining in community colleges involved a request by part-time faculty who teach at least six hours per semester on a regular basis to form their own unit. An administrative law judge authorized an election, but the state Educational Labor Relations Board (ELRB) reversed in calling for a modified unit. On further review, an appellate court reversed in holding that adjunct faculty who teach every term are entitled to representation under state law.[146]

Two bargaining units at a community college in Illinois challenged the ELRB's dismissal of their self-determination petition to merge. An appellate court pointed out that since a sufficient community of interest existed between the units, their petition should have been allowed to proceed.[147]

A community college sought further review of an adjudication by the ELRB that permitted the merger of units representing "regular" part-time instructors into the same unit as full-time faculty. An appellate court in Illinois affirmed that the merger constituted an appropriate bargaining unit.[148]

Unfair Labor Practices

Where the Hawaii Labor Relations Board (HLRB) ruled in favor of the board of regents in a dispute over whether it committed a prohibited practice in announcing new policies that complied with the Drug-Free Workplace Act, a bargaining unit appealed. The Supreme Court of Hawaii affirmed that because the policy was in compliance with a federal statute,

---

[145] California Sch. Employees Ass'n v. Kern Community College Dist. Bd. of Trustees, 48 Cal. Rptr.2d 889 [105 Educ. L. Rep. 1128] (Cal. Ct. App. 1996).

[146] William Rainey Harper Community College v. Harper College Adjunct Faculty Ass'n, 653 N.E.2d 411 [102 Educ. L. Rep. 720] (Ill. App. Ct. 1995).

[147] Black Hawk College Professional Tech. Unit v. Illinois Educ. Labor Relations Bd., 655 N.E.2d 1054 [103 Educ. L. Rep. 1135] (Ill. App. Ct. 1995).

[148] Community College Dist. No. 509 v. Illinois Educ. Labor Relations Bd., 660 N.E.2d 265 [106 Educ. L. Rep. 844] (Ill. App. Ct. 1996).

it was not subject to bargaining.[149] However, the court reversed in observing that since the policy affected topics subject to mandatory bargaining, the union did not have to wait until the board attempted implementation to begin bargaining.

A medical facility appealed a finding that it committed an unfair labor practice when it failed to notify an interns' union before it disciplined one of its members over an academic matter. The Supreme Court of New Jersey affirmed that the union should have received notice and could be present at the hearing.[150] At the same time, the court added that the right to representation ends as soon as it becomes apparent that a dispute involves academic or medical matters involving an intern's judgment.

A second case from New Jersey dealt with a university's challenge to an order compelling it to provide a faculty union with records, some of which were public documents. An appellate court reversed in holding that the university was not required to provide the union or its representative with material that was already available as public documents.[151]

The union representing faculty and chairs sued claiming that the state system of higher education committed an unfair labor practice when it created a new classification of employees and placed them in a preexisting bargaining unit. After a hearing officer dismissed the charge as premature, the union sought further review. An appellate court in Pennsylvania affirmed that the claim was premature insofar as there was no evidence that any of the bargaining unit's work had been assigned to a nonmember.[152]

In Illinois, a university challenged a default judgment against it based on its inability to demonstrate good cause for being late in responding to an unfair labor complaint over deductions for the cost of health insurance. An appellate court affirmed that since the university did not show good cause for its action, there was no reason to disturb the decision in favor of the union.[153]

A university challenged an adjudication that it committed an unfair labor practice because it refused to honor the employee leave provisions

---

[149] University of Hawaii Prof'l Assembly v. Tomasu, 900 P.2d 161 [102 EDUC. L. REP. 831] (Hawaii 1995).

[150] *In re* University of Med. and Dentistry of N.J., 677 A.2d 721 [110 EDUC. L. REP. 725] (N.J. 1996).

[151] Keddie v. Rutgers, 669 A.2d 247 [106 EDUC. L. REP. 238] (N.J. Super. App. Div. 1996).

[152] Association of Pa. State College and Univ. Faculty v. Pennsylvania Labor Relations Bd., 661 A.2d 898 [102 EDUC. L. REP. 202] (Pa. Commw. Ct. 1995).

[153] Board of Trustees of the Univ. of Ill. v. Illinois Educ. Labor Relations Bd., 653 N.E.2d 882 [102 EDUC. L. REP. 726] (Ill. Ct. App. 1995).

in an expired collective bargaining contract. An appellate court in Michigan affirmed.[154] The court agreed that since payment for release time was a mandatory subject of bargaining, it survived the expiration of the contract.

Grievance Procedures

A community college appealed an arbitration award that ordered it to appoint an electronics technology faculty member who lost his job as part of a reduction-in-force as the replacement for a colleague in the mathematics department who died. The Supreme Judicial Court of Massachusetts vacated in favor of the college on the basis that the arbitrator violated the principal of nondelegability in permitting the electronics professor to fill the vacancy in mathematics.[155]

In Minnesota, a university challenged an arbitration award that ordered the reinstatement of an employee who was dismissed for sleeping on the job. The federal district court vacated in asserting that the university complied with the terms of its bargaining agreement by giving the employee proper warning and notice before he was dismissed.[156]

Administration and Staff

Issues involving individual rights under the federal and state constitutions, contacts, and state laws were litigated in cases dealing with the dismissal of administrators and staff at colleges and universities.

Individual Rights
Procedural Issues

A doctor who lost his block time in the operating room following his dismissal as department head sought a preliminary injunction ordering his reinstatement. The university requested a dismissal on the ground that the doctor failed to state a cause of action. A trial court in New York decided that the hospital would be given the opportunity to inform both the doctor and the judge as to why the administrators acted as they did.[157]

---

[154] United Auto Workers, Local 688 v. Central Mich. Univ., 550 N.W.2d 835 [111 EDUC. L. REP. 486] (Mich. Ct. App. 1996).
[155] Higher Educ. Coordinating Council/Roxbury Community College v. Teachers Ass'n/ Mass. Community College Council, 666 N.E.2d 479 [110 EDUC. L. REP. 777] (Mass. 1996).
[156] International Bd. of Teamsters, Local No. 120, St. Paul, Minn. v. University of St. Thomas, 894 F. Supp. 346 [102 EDUC. L. REP. 1086] (D. Minn. 1994).
[157] Hanna v. Board of Trustees of N.Y. Univ. Hosp., 633 N.Y.S.2d 738 [104 EDUC. L. REP. 1288] (N.Y. Sup. Ct. 1995).

Property Rights

In Ohio, a university appealed the dismissal of its motion for summary judgment after a former civil service employee claimed that she was denied due process. The Sixth Circuit reversed.[158] The court concluded that the employee did not have a property right in her job and that she was not denied due process when her position was abolished.

A former instructor at a community college who claimed that his right to due process was violated when he was dismissed summarily challenged a ruling in favor of the institution. The Eighth Circuit affirmed.[159] The court agreed that, as an arm of the state, the college was entitled to sovereign immunity under the Eleventh Amendment.

In Utah, a nurse who was dismissed and lost her license for violating a university hospital policy by delivering a baby appealed a grant of summary judgment in favor of the institution. The Tenth Circuit affirmed that the nurse failed to demonstrate a property interest in her position.[160] However, the court reversed and remanded in contending that administrators were not entitled to qualified immunity on the nurse's claim that they violated her liberty interest in the protection of her professional reputation and the freedom to take advantage of other employment opportunities in obstetrics.

A former employee challenged an administrative determination that led to his dismissal for insubordination. The Supreme Court of Alaska agreed that substantial evidence supported the finding that the computer specialist's insubordination in refusing to honor his supervisor's request to write a memorandum justified his dismissal.[161]

After being discharged from his position as a vice president of a community college, a former administrator alleged that he was denied due process. A federal district court in New York granted the college's motion to dismiss.[162] The court held that the county's employee handbook did not provide the former vice president with a property interest that gave rise to a right to due process.

A university medical center questioned a preliminary injunction that ordered it to reinstate a physician who was relieved of his administrative

---

[158] Christophel v. Kukulinsky, 61 F.3d 479 [102 EDUC. L. REP. 58] (6th Cir. 1995).

[159] Hadley v. North Ark. Community Tech. College, 76 F.3d 1437 [107 EDUC. L. REP. 75] (8th Cir. 1996).

[160] Watson v. University of Utah Med. Ctr., 75 F.3d 569 [106 EDUC. L. REP. 1030] (10th Cir. 1996).

[161] Helmuth v. University of Alaska, Fairbanks, 908 P.2d 1017 [106 EDUC. L. REP. 343] (Ala. 1995).

[162] McCarthy v. Board of Trustees of Erie Community College, 914 F. Supp. 937 [107 EDUC. L. REP. 156] (W.D.N.Y. 1996).

duties. An appellate court in California reversed in favor of the hospital.[163] The court ruled that since the doctor retained his job as a faculty member, he was not entitled to due process before he was removed from his administrative positions.

Freedom of Speech

An African-American who was an assistant men's basketball coach sued a state university and its white head coach alleging employment discrimination and violations of First Amendment rights of free speech and association. The assistant claimed that he was mistreated for exercising his speech right by advising players of their eligibility for financial assistance and for exercising his association right by having close, personal relationships with several members of the team. The coach also argued that his contract was not renewed due to his race. A federal district court in Texas granted summary judgment in favor of the defendants and the Fifth Circuit affirmed.[164] The court agreed that there was an absence of evidence to support the coach's discrimination claim. On the First Amendment charge, the court was of the opinion that the coach's comments were not on matters of public concern for the purposes of speech and that the association charge, based on his social relationships with players, was not entitled to constitutional protection.

A faculty member, who was removed as head of a social work program after she sent a memo to an accrediting agency that raised questions about whether her program should be maintained, claimed that the university violated her rights under the First Amendment and the Fourteenth Amendment. A federal district court in Mississippi maintained that sovereign immunity prohibited the professor's claims against the university and its officials in their official capacity.[165] The court added that the faculty member failed to state a free speech claim under the First Amendment since the memo to the accrediting agency was a personal matter, not a matter of public concern.

Following remand from the federal court, a former administrator at a university's medical facility challenged a grant of summary judgment in favor of the institution where she claimed that it violated her right to free speech. An appellate court in North Carolina reversed in favor of the administrator.[166] The court posited that since the former administrator's

---

[163] Shoemaker v. County of Los Angeles, 43 Cal. Rptr.2d 774 [102 Educ. L. Rep. 259] (Cal. Ct. App. 1995).
[164] Wallace v. Texas Tech Univ., 80 F.3d 1042 [108 Educ. L. Rep. 1069] (5th Cir. 1996).
[165] Harris v. Mississippi Valley State Univ., 899 F. Supp. 1561 [104 Educ. L. Rep. 261] (N.D. Miss. 1995).
[166] Evans v. Cowan, 468 S.E.2d 575 [108 Educ. L. Rep. 991] (N.C. Ct. App. 1996).

free speech charges in feeral and state court were not identical, res judicata did not bar her state constitutional claims.

A former law clerk who was also a reporter for student newspapers alleged that her right to free speech was violated when she was dismissed from her position in the office of the university's chief counsel. A trial court granted the university's motion for summary judgment. On further review, an appellate tribunal in Ohio affirmed.[167] The court agreed that the dismissal did not violate the student's First Amendment rights since the university's attorney/client privilege was jeopardized by having a reporter serving as a law clerk.

Discrimination

A former research technician in Wisconsin appealed a grant of summary judgment in favor of a medical college wherein she claimed that she lost her job due to age discrimination. The Seventh Circuit affirmed.[168] The court observed that the technician failed to establish that the university's proffered reason for her dismissal, the discontinuation of external funding for her project, was a pretext for age discrimination.

After a college dismissed a staff member when administrators were unable to confirm her ability to perform her job due to complications surrounding her pregnancy, she brought suit for gender-based claims of emotional distress. The federal trial court in the District of Columbia declared that even though the employee's claim was not barred by the Workers' Compensation Act, the administrator's statement about her ability to handle the stress of the job was not so atrocious as to give rise to a claim for intentional infliction of emotional distress.[169]

In Missouri, a pulmonary function assistant at a university hospital filed suit alleging discrimination based on age and national origin when she was dismissed from her position. A federal trial court granted the hospital's motion for summary judgment.[170] The court reasoned that the employee failed to establish a prima facie case of age or national origin discrimination because she lost her job as part of a legitimate reduction-in-force.

An African-American secretary at a state university sought further review of the rejection of her claim of racial discrimination when she was passed over for promotion in favor of a white woman. An appellate court

---

[167] Edwards v. Buckley, 667 N.E.2d 423 [111 Educ. L. Rep. 458] (Ohio Ct. App. 1995).
[168] Weisbrot v. Medical College of Wisc., 79 F.3d 677 [108 Educ. L. Rep. 39] (7th Cir. 1996).
[169] Harvey v. Strayer College, 911 F. Supp. 24 [106 Educ. L. Rep. 610] (D.D.C. 1996).
[170] Herrero v. St. Louis Univ. Hosp., 929 F. Supp. 1260 [110 Educ. L. Rep. 1121] (E.D. Mo. 1996).

in North Carolina affirmed that the evidence supported the finding that the woman who was hired for the job was more qualified than the secretary.[171]

Retaliation

A former associate dean unsuccessfully claimed that he was dismissed in retaliation for whistleblowing after he reported alleged conflicts of interest involving various medical school personnel. An appellate court in North Carolina affirmed.[172] The court noted that the administrator failed to prove that whistleblowing was a substantial factor in his dismissal.

University employees brought two separate actions under the Whistleblowers' Protection Act (WPA) in connection with their requests for jury trials. In a consolidated opinion, an appellate court in Michigan found that the employees retained their rights to a jury trial under the WPA.[173]

Contracts

Breach of Contract

In California, a physicist who worked for a federally funded project appealed the dismissal of his section 1983 breach of contract claim against a state university and its director of laboratories. The Ninth Circuit reversed in favor of the physicist.[174] According to the court, since the university did not have sovereign immunity, both it and the laboratory director could be liable under section 1983.

A physician sued a university hospital for not renewing her contract for the final year of her residency program. The federal trial court in the District of Columbia held that although the hospital breached its contract by not performing evaluations every two months, the doctor was only entitled to a nominal award because she did not suffer any damages as a result of the breach.[175]

In the first of two suits from Missouri, a former administrator challenged the dismissal of his breach of contract action. An appellate court affirmed that the administrator's charge lacked merit because he was employed under an at-will contract that could have been terminated at any time.[176]

---

[171] Dorsey v. UNC-Wilmington, 468 S.E.2d 557 [108 EDUC. L. REP. 985] (N.C. Ct. App. 1996).

[172] Aune v. University of N.C. at Chapel Hill, 462 S.E.2d 678 [103 EDUC. L. REP. 1262] (N.C. Ct. App. 1995).

[173] Anzaldua v. Band, 550 N.W.2d 544 [110 EDUC. L. REP. 1258] (Mich. Ct. App. 1996).

[174] Doe v. Lawrence Livermore Nat'l Lab., 65 F.3d 771 [103 EDUC. L. REP. 583] (9th Cir. 1995).

[175] Patel v. Howard, 896 F. Supp. 199 [103 EDUC. L. REP. 678] (D.D.C. 1995).

[176] Clark v. Washington Univ., 906 S.W.2d 789 [103 EDUC. L. REP. 1268] (Mo. Ct. App. 1995).

A junior college sought further review of a jury verdict in favor of an audit manager whose one-year employment contract had not been renewed. An appellate court in Missouri reversed in favor of the college.[177] The court contended that since there was no record that the auditor ever accepted the college's offer of a three-year contract, his suit was without merit.

Procedural Issues

Farm workers brought a class action suit against a university's extension service when it identified them as independent contractors in order to avoid having to comply with the minimum wage provisions of the Fair Labor Standards Act (FLSA). A federal district court in Texas approved the settlement agreement when it decreed that the university violated the FLSA by classifying the farm workers as independent contractors.[178]

A university sought further review of a ruling in favor of a resident physician who requested access to her own records and those of her peers after she was dismissed from a training program. An appellate court in California reversed in favor of the university.[179] The court offered that the resident could not claim exceptions to the nondiscovery provisions applicable to hospitals where a peer review committee evaluated the quality of care that she provided as part of her request for staff privileges at the medical facility.

Denial of Benefits

A variety of issues involving benefits were litigated again this year. In the first of four cases from New York, an inmate who served as a tutor in an education program appealed a grant of summary judgment in favor of the prison when he demanded minimum wages under the FLSA. The Second Circuit affirmed that prison labor is not subject to the FLSA.[180] Moreover, the court found that since the inmate's working as a tutor served only the institutional purpose of rehabilitation, he was not an employee within the meaning of the law.

Unemployment compensation was before the courts in four cases, the first three of which were from New York. For example, a secretary who took early retirement from her university and subsequently filled a

---

[177] Wiseman v. Junior College Dist. of St. Louis, 916 S.W.2d 267 [107 Educ. L. Rep. 1047] (Mo. Ct. App. 1995).

[178] Murillo v. Texas A & M Univ. Sys., 921 F. Supp. 443 [108 Educ. L. Rep. 1162] (S.D. Tex. 1996).

[179] University of S. Cal. v. Superior Ct. of Los Angeles County, 53 Cal. Rptr.2d 260 [109 Educ. L. Rep. 856] (Cal. Ct. App. 1996).

[180] Danneskjold v. Hausrath, 82 F.3d 37 [108 Educ. L. Rep. 1105] (2nd Cir. 1996).

part-time position on a temporary basis challenged the denial of her request for unemployment benefits when she was released after a full-time employee was hired. An appellate court affirmed that the secretary was not qualified for unemployment benefits since she retired voluntarily.[181]

A voluntary, unpaid adjunct professor sought further review of the dismissal of his suit for unemployment compensation from a university and its research foundation after he lost his full-time job. An appellate court in New York affirmed.[182] The court decided that the faculty member was not entitled to unemployment compensation from the university because he never worked there in a full-time, paid capacity.

In New York, a university disputed an award of unemployment compensation to an engineering assistant who was enrolled in a cooperative education program. An appellate court reversed in favor of the university.[183] The court determined that since the program combined academic instruction with work experience, the full-time student was not an employee for purposes of unemployment compensation.

In Illinois, a transportation authority sought further review of an award in favor of a college student who was granted unemployment compensation when she elected not to return to school. An appellate court affirmed in favor of the student.[184] The court agreed that the student was not disqualified for benefits under the voluntary leave section of the Unemployment Compensation Act when she decided not to return to school and asked the authority for a permanent position before she left her summer job.

Retirement benefits were before the court when a professor at a community college who was injured in the college's cafeteria was denied accidental disability retirement benefits. The Supreme Judicial Court of Massachusetts affirmed.[185] The court ruled that the faculty member was not entitled to accidental disability retirement benefits since she was not injured while performing the duties associated with her position.

In Pennsylvania, a professor challenged the denial of his petition to buy nonstate service credits for the academic year he spent overseas on a Fulbright Scholarship. An appellate court reversed in favor of the faculty member.[186] The court observed that the state employees retirement code,

---

[181] *In re* Wilson, 639 N.Y.S.2d 177 [107 Educ. L. Rep. 954] (N.Y. App. Div. 1996).

[182] Vartanian v. Research Found. of State Univ. of N.Y., 642 N.Y.S.2d 726 [109 Educ. L. Rep. 904] (N.Y. App. Div. 1996).

[183] *In re* Killian, 645 N.Y.S.2d 627 [111 Educ. L. Rep. 942] (N.Y. App. Div. 1996).

[184] Chicago Transit Auth. v. Didrickson, 659 N.E.2d 28 [105 Educ. L. Rep. 1169] (Ill. App. Ct. 1995).

[185] Namvar v. Contributory Retirement Appeal Bd., 663 N.E.2d 263 [108 Educ. L. Rep. 861] (Mass. 1996).

[186] Shafer v. State Employees' Retirement Bd., 667 A.2d 1209 [105 Educ. L. Rep. 614] (Pa. Commw. Ct. 1995).

which allows individuals to purchase credit for service in public schools or as an administrator or instructor for an agency of the United States, did not intend for an employment relationship to exist between the two parties. As such, the court concluded that the professor was entitled to purchase nonstate service credit.

A proprietary college appealed a judgment in favor of a former recruiter after it refused to pay her a bonus following the termination of her employment. The Supreme Court of South Dakota affirmed.[187] The panel stated that the clause in the recruiter's contract, providing that she was not entitled to a bonus after she left the job, was waived since the admissions director promised to pay her even after her employment had been terminated. However, the court also reversed in finding that the college's failure to pay the bonus was not such oppressive conduct that warranted the doubling of damages.

Sexual Harassment

The lead case here involved allegations of sexual harassment against a tenured faculty member who used a confrontational teaching style in an English writing class. In light of his having students write on controversial topics such as obscenity, cannibalism, and consensual sex with children, a female charged that the professor's comments, use of profanity, and discussions of a sexual nature were aimed at her and other women in the class. The college, based on its sexual harassment policy, agreed that the professor had fostered a hostile and offensive learning environment. As such, the college ordered the professor to provide a syllabus outlining the style, content, and methods used in his class; attend a seminar on sexual harassment; undergo formal evaluation procedures for faculty; become sensitive to student needs and backgrounds; and modify his teaching techniques to avoid impairing students from learning. The professor appealed after a federal district court in California granted the college's motion for summary judgment in his suit that challenged the sexual harassment policy on the ground that it inhibited his right to free speech under the First Amendment. The Ninth Circuit reversed in favor of the faculty member. The court ruled that the policy, which prohibited conduct that had the " . . . effect of unreasonably interfering with an individual's academic performance or creating an intimidating, hostile, or offensive learning environment,"[188] was unconstitutionally

---

[187] Baldwin v. National College, 537 N.W.2d 14 [103 EDUC. L. REP. 392] (S.D. 1995).
[188] Cohen v. San Bernadino Valley College, 92 F.3d 968, 972 [111 EDUC. L. REP. 762] (9th Cir. 1996).

vague in relation to the professor's actions in class. The court reflected that rather than prohibit the college from punishing the type of speech used by the professor, it could do so only through a policy that was precisely construed to identify the conduct or speech to be controlled.

After a group of female students had trouble with the equipment in a summer physiology of exercise class, a professor was summoned. Yet, even though the faculty member was warned that one of the females was not fully clothed, he barged into the room, removed a covering, and made lewd comments about the young woman. Subsequently, the professor appealed an administrative determination that he engaged in sexual harassment. The Supreme Court of Tennessee affirmed that the notice of hearing given to the professor comported with due process and that his conduct, which violated the university's policy, was sexual harassment.[189]

Title VII and Title IX

A female librarian claimed that along with being sexually harassed by a woman supervisor, a female consultant created a hostile work environment. The federal district court in Puerto Rico rejected the university's motion to dismiss when it held that same sex sexual harassment was a valid claim under title VII.[190] At the same time, the court dismissed charges against defendants who were not included in the librarian's EEOC claim on the basis that the Eleventh Amendment barred the librarian's claim for monetary damages.

In Pennsylvania, a student sued her community college and a professor for sexual harassment. The court rebuffed the student's section 1983, equal protection, ADA, title IX, and section 504 Rehabilitation Act claims for lack of sufficient detail and failure to state causes of action.[191] However, the court refused to dismiss the title IX quid pro quo charge because the student, who graduated with a 4.00 grade point average, raised material issues of fact as to whether the harassment limited the variety of course work she might have taken while enrolled in the community college.

A former female clerical employee at a university medical school filed suit alleging a title VII hostile work environment and constructive discharge along with a variety of claims involving a coworker and his supervisor. A federal district court in Georgia dismissed the claims against

---

[189] McClellan v. Board of Regents of the State Univ., 921 S.W.2d 684 [111 Educ. L. Rep. 997] (Tenn. 1996).
[190] Nogueras v. University of P.R., 890 F. Supp. 60 [102 Educ. L. Rep. 90] (D.P.R. 1995).
[191] Slater v. Marshall, 906 F. Supp. 256 [105 Educ. L. Rep. 501] (E.D. Pa. 1995).

the supervisor but not against the medical center.[192] The court acknowledged that genuine issues of material fact precluded summary judgment on the allegations under title VII for a hostile work environment and constructive discharge as well as for the state law charges dealing with the intentional infliction of emotional distress, invasion of privacy, and negligent retention and supervision.

A former executive secretary to the dean of a law school claimed that acts of sexual harassment by the dean created a hostile work environment under title VII and title IX. The secretary alleged that she was fired after she failed to submit to his advances that included explicit remarks, innuendoes, fondling his sex organ in her presence, and touching her in an offensive and unwanted way. The federal trial court in the District of Columbia denied the dean's motion for partial summary judgment in declaring that genuine issues of material facts existed on the claims of improper dismissal under title VII and title IX, sexual harassment, and hostile work environment.[193] The court added that it was unclear whether the school vigorously discouraged sexual harassment in the work environment.

Two students, one of whom also worked for a college, unsuccessfully sued the college and a professor for sexual harassment under title VII and title IX. A federal district court in New York granted the college's motion to dismiss.[194] The court judged that the student-employee's title VII charge terminated when she resigned from her job. Further, the court contended that the college supported the efforts of the students to complain under its sexual harassment policy and suspended the professor based on his inappropriate behavior.

In a second case from New York, a former employee of a university claimed that she was harassed by a male supervisor with whom she had a sexual relationship. Following a jury verdict that found that the woman had not been sexually harassed, a federal district court rejected her motion for a new trial.[195] The court was of the opinion that the university could not be liable for failing to take investigative or remedial action after it decided that sexual harassment did not occur.

Judicial Procedures

The first of three actions involving judicial procedures was filed by an African-American female employee who sought to amend her

---

[192] Simon v. Morehouse Sch. of Med., 908 F. Supp. 959 [105 Educ. L. Rep. 1067] (N.D. Ga. 1995).

[193] Pinkney v. Robinson, 913 F. Supp. 25 [106 Educ. L. Rep. 1119] (D.D.C. 1996).

[194] Pallett v. Palma, 914 F. Supp. 1018 [107 Educ. L. Rep. 165] (S.D.N.Y. 1996).

[195] Karibian v. Columbia Univ., 930 F. Supp. 134 [111 Educ. L. Rep. 221] (S.D.N.Y. 1996).

complaint against a university. A federal district court pointed out that permitting the woman to add an allegation under the Pennsylvania Human Rights Act, along with a charge of negligent retention to her title VII claims of discrimination and sexual harassment, was not prejudicial to the university's case.[196] The court reasoned that the additions were proper since the supposedly discriminatory conduct occurred within the limitations periods.

In a follow up to the previous case, the employee made a motion for attorney fees after she prevailed in a jury trial. A federal district court in Pennsylvania granted the woman's request but reduced the lodestar amount based on the partial success of her claim.[197]

Complainants in a sexual harassment suit against a university challenged a ruling in favor of a board of regents that enforced the terms of a dictated settlement agreement. An appellate court in California affirmed in favor of the board.[198] The court agreed that the parties had reached a binding agreement at the conclusion of a mediation and settlement conference even though some participants expressed misgivings before the typed release was prepared.

Sexual Assault

A university in Texas appealed the dismissal of its motion for summary judgment where a student alleged that she had been sexually assaulted by a male classmate at a party that was sponsored by her department. However, the investigation ceased after the woman failed to bring charges against the male when other students reported that the sexual activity was consensual. The student later filed civil rights charges against police officers from the university and the former chief of the department as well as a professor who allegedly attempted to intimidate her because she complained about the male's behavior. The Fifth Circuit reversed in favor of the defendants.[199] The court posited that the police officers and chief were entitled to qualified immunity on the invasion of privacy, defamation, and intent to inflict emotional distress charges since they acted in their official capacities in investigating the complaint. The court added that the student failed to state a claim of intention to inflict emotional distress against the professor.

---

[196] Schofield v. Trustees of the Univ. of Pa., 894 F. Supp. 194 [102 Educ. L. Rep. 1082] (E.D. Pa. 1995).

[197] Schofield v. Trustees of the Univ. of Pa., 919 F. Supp. 821 [108 Educ. L. Rep. 581] (E.D. Pa. 1996).

[198] Regents of the Univ. of Cal. v. Sumner, 50 Cal. Rptr.2d 200 [106 Educ. L. Rep. 1259] (Cal. Ct. App. 1996).

[199] Cantu v. Rocha, 77 F.3d 795 [107 Educ. L. Rep. 459] (5th Cir. 1996).

Students

Admissions

The Supreme Court took some action on two important and well
known cases dealing with admissions. This year brought the final ruling
in *Hopwood v. Texas*,[200] a suit that was brought by four white applicants
who were denied admission to the law school at the University of Texas.
The prospective students claimed that the school's dual admissions process
violated the Equal Protection Clause of the Fourteenth Amendment. The
Fifth Circuit prohibited the use of race as a criterion in admissions. In
denying the university's appeal, the Court stated that it would not hear
the case due to a lack of judgments and/or opinions in the controversy
since the law school had changed its policy.

There was no additional litigation during 1996 in the case of a female
student who was admitted to The Citadel, a state-supported, all-male
military college in South Carolina.[201] Yet, the Court rejected the petition
for a writ of certiorari to permit another party to intervene when it observed
that the issues involved in the initial litigation were moot.[202]

An applicant who was blind appealed the denial of her admission to
medical school. The applicant claimed that she was rejected due to her
handicap and that, but for her visual impairment, she was otherwise
qualified. The university retorted that its admissions guidelines, which
were extracted from those of the Association of American Medical
Colleges, require students to be able to observe various procedures. The
Supreme Court of Ohio affirmed that the applicant's civil rights were not
violated when she was denied admission based on her inability to
observe.[203] The court added that accommodation was not possible and
that the college did nor err in refusing to interview a blind psychiatrist
prior to acting on the student's application.

In North Carolina, a student who was denied admission into a nursing
school despite having met its basic requirements sought further review
of a grant of summary judgment in her breach of contract action against
the university. An appellate court affirmed in holding that the faculty
members who allegedly assured the applicant that she would be admitted
lacked apparent authority to do so pursuant to written admission criteria

[200] Hopwood v. Texas, 78 F.3d 932 [107 EDUC. L. REP. 552] (5th Cir. 1996), *cert. denied*, 116 S. Ct. 2581 (1996).
[201] Faulkner v. Jones, 51 F.3d 440 [99 EDUC. L. REP. 99] (4th Cir. 1995).
[202] Faulkner v. Jones, 116 S. Ct. 331 [105 EDUC. L. REP. 395] (1995).
[203] Ohio Civil Rights Comm'n v. Case W. Reserve Univ., 666 N.E.2d 1376 [110 EDUC. L. REP. 1202] (Ohio 1996).

in the student handbook.[204] Further, the court maintained that all sixty of the seventy-seven qualified applicants who were admitted had higher cumulative grade point averages than the student.

A student challenged a grant of summary judgment in favor of a university after she sued it for refusing to accept academic work that she completed at an unaccredited institution. An appellate court in New York affirmed that any claim for refusal to accept the credits was barred by the statute of limitations.[205] In addition, the panel indicated that while the Court of Claims was the proper venue for her suit, the student failed to meet her statutory obligation of specifying the defamatory words.

Financial Aid

Policies and Regulations

Institutions unsuccessfully challenged the administration of new regulations enacted pursuant to the Higher Education Act (HEA) that were designed to improve accountability and integrity of schools participating in federally funded student financial aid programs. The Circuit Court for the District of Columbia upheld a grant of summary judgment in favor of the DOE.[206] The court ruled that the rules should be left in place because they were promulgated in proper form within the time limit set by the master calendar provision in the federal regulations.

Proprietary vocational schools appealed a grant of summary judgment in favor of the DOE in their dispute over regulations dealing with the administration of amendments to the HEA. The changes, which were designed to improve the accountability of colleges and universities that are involved in federally funded student financial aid programs, shift the burden of collection of loans from the federal government and affiliated lending agencies to the schools. The Circuit Court for the District of Columbia affirmed.[207] The court agreed that the institutions could not assume that students would repay financial assistance to the government if they withdrew from programs during the academic year. Accordingly, the court concluded that the schools were to repay the government and then collect the funds from the students.

Student loan servicers in Indiana unsuccessfully appealed the rejection of their suit to invalidate regulations issued by the DOE. The

---

[204] Long v. University of N.C. at Wilmington, 461 S.E.2d 773 [103 Educ. L. Rep. 490] (N.C. Ct. App. 1995).

[205] Washington v. Baruch, 633 N.Y.S.2d 286 [104 Educ. L. Rep. 1268] (N.Y. App. Div. 1995).

[206] Career College Ass'n v. Riley, 74 F.3d 1265 [106 Educ. L. Rep. 981] (D.C. Cir. 1996).

[207] Career College Ass'n v. Riley, 82 F.3d 476 [109 Educ. L. Rep. 27] (D.C. Cir. 1996).

regulations obligated the servicers to avoid careless mistakes and outright fraud by their employees that resulted in the loss of federal money. The Seventh Circuit affirmed that the regulations neither exceeded the ordinary common liabilities imposed on loan servicers nor were they arbitrary or capricious.[208]

A not-for-profit corporation that operated a vocational school challenged a regulation of the DOE that required it to derive a percentage of its tuition from nonfederal sources before it could be eligible to participate in guaranteed federal aid programs. The federal district court in Kansas granted the school's motion for declaratory and injunctive relief.[209] The court ruled that the rule contravened the plain language of the HEA.

Institutional Eligibility

In the first of two cases from California, the DOE appealed a grant of summary judgment in favor of trustees who challenged an administrative determination that the university was responsible for interest earned on undisbursed Pell Grant funds. The Ninth Circuit affirmed that the DOE not only miscalculated the interest but also misinterpreted federal law regarding the state's accountability for interest on such grants.[210]

The trustee of a private vocational college in California that was denied access to student loans because of the high default rate among its pupils disputed the dismissal of his section 1983 suit for lack of standing. The Ninth Circuit affirmed that since the students, not the school, were the intended beneficiaries, the trustee could not maintain the section 1983 action.[211]

A vocational school that lost its eligibility to participate in federal student loan programs sued the DOE seeking reinstatement. The federal trial court for the District of Columbia held that since the school was ineligible when the 1983 amendments to the HEA went into effect, it was not entitled to reinstatement pending the result of its appeal.[212]

The Student Loan Marketing Association (Sallie Mae) brought suit against the DOE over a statute that imposed an annual fee for transferred student loans to a wholly owned subsidiary under the Federal Family Education Loan (FFEL) program. The federal trial court in the District

---

[208] USA Group Loan Serv. v. Riley, 82 F.3d 708 [109 EDUC. L. REP. 30] (7th Cir. 1996).
[209] Mission Group Kan. v. Riley, 909 F. Supp. 835 [106 EDUC. L. REP. 163] (D. Kan. 1995).
[210] Trustees of Cal. State Univ. v. Riley, 74 F.3d 960 [106 EDUC. L. REP. 478] (9th Cir. 1996).
[211] Dumas v. Kipp, 90 F.3d 386 [111 EDUC. L. REP. 124] (9th Cir. 1996).
[212] The Bilingual Inst. v. Riley, 930 F. Supp. 9 [111 EDUC. L. REP. 192] (D.D.C. 1996).

of Columbia granted the DOE's motion for summary judgment.[213] The court ascertained that the law did not amount to an unconstitutional taking of private property, did not violate Sallie Mae's right to equal protection, and was neither arbitrary nor capricious.

In a second suit involving Sallie Mae, the corporation successfully sued a service contract debtor over the recalculation of interest. An appellate court in Missouri affirmed in favor of Sallie Mae.[214] The court not only agreed that the recalculation of principal and interest due on the coagulation of three notes was proper but added that a case could have been made against the debtor for accrued interest.

Individual Eligibility

In Mississippi, a student sought injunctive relief where guaranty agencies refused to issue him a loan after they sent him a letter for failing to repay past debts that were in default. A federal district court granted the agencies' motions for summary judgment.[215] According to the court, the student was ineligible for a loan because he was in default on a prior obligation when he submitted an application for assistance.

An inmate in a state prison unsuccessfully questioned the constitutionality of an amendment to the HEA that prohibited prisoners from receiving Pell Grants. A federal district court in New York granted the DOE's motion to dismiss for failure to state a cause of action.[216] The court decreed that the denial of Pell Grants to inmates was neither an ex post facto punishment nor cruel and unusual.

In Pennsylvania, a college student who was blind sought judicial review of an administrative determination of a state statute. The student, who had fallen behind the time schedule to complete his degree, was informed in typed, instead of in a Braille, communication that the deficient credits would be made up at his, rather than the agency's, expense. An appellate court in Pennsylvania affirmed in favor of the agency.[217] The court noted that the denial of continued funding was not a breach of due process nor was the agency's limiting participation in the tuition payment program so inflexibile as to be facially invalid under the Rehabilitation Act.

---

[213] Student Loan Mktg. Ass'n v. Riley, 907 F. Supp. 464 [105 EDUC. L. REP. 927] (D.D.C 1995).

[214] Student Loan Mktg. Ass'n v. Raja, 914 S.W.2d 825 [108 EDUC. L. REP. 1302] (Mo. Ct. App. 1996).

[215] Pace v. Suntech, 900 F. Supp. 20 [104 EDUC. L. REP. 279] (S.D. Miss. 1995).

[216] Tremblay v. Riley, 917 F. Supp. 195 [107 EDUC. L. REP. 817] (W.D.N.Y. 1996).

[217] Murdy v. Bureau of Blindness & Visual Servs., 677 A.2d 1280 [110 EDUC. L. REP. 739] (Pa. Commw. Ct. 1996).

Bankruptcy

Chapter 7

Once again, a significant number of Chapter 7 bankruptcy disputes were litigated. In two suits, the courts permitted loans to be discharged since the debtors substantiated hardship based on mental illness[218] and age.[219] However, in six cases, courts refused to excuse loans where debtors were unable to demonstrate undue hardships and/or good faith efforts to repay their obligations.[220] Five actions involved the nondischarge of loans based on a seven-year moratorium from the date when their principal become due.[221] In two additional matters, judges reduced the amount of nondischarge as the debtors had other available resources or repayments would not have lowered their standards of living.[222]

Along with the more typical Chapter 7 cases, this year witnessed litigation where parents filed for bankruptcy and tried to claim dischargeability for the college debts of their children. One case involved loans for unpaid tuition by the student[223] while another was by the parents.[224] And, in three disputes, the courts held that the debts were nondischargeable.[225] In a fourth action, the court deferred a payment for six months after the debtor demonstrated that her current financial circumstances, with the added burden of having to repay the loan, would create an undue hardship.[226]

A bankruptcy court in Ohio granted partial relief even though there was no justification to discharge a student loan after the debtor did not complete his medical education. On appeal, the Sixth Circuit affirmed

---

[218] *In re* Mayer, 198 B.R. 116 [111 Educ. L. Rep. 333] (Bankr. E.D. Pa. 1996).

[219] *In re* Taylor, 198 B.R. 700 [111 Educ. L. Rep. 841] (Bankr. N.D. Ohio 1996).

[220] *In re* Hawkins, 187 B.R. 294 [103 Educ. L. Rep. 1090] (Bankr. N.D. Iowa 1995); *In re* Melton, 187 B.R. 98 [103 Educ. L. Rep. 1082] (Bankr. W.D.N.Y. 1996); Commonwealth of Va. State Educ. Assistance Auth. v. Dillon, 189 B.R. 382 [105 Educ. L. Rep. 206] (W.D. Va. 1995); *In re* Maulin, 190 B.R. 153 [105 Educ. L. Rep. 1098] (Bankr. W.D.N.Y. 1995); *In re* Robinson, 193 B.R. 967 [108 Educ. L. Rep. 278] (Bankr. N.D. Ala. 1996); *In re* Griffin, 197 B.R. 144 [110 Educ. L. Rep. 210] (Bankr. E.D. Okla. 1996).

[221] *In re* Flynn, 190 B.R. 139 [105 Educ. L. Rep. 1093] (Bankr. D.N.H. 1995); *In re* Schirmer, 191 B.R. 155 [106 Educ. L. Rep. 699] (Bankr. D. Minn. 1996); *In re* Thorson, 195 B.R. 101 [109 Educ. L. Rep. 248] (Bankr. 9th Cir. 1996); *In re* Williams, 195 B.R. 644 [109 Educ. L. Rep. 763] (Bankr. N.D. Tex. 1996); *In re* Cobb, 196 B.R. 34 [109 Educ. L. Rep. 1272] (Bankr. E.D. Va. 1996).

[222] *In re* Ammirati, 187 B.R. 902 [104 Educ. L. Rep. 425] (D.S.C. 1995); *In re* Fox, 189 B.R. 115 [105 Educ. L. Rep. 192] (Bankr. N.D. Ohio 1995).

[223] *In re* Van Ess, 186 B.R. 375 [103 Educ. L. Rep. 765] (Bankr. D.N.J. 1994).

[224] *In re* Peller, 184 B.R. 663 [102 Educ. L. Rep. 180] (Bankr. D.N.J. 1994).

[225] *In re* Pichardo, 186 B.R. 279 [103 Educ. L. Rep. 240] (Bankr. M.D. Fla. 1995); *In re* Uterhark, 185 B.R. 39 [102 Educ. L. Rep. 600] (Bankr. N.D. Ohio 1995); TI Fed. Credit Union v. Delbonis, 72 F.3d 921 [106 Educ. L. Rep. 33] (1st Cir. 1995).

[226] *In re* O'Donnell, 198 B.R. 1 [111 Educ. L. Rep. 328] (Bankr. D.N.H. 1996).

that the loan could not be discharged solely on the ground of unconscionability where the joint income of the former student and his spouse would not result in a hardship if the debt were repaid.[227]

The bankruptcy court in South Dakota reviewed the case of a Chapter 7 debtor to determine the dischargeability of her loan for tuition, room, board, fees, books, and supplies.[228] The court agreed that the student loan could be discharged since none of the items were educational benefits.

Chapter 13

A debtor in Virginia filed suit over the dischargeability of her student loans in a case that involved whether her Chapter 13 action could include the previous years under which she was in Chapter 7 proceedings. The court mandated that the previous years could not be included in assessing the dischargeability of the student's loan.[229]

In two separate suits involving Health Education Assistance Loans (HEAL), dentists tried to have nondischargeable debts converted to dischargeable loans. Courts in New Hampshire[230] and Wisconsin[231] declared that the debtors could not silently change the nature of their obligations by entering settlement agreements.

In cases brought on behalf of an Egyptian physician in Ohio[232] and a sixty-seven-year-old, partially blind widow in Florida,[233] courts permitted debtors to discharge their student loans based on undue hardship. Yet, in New Hampshire, the court ruled that since the parent of a student was unable to demonstrate undue hardship where the lender was willing to accept a deferred repayment schedule, there was no reason to discharge educational loans in a Chapter 13 proceeding.[234]

Chapter 13 litigation also included actions by debtors who requested adjustments in the percentage of dischargeable debts and nondischargeable student loans. At issue in both suits was the disparate treatment of nondischargeable loans and unsecured credit when the student loan would be paid off at one-hundred percent, while the other debts would be paid at eighteen percent in one case and ten percent in the other. Courts in Florida[235] and Oklahoma[236] concluded that the favorable treatment of nondischargeable

---

[227] *In re* Rice, 78 F.3d 1144 [107 Educ. L. Rep. 589] (6th Cir. 1996).

[228] *In re* Nelson, 188 B.R. 32 [104 Educ. L. Rep. 431] (D.S.D. 1995).

[229] *In re* Gibson, 184 B.R. 716 [102 Educ. L. Rep. 188] (E.D. Va. 1995).

[230] *In re* Roy, 189 B.R. 245 [105 Educ. L. Rep. 202] (Bankr. D.N.H. 1995).

[231] *In re* Tanski, 195 B.R. 408 [109 Educ. L. Rep. 254] (Bankr. E.D. Wis. 1996).

[232] *In re* Elebrashy, 189 B.R. 922 [105 Educ. L. Rep. 1083] (Bankr. N.D. Ohio 1995).

[233] *In re* Fuertes, 198 B.R. 379 [111 Educ. L. Rep. 346] (Bankr. S.D. Fla. 1996).

[234] *In re* LaFlamme, 188 B.R. 867 [105 Educ. L. Rptr. 185] (Bankr. D.N.H. 1995).

[235] *In re* Cox, 186 B.R. 744 [103 Educ. L. Rep. 772] (Bankr. N.D. Fla. 1995).

[236] *In re* Willis, 189 B.R. 203 [105 Educ. L. Rep. 198] (Bankr. N.D. Okla. 1995).

loans over unsecured debt was not unfair discrimination. Conversely, a bankruptcy court in California observed that favoring nondischargeable loans over unsecured creditors was unfair discrimination.[237]

Service Scholarships

The first of two cases involving the National Health Services Corps (NHSC) was filed by a doctor and her spouse who requested an income tax refund from liability and interest payments on their service obligation as an unreimbursed business expense. The federal district court in South Carolina reasoned that repayment of an unfulfilled service obligation to the NHSC is not tax deductible and that the Internal Revenue Service (IRS) had properly assessed the penalty.[238]

Where the federal government sued a physician to collect on a NHSC loan, a federal district court in Louisiana offered that there could be no estoppel after it denied his claim for a hardship.[239] The court added that the physician was not entitled to service credit for time spent at a clinic since he failed to receive prior approval for his placement.

The government sued a physician for repayment of loans issued under the Uniformed Services University of the Health Sciences since he was no longer meeting his active duty obligation. A federal district court in Missouri stated that the physician's failure to remain on active duty warranted the statutory doubling of his indebtedness.[240]

Collections

A former student sued the trustees of her university alleging racial discrimination, a violation of a bankruptcy stay that had been granted under Chapter 7, and defamation. After acknowledging that the discrimination claim was unsubstantiated, a federal district court in New York posited that it lacked jurisdiction over the default judgment that the university had been awarded in a state court on the defamation claim.[241] In addition, the court asserted that the university's computerized automatic debt collection program did not violate the bankruptcy stay.

After a federal employee defaulted on a student loan, he sued the DOE in an attempt to overturn wage garnishment on the basis that it created a hardship. A federal district court in Illinois granted the DOE's

---

[237] *In re* Bernal, 189 B.R. 507 [105 Educ. L. Rep. 211] (Bankr. S.D. Cal. 1995).

[238] Stroud v. United States, 906 F. Supp. 990 [105 Educ. L. Rep. 526] (D.S.C. 1995).

[239] United States v. Bloom, 925 F. Supp. 426 [109 Educ. L. Rep. 1260] (E.D. La. 1996).

[240] United States v. Fattman, 905 F. Supp. 646 [105 Educ. L. Rep. 148] (W.D. Mo. 1995).

[241] Odom v. Columbia Univ., 906 F. Supp. 188 [105 Educ. L. Rep. 491] (S.D.N.Y. 1995).

motion for summary judgment.[242] The court was of the opinion that the debtor failed to demonstrate how the garnishment would create an extreme financial hardship.

In the first of two cases involving alleged violations of the Fair Debt Collection Practices Act (FDCPA), the federal district court in Kansas dismissed a suit filed by a debtor who sued the DOE.[243] The court indicated that the debtor failed to state a claim for injunctive relief and that the statute of limitations on his charge had expired.

A student successfully challenged a college that assigned his debt to an agency that added a collection fee equal to one third of his obligation. The federal district court in Wisconsin held that attempts by the college to collect the debt violated both the FDCPA and state law.[244] The court further contended that the student was entitled to recover both the amount of interest and collection fees that he paid.

Students sued their college, the DOE, the state higher education assistance authority, and Sallie Mae for declaratory and injunctive relief under the Georgia Uniform Deceptive Trade Practices Act. The students alleged education malpractice after the school recruited them and induced them to sign up for federally guaranteed loans but failed to deliver on promised education and job placement. A federal district court dismissed in favor of the defendants.[245] The court decided that the students lacked a private right of action under the HEA and that their relationship with the college did not provide the basis for a fraud claim.

A student loan authority sought further review of a grant of summary judgment in favor of a debtor. An appellate court in Oklahoma reversed in favor of the loan authority.[246] The court pointed out that since the authority enforces the right of the state in recovering publicly funded educational loans, the debtor could not employ laches, the statute of limitations, or estoppel as defenses.

In the first of two cases where Sallie Mae sued debtors to recover on defaulted student loans, an appellate court in Pennsylvania affirmed a discharge of indebtedness because the borrower was permanently

---

[242] Sibley v. United States Dep't of Educ., 913 F. Supp. 1181 [106 EDUC. L. REP. 1175] (N.D. Ill. 1995).
[243] Whayne v. United States Dep't of Educ., 915 F. Supp. 1143 [107 EDUC. L. REP. 678] (D. Kan. 1996).
[244] Patzka v. Viterbo College, 917 F. Supp. 654 [107 EDUC. L. REP. 836] (W.D. Wis. 1996).
[245] Bartels v. Alabama Commercial College, 918 F. Supp. 1565 [108 EDUC. L. REP. 249] (S.D. Ga. 1995).
[246] Oklahoma ex rel. Okla. Student Loan Auth. v. Akers, 900 P.2d 468 [102 EDUC. L. REP. 841] (Okla. Ct. App. 1995).

disabled.[247] In the second, an appellate court in Florida reversed in noting that the agency's failure to attach payment schedules to a complaint was insufficient cause to dismiss its motion to recover debt.[248] The court found that Sallie Mae had sufficiently performed all conditions of the promissory note and was entitled to repayment.

A guarantor from New York challenged a dismissal in favor of a student who sued for the reimbursement of funds that it advanced to a lender after the student defaulted on his debts. An appellate court in New Jersey reversed in favor of the guarantor.[249] The court determined that the guarantor had established that the five-year discharge clock was based on the anticipated graduation date set forth in his loan contract, not on the earlier date when the student withdrew from school.

In Arkansas, a nonresident challenged the denial of his motion to dismiss an action by a student loan guarantee foundation to collect on notes that were allegedly in default. An appellate court reversed in favor of the nonresident.[250] It judged that the trial court lacked personal jurisdiction since the former student was not a resident of the state.

Child Support

Following their father's death, his children in Arkansas appealed a judgment in favor of his second wife when they claimed that his marital termination agreement with their mother imposed a constructive trust over his life insurance proceeds. The Eighth Circuit affirmed in favor of the second wife.[251] The court asserted that the marriage termination agreement did not require the father to make the proceeds of his life insurance payable to the children because they did not meet their obligation by attending approved colleges, on a full-time basis, while making normal progress toward obtaining their degrees.

In two similar cases, ex-wives appealed orders ending the settlement obligations of their former spouses to pay the college expenses of their children. In the first, an appellate tribunal in Florida affirmed that a lower court acted within its discretion in terminating the ex-husband's obligations for child support but not for a contractual obligation

---

[247] Student Loan Marketing Ass'n v. Farr, 663 A.2d 750 [103 EDUC. L. REP. 284] (Pa. Super. Ct. 1995).

[248] Student Loan Marketing Ass'n v. Morris, 662 So. 2d 990 [104 EDUC. L. REP. 1420] (Fla. Dist. Ct. App. 1995).

[249] New York State Higher Educ. Servs. Corp. v. Lucianna, 66 A.2d 173 [104 EDUC. L. REP. 771] (N.J. Super. Ct. App. Div. 1995).

[250] Glenn v. Student Loan Guarantee Found. of Ark., 920 S.W.2d 500 [109 EDUC. L. REP. 460] (Ark. Ct. App. 1996).

[251] Krupnick v. Ray, 61 F.3d 662 [102 EDUC. L. REP. 76] (8th Cir. 1995).

enforceable by the daughter as a third-party beneficiary.[252] In the second, an appellate court in New Jersey agreed that the husband's obligation ended when his ex-wife failed to communicate their daughter's educational plans.[253]

Former spouses in Missouri both challenged a post-marital dissolution action, child support, and maintenance. An appellate court affirmed that if their son enrolled in vocational or higher education prior to the October following his high school graduation, the father was obligated to pay his expenses until he graduated or reached the age of twenty-two, which ever came first.[254]

Freedom of Speech

A graduate filed a section 1983 action against the editors of his law school newspaper alleging that their refusal to publish a classified advertisement critical of its faculty and staff violated his First Amendment rights. The student editors rejected the advertisement because they feared that it was inflammatory and would expose the paper to litigation. A federal district court in New York dismissed in favor of the editors on the basis that they were not state actors for the purpose of liability under section 1983.[255]

In Indiana, a professor and students unsuccessfully sought to enjoin the offering of an invocation and benediction as part of official university-wide commencement activities.[256] A federal district court decreed that the invocation and benediction did not violate either the coercion test under *Lee v. Weisman*[257] or the three part standards enunciated in *Lemon v. Kurtzman*.[258]

Freedom of Association

The primary litigation in the area of freedom of association involved three actions by a gay-lesbian bisexual student organization in Alabama against the state's Attorney General. In the first, the group sought declaratory and injunctive relief from the state statute that prohibited colleges from spending public funds or using facilities to sanction, recognize, or support any group that promotes a life-style or action

---

[252] Farnsworth v. Farnsworth, 657 So. 2d 1273 [102 EDUC. L. REP. 402] (Fla. Dist. Ct. App. 1995).

[253] Moss v. Nedas, 674 A.2d 174 [108 EDUC. L. REP. 787] (N.J. Super. Ct. App. Div. 1996).

[254] Monsees v. Monsees, 908 S.W.2d 812 [104 EDUC. L. REP. 920] (Mo. Ct. App. 1995).

[255] Leeds v. Meltz, 898 F. Supp. 146 [103 EDUC. L. REP. 1033] (E.D.N.Y. 1995).

[256] Tanford v. Brand, 932 F. Supp. 1139 [111 EDUC. L. REP. 1203] (S.D. Ind. 1996).

[257] 505 U.S. 577 [75 EDUC. L. REP. 43] (1992).

[258] 403 U.S. 602 (1971).

contrary to the state's sodomy and sexual misconduct laws. A federal district court declared the statute unconstitutional for violating the First Amendment not only because it prohibited speech based solely on viewpoint but also because it failed to distinguish between advocacy and the incitement, promotion, and production of imminent lawless action.[259] Subsequently, the court refused to stay its order on the ground that the Attorney General had not adequately demonstrated the merits of an appeal.[260] In the third suit, the court awarded attorney fees to the student group since it was the prevailing party.[261]

In Nebraska, a first-year student who wished to live off-campus in a Christian housing facility successfully challenged the state university's parietal rule that would have required him to live on-campus.[262] The federal district court reasoned that the rule neither passed the general applicability test nor met the requirements of neutrality given the excessive number of exceptions that had already been granted to other students. The court added that the rule was not sufficiently narrowly tailored to further a compelling governmental interest.

Discipline

Nonacademic Infractions

A former student who had been charged with harassment claimed that the disciplinary investigation conducted by a private college violated his right to due process on the basis that it did not comply with procedures described in the school's handbook or New York statutes. A federal trial court granted the college's motion for summary judgment.[263] The court held that the student failed to demonstrate that the college deviated from procedures identified in the handbook.

In Tennessee, a former student who was suspended for violating a church-affiliated college's policy against premarital sexual intercourse alleged that the school engaged in unlawful gender discrimination. A federal district court ruled that absent evidence that the student was suspended because she was female or that a male would have received the same treatment, the policy did not violate title IX.

[259] Gay Lesbian Bisexual Alliance v. Sessions, 917 F. Supp. 1548 [108 Educ. L. Rep. 113] (M.D. Ala. 1996).
[260] Gay Lesbian Bisexual Alliance v. Sessions, 917 F. Supp. 1558 [108 Educ. L. Rep. 123] (M.D. Ala. 1996).
[261] Gay Lesbian Bisexual Alliance v. Sessions, 930 F. Supp. 1492 [111 Educ. L. Rep. 321] (M.D. Ala. 1996).
[262] Rader v. Johnston, 924 F. Supp. 1540 [109 Educ. L. Rep. 1228] (D. Neb. 1996).
[263] Fraad-Wolff v. Vassar College, 932 F. Supp. 88 [111 Educ. L. Rep. 815] (S.D.N.Y. 1996).

A student at a private art college unsuccessfully sought further review of the dismissal of his challenge to his suspension. An appellate court in Pennsylvania decided that the college acted within its discretion in suspending the student for using deception and coercion in making repeated unauthorized entries into areas housing unique and priceless art collections.[264]

In New York, a student at a public university successfully challenged his summary suspension after he was arrested and charged with various narcotics offenses.[265] A trial court observed that the student was entitled to advance notice and a hearing before an impartial body before he could be suspended.

A student at a private college sought further review of his suspension for allegedly physically and sexually assaulting a classmate off-campus. An appellate court in Ohio affirmed that the college's action was neither arbitrary nor capricious.[266]

Academic Dismissal

A former student sued faculty and administrators after he was dismissed from a graduate program. The student submitted a manuscript to an academic journal and indicated that it was based on the study that he was completing, despite being warned not to do so because the faculty believed that his dissertation needed work. Yet, even after making changes to the study that the new department head suggested, the student was dismissed from the program because his work was unacceptable. The federal district court in Colorado stated that the university's failure to provide the student with a hearing prior to his dismissal violated due process but granted its motion for summary judgment since his claim was time barred.[267]

In Kansas, a former student unsuccessfully sought relief from an earlier judgment in her suit against the university where she was unable to complete her studies due to academic difficulties. The federal district court rejected the student's contention that she was entitled to relief based on newly discovered evidence provided by her cardiologist regarding her difficulty in taking timed examinations.[268]

---

[264] *In re* Barnes Found., 661 A.2d 889 [102 Educ. L. Rep. 193] (Pa. Super. Ct. 1995).
[265] Held v. State Univ. of N.Y., College at Fredonia, 630 N.Y.S.2d 196 [102 Educ. L. Rep. 748] (N.Y. Sup. Ct. 1995).
[266] Ray v. Wilmington College, 667 N.E.2d 39 [110 Educ. L. Rep. 1222] (Ohio Ct. App. 1995).
[267] Siblerud v. Colorado State Bd. of Agric., 896 F. Supp. 1506 [103 Educ. L. Rep. 726] (D. Colo. 1995).
[268] Nutter v. Wefald, 163 F.R.D 609 [104 Educ. L. Rep. 1232] (D. Kan. 1995).

A former graduate student sued faculty members claiming that they deprived him of a property right and a liberty interest in an education when he was dismissed allegedly in retaliation for exercising his right to free speech regarding research misconduct by his advisor. A federal district court in Illinois found that the student's right to free speech under the First Amendment had been violated but that the university had not deprived him of due process in the dismissal proceedings.[269]

In the first of four cases involving medical schools, a student who was dismissed for uneven academic performance claimed that his rights to procedural and substantive due process had been violated. A federal district court in Virginia dismissed in favor of the school on the basis that the college's action comported with requirements for procedural due process and was not a substantial departure from accepted academic norms.[270] However, the court added that the student stated a cause of action under the Family Educational Rights and Privacy Act based on his allegation that he was denied the right to challenge an error in scoring one of his examinations.

A medical student in Georgia with dyslexia who was dismissed due to poor academic performance claimed that the school violated his rights under the ADA and the Rehabilitation Act. A federal district court granted the school's motion for summary judgment.[271] The court noted that the young man failed to establish a prima facie case that his performance difficulties were related to his dyslexia or that he could meet the essential requirements of a medical student. As such, the court concluded that the student was not an otherwise qualified individual as there was no accommodation that would have allowed him to achieve passing grades without drastically altering the fundamental nature of the academic program.

In Indiana, a medical student who received failing grades after being accused of the appearance of cheating sought further review of the denial of her motion for a preliminary injunction to prohibit her expulsion. An appellate court affirmed.[272] The court acknowledged that the student's right to due process had been satisfied even though she did not have the opportunity to cross-examine the two professors whose classes she failed.

---

[269] Qvyjt v. Lin, 932 F. Supp. 1100 [111 EDUC. L. REP. 1192] (N.D. Ill. 1996).

[270] Lewin v. Medical College of Hampton Roads, 910 F. Supp. 1161 [106 EDUC. L. REP. 581] (E.D. Va. 1996).

[271] Ellis v. Morehouse Sch. of Med., 925 F. Supp. 1529 [110 EDUC. L. REP. 106] (N.D. Ga. 1996).

[272] Reilly v. Daly, 666 N.E.2d 439 [110 EDUC. L. REP. 769] (Ind. Ct. App. 1996).

A student in New York who was dismissed for repeated academic failures unsuccessfully sought to annul the medical school's action. An appellate court affirmed that the student failed to demonstrate that the actions of the school were arbitrary or capricious.[273]

In a second case from New York, a former student sued her college alleging that it violated her rights under the ADA and Rehabilitation Act. Following her dismissal from an occupational therapy program, the student claimed that officials knew of her learning disability. A federal district court in New York granted the college's motion for summary judgment.[274] The court indicated that the student failed to establish a prima facie case under either law since she did not demonstrate that the college knew about her disability prior to her expulsion.

A graduate student in Louisiana who was expelled for failing to maintain her academic standing challenged a grant of summary judgment in favor of the university in her breach of contract suit. An appellate court reversed in favor of the student.[275] The court pointed out that there were material issues of fact in need of resolution as to whether the associate dean verbally promised the student that she could remain in her social work program if she met the prerequisites established by the university's candidacy committee or whether she could merely reapply for admission.

In Ohio, a former nursing student who was dismissed due to poor academic performance just days before graduation sought further review of a grant of summary judgment in favor of the school. The former student claimed that her right to due process had been violated since she had not received a hearing prior to her dismissal. An appellate court applied academic deference in agreeing that the college's actions were neither arbitrary nor capricious.[276]

As illustrated by the next two cases, law schools also witnessed their share of litigation involving dismissals for academic infractions. A former student who claimed that he suffered from Post-Traumatic Stress Syndrome as the result of being the child of an alcoholic sued his law school for an alleged breach of contract related to his dismissal and for violating the Rehabilitation Act when he was denied readmission. The federal district court in New Hampshire maintained that even if the school's academic rules and regulations constituted a contract, it was not breached since he did not submit a plan on how he might overcome his

---

[273] *In re* McDermott, 644 N.Y.S.2d 834 [110 EDUC. L. REP. 1185] (N.Y. App. Div. 1996).
[274] Goodwin v. Keuka College, 929 F. Supp. 90 [110 EDUC. L. REP. 1084] (W.D.N.Y. 1995).
[275] Frentz v. Tulane Univ., 661 So. 2d 1097 [104 EDUC. L. REP. 536] (La. Ct. App. 1995).
[276] Frabotta v. Meridia Huron Hosp. Sch. of Nursing, 657 N.E.2d 816 [104 EDUC. L. REP. 1313] (Ohio Ct. App. 1995).

academic deficiencies.[277] The court added that the school did not violate the Rehabilitation Act because the former student was not otherwise qualified within the meaning of the law.

In Ohio, a fifty-six-year-old student with only one more semester to complete and who received a nonpassing grade that resulted in her expulsion from law school, sought further review of the dismissal of her suit alleging that her rights to due process had been violated. An appellate tribunal affirmed that a trial court lacked subject matter jurisdiction since the student's complaint set forth state constitutional claims against public employees.[278]

Other Academic Issues

A student at a community college in Texas appealed the dismissal of his suit claiming that his civil rights were violated when his grade in an English class was reduced due to his poor attendance record. The Fifth Circuit affirmed that the action was frivolous, insubstantial, insufficient, and did not involve a federal question.[279]

In Pennsylvania, a graduate sued his law school, its dean, and others for breach of contract and interference with contractual obligations where he was allegedly forced to withdraw from all but one of his classes during his final semester and was denied access to the university's facilities. A federal district court granted the defendants' motions for summary judgment.[280] The court offered that the student failed to spell out the nature of the contractual relationship with the law school or the specific way in which it had been breached.

A graduate social worker challenged the dismissal of her suit against both her professional association for a breach of its rules, regulations, and procedures and her faculty adviser for breach of fiduciary duty. The association censured the student in a private letter when she violated its rules by continuing to treat a suicidal client after the completion of her internship. An appellate court in Missouri affirmed that the student's petition did not allege any clear violations of how the association violated its rules.[281] In addition, the court ascertained that the student failed to establish that her faculty adviser owed her a fiduciary duty.

---

[277] Gill v. Franklin Pierce Law Ctr., 899 F. Supp. 850 [104 EDUC. L. REP. 234] (D.N.H. 1995).

[278] Kellon v. Cleveland Marshall College of Law, 657 N.E.2d 835 [104 EDUC. L. REP. 1318] (Ohio Ct. App. 1995).

[279] Dilworth v. Dallas County Community College Dist., 81 F.3d 616 [108 EDUC. L. REP. 531] (5th Cir. 1996).

[280] Gundlach v. Reinstein, 924 F. Supp. 684 [109 EDUC. L. REP. 1194] (E.D. Pa. 1996).

[281] Shapiro v. Butterfield, 921 S.W.2d 649 [109 EDUC. L. REP. 993] (Mo. Ct. App. 1996).

Constitutional Issues

An itinerant Pentecostal preacher in Virginia sued a public university and its officials alleging that their refusal to permit him to use facilities on campus because he did not have the sponsorship of two student groups violated his rights under the First Amendment. After a federal district court upheld the regulations, the Fourth Circuit vacated and remanded.[282] The court found that since the preacher did not have standing, the case should have been dismissed.

In the first of two cases from New York, a federal trial court dealt with an award of attorney fees to students who partially succeeded in questioning the use of some of their fees for a Public Interest Research Group.[283] The court declared that even though the students were entitled to partial attorney fees, their failure to itemize covered and noncovered issues meant that it would exercise its discretion in making the award.

Students brought a civil rights action against a city, a state university, and law enforcement officials alleging racial discrimination in the conduct of a criminal investigation. In reconsidering its own prior judgment, a federal district court in New York posited that since releasing the names of black male students to the police as potential suspects by the university did not necessarily violate their civil rights, the merits of the claim would have to be evaluated by a finder of fact.[284]

In a second case involving a criminal investigation on a campus, the state appealed the suppression of evidence and contraband that was obtained in the search of the dormitory room of a student at a state college. The Supreme Judicial Court of Massachusetts affirmed.[285] The court concluded that even though campus officials who were in the room checking for illegal pets stopped and called the campus police when they discovered marijuana plants, lights, and fertilizer in a closet, the subsequent search and confiscation violated the Fourth Amendment.

A university appealed a permanent injunction entered on behalf of a gay student group that prevented the military from using on-campus facilities for recruitment. The students argued that the military's discrimination against gay men and lesbians contradicted the school's nondiscrimination policy. The Supreme Court of Connecticut upheld the injunction.[286] The court asserted that the military had to meet the same standards as other employers.

---

[282] Gilles v. Torgersen, 71 F.3d 497 [105 Educ. L. Rep. 406] (4th Cir. 1995).

[283] Carroll v. Blinken, 899 F. Supp. 1214 [104 Educ. L. Rep. 242] (S.D.N.Y. 1995).

[284] Brown v. City of Oneonta, 916 F. Supp. 176 [107 Educ. L. Rep. 748] (N.D.N.Y. 1996).

[285] Commonwealth v. Neilson, 666 N.E.2d 984 [110 Educ. L. Rep. 790] (Mass. 1996).

[286] Gay and Lesbian Law Students Ass'n at the Univ. of Conn. Law Sch. v. Board of Trustees, Univ. of Conn., 673 A.2d 484 [108 Educ. L. Rep. 724] (Conn. 1996).

In Tennessee, a student sought further review of the dismissal of her damage suit against the university after she received a failing grade for refusing to read a book about a relationship between a white woman and a black man that she considered obscene. An appellate court affirmed that the student was not entitled to damages since she did not have a right to judicial review of a grade.[287]

Federal Statutory Issues
Title IX
A student in Virginia sued her professor and university for sexual harassment under title IX after her professor spanked her for failing to achieve a satisfactory score on a makeup examination. A federal district court stated that material issues of fact precluded the university's motion for summary judgment as to whether it could be liable for quid pro quo sexual harassment.[288] However, the court also mandated that the student failed to establish that the university violated title IX by creating an intentionally hostile environment.

Females filed a title IX class action suit in an attempt to compel their university to organize fast-pitch softball and soccer teams. Even though a federal district court in Louisiana held that the university violated title IX by not providing a fast-pitch softball team, it chose not to join the majority of courts that have relied upon numerical proportionality as a "safe harbor."[289] Under this theory, courts have reflected that as long as student-athletes are represented in the same proportion as in the general population on campus, then a university has complied with the "opportunity" aspect of title IX. The court judges that there was no evidence to support the assumption that interest and ability to participate in sports is equal between all students on campuses. Yet, the court ruled in favor of the women when it pointed out that the university did not present any credible evidence to establish what the interests and abilities of the student population are or have been. In contrast, the court acknowledged that the students presented credible evidence of their interest in and substantial ability to play softball. The court added that the women lacked standing to pursue the claim about the soccer team.

A student in Pennsylvania sued her university and an administrator who allegedly retaliated against her for filing an administrative complaint that he engaged in sexual harassment. A federal district court found that

---

[287] Lester v. Walker, 907 S.W.2d 812 [104 EDUC. L. REP. 522] (Tenn. Ct. App. 1995).

[288] Kadiki v. Virginia Commonwealth Univ., 892 F. Supp. 746 [102 EDUC. L. REP. 557] (E.D. Va. 1995).

[289] Pederson v. Louisiana State Univ., 912 F. Supp. 892 [106 EDUC. L. REP. 1060] (M.D. La. 1996).

title IX did not support the student's cause of action against the university.[290] However, the court retained jurisdiction over the student's claims against the administrator.

Family Educational Rights and Privacy Act

A former student sued his medical college alleging that his rights under the Family Educational Rights and Privacy Act were violated after he failed a "challenge exam" that he was required to take because he had taken a course at another school. A federal district court in Virginia granted the college's motion for summary judgment.[291] The court decided that the student failed to state a cause of action because his suit, which was fundamentally a challenge to the substance of a professor's evaluation of his knowledge, was beyond the scope of the Act.

Protection from Abuse Act

A male student challenged a protective order obtained by his former girlfriend at their university that directed him to cease all contact or communication with her. An appellate court in Pennsylvania affirmed that the female was entitled to the order because she had proven that her boyfriend had engaged in relational abuse.[292]

Civil Rights

An African-American student unsuccessfully filed a section 1983 action alleging that his university and coach violated his civil rights when, based on his race, he suffered indignities, disparate treatment, the loss of his scholarship, and demotion from the gymnastics team. A federal district court in Ohio dismissed on the basis that the university and coach were protected from immunity by the Eleventh Amendment.[293] According to the court, the case was moot since the injunctive relief sought by the student could not be granted in light of the fact that the gymnastic team no longer existed.

---

[290] Nelson v. Temple Univ., 920 F. Supp. 633 [108 EDUC. L. REP. 674] (E.D. Pa. 1996).
[291] Lewin v. Medical College of Hampton Roads, 931 F. Supp. 443 [111 EDUC. L. REP. 783] (E.D. Va. 1996).
[292] R.G. v. T.D., 672 A.2d 341 [107 EDUC. L. REP. 876] (Pa. Super. Ct. 1996).
[293] Davis v. Kent State Univ., 928 F. Supp. 729 [110 EDUC. L. REP. 689] (N.D. Ohio 1996).

Liability

Personal Injury
Alcohol

A fraternity house sought further review of the denial of its motion for summary judgment after the spouse of a motorist who was killed in a collision with an intoxicated student sued because the driver consumed the alcohol on its premises. An appellate court in Georgia reversed on the basis that the evidence did not support the allegation that the fraternity furnished the alcohol.[294]

Strict Liability

In Minnesota, a university filed a strict products liability claim against the manufacturer of a gas dryer blower unit to recover for property damage when the equipment allegedly caught fire. The federal district court reasoned that, as a "merchant in goods of the kind" with respect to its purchase of the unit, state law precluded the university from recovering on its tort claim of property damage to anything other than the dryer.[295]

The company that owned a motel that was leased to a university as a dormitory for student-athletes challenged a ruling that it was the sole cause of injuries sustained by a young man who fell through a glass door after he tripped on buckled carpet in a hallway. An appellate court in Louisiana amended and affirmed that the evidence was insufficient to establish negligence but that strict liability applied where the defect in the carpeting was unreasonably dangerous.[296]

In a second case from Louisiana, a nursing student who suffered neck and back injuries when a classroom chair she sat in broke challenged a judgment that apportioned sixty percent of fault to the school and the remaining forty percent to the company that provided building maintenance. An appellate court affirmed.[297] The court indicated that the state was strictly liable and that the apportionment of fault as well as the awards for medical expenses and loss of earning capacity damages were proper as they were supported by the evidence.

---

[294] Kappa Sigma Int'l Fraternity v. Tootle, 473 S.E.2d 213 [111 EDUC. L. REP. 988] (Ga. Ct. App. 1996).

[295] Board of Regents of the Univ. of Minn. v. Chief Indus., 907 F. Supp. 1298 [105 EDUC. L. REP. 1001] (D. Minn. 1995).

[296] Jones v. Peyton Place, Inc., 675 So. 2d 754 [110 EDUC. L. REP. 882] (La. Ct. App. 1996).

[297] Davis v. Lousiana *ex rel.* Charity-Delgado Sch. of Nursing, 675 So. 2d 1227 [110 EDUC. L. REP. 1306] (La. Ct. App. 1996).

Sexual Assault

A university and a company that provided security objected to a ruling by a magistrate that permitted a rape victim to amend her complaint to add a claim for punitive damages based on evidence that emerged during discovery. A federal district court in New York denied the defendants' objections.[298] The court observed that the woman's showing of merit in support of her request for punitive damages outweighed the prejudice that the university and security company would experience.

Procedural questions surrounded a case where a woman brought assault, battery, and negligence charges against a university. The woman, who alleged that she was raped in a fraternity house leased from the university, refused to respond to pretrial questions posed by the defendants concerning the identities of individuals with whom she had engaged in sexual intercourse, both before and after the alleged rape. When the woman refused to respond, the defendants sought further review. An appellate panel in New York affirmed that the trial court did not abuse its discretion in refusing to compel the woman to disclose the information demanded by the defendants.[299]

Parents challenged a grant of summary judgment in their suit against a college and a hospital where their son was assaulted by a campus minister/ chaplain who also served as a parish priest. An appellate court in Ohio affirmed that neither the college nor the hospital were liable under respondeat superior because the assault did not promote or facilitate their activities.[300] Further, the court was of the opinion that since the assault took place in the evening at the priest's parish residence and the victim was neither a patient of the hospital nor a student of the college, they had no responsibility to supervise his activity.

Scope of Duty

A mother appealed an adverse judgment where she sued Los Alamos National Laboratory under federal and state law alleging that her daughter died as a result of exposure to radiation and other hazardous substances. The Tenth Circuit agreed that since the woman's state law claims were subsumed in the federal charges, both were untimely under New Mexico's statute of limitations.[301]

---

[298] Doe v. Columbia Univ., 165 F.R.D. 394 [108 Educ. L. Rep. 1173] (S.D.N.Y. 1996).

[299] Andersen v. Cornell Univ., 638 N.Y.S.2d 852 [107 Educ. L. Rep. 940] (N.Y. App. Div. 1996).

[300] Gebhart v. College of Mt. St. Joseph, 665 N.E.2d 223 [109 Educ. L. Rep. 931] (Ohio Ct. App. 1996).

[301] Lujan v. Regents of the Univ. of Cal., 69 F.3d 1511 [104 Educ. L. Rep. 992] (10th Cir. 1995).

Bodily Injury
On Campus

A man who was injured when he fell into a hole created by the removal of a grate on the floor of a building maintained by the Board of Regents appealed the dismissal of his claim on the basis that it was time barred. The Supreme Court of Nebraska affirmed that the board was not estopped from asserting the statute of limitations as a defense where the man withdrew the charge that he filed with the State Claims Board and brought suit after time had expired.[302]

After a student was rendered quadriplegic as a result of a sledding accident in which he hit a light pole in a parking lot at the bottom of a hill on campus, an appellate court pointed out that the institution had a duty to protect him from or warn him of the risk of injury. On remand, a trial court disregarded the directions of the appellate tribunal and held that the university did not owe the injured student a duty. On further review, an appellate panel again reversed on the basis that the lower court should not have revisited the question of duty and awarded damages to the student. The Supreme Court of Louisiana reversed in ascertaining that the university had no duty of care.[303] Using a duty-risk analysis, the court offered that the light pole was of great social utility as it served important safety interests by providing light to pedestrians and users of the parking lot. Further, the court judged that the likelihood of harm was minimal since the pole was obvious to those sledding on the hill and the risks of colliding with it were well known. The court added that since the condition was not unreasonably dangerous, the university had no duty to the injured student.

In a second case from Louisiana, an employee of a subcontractor who was injured while working on campus sought further review of a grant of summary judgment in favor of a university after the contractor was dismissed from the suit. An appellate court affirmed.[304] The court stated that the university was not liable for the injury since it did not exercise or retain any control over the contractor's activities at the job site.

A third case from Louisiana involved a university that challenged a ruling in favor of a student and her husband who brought a personal injury suit that included a claim for loss of consortium when she was injured after tripping on a depression in a sidewalk on campus. An

---

[302] Hullinger v. Board of Regents of the Univ. of Neb., 546 N.W.2d 779 [108 EDUC. L. REP. 1267] (Neb. 1996).
[303] Pitre v. Louisiana Tech Univ., 673 So. 2d 585 [109 EDUC. L. REP. 1398] (La. 1996).
[304] Perrit v. Bernhard Mechanical Contractors, 669 So. 2d 599 [107 EDUC. L. REP. 1081] (La. Ct. App. 1996).

appellate court affirmed.[305] The court agreed that there was evidence that the university had sufficient notice of the dangerous condition and the student was not contributorily negligent.

Jurisdiction was at issue when a resident of Maryland filed suit in federal district court seeking to recover for personal injuries that he sustained while attending a rock concert at the university he attended in Pennsylvania. The federal district court transferred the case to a venue in Pennsylvania on the basis that it lacked jurisdiction.[306] The court maintained that it did not have jurisdiction simply because the student received a letter of acceptance while he was a resident of Maryland.

A student who was injured when she jumped over a wall on campus to avoid protestors unsuccessfully alleged that her injury was caused by the university's negligence. An appellate court in Pennsylvania affirmed in favor of the university.[307] The court found that in light of the feasible alternative routes available, the university did not have a duty to warn the student of the risk of injury where it reasonably could have expected her to recognize the obvious and known risk of her action.

In the first of two suits from Ohio, a citizen brought a personal injury suit against a state university after he fell into an uncovered air ventilation shaft on its campus. The citizen, who had slept on the vent in the past, fell when he climbed over a wall to sleep on it after someone, without the university's knowledge, stole the covering. The Court of Claims ruled in favor of the university on the basis that the university had not breached any duty and that the citizen's voluntary act was the proximate cause of his injury.[308]

A student brought a negligence action against a state university when she was injured because she failed to follow the pedestrian walkway to an exit and fell in a hole in the loading area of a parking garage. Relying on the principles of comparative negligence, the Court of Claims of Ohio deemed that since both the student and university were at fault, it was necessary to set a trial date to determine damages.[309]

In Massachusetts, a father and son sought further review of a grant of summary judgment in their negligence claim against a college in New

---

[305] Boyle v. Board of Supervisors of La. State Univ. and Agric. and Mechanical College, 672 So. 2d 254 [109 EDUC. L. REP. 484] (La. Ct. App. 1996).
[306] Hardnett v. Duquesne Univ., 897 F. Supp. 920 [103 EDUC. L. REP. 964] (D. Md. 1995).
[307] Banks v. Trustees of the Univ. of Pa., 666 A.2d 329 [104 EDUC. L. REP. 789] (Pa. Super. Ct. 1995).
[308] Pride v. Cleveland State Univ., 657 N.E.2d 878 [104 EDUC. L. REP. 1330] (Ohio. Ct. Cl. 1995).
[309] Malley v. Youngstown State Univ., 658 N.E.2d 333 [105 EDUC. L. REP. 277] (Ohio Ct. Cl. 1995).

York. The suit alleged that the school's inadequate security led to the beating and knifing that the student sustained at the hands of three basketball players on campus. An appellate court affirmed that the case should have been dismissed because it should have been filed in New York.[310] However, the court modified in noting that the dismissal should have been conditioned on the defendants waiving a defense based on the statute of limitations in New York.

The first of four cases from New York was filed by a student who became a quadriplegic when, while riding his bike at night on campus, he veered off of a path on to the grass, struck a root, and was thrown from his bike. The student sought further review of a grant of summary judgment in favor of the college and the company that cared for its grounds. An appellate court affirmed with modifications.[311] The court asserted that summary judgment in favor of the grounds company was precluded where there were material issues of fact as to whether the student's riding his bike between trees at night was the proximate cause of his injury and whether it failed to maintain a safe path. Yet, the court agreed that the recreational immunity statute protected the college from liability for the student's injuries.

A member challenged a grant of summary judgment in favor of his fraternity after he sued to recover for injuries that he suffered when he stepped on a nail in a pile of debris that accumulated from a remodeling project. An appellate court in New York affirmed that the fraternity did not have a duty to warn its member where the dangers associated with a pile of debris were obvious.[312]

Following the dismissal of its motion for conditional judgment of common law indemnification in a suit filed by a construction worker who was injured after he fell from a scaffold on campus, a college sought further review. An appellate court in New York reversed in favor of the college.[313] The court decided that since the college was only vicariously liable for the worker's injuries under the state's scaffold law, it was entitled

---

[310] Green v. Manhattanville College, 661 N.E.2d 123 [106 EDUC. L. REP. 1310] (Mass. App. Ct. 1996).

[311] Weller v. Colleges of the Senecas, 635 N.Y.S.2d 990 [106 EDUC. L. REP. 282] (N.Y. App. Div. 1995).

[312] Pellicane v. Lambda Chi Alpha Fraternity, 644 N.Y.S.2d 769 [110 EDUC. L. REP. 1180] (N.Y. App. Div. 1996).

[313] Keck v. Board of Trustees of Corning Community College, 645 N.Y.S.2d 177 [111 EDUC. L. REP. 445] (N.Y. App. Div. 1996). *See also* Singh v. City Univ. of N.Y./ Bronx Community College, 636 N.Y.S.2d 131 [106 EDUC. L. REP. 294] (N.Y. App. Div. 1995) (where a worker who was injured on college grounds when scaffolding collapsed was entitled to serve late notice of claim because the college had actual knowledge of the accident).

to common law indemnification from the contractor who supervised, directed, and controlled the work that led to the injury.

A college challenged the dismissal of its motion for summary judgment when an adjunct faculty member filed suit after she broke her ankle when she slipped and fell on the stairs in one of its buildings. An appellate court reversed in favor of the college.[314] The court acknowledged that the faculty member's suit was barred since she received workers' compensation benefits in connection with her injury.

Injury in Class

A student who severed his thumb on a milling machine appealed a ruling in favor of his junior college in his negligence action. The Supreme Court of Mississippi reversed in favor of the student.[315] The court declared that summary judgment was precluded where there were material issues of fact as to the college's duty to provide instructions on the safe use of the machine and the level of supervision that it provided.

In the first of two cases from California, a university challenged the denial of its motion for summary judgment where the survivor of a student who was killed during a rock climbing class brought a wrongful death action. An appellate court granted the university's motion for writ of mandate.[316] The court posited that, under the doctrine of primary assumption of risk, the university did not owe the student a duty.

A student in an advanced football class unsuccessfully sued for an eye injury that he sustained from a collision during a noncontact drill. In upholding a grant of summary judgment in favor of the college, an appellate court observed that injuries are an inherent risk of the sport.[317] As such, the court reasoned that assumption of risk prevented the student from recovering since he voluntarily took part in the class.

In Indiana, a student who was injured on a motorcycle training course challenged a grant of summary judgment in favor of the university in his negligence action. An appellate court affirmed that the university did not have a statutory duty that overrode the liability waiver executed by the

---

[314] Kuznetz v. County of Nassau, 645 N.Y.S.2d 520 [111 Educ. L. Rep. 937] (N.Y. App. Div. 1996). For a similar ruling involving a state employee who was injured while at work, *see* Rodriguez v. Board of Directors of the Auraria Higher Educ. Ctr., 917 P.2d 358 [110 Educ. L. Rep. 431] (Colo. Ct. App. 1996).

[315] Garrett v. Northwest Miss. Junior College, 674 So. 2d 1 [110 Educ. L. Rep. 493] (Miss. 1996).

[316] Regents of the Univ. of Cal. v. Superior Ct., 48 Cal. Rptr.2d 922 [105 Educ. L. Rep. 1135] (Cal. Ct. App 1996).

[317] Fortier v. Los Rios Community College Dist., 52 Cal. Rptr.2d 812 [109 Educ. L. Rep. 298] (Cal. Ct. App. 1996).

student.[318] The court added that the waiver was not an unconscionable adhesion contract.

A doctoral student sought further review of a directed verdict in favor of the board of regents after he suffered severe injuries during a laboratory experiment. An appellate court in Georgia agreed that neither the university nor the supervising professor had a duty to warn the student about the mixing of hazardous materials because, in light of his education and training, the student should have known of the dangers involved in his actions.[319]

Residence Halls or Living Units

An architectural student sought further review of a grant of summary judgment where he sued the university for negligence after he was injured when rubber cement caught fire in his residence hall room while he and a friend worked on a class project. An appellate court in New York affirmed.[320] The court indicated that insofar as the university did not stand in loco parentis with regard to the student, it did not have a duty to instruct him in the safe use of rubber cement.

The mother of a student was injured when, despite several requests to repair a leaking air conditioning unit, she fell on water from it while visiting her daughter's dormitory room. The university challenged a jury verdict in favor of the mother because it was not allowed to present any witnesses since it provided her attorney with their names only six days prior to the trial. An appellate court in Louisiana reversed and remanded in determining that, under the circumstances, the sanctions against the university were inappropriate.[321]

Sports Activity

In Missouri, a former football player who was injured alleged that by requiring him to practice with the team despite his academic ineligibility, the board of regents and coach violated his rights under the Fourteenth Amendment, breached their contract, and were negligent. A federal district court dismissed the section 1983 claim in which the student asserted that he had a protected liberty interest in refusing to practice

---

[318] Terry v. Indiana State Univ., 666 N.E.2d 87 [110 Educ. L. Rep. 390] (Ind. Ct. App. 1996).

[319] Niles v. Board of Regents of the Univ. Sys. of Ga., 473 S.E.2d 173 [111 Educ. L. Rep. 984] (Ga. Ct. App. 1996).

[320] Talbot v. New York Inst. of Tech., 639 N.Y.S.2d 135 [107 Educ. L. Rep. 951] (N.Y. App. Div. 1996).

[321] Varnell v. Louisiana Tech Univ., 671 So. 2d 1238 [109 Educ. L. Rep. 479] (La. Ct. App. 1996).

football while he was academically ineligible.[322] The court responded that the history of the Due Process Clause did not support the student's claim. In addition, the court chose not to exercise supplemental jurisdiction over the state law charges.

A hockey player at a university in North Dakota filed suit in Minnesota alleging that he was injured due to the negligence of his coaches. The player was hurt when he took part in a ten kilometer race as part of preseason conditioning and suffered extensive internal damage due to dehydration. An appellate court affirmed the dismissal on jurisdictional grounds.[323] The court concluded that since the claims arose in North Dakota, its laws applied and the Minnesota courts should not have exercised jurisdiction as a matter of comity.

In Ohio, an intercollegiate basketball player who was injured while weight-lifting claimed that the manager of the university's program failed to spot the lift as he had promised. As such, the student alleged that a substantial weight fell on him and caused a pectoral muscle to rupture. After a trial court granted summary judgment in favor of the university and its employee, the student sought further review. An appellate court reversed and remanded.[324] The court held that summary judgment was precluded where there was an issue of fact as to whether the supervisor had been reckless in failing to perform as a spotter after agreeing to do so.

Off-Campus Institution Sponsored or Sanctioned Events

A fraternity appealed a judgment in favor of a guest who was injured in a fight at a party that it sponsored. The Supreme Court of Alabama reversed.[325] The court pointed out that permitting the guest's attorney to make references to its risk management manual on underage drinking and liability insurance, combined with other admissible evidence, was prejudicial to the fraternity.

University students who were injured while touring a nuclear reactor sued for damages under state safety regulations and the Atomic Energy Act. The students were subjected to radioactive gases during a routine process that was part of the repair of a design flaw and leakage in the reactor. In response to the operator's motion's to dismiss, the federal district court in Maine found that federal law preempted the students'

---

[322] Canada v. Thomas, 915 F. Supp. 145 [107 EDUC. L. REP. 209] (W.D. Mo. 1996).
[323] Reed v. University of N. Dakota, 543 N.W.2d 106 [106 EDUC. L. REP. 891] (Minn. Ct. App. 1996).
[324] Sicard v. University of Dayton, 660 N.E.2d 1241 [106 EDUC. L. REP. 1305] (Ohio Ct. App. 1995).
[325] Pi Kappa Phi Fraternity v. Baker, 661 So. 2d 745 [104 EDUC. L. REP. 532] (Ala. 1995).

claims based on strict liability.[326] At the same time, the court ascertained that federal law did not preclude the students' allegations of intentional infliction of emotional distress, battery, and fraud.

A community college disputed a ruling in favor of a student who was injured when he was struck by a dump truck while on a bicycle trip that it organized. An appellate court in New York affirmed the denial of the college's motion for summary judgment.[327] The panel was of the opinion that since the college had the duty to take appropriate safety precautions during the bike trip, the trial court had to consider not only whether the school breached its duty to supervise but also whether that breach was the proximate cause of the student's injury.

Medical Malpractice

The substantial number of malpractice suits in this area indicates the degree to which universities are involved in medical education. A patient at a state university hospital who was burned during cauterizing procedures that were part of her hysterectomy appealed a grant of summary judgment in favor of her physician. The Supreme Court of Oklahoma reversed in favor of the patient.[328] The court maintained that the state Governmental Tort Claims Act did not provide the doctor with immunity where the patient established a basis for her claim under the doctrine of res ipsa loquitur.

A patient who received an allegedly defective hip transplant at a university medical center challenged a finding that her negligence action first had to be submitted to a medical review panel. An appellate court in Louisiana affirmed.[329] The court agreed that since the dispute fell within the purview of the state's Medical Malpractice Act, it had to be submitted to the review panel.

After a patient in North Carolina filed a malpractice claim over a bone marrow transplant, an appellate court upheld a partial grant of summary judgment in favor of a university medical center. When the patient's second amended complaint was voluntarily dismissed, the medical center sought to prevent her from refiling it on the basis that it was time barred. This time an appellate court reversed in favor of the patient on the ground that the second complaint related back to the date

---

[326] Bohrmann v. Maine Yankee Atomic Power Co., 926 F. Supp. 211 [110 EDUC. L. REP. 133] (D. Me. 1996).
[327] Hores v. Sargent, 646 N.Y.S.2d 165 [111 EDUC. L. REP. 1320] (N.Y. App. Div. 1996).
[328] Jackson v. Oklahoma Mem'l Hosp., 909 P.2d 765 [106 EDUC. L. REP. 364] (Okla. 1995).
[329] Huffaker v. ABC Ins., 659 So. 2d 544 [102 EDUC. L. REP. 1262] (La. Ct. App. 1995).

of the original charge.[330] The court added that the patient's failure to seek a ruling on her second amended complaint did not mean that she forfeited her right to bring a later action where the doctor did not raise the statute of limitations as a defense until after the latter case was filed.

A patient who was awarded medical expenses, lost wages, and home service in a malpractice action against a university hospital challenged a jury's failure to provide damages for pain and suffering. An appellate court in the District of Columbia affirmed that the evidence did not support such an award.[331] Further, the court rejected the patient's argument that media coverage over the economic impact of medical malpractice verdicts led to a reduction in the amount of damages that she received.

In Michigan, a family that brought a wrongful death action sought further review of a grant of summary judgment in favor of a doctor from a university medical center who also worked at a private hospital. An appellate court affirmed that the Tort Liability Act provided a rational basis for the distinction between a physician who is employed by the state and one who works at a private facility.[332] As such, the court noted that since the training program at the private hospital was part of the governmental function of the state university's medical college, the doctor was entitled to immunity insofar as his actions were within the scope of his job.

A student in New York who voluntarily participated in a diet research project challenged the dismissal of her malpractice suit against the university on the ground that it was time barred. An appellate court reversed in favor of the student.[333] The court declared that since the student's claim was more properly one for negligence rather than medical malpractice, it was governed by the three- rather than two-and-one-half-year statute of limitations. As such, the court conceded that the action was filed in a timely manner.

In the first of three cases surrounding AIDS, a pregnant patient who received a false-positive in a test for HIV sued several parties, including a university's board of regents. After the board successfully motioned for summary judgment, but not costs, it sought further review. An appellate court in California reversed in favor of the board.[334] The court stated that

---

[330] Bowlin v. Duke Univ., 457 S.E.2d 737 [105 Educ. L. Rep. 1281] (N.C. Ct. App. 1995).

[331] Shomaker v. George Washington Univ., 669 A.2d 1291 [106 Educ. L. Rep. 726] (D.C. Ct. App. 1995).

[332] Vargo v. Sauer, 547 N.W.2d 40 [109 Educ. L. Rep. 378] (Mich. Ct. App. 1996).

[333] Payette v. Rockefeller Univ., 643 N.Y.S.2d 79 [110 Educ. L. Rep. 318] (N.Y. App. Div. 1996).

[334] Hall v. Regents of the Univ. of Cal., 51 Cal. Rptr.2d 387 [108 Educ. L. Rep. 319] (Cal. Ct. App. 1996).

since the patient's tactical decision to keep the board in her claim to prevent the other defendants from asserting the empty chair argument did not constitute reasonable cause to do so as a matter of law, it was entitled to costs.

In Ohio, a patient with AIDS challenged a ruling in favor of a university hospital that inadvertently tested him for HIV without his consent. When the treating physician, who knew that the patient had AIDS, asked a nurse to make such a notation on his surgical chart, she did so in the wrong place. Consequently, since the laboratory checked for HIV as part of other blood tests, it notified the state Department of Health of the positive results. On further review, an appellate court affirmed in favor of the hospital.[335] The court agreed that the hospital and physician were not liable because they did not knowingly violate the statutory provisions requiring a patient's consent before conducting a test for HIV.

A student in a medical support personnel training program acquired AIDS when the patient he was asked to restrain became violent and projected bodily fluid, including blood, into his eye. Subsequently, the student sought further review of a ruling in favor of the school when he alleged that it was negligent because it knew, but failed to warn him, that the patient had AIDS. An appellate court in Louisiana reversed in favor of the student.[336] The court rejected the argument that the student was a borrowed employee who could only collect under workers' compensation. It reasoned that since he was a student, rather than an employee of the training school or the medical facility, his negligence claim could proceed to trial.

Negligence

In Vermont, a university student who was a member of the Naval Reserve Officers' Training Corps program was injured when the naval car she was riding in was in an accident as she was returning from a physical examination prior to her being commissioned. The student appealed the dismissal of her personal injury suit against the government and various military personnel. The Second Circuit affirmed[337] that the Feres doctrine[338] barred the student's claim under the Federal Tort Claim Act.

A graduate student who served as a teaching and research assistant received workers' compensation benefits after she was allegedly exposed

---

[335] Doe v. Ohio State Univ. Hosps. and Clinics, 663 N.E.2d 1369 [109 EDUC. L. REP. 354] (Ohio Ct. App. 1995).

[336] Dustin v. DHCI Home Health Serv., 673 So. 2d 356 [109 EDUC. L. REP. 1025] (La. Ct. App. 1996).

[337] Wake v. United States, 89 F.3d 53 [110 EDUC. L. REP. 1026] (2nd Cir. 1996).

[338] Freres v. United States, 340 U.S. 135 (1950) (holding that the government is not liable under the Federal Torts Claims Act for injuries sustained by service personnel arising out of or in the course of activity incident to their military service).

to toxic substances. The student also filed an unsuccessful negligence suit against the university. The Supreme Court of Montana affirmed that the student's claim was barred not only by the Occupation Disease Act but also by having received workers' compensation for her injury.[339]

A patient who was injured as she fell out of bed appealed a dismissal in favor of a university's medical center. The Supreme Court of North Dakota affirmed that under the law that predated the abolition of sovereign immunity, the hospital was an arm of the state that was entitled to protection regardless of the alleged proprietary nature of its function.[340] The court added that the hospital's participation in a self-insurance pool did not waive its immunity.

Workers in a building that was being renovated sued a university alleging that the levels of asbestos emissions from the project violated the Clean Air Act. A federal district court in Alabama denied the university's motion to dismiss.[341] The court posited that in light of the dangerous substances that were being discharged and the need for immediate action, it would make an exception to the sixty-day notice provision of the Act.

A nurse's aid sought further review of a grant of summary judgment in her negligence action against a university hospital and a therapist after she was assaulted by a patient who was improperly restrained. An appellate court in Wisconsin affirmed that the hospital was entitled to sovereign immunity.[342] At the same time, the court reversed in determining that since the therapist's duty to restrain the patient was ministerial, she was not immune from personal liability.

Vicarious Liability

A student sued a university alleging that it was vicariously liable when he was assaulted by the instructor in a noncredit summer karate class that was conducted in its gym. The Court of Claims of New York dismissed in favor of the university.[343] The court declared that since the instructor was an independent contractor whose acts were beyond the scope of his employment, the university could not be held vicariously liable.

---

[339] Torres v. Montana, 902 P.2d 999 [103 EDUC. L. REP. 843] (Mont. 1995).
[340] Stratton v. Medical Ctr. Rehabilitation Hosp., 547 N.W.2d 748 [109 EDUC. L. REP. 935] (N.D. 1996).
[341] Adair v. Troy State Univ. of Montgomery, 892 F. Supp. 1401 [102 EDUC. L. REP. 591] (M.D. Ala. 1995).
[342] Walker v. University of Wis. Hosp., 542 N.W.2d 207 [106 EDUC. L. REP. 320] (Wis. Ct. App. 1995).
[343] Forester v. State of N.Y., 645 N.Y.S.2d 971 [111 EDUC. L. REP. 956] (N.Y. Ct. Cl. 1996).

Workers' Compensation

A university medical center sought further review of an award of workers' compensation to an electrician who injured his back while on the job. An appellate court in Louisiana affirmed that the electrician should have been awarded supplemental earnings as part of his claim.[344] At the same time, the court reversed on the basis that the rehabilitation award, granted in lieu of job placement, needed to be adjudicated. The court found that since the Office of Workers' Compensation had not adequately considered job placement for the electrician, it was unclear whether job placement or rehabilitation was the appropriate relief.

After filing a workers' compensation claim, a former employee of a state university brought a section 1983 suit alleging that he was stabbed by his former supervisor. A federal district court in Tennessee concluded that Eleventh Amendment immunity barred the claims against the university and its employees in their official capacities.[345] The court added that the employee waived his right to sue under section 1983 when he filed the workers' compensation claim.

In Texas, a former employee of a university challenged a grant of summary judgment when she claimed that she was fired in retaliation for filing a workers' compensation claim. An appellate court affirmed that the university and its employees were immune from suit since the employee filed the workers' compensation claim.[346] However, the court also found that summary judgment was precluded where there were material questions of fact as to whether the dean, in his unofficial capacity, intentionally inflicted emotional distress on the employee.

A university disputed a ruling that an injured employee's accrued leave time should have been included in the calculation of his average weekly salary. An appellate court in Florida affirmed that since leave time was part of the worker's contract, it was consideration received as compensation for his efforts.[347]

Intentional Torts

Defamation

In the first of two cases involving coaches, a woman appealed a grant of summary judgment in favor of the publishers of a preseason

---

[344] Bigner v. Louisiana State Univ. Med. Ctr., 658 So. 2d 218 [102 EDUC. L. REP. 889] (La. Ct. App. 1995).
[345] Hiefner v. University of Tenn., 914 F. Supp. 1513 [107 EDUC. L. REP. 200] (E.D. Tenn. 1995).
[346] Clark v. University of Tex. Health Science Ctr. at Houston, 919 S.W.2d 185 [108 EDUC. L. REP. 1017] (Tex. Ct. App. 1996).
[347] University of Fla. v. Bowens, 677 So. 2d 942 [111 EDUC. L. REP. 1391] (Fla. Dist. Ct. App. 1996).

publication after she filed a defamation suit based on an author's comment that she "usually finds a way to screw things up." The Circuit Court for the District of Columbia affirmed that the statements were not actionable since the coach was unable to show that they were objectively verifiable and false.[348] The court added that ambiguity in the facts surrounding the coach's performance was fatal to her claim.

The second case involving defamation and a coach arose in California. The coach of a men's basketball team unsuccessfully brought a defamation action against the university and its athletic director for comments that were made after he was fired. An appellate court affirmed in favor of the university.[349] The court agreed that the statements made by the vice president and the athletic director about the environment that the coach created between himself and the players were not factual assertions subject to defamation.

A purchasing agent appealed the dismissal of his defamation claim after a state agency charged him with improper bidding practices. The Supreme Court of Louisiana affirmed.[350] The court reasoned that the state investigator's report was not defamatory nor was there malice in its making.

In Connecticut, a faculty member who claimed that a colleague plagiarized his ideas for a course sought further review of a verdict in favor of the accused. An appellate court affirmed.[351] The tribunal ruled that as a public figure, the professor's attorney established that his accuser acted with the requisite level of actual malice to justify the verdict.

A bank brought false advertising and unfair competition claims against the state agency that administers a prepaid tuition program. The agency filed counter claims of defamation, product disparagement, and trade libel. On a motion to dismiss the counterclaims, the federal district court in New Jersey judged that the Free Speech Clause of the First Amendment barred the agency from bringing its charges against a private competitor.[352] The court further noted that an amendment to the Lanham Act, which allows suits where parties misrepresent the goods and services that they provide, barred the agency's product disparagement and trade libel claims.

In South Carolina, a former resident physician at a university medical center filed a defamation action after her controversial opinion piece on

---

[348] Washington v Smith, 80 F.3d 555 [108 EDUC. L. REP. 499] (D.C. Cir. 1996).

[349] Campanelli v. Regents of the Univ. of Cal., 51 Cal. Rep.2d 891 [108 EDUC. L. REP. 801] (Cal. Ct. App. 1996).

[350] Davis v. Borskey, 660 So. 2d 17 [103 EDUC. L. REP. 538] (La. 1995).

[351] Abdelsayed v. Narumanchi, 668 A.2d 378 [105 EDUC. L. REP. 1103] (Conn. App. Ct. 1995).

[352] College Savings Bank v. Florida Prepaid Postsecondary Educ. Expense Bd., 919 F. Supp. 756 [108 EDUC. L. REP. 541] (D.N.J. 1996).

homosexuality in a local newspaper stimulated a number of negative editorial responses. The doctor claimed, in part, that the controversy led to the nonrenewal of her contract. The federal district court granted motions for summary judgment entered by the newspapers and the author of one of the letters to the editor.[353] The court found that as a limited purpose public figure, the doctor was unable to demonstrate that she suffered any harm.

Deceptive Practices

A student challenged the dismissal of his suit that claimed his university breached its promise to provide a quality educational environment and falsely described its atmosphere and disciplinary process. An appellate court in New York affirmed that the student's claims improperly tried to circumvent the principle that there is no cognizable tort claim for educational malpractice.[354]

In California, an applicant unsuccessfully sued a university for misleading advertising over a statement that it did not discriminate on the basis of race in admitting students to its law and medical schools. An appellate court affirmed the university's demurrer that led to the denial of the applicant's request for specific performance and restitution for his application fees.[355] The court maintained that the statute prohibiting false or misleading advertising did not govern the state's public universities. The court reflected that the constitutional authority of the legislature to control the administration of colleges and universities was through the Board of Regents.

A former student challenged a grant of summary in favor of his vocational school claiming that it violated the federal Consumer Fraud and Deceptive Practices Act by certifying that its graduates would benefit from their programs. An appellate court in Illinois affirmed on the ground that the student's state cause of action was preempted by federal law.[356]

Contract Liability
Breach of Warranty or Fraud

A university appealed a ruling in favor of a dissolved out-of-state corporation that it sued over the installation of allegedly faulty panels. The Supreme Court of Alaska reversed in favor of the university.[357] The

---

[353] Faltas v. State Newspaper, 928 F. Supp. 637 [110 Educ. L. Rep. 668] (D.S.C. 1996).

[354] Sirohi v. Lee, 634 N.Y.S.2d 119 [105 Educ. L. Rep. 255] (N.Y. App. Div. 1995).

[355] Favish v. Regents of the Univ. of Cal., 53 Cal. Rptr.2d 757 [110 Educ. L. Rep. 248] (Cal. Ct. App. 1996)

[356] Wilson v. Chism, 665 N.E.2d 446 [110 Educ. L. Rep. 287] (Ill. App. Ct. 1996).

[357] University of Alaska v. Thomas Architectural Prods., 907 P.2d 448 [105 Educ. L. Rep. 765] (Alaska 1995).

court asserted that whether the suit could be filed against the corporation would have to be decided in Washington state, the home of the dissolved organization. The court added that the corporation's failure to comply with statutory windup requirements rendered it susceptible to suits by known creditors who did had not received notice that it went out of business.

In New York, a lessee sought a declamatory judgment against a university over the boundaries of leased property. On further review of partial grants of summary judgment in favor of both parties, an appellate court affirmed that the boundaries of the leased property should have been determined by measuring the distance from the building that existed at the time of the lease, not the boundaries of a new structure.[358] Further, the court posited that material issues of fact over the dimensions of the property precluded summary judgment on the issue.

Breach of Contract

A contracting company appealed the dismissal of its section 1983 due process and breach of contract claims against a university in Arkansas when it accepted bids on a service contract following the expiration of a five-year contract. The company claimed that the university failed to provide written notice that it would not renew the contract. The Eleventh Circuit affirmed that the contractor did not have a viable due process claim under section 1983 because the simple breach of contract action did not rise to the level of a constitutional deprivation.[359] According to the court, the university and its trustees were protected from the breach of contract claim by Eleventh Amendment immunity.

The Federal Deposit Insurance Corporation, in its capacity as receiver for the assignee of an equipment lease, filed suit against the lessee that brought a third-party action against the lessor. The federal district court in Kansas sustained the lessor's motion to strike the lessee's third-party demand for a jury trial.[360] The court reasoned that the provision in the lease that waived the right to a jury trial was enforceable.

Where a university entered into a contract with a company for computer maintenance, the final agreement called for the assignment of payments to a bank. Subsequently, when the service company went out of business, the bank sued the university to collect the remainder due on

[358] North Shore Equestrian Ctr., v. Long Island Univ., 639 N.Y.S.2d 243 [107 Educ. L. Rep. 959] (N.Y. App. Div. 1996.
[359] Dover Elevator Co. v. Arkansas State Univ., 64 F.3d 442 [103 Educ. L. Rep. 49] (11th Cir. 1995).
[360] Federal Deposit Ins. Corp. v. Ottawa Univ., 906 F. Supp. 601 [105 Educ. L. Rep. 512] (D. Kan. 1995).

the assigned contract. The federal district court in Delaware granted the university's motion for summary judgment.[361] The court declared that the clause in the contract waiving the university's defenses against any assignee was unenforceable under the Uniform Commercial Code.

The state challenged a grant of summary judgment in favor of a public university in a dispute over whether it had to comply with the Prevailing Wage Act on a construction project. An appellate court in Michigan affirmed.[362] The court asserted that the Act was inapplicable since the state had not provided any of the direct capital outlays for the project that was funded with assessed student fees.

A college of art design sought further review of a partial grant of summary judgment in favor of a school of visual arts that it sued for tortuous interference with existing and potential relationships with students, faculty, staff, accreditation agencies, and banks. An appellate court in Georgia reversed in favor of the college.[363] The court posited that if the college could demonstrate that the school had knowledge of a concerted effort to destroy it, then the school could be liable for all torts committed in furtherance of the conspiracy.

In the first of two cases from Ohio, a clothing company sued a sorority that refused to pay for sweaters when it discovered that the agreed upon design had been changed. A trial court entered judgment in favor of the sorority on the ground that the clothing company breached the contract by changing the design on the sweaters.[364] The court added that the sorority could reject the order since physically receiving it was not acceptance and that until such time as the company returned the down payment, the organization could retain possession of the sweaters.

A contractor sought further review of a trial court's refusal to act upon its motion to enforce a settlement agreement that it had entered into with a university. An appellate court in Ohio reversed.[365] The court pointed out that since there was a factual dispute over the terms of the settlement

---

[361] Suburban Trust and Savings Bank v. University of Del., 910 F. Supp. 1009 [106 EDUC. L. REP. 560] (D. Del. 1995).

[362] Western Mich. Board of Control v. Michigan, 536 N.W.2d 609 [102 EDUC. L. REP. 1172] (Mich. Ct. App. 1995). For a similar result, *see* Regents of the Univ. of Cal. v. Aubry, 49 Cal. Rptr.2d 703 [106 EDUC. L. REP. 796] (Cal. Ct. App. 1996) (holding that a state agency could not order a university to pay prevailing wages on a construction project).

[363] Savannah College of Art & Design v. School of Visual Arts of Savannah, 464 S.E.2d 895 [105 EDUC. L. REP. 1286] (Ga. Ct. App. 1995).

[364] Furlong v. Alpha Chi Omega Sorority, 657 N.E.2d 866 [104 EDUC. L. REP. 1322] (Ohio Mun. Ct. 1993).

[365] United States Fidelity & Guar. Corp. v. BOHM-NBBJ, 662 N.E.2d 71 [107 EDUC. L. REP. 985] (Ohio Ct. App. 1995).

and how they impacted the existence of liens that the subcontractor filed against the contractor, the dispute had to be remanded for trial.

Insurance Contracts

In Missouri, a university appealed a grant of summary judgment in favor of its insurance company after it mistakenly reported that a medical malpractice claim occurred before the policy in question was in effect. The Eighth Circuit affirmed that, under state law, the university's defective notice precluded coverage.[366]

An insurance company appealed the denial of its motion to dismiss a suit that a university filed against it for breach of an employee dishonesty policy, bad faith, deceptive business practices, and fraud. The criminal liability insurance policy became the focus of attention when the manager of its bookstore and a supplier allegedly billed the university for goods that it never received. The Court of Appeals of New York reversed in favor of the insurance company on the ground that the state law prohibiting unfair claim settlement practices does not recognize a tort duty of care to an insured party apart from the provisions of its insurance contract.[367] The court added that punitive damages were unavailable since the university failed to allege any tort other than breach of contract and that the deceptive acts and practices prohibitions did not control the sale of the policy or the handling of the claim.

In a second case involving an insurance policy dealing with the criminal acts of an employee, a technical institute sought to collect an amount in excess of its coverage after an accounting manager embezzled funds. The federal district court in Arizona granted the insurance company's motion for summary judgment.[368] The court held that since the policy that was in effect when the embezzlement took place did not provide coverage for the university's entire loss, it was not entitled to recover the full amount that it requested.

A university sued its insurance broker for breach of contract and negligence over a policy to cover a promoter's nonperformance in connection with a football game that its team was scheduled to play in Ireland. The university alleged that it believed that the broker had obtained insurance to cover funds it spent preparing for the game. After a jury returned a verdict in favor of the university, an appellate court in Indiana

---

[366] Lexington Ins. Co. v. St. Louis Univ., 88 F.3d 632 [110 EDUC. L. REP. 995] (8th Cir. 1996).
[367] New York Univ. v. Continental Ins. Co., 639 N.Y.S.2d 283 [108 EDUC. L. REP. 342] (N.Y. 1995).
[368] Lincoln Technical Inst. of Ariz. v. Federal Ins. Co., 927 F. Supp. 376 [110 EDUC. L. REP. 203] (D. Ariz. 1994).

affirmed.[369] The court rejected the insurance company's argument that the university should not have recovered because it could have reviewed the policy at any time. The court acknowledged that an insured's duty to acquaint itself with a policy may be excused when the strength of the agent's oral assurances lulls it into not reading, or reading inattentively, dense and rebarbative language. As such, the court concluded that the evidence supported the finding that the agent had assured the university that the policy had the nonperformance clause that it requested.

In New Jersey, a university challenged a grant of summary judgment in favor of an insurance company that refused to defend it against an environmental cleanup claim. An appellate court affirmed that the comprehensive general liability policy did not include a duty to defend the university against a claim for environmental cleanup.[370]

Bidding

A carrier appealed the dismissal of its claim for interference with a contractual relationship against a railroad after the railroad protested a university entering into a sole source contract with a trucker for the delivery of coal. The Supreme Court of Alaska affirmed that the railroad was immune under the Noerr-Pennington[371] Doctrine.[372] The court reasoned that the railroad's alleged misrepresentations about its ability and intention to bid a competitive price for the delivery of coal did not render its protest a sham, thereby depriving it of immunity.

In Florida, a former athletic director at a state university challenged an order of the Commission on Ethics that he violated a statute on unauthorized compensation. The administrator had a new roof placed on his home at a low price from a construction company that had been awarded a contract to complete extensive renovations on campus. An appellate court reversed in favor of the athletic director.[373] The court noted that the Commission exceeded its authority when it substituted its judgment for that of a hearing officer, who decided that the athletic director lacked constructive knowledge that he was receiving unauthorized compensation, and decreed that he violated the ethics code.

---

[369] Rollins Burdick Hunter of Utah v. Board of Trustees of Ball State Univ., 665 N.E.2d 914 [110 EDUC. L. REP. 373] (Ind. Ct. App. 1996).

[370] Trustees of Princeton Univ. v. AETNA Casaulty & Sur. Co., 680 A.2d 783 [111 EDUC. L. REP. 1249] (N.J. Super. Ct. App. Div. 1996).

[371] See Eastern Railroad Presidents Conference v. Noerr Motor Freight, 365 U.S. 127 (1961) and United Mine Workers v. Pennington, 381 U.S. 657 (1965).

[372] Gunderson v. University of Alaska, Fairbanks, 902 P.2d 323 [103 EDUC. L. REP. 826] (Alaska 1995).

[373] Goin v. Commission on Ethics, 658 So. 2d 1131 [102 EDUC. L. REP. 1242] (Fla. Dist. Ct. App. 1995).

Antitrust

Basketball coaches and universities prevailed in their challenge to a rule of the NCAA that set a salary cap for entry-level positions. The action was based on antitrust grounds as the plaintiffs alleged that the rule violated the Sherman Act as an illegal restraint of trade. The federal district court in Kansas granted summary judgment in favor of the coaches and universities on the basis that the NCAA failed to establish that the rule enhanced competition or promoted a legitimate, pro-competitive goal.[374]

When the NCAA failed to answer interrogatories necessary to determine relief in the previous case, the parties were back in court to determine sanctions. The federal district court in Kansas observed that the NCAA was not excused from disclosing information on the basis that it lacked the legal authority to require its constituents to provide the data since the NCAA helped create the situation by discouraging member schools' from assisting in this endeavor. As such, the court ordered the NCAA to comply with the discovery requests and imposed sanctions for not doing so in a timely manner.[375]

In a companion case, men's baseball coaches with restricted earnings sought certification as a class in their antitrust action against the NCAA for its salary cap rule. The court granted the coaches' motion for class certification as to the injunctive and declaratory aspects of the claim but refused to do so as to the damages issues.[376]

A corporation in Louisiana brought an antitrust conspiracy claim against a university that was organized as a not-for-profit corporation in Utah and business organizations in California, Nevada, and Pennsylvania. The controversy surrounded the defendants' alleged conspiracy to slow down the corporation's development and sales of a new open architecture computer operating system used in robotics and machine tool operations. A federal district court ruled that it had jurisdiction over the nonresident corporations under the "worldwide provisions" of the Clayton Act.[377] In addition, the court ascertained that it would not have been any more convenient for witnesses if the case were moved to Utah.

[374] Law v. National Collegiate Athletic Ass'n, 902 F. Supp. 1394 [104 EDUC. L. REP. 1104] (D. Kan. 1995).
[375] Law v. National Collegiate Athletic Ass'n, 167 F.R.D. 464 [111 EDUC. L. REP. 822] (D. Kan. 1996).
[376] Schreiber v. National Collegiate Athletic Ass'n, 167 F.R.D. 169 [110 EDUC. L. REP. 710] (D. Kan. 1996).
[377] ICON Indus. Control Corp. v. Cimetrix, 921 F. Supp. 375 [108 EDUC. L. REP. 1151] (W.D. La. 1996).

Patents and Copyrights

The author of an instructional video in California appealed a grant of summary judgment in his copyright infringement suit against a language school. After paying the author to produce the video for use in its classes, the school relied on the copyright notice at the front of the videos that they sold to other programs. The Ninth Circuit affirmed that the operator of the school that purchased the videos came under the innocent infringement defense when he relied on the copyright notice.[378] However, the court reversed in deciding that there were material issues of fact over the rights of the author and the school under their initial agreement and whether the school acted in good faith by relying on the copyright notice which read that it reserved all rights when it allegedly sold the videos without authorization.

Under the Lanham Act, a university in Florida unsuccessfully sued the publisher of study guides that purchased class notes from students. The Eleventh Circuit affirmed.[379] The court maintained that the use of course numbers, locations, and meeting times did not create the illusion that the notes were either published or sanctioned by the university. The court offered that the university could not sustain a claim of unfair competition under the Lanham Act absent a showing that the information was nonfunctional and distinctive.

In the first of two cases from New York, a standardized testing organization moved for partial reconsideration of an order requiring it to make limited disclosures of test forms. A federal district court in New York decided that laches did not bar the state from raising its objections to the organization's proposal for complying with the order.[380] The court chose to preserve the status quo rather than preclude the state from enforcing the law which required testing companies to disclose the contents of examinations after they are administered.

A graduate sued his law school and one of its journals claiming that editors not only mutilated his Comment in contravention of the Lanham Act but also that they violated his moral rights. A federal district court in New York granted the school's motion for summary judgment.[381] The court asserted that the author failed to state a claim under the Lanham Act since his revised Comment did not depart substantially enough from

---

[378] Bagdadi v. Nazar, 84 F.3d 1194 [109 Educ. L. Rep. 1094] (9th Cir. 1996).
[379] University of Fla. v. KPB, Inc., 89 F.3d 773 [110 Educ. L. Rep. 1079] (11th Cir. 1996).
[380] College Entrance Examination Bd. v. Pataki, 893 F. Supp. 152 [102 Educ. L. Rep. 967] (N.D.N.Y. 1995).
[381] Choe v. Fordham Univ. Sch. of Law, 920 F. Supp. 44 [108 Educ. L. Rep. 652] (S.D.N.Y. 1995).

the original such that it could no longer be called his work. The court added that there is no federal claim for moral rights.

In Michigan, a university sued both the corporation that it contracted with to patent an invention by of one of its faculty members and the company to which that agreement was assigned. In fact, the university continued dealing with the second corporation as though it were a party to the contact. Yet, the university rejected the second company's request for arbitration over a dispute in the terms of their contract.[382] A federal district court in Michigan was of the opinion that the university's acceptance of the original assignment meant that it was required to submit to the second corporation's request for arbitration.

University professors unsuccessfully alleged conversion, fraud, wrongful naming of an inventor, copyright infringement, misappropriation, patent infringement, breach of confidentiality obligation, and unjust enrichment where patentees reformulated their vitamin product. On reconsideration of an earlier grant of summary judgment in favor of the professors, the federal district court in Colorado agreed that they were not entitled to equitable relief because they did not have the title to the patent.[383] At the same time, the court found that the professors maintained an infringement claim against the patentee for using charts and graphs from their copyrighted journal article.

Gifts

A taxpayer challenged an IRS disallowance of a deduction that he claimed on his federal tax return for common stock that he donated to a university in Delaware. The United States Court of Federal Claims ascertained that since actual sales were inconclusive in trying to value the stocks on the date that the gift was made, it based its judgment on the adjusted net worth method of analysis.[384] Accordingly, the court concluded that the donor was entitled to a deduction.

A donor challenged the denial of his request for injunctive and other relief to enforce the provisions of a restricted charitable gift that he made to a university. The dispute arose when the university discontinued its nursing program and folded the money available for disadvantaged students into its general scholarship program. An appellate court in Connecticut reversed in favor of the donor.[385] The court held that the

---

[382] Board of Trustees of Mich. State Univ. v. Research Corp., 898 F. Supp. 519 [103 Educ. L. Rep. 1055] (W.D. Mich. 1995).
[383] University of Colo. Found. v. American Cyanamid, 902 F. Supp. 221 [105 Educ. L. Rep. 435] (D. Colo. 1995).
[384] Krapf v. United States, 35 Fed. Cl. Rep. 286 [108 Educ. L. Rep. 714] (Fed. Cl. 1996).
[385] Carl J. Herzog Found. v. University of Bridgeport, 677 A.2d 1378 [110 Educ. L. Rep. 1145] (Conn. App. Ct. 1996).

donor had standing to enforce the restriction since the university did not have his written consent to deviate from the restriction.

Conclusion

This year's review of case law in higher education reveals a steady stream of heavy litigation in such areas as sexual harassment, by faculty and peers, and matters surrounding financial aid. The Supreme Court's challenge to the use of sovereign immunity as a defense by states in suits under federal laws may have some interesting ramifications for higher education. Moreover, affirmative action will require further clarification. Yet, a few suits relating to employment and academic dismissal border on being frivolous and may cast higher education in a less favorable light. One thing is for certain: the seemingly endless supply of cases guarantees that the landscape of American higher education will continue to evolve.

9
FEDERAL AND STATE LEGISLATION

Gus Douvanis

Introduction

This chapter summarizes the major actions taken by the United States Congress, the fifty state legislatures, and the District of Columbia that are likely to have an impact on education at both the K-12 and post-secondary levels.

Federal Legislation

The second session of the 104th Congress did not generate a substantial body of law involving public education. In fact, this session is notable for the legislation that Congress failed to enact, perhaps the most notable of which was its inability to reauthorize or make improvements to the Individuals with Disabilities Education Act (IDEA)[1] coupled with its refusal to respond to calls to abolish the federal Department of Education (DOE).

In the actions that it did undertake, Congress passed few significant bills, other than appropriations for funding, that are likely to have a major impact on education. The major statues enacted by Congress include the following:

1. The Personal Responsibility and Work Opportunity Act is designed to reduce reimbursements to districts that receive Medicare payments for school clinics.[2] The law also modifies the National School Lunch Act by rounding down reimbursement rates to the nearest whole cent.

2. The Contract with America Advancement Act of 1996 permits Congress to review the rules of federal agencies before they become effective.[3] This act is designed to limit the number of new federal regulations that are applicable to state and local governments.

3. The Goals 2000 Amendments permit local school districts in states that originally decided not to participate in Goals 2000 to apply directly to the United States Department of Education for funding.[4] The amount of the grant money available will be based on a proportion of a state's allotment and a school system's enrollment.

4. The Healthy Meals for Healthy Children Act provides greater flexibility for school districts that are seeking to comply with Department of Agriculture guidelines dealing with meal planning.[5] In addition, the law is intended to help school systems save money as they plan meals for students.

5. The National Education Standards Act increased the maximum amount available for Pell Grants to at least $2,440.[6]

The major piece of legislation affecting education was the 1997 Education Appropriations Act.[7] This act increased spending for the 1997-98 fiscal year by 3.5 billion dollars, or almost 15%, over fiscal year 1996-97. The largest increases in expenditures are in educational technology, special education, charter schools, and bilingual and immigrant education.

---

[1] 1. 20 U.S.C. § 1400 *et seq.*
[2] P.L. 104-193.
[3] P.L. 104-121.
[4] P.L. 104-134.
[5] P.L. 104-149.
[6] P.L. 104-99.
[7] P.L. 104-208.

State Legislation

This section summarizes the major pieces of legislation dealing with education that have been passed by the states and the District of Columbia. Grouped by topic area, these laws reflect policy trends that have evolved over the past year.

Crime and Violence Prevention

Legislatures in seven states enacted laws responding to public concerns about perceived violence in public schools. The approaches taken by these states continue the trend toward promoting safer schools that was established by Congress in the Improving America's Schools Act.[8]

Alabama mandates the imposition of felony penalties for any person who acts with intent and causes physical injury to teachers or other public employees.[9] Any such act is considered assault in the second degree.

Both **Alabama** and **California** enacted legislation to address criminal sexual offenders in and around public schools. **Alabama's** law prohibits released sex offenders from establishing legal residences within 1,000 feet of any public or private school, day care center, or any other child care facility.[10] **California's** new law requires courts to provide written notice to school superintendents informing them if a student in a given district has committed a sex offense.[11]

Another new bill in **California** prevents unauthorized individuals from loitering in schools or public places frequented by children. Under the bill, individuals who are directed to leave such places are to be informed they will be charged with a crime if they re-enter the premises.[12] The law also requires educators to report assaults at schools to appropriate local law enforcement authorities where the incidents occurred. Failure to make reports is punishable by a fine.[13]

Delaware now permits the use of video cameras on public school property as a means of helping to reduce incidents of crime, violence, and vandalism.[14] The statute authorizes school boards to " . . . implement programs to use video cameras for surveillance on public school property, including but not limited to classrooms, halls, auditoriums, cafeterias, gymnasiums, and parking lots"[15] in order to monitor student activity. The

---

[8] 20 U.S.C. § 8921.
[9] 1996 Ala. Pub. Act 533 (1996 Ala. H.B. 296).
[10] 1996 Ala. Pub. Act 793 (1996 Ala. S.B. 393).
[11] 1996 Cal. S.B. 1938 ch. 599.
[12] 1996 Cal. A.B. 3103 ch. 305.
[13] 1996 Cal. S.B. 691 ch. 17.
[14] 1996 Del. Laws 377 (1995 Del. H. B. 371).
[15] *Id.* § 4120.

bill acknowledges that while supervision is an essential component of an educator's duty, monitoring all areas of school property can be difficult. As such, the law provides that the information obtained by the use of the video cameras may be used in student disciplinary actions and in criminal proceedings.

Illinois' law dealing with students who bring weapons to school permits expulsions for not less than one year; at the same time, boards may modify the time out of school on a case by case basis.[16] The statute covers "look-alike" weapons and items such as baseball bats, pipes, bottles, sticks, pencils, and pens if they are used to in an attempt to cause bodily harm.[17] In addition, the bill addresses searches of school controlled property used by students by asserting that as a matter of public policy students have no expectation of privacy in desks, lockers, parking lots, or in personal effects left in those places or areas. The statute goes on to state that these locations may be searched without notice to or consent of students and without a warrant. The bill does permit school authorities to request the assistance of law enforcement officials when conducting such searches.[18] Another part of the bill mandates the creation of parent-teacher advisory committees to develop policy guidelines on student discipline. School boards, in conjunction with these advisory committees, must, on an annual basis, review pupil discipline policies, their implementation, and any other factors related to the safety of the school, pupils, and staff.

Maryland now forbids the possession of " . . . any rifle, gun, knife, or deadly weapon of any kind on any public school property" and provides for an expulsion of a minimum of one year for any student who brings one of these items to school.[19] In Prince George's County, a student who is expelled is forbidden from entering school property while classes are in session.[20] The law also authorizes county superintendents to expel an identified student with disabilities who bring firearms onto school property; however, the administrator, may, on a case by case basis, reduce the period of expulsion.[21] The statute calls for a placement in an interim alternative educational setting in accordance with state law for not more than the maximum number of days specified in the state IDEA.[22] Further, if a due process hearing is requested to contest an expulsion, the bill requires a student to remain in the alternative placement during the pendency of the proceedings.[23] In an unrelated change, Maryland now

---

[16] 1996 Ill. Laws 610 (1995 Ill. H.B. 2596).
[17] *Id.* § 10-22.6(e).
[18] *Id.* § 10-20.14.
[19] 1996 Md. Laws 561 (1996 Md. S.B 215).
[20] 1996 Md. Laws 323 (1996 Md. H.B. 1245).
[21] *Id.* § 3.
[22] 1996 Md. Laws 323 (1996 Md. H.B. 1224).

requires criminal records checks for employers and employees in child care facilities as well as for school volunteers.[24]

Mississippi passed legislation to provide for a one calendar year expulsions for students who bring weapons to schools.[25]

Oregon adopted legislation similar to the Federal Gun Free Schools Act of 1994,[26] which mandated that schools receiving funds under the Improving America's Schools Act must adopt policies to provide for the one-year minimum expulsion of students who bring firearms to school. If a pupil is deemed to have violated the law, a school system must provide a statement of alternative programs of instruction or counseling that are appropriate and accessible.[27] Further, the statute permits school districts to deny admission to students who have been expelled by another system for violating the Act.[28] Finally, the law authorizes employees and volunteers to use reasonable physical force to restrain a student if it is necessary to maintain order, regardless of whether an activity takes place on school property.[29]

Oregon passed a law to authorize the suspension or expulsion of any student who assaults or menaces a school employee or another pupil. The statute defines menace as words or conduct that intentionally place a school employee or another student in fear of imminent serious physical injury.[30]

Student Discipline

As with school safety, legislatures demonstrated great concern over issues surrounding student discipline.

Connecticut's legislature determined that there are few legitimate reasons for students to have pagers on school property. As such, it passed a new law banning the possession of paging devices by students in public schools unless an individual pupil has obtained the written consent of the principal.[31]

Illinois and **Maryland** passed bills dealing with school uniforms. In both states, the legislatures were of the opinion that uniforms have a positive effect on school order and administration and that they help to create an atmosphere that is conducive to learning. The law in **Illinois** maintains that upon the request of parents or officials of an individual

---

[23] *Id.* § 4(1).
[24] 1996 Md. Laws 13 (1996 Md. S.B. 160).
[25] 1996 Miss. Laws 534 (1996 Miss. S.B. 2445).
[26] 20 U.S.C. § 6301.
[27] 1996 Ore. Laws 16 (1996 Ore. S.B. 1159).
[28] *Id.* § 6.
[29] *Id.* § 10.
[30] 1996 Or. Laws 16 (1996 Or. S.B. 1159).
[31] 1996 Conn. P.A. 108 (1996 Conn. S.B. 291).

attendance center, a school board may adopt a policy on uniforms or a dress code.[32] The law indicates that the enactment of such a code must be necessary to maintain the orderly process of the school or prevent endangerment of student health or safety. The statute adds that if a policy is adopted, students will be given reasonable time to comply, that the school will accommodate the needs of youngsters who are indigent, and that pupils whose parents object to uniforms on religious grounds will not be required to comply with the policy if they present a signed statement of objection to the school board.[33] The **Maryland** law is much more limited insofar as it applies only to Prince George's County and authorizes the board there to implement the use of uniforms by all students in its public schools.[34]

Kentucky's General Assembly ordered its Department of Education to develop statewide student discipline guidelines. In addition, the Department must implement recommendations designed to reduce the dropout rate in the state's public schools.[35]

Maryland passed legislation that requires the state Board of Education to adopt regulations including a code of student discipline.[36] County boards must provide a continuum model of prevention and intervention activities coupled with programs to encourage and promote positive behavior and reduce disruption.[37] The statute authorizes county superintendents to deny admission to students who commit violent acts and to forward information to other school systems regarding pupils who have been expelled and are attempting to enroll elsewhere.[38]

Both **Mississippi** and **Illinois** have established a requirement to report school-related misbehavior. **Mississippi** now obligates school officials to report expulsions and the acts leading up to them to the appropriate youth court.[39] The new law in **Illinois** deals with students who are suspended or expelled for possession of a weapon on school property or for several other enumerated offenses.[40] If such a pupil attempts to transfer into another public school, the records that are transferred must include the date and duration of the suspension or expulsion. Additionally, the student is not allowed to attend class in the school in which he or she is transferring until the entire period of suspension or expulsion has been served.

---

[32] 1996 Ill. Laws 610 (1995 Ill. H.B. 2596).
[33] *Id.* § 10-22.25b.
[34] 1996 Md. Laws 265 (1996 Md. H.B. 736).
[35] 1996 Ky. Acts 8 (1996 Ky. H.B. 96).
[36] 1996 Md. Laws 5 (1996 Md. H.B. 298).
[37] 1996 Md. Laws 54 (1996 Md. S.B. 221).
[38] *Id.* § 1(a).
[39] 1996 Miss. Laws 514 (1996 Miss. S.B. 2572).
[40] 1996 Ill. Laws 622 (1996 Ill. H.B. 3052).

Missouri passed extensive legislation dealing with student discipline and conduct aimed at providing safer schools. The legislation requires local boards of education to establish written discipline policies, including determinations on the application of corporal punishment and the procedures accompanying its use. Moreover, the law requires all students and their parents to be notified of the district's policies. Finally, the statute mandates that all district employees must receive annual instruction related to the contents of the policies including approved methods of dealing with acts of school violence, disciplining students with disabilities, and confidentiality.[41]

The Missouri statute goes on to declare that school administrators are required to report acts of school violence on a "need to know" basis to teachers and other system employees, defined as those personnel who are directly responsible for a student's education or who otherwise interact with the pupil on a professional basis in the scope of their assigned duties.[42] Further, the statute requires administrators to report specific felonies committed on school properties to law enforcement agencies.[43] At the same time, the statute imposes a suspension of not less than one year for any student who brings a weapon to school. However, the law does empower superintendents to modify suspensions on a case by case basis.[44]

Utah has amended its laws to provide that pupils may be suspended or expelled from public schools for offenses such as frequent or flagrant use of foul, profane, or abusive language.[45] Students may also be suspended or expelled for frequent or flagrant willful disobedience, defiance of proper authority, or disruptive behavior.[46]

Employment Issues

Amended legislation in **Alaska** requires school systems to notify teachers who are to be laid off by March 31.[47] Under the change, these teachers will lose their right to return to work automatically if they do not accept re-employment within thirty days of receiving a contract of re-employment.[48] In addition, the statute amended the grounds for loss of tenure by permitting a school system to reduce the number of tenured

---

[41] 1996 Mo. H.B. 1301.
[42] *Id.* § 160.261(1).
[43] *Id.* § 160.261(2).
[44] *Id.* § 160.261(7).
[45] 1996 Utah S.B. 33.
[46] *Id.* § 1(a).
[47] 1996 Alaska Sess. Laws 3 (1995 Alaska H.B. 465).
[48] *Id.* § 14.20.145.

teachers that it employs if there has been a decrease in attendance or if a district's basic needs decrease by three percent or more in a year.[49]

California now requires the Commission on Teacher Credentialing to send a monthly listing to all public and private schools in the state identifying individuals who have had their credentials suspended or revoked.[50]

Illinois has revised its definition of unprofessional conduct that can lead to the suspension of a teaching or administrative certificate to include " . . . conduct that violates the standards, ethics, or rules applicable to the security, administration, monitoring, or scoring . . . of scores from any assessment test."[51] Teachers who have had their certificates suspended for convictions of Class X felonies will now be able to have the suspensions lifted if they are acquitted in new trials or have the charges dismissed. However, when a conviction becomes final, the state superintendent of education is required to revoke the certificate.[52]

Kentucky established a Principals Assessment Center to certify administrators for public schools. The center allows flexibility in the certification of principals who have comparable credentials from other states or where a local superintendent informs the Professional Standards Board that there are a limited number of local applicants available to fill administrative positions.[53]

Pennsylvania has made substantial changes to its process for granting tenure to professional employees in its public schools. Temporary professional employees, defined as individuals with less than four years of service and whose superintendents have certified that they are performing satisfactorily, can now be granted professional employee status during the last four months of their third year of service.[54] Along with providing these employees tenure in their certifying school systems, theses educators do not have to undergo the tenure process in any other district in Pennsylvania where they may be offered jobs.[55] Further, temporary professional employees who are not offered contracts at the end of three years of service must be given written statements from their boards setting forth the reasons for their dismissals.[56] Valid causes for the termination of the contract of a professional employee are unacceptable teaching performance based on two consecutive unsatisfactory ratings; persistent or willful negligence in the performance of duties; conviction of a felony

---

[49] *Id.* § 14.20.177.
[50] 1996 Cal. S.B. 1444 ch. 1075.
[51] 1996 Ill. Laws 610 § 21-23(a).
[52] *Id.* § 21-23(b).
[53] 1996 Ky. Acts 343 (1996 Ky. H.B. 327).
[54] 1996 Pa. Laws 16 (1995 Pa. S.B. 708).
[55] *Id.* § 1108(b)(3).
[56] *Id.* § 1108(b)(2).

or entering a plea of guilty or nolo contendere; persistent and willful failure to comply with school laws. The final ground for dismissal is physical or mental disability that has been documented by competent medical evidence and which, even after school officials have made reasonable attempts to accommodate, substantially interferes with the educator's ability to perform the essential functions of the job.[57]

The **Utah** legislature clarified the evidentiary standards under which its state board of education can receive and act upon charges and recommendations regarding immoral, unprofessional, or incompetent conduct or other violations of the state's standards of ethical conduct and professional competence.[58] The law was amended to require the use of the preponderance of evidence standard in state board hearings as the basis of recommendations leading to the revocation or suspension of an educator's certificate or leading to the placement of a prohibition or restriction on an individual's request for recertification.[59]

Virginia[60] and **Connecticut**[61] enacted laws calling for the suspension of teachers who are convicted of crimes involving moral turpitude or sexual molestation and the suspension of certified school employees involved in child abuse.

Curriculum

Six legislatures passed laws relating to issues of culture, values, and history in public school curricula.

Illinois mandated that beginning with the 1998-99 school year, the state Board of Education will conduct annual assessments of students in the third and fifth grades in reading, writing, and mathematics along with academic standards applicable to these areas.[62] Beginning in 1998, students who demonstrate a proficiency level, based on average pupil performance, of two or more grades below current placement will be provided with remediation programs developed in consultation with the parents or guardians. Remediation may include increased instructional time, a summer school program, tutorials, retention in grade, or modifications to instructional materials.[63]

The General Assembly in **Kentucky** was very active with regard to curricular issues. A new law permits students to engage in a period of

---

[57] *Id.* § 1122.
[58] 1996 Utah Laws 106 (1996 Ut. H.B. 124).
[59] *Id.* § 3(a).
[60] 1996 Va. Acts 960 (1996 Va. H.B. 290).
[61] 1996 Conn. P.A. 246 (1996 Conn. H.B. 404).
[62] 1996 Ill. Laws 610 (1995 Ill. H.B. 2596).
[63] *Id.* § 2-3.64(c).

silence or reflection not to exceed one minute. The law also mandates that at the start of each class in every public school, the teacher in charge of the room shall notify students of their right to participate in a moment of silent reflection.[64] In a related measure, local school boards can now authorize the recitation of the " . . . traditional Lord's prayer and the pledge of allegiance to the American flag in public elementary schools."[65] The law further directs local boards to establish policies and procedures whereby students at all grade levels may participate in the pledge of allegiance to the American flag.[66] Finally, the legislation orders private and parochial schools to offer instruction in English while increasing the minimum length of the school year to 185 days.[67]

Rhode Island found that three quarters of its workforce lacks a baccalaureate degree and that many others do not have the academic or occupational skills to succeed in a changing workplace.[68] It also observed that twenty-eight percent of its students do not complete high school[69] and unemployment among youths is high.[70] In order to make an effective transition from school to work, the legislature mandated a work-based learning approach modeled after " . . . [t]he time-honored apprenticeship concept" to integrate theoretical instruction with practice.[71]

Utah was the most active state in the area of curriculum. A new law modifies the curriculum by calling for the study of American heritage documents and the display of excerpts from these writings.[72] More specifically, the statute dictates that there shall not be any content-based censorship of American history and heritage documents due to their religious and/or cultural nature. Among the historical documents to be displayed are the Declaration of Independence; the United States Constitution; writings, speeches, documents, and proclamations of the founders and presidents of the United States; organic documents from the pre-colonial, colonial, revolutionary, federalist, and post-federalist eras; decisions of the United States Supreme Court; and acts of the United States Congress. A related provision calls for the study of Utah history from 1847 to the present in connection with regular school work.[73] Like Kentucky, another section in the law permits public schools to observe a

---

[64] 1996 Ky. Acts 85 (1996 Ky. H.B. 28).
[65] *Id.* § 1.
[66] *Id.* § 2.
[67] 1996 Ky. Acts 10 (1996 Ky. H.B. 102).
[68] 1996 R.I. Pub. L. 251 (1996 R.I. S.B. 2650).
[69] *Id.* § 16-80-2(a).
[70] *Id.* § 16-80-2(b).
[71] *Id.* § 16-80-2(h).
[72] 1996 Utah Laws 5 (1996 Ut. H.B. 14).
[73] 1996 Utah Laws 28 (1996 Ut. H.B. 63).

period of silence to reflect upon the activities of the day.[74] A final provision amended existing law regarding health instruction by requiring teachers to stress the importance of abstinence from all sexual activity before marriage and fidelity afterwards as methods of preventing certain communicable diseases.[75]

In response to concerns about accountability and student academic achievement, **Utah** also enacted legislation to require each of its school districts to establish policies providing for the implementation of a personalized student education plans. These plans are designed to implement a comprehensive system of accountability in which students advance through school by demonstrating competency of skills and mastery of knowledge. Under the bill, assessment will rely upon criterion-referenced tests, projects, and portfolios. The law also encourages schools and districts to develop and implement programs integrating technology into the curriculum and creating a choice program to give parents, teachers, and students greater flexibility in designing and choosing among programs with different focuses.[76]

Respect for the American flag and the pledge of allegiance were acted upon in **Virginia** and **New York**. **Virginia** directs the State Board of Education to develop guidelines on constitutional rights and restrictions relating to the recitation of the pledge in public schools.[77] The **New York** law ordered the Commissioner of Education to prepare a program that, in addition to a daily pledge of allegiance to the American flag, has specific instructions regarding respect for the flag along with its display and use.[78]

Funding

There was not a substantial amount of legislative funding activity other than normal budget legislation. Two exceptions occurred in **New Jersey** and **Florida**.

New Jersey passed the Comprehensive Educational Improvement and Financing Act of 1996 which observed that the state constitution requires the legislature to provide for " ... the maintenance and support of a thorough and efficient system of free public schools"[79] even though the Supreme Court of New Jersey has held that the existing system of funding did not meet this standard. The legislature decided that all children in the state are entitled to educational opportunities based on academic standards that meet

[74] 1996 Utah Laws 8 (1996 Ut. H.B. 20).
[75] 1996 Utah Laws 5 § (4)(5).
[76] 1996 Utah H.B. 117.
[77] 1996 Va. Acts 122 (1996 Va. H.B. 433).
[78] 1996 N.Y. Laws 601.
[79] 1996 N.J. Laws 138 (1996 N.J. S.N. 40).

the constitutional requirement regardless of where they reside. As such, the legislature provides for a system of funding to support this mandate.

Florida's new law created a post-secondary scholarship program funded by a lottery. The program provides financial assistance to high school graduates that does not exceed the cost of tuition, books, and fees at post-secondary institutions in the state. In order to be eligible to participate in the program, a student must receive a high school diploma or its equivalent in Florida; must have achieved a minimum of a 3.0 grade point average; and must have attained at least the minimum score established by the Florida Department of Education on the American College Test or The Scholastic Assessment Test.[80]

Governance

Hawaii, which traditionally convened an annual conference of students to address their needs, passed a bill to suspend that meeting. In its place, the legislature substituted a student governance summit to review the structure and roles of the conference in creating student-centered schools.[81] The purpose of the summit was to shift the focus of education from the administration of the system to the education of students.[82]

Mississippi passed legislation dealing with the state's takeover of school districts that failed to meet accreditation standards. The legislation provides that in an emergency situation, the state Board of Education has the authority to abolish a district, appoint an interim conservator, and/or to establish a probationary period during which the school system will be given an opportunity to remove the reported deficiencies.[83] According to the statute, a state of extreme emergency exists when the state Board of Education finds that a school district jeopardizes the safety, security, or educational interests of its students and is related to violations of accreditation standards or state or federal law.[84] Under the statute, declarations of emergency are not limited to impairments related to a lack of financial standards but may also be based on failure to meet minimum academic standards as evidenced by a continued pattern of poor student performance.

Recognizing that **New Mexico** had been involved in educational restructuring and systematic change over the years, its legislature passed a law creating the Public Education Strategic Planning Team to concentrate the efforts, resources, activities, and energies of the state

---

[80] 1996 Fla. Laws ch 341 (1996 Fla. H.B. 2405).
[81] 1996 Haw. Act 47 (1995 Haw. S.B. 3267).
[82] *Id.* § 1.
[83] 1996 Miss. Laws 302 (1996 Miss. S.B. 3135).
[84] *Id.* § 1(14).

into one framework. The objective of the law is to develop a statewide strategic plan to achieve national preeminence in education.[85] The Team is charged with reviewing and approving action plans along with recommending a schedule of implementation that includes a budgeting system and reporting back to the legislature in the first part of its forty-third session.[86]

School Choice

The charter school movement continued to gain momentum in 1996 as six states and the District of Columbia passed new legislation or amended existing laws in this area.

Arizona clarified funding and transportation allotments for charter schools. The new law allows districts that sponsor charter schools to apply for funds for students whose attendance was not reflected in the previous year's count of full-time equivalent attendance figures. In addition, the amended law offers enrollment preferences to students who are returning to the charter schools and to the siblings of pupils already enrolled there.[87]

Colorado's legislature observed that the restrictions and requirements of state laws and regulations often prevent school districts from achieving educational reforms. As such, a new law directs the state Board of Education, beginning with the 1997-98 school year, to create a pilot program of five systems to test the effectiveness of charter school districts.[88] Each school is to operate as public, nonsectarian, nonreligious institution with control of instruction vested in a local board of education, under the general supervision of the state board. Applicants for designation as a charter school must provide the state board with a statement of the mission and purpose of the school, including its goals and objectives; evidence of broad-based support among parents, teachers, and students; and evidence that the charter is educationally sound.

Connecticut defined a charter school as " . . . a public, nonsectarian school which is established under a charter . . . and [is] organized as a nonprofit entity.[89] The statute specifically decrees that charter schools are subject to all federal and state laws governing public schools.[90]

---

[85] 1996 N.M. Laws 86 (1996 N.M. H.B. 83).
[86] *Id.* § C(1).
[87] 1996 Ariz. Sess. Laws 284 (1996 Ariz. H.B. 2417).
[88] 1996 Colo. S.B. 77.
[89] 1996 Conn. P.A. 214 (1996 Conn. S.B. 19).
[90] *Id.* § 2(a).

Florida's law on charter schools,[91] which intends to improve learning by increasing learning opportunities for all students, places special emphasis on low achievers;[92] it also encourage the use of different and innovative learning methods.[93] Moreover, the legislation orders controlled open enrollment. Designed to allow a variety of programs tailored to the individual needs of communities, the open enrollment program is offered along with choice programs such as magnet and alternative schools as well as advanced placement programs.[94]

Similarly, the **District of Columbia** called for the creation of charter schools to improve the quality of public education, to provide parents and students with choices, and to offer the option of public schools free from the rules and regulations of its Board of Education.[95] Some purposes of the statute are to improve the quality of learning; to encourage diverse approaches in learning, including the innovative use of technology; and to offer new professional opportunities to teachers.

The general assembly of **Illinois** authorized the creation of charter schools[96] in order to encourage educational excellence by creating schools with high, rigorous standards for pupil performance;[97] by increasing learning opportunities for all pupils, with special emphasis on at-risk students;[98] by fostering the use of innovative teaching methods;[99] and by inviting parental involvement in the schools.[100]

South Carolina's Charter Schools Act calls for "parents, teachers, community members to take responsible risks and create new, innovative, and more flexible ways of educating all children."[101] Each charter school created under this legislation will be a part of the district in which it is located and is accountable to the local board.[102]

Attendance

Alternative placements for students and home schooling were the subject of legislation in four states.

---

[91] 1996 Fla. Laws Chap. 186 (1996 Fla. H.B. 403).
[92] *Id.* § 2(A).
[93] *Id.* § 2(B).
[94] *Id.* § 7(2).
[95] 1996 D.C. Stat. 135 (1996 D.C. Law 135).
[96] 1996 Ill. Laws 450 (1995 Ill.S.B. 19).
[97] *Id.* § B(1).
[98] *Id.* § B(2).
[99] *Id.* § B(3).
[100] *Id.* § B(5).
[101] 1996 S.C. Acts 447 (1996 S.C. H.B. 4443).
[102] *Id.* § 1(a).

Both **Alabama**[103] and **New Hampshire** passed laws designed to provide appropriate educational opportunities for students who are in youth centers or juvenile facilities. **New Hampshire's** new law also established a committee to study issues relating to providing a free, appropriate public education (FAPE) for educationally disabled students who are in the state prison, a county correctional facility, a youth development center, or a youth services center.[104]

Another new law in **New Hampshire** requires parents who begin a home school program for their children, or who withdraw students from the public schools, to notify the Commissioner of Education, superintendent, or principal before acting.[105]

Illinois is attempting to address the problem of students who are academically at risk in critical subject areas such as language arts and mathematics by requiring attendance in summer school programs. The new law mandates the creation of a program to raise the level of achievement of at-risk students who have not been identified as disabled.[106] Further, schools are discouraged from promoting students based upon age or social reasons unrelated to academic performance.[107]

The legislature in **Oklahoma** asserted that there is no legal preference or presumption for or against private, public, or home-schooling in awarding child custody or in appointing a guardian for a youngster.[108]

Students with Disabilities

Five states passed laws dealing with the education of students with disabilities.

In addition to clarifying and redefining who an "exceptional child" requiring special education is, **Connecticut** provides for the training of hearing officers in administrative procedures, including due process, and in the educational needs of children.[109]

Illinois amended its impartial due process hearing procedures, particularly with regard to the screening and training of a corps of hearing officers.[110] The bill not only requires the regular evaluation of hearing officers but also enumerates the conditions under which their employment can be terminated.[111]

---

[103] 1996 Ala. Acts 769 (1996 Ala. H.B. 149).
[104] 1996 N.H. Laws 273 (1995 N.H. H.B. 1101).
[105] 1996 N.H. Laws 222 (1996 N.H. H.B. 1203).
[106] 1996 Ill. Laws 610 (1995 Ill. H.B. 2596).
[107] *Id.* § 10-20.14.
[108] 1996 Okla. Laws 131 (1995 Okla. S.B. 73).
[109] 1996 Conn. P.A. 146 (1996 Conn. S.B. 245).
[110] 1996 Ill. Laws 698 (1995 Ill. H.B. 207).
[111] *Id.* § 14-8.02d.

Missouri and **Maryland** enacted legislation to provide for the use of mediation in resolving disputes involving issues arising out of the IDEA. The **Missouri** law[112] maintains that mediation must be mutually agreed upon by both parties and is to be provided at no cost to the parents or participating school district.[113] The law adds that no statements made by either party may be used as evidence in any hearing, review of hearing decision, or civil suit[114] and no attorney may attend or participate on behalf of any party at the mediation proceeding.[115] The statute in **Maryland**[116] requires the parties in a dispute arising under the IDEA to request the use of mediation prior to resorting to a due process hearing on matters concerning the identification, evaluation, or educational placement of a student or the provision of a FAPE.[117] Amended legislation also clarifies the rights of the parties by pointing out that if the hearing concerns the child's initial placement, the student, with the consent of his or her parents, must be placed in a public school program until the proceedings have been completed.[118]

The **Rhode Island** American Sign Language Instruction Act of 1996 acknowledges the that American Sign Language is " . . . a valid format and natural language, the use of which is vital to the preservation of the culture and heritage of the deaf community."[119] Moreover, the legislature passed a law creating a committee to develop a curriculum, adopt teacher qualification standards, and implement policies and procedures for the teaching of American Sign Language in the state's public elementary and secondary schools.[120]

Higher Education

New York's Merit Scholarship Program, designed to begin in 1997, will fund five-thousand scholarships for academic excellence.[121] The criteria for an award will be determined by taking the weighted average of the student's score on the Regents Examination in comprehensive English, Global Studies, United States History and Government, Level Three

---

[112] 1996 Mo. Laws 1376 (1996 Mo. H.B. 1501).
[113] *Id.* § 162.959.2.
[114] *Id.* § 162.959.3.
[115] *Id.* § 162.959.9.
[116] 1996 Md. Laws 16 (1996 Md. S.B. 99).
[117] *Id.* § B(1).
[118] 1996 Md. Laws 190 (1996 Md. H.B. 159).
[119] 1996 R.I. Pub. Laws 317 (1995 R.I. H.B. 8349).
[120] *Id.* § 16-25.4-3.
[121] 1996 N.Y. Laws 309 (1996 N.Y.A.N. 11319).

Mathematics, and Science.[122] The scholarships, which may not exceed four years, range in amounts from five-hundred to one-thousand dollars.[123]

Utah's legislature expressed concern about the limited resources that the state has to provide funding for higher education.[124] Therefore, lawmakers created a public trust fund that citizens may invest in to help pay for higher education.[125]

The General Assembly in **South Carolina** issued a pronouncement that the mission of higher education is to assist the state in becoming a global leader by providing a coordinated, comprehensive system of excellence in education. As such, the General Assembly created a commission to study higher education there.[126] The goals of the commission are to promote high academic quality, affordable and accessible education, instructional excellence, and coordination and cooperation with public education.[127]

Miscellaneous

California forbids teachers or others from soliciting students on school premises to subscribe or contribute to the funds of, to become members of, or to work for any organization that is not directly under the control of educational authorities.[128] The ban goes into effect an hour before classes begin and lasts until an hour after the school day ends.

Although the United States Congress did not abolish the DOE, the **New Hampshire** legislature, in a joint resolution, urged the Congress to do so. Among other points, the resolution maintained that the DOE has shown a tendency toward direct, federal control of schools and that the states are better suited to determine their own costs and curricula. The legislature resolved: "[t]hat the United States Department of Education be abolished and that the funds now distributed by the Department be granted directly to the states on a per capita basis, without restriction, except that the funds shall be applied only to public education."[129]

In **Virginia,** the General Assembly found that educational research supported the conclusion that poor children are more at risk of educational failure than youngsters from more affluent homes and that reduced pupil-teacher ratios and class sizes result in improved academic performance

---

[122] *Id.* § 670-B(2).
[123] *Id.* 670-B(3).
[124] 1996 Utah H.B. 1003.
[125] *Id.* § 3(A).
[126] 1996 S.C. S.B. 1195.
[127] *Id.* § 59-103-15.(A)(1).
[128] 1996 Cal. A.B. 2478 ch. 83.
[129] 1996 N.H. Ch. 60 (1995 H.J.R. 21).

among young children. As such, the General Assembly established the long-term goal of reducing pupil-teacher ratios and class sizes for grades K-3 in schools with high or moderate concentrations of at-risk students.[130]

Conclusion

The 1996 legislative year was active in terms of the amount and the diversity of the bills that were enacted. Even though the United States Congress took little action that is likely to have a substantial immediate impact on public education, state legislatures responded to the concerns of the general public about perceived problems in the schools.

Several state legislatures passed laws dealing with safety and violence in the public schools. Further, more states are acknowledging that parents and students are seeking choice in educational opportunities as boards are trying to reduce the constraints of rules and regulations of departments of education by enacting legislation calling for the creation of charter schools.

The laws that were enacted during the 1996 legislative year indicate that the public, through its elected representatives, continues to be concerned with the current status and future direction of public education in the United States.

---

[130] 1996 Va. Acts 974 (1996 Va. H.B. 512).

10
EDUCATION RELATED

Paul R. Downing

Introduction

This chapter reviews decisions from the federal courts on topics that may influence education. While schools, colleges, and universities are not directly involved in these rulings, the cases are highlighted for their relevance to education and their potential significance for students, employees, or institutions.

The chapter address a variety of issues under the First Amendment including free speech guidelines in the workplace, the relationship between independent contractors and government agents, and entanglements involving religious groups and government bodies. Another area that this chapter examines is the interplay between the Equal Protection Clause and the Due Process Clause of the Fourteenth Amendment. The chapter next looks at how the courts have clarified the search and seizure provisions of the Fourth Amendment. Given the fact that an increasing number of cases involve the Religious Freedom Restoration Act, which pertains to the relationship between the government and religious expression, the chapter also visits cases in this area. Among the employment issues that are discussed are discrimination in the workplace, collective bargaining, and the Employee Retirement Income Security Act. The last part of the chapter examines Supreme Court cases on voting rights, psychological privilege, and damages awards.

First Amendment

The courts have ruled that the First Amendment protects the rights of both independent contractors and government agents from retaliatory actions as long as their speech in the workplace is on matters of public concern. As such, the courts continue to rely on the *Pickering*[1] balancing test to determine whether the government's interests in maintaining an effective and efficient operation outweigh the rights of employees. Moreover, content-based restrictions on speech and expression in nonpublic forums, which are subject to strict scrutiny, must be neutral and reasonable.

Parties continue litigating disputes under the First Amendment religion clauses. These suits typically focus on whether governmental action has a secular legislative purpose, neither inhibits nor advances religion, and avoids excessive entanglement.

Freedom of Speech
Independent Contractors

A towing contractor alleged that a city removed the name of his company from a list of vendors used by the police for removing vehicles in retaliation for his refusing to contribute to the mayor's re-election campaign coupled with his support for the other candidate. A federal district court in Illinois dismissed the contractor's charge for failure to state a

---

[1] Pickering v. Board of Educ. of Township High Sch. Dist. 205, Will County, 391 U.S. 563 (1968).

claim and the Seventh Circuit affirmed. On further review, the Supreme Court, in *O'Hare Truck Service v. City of Northlake,*[2] reversed. Writing for the Court in its seven-to-two decision, Justice Kennedy held that independent contractors in employment relationships with government agents have an expectation of freedom of speech that is protected by the First Amendment. He noted that mandating affiliation with a political party may be acceptable in hiring or dismissing regular employees. However, he reasoned that the relevance of such an affiliation must be both an appropriate requirement and bear a substantial relationship to the effective performance of the job. Kennedy recognized that making a distinction between the independent contractors and governmental employees could invite the manipulation of job classifications and labels that might have a chilling effect on their free speech and association rights.

In a second case involving independent contractors, a board of commissioners voted to terminate the contract of a trash hauler who was critical of their actions. The federal district court in Kansas granted the board's motion for summary judgment but the Tenth Circuit reversed. In *Board of County Commissioners, Wabaunsee County v. Umbehr,*[3] the Supreme Court affirmed. In a seven-to-two ruling, Justice O'Connor wrote that the First Amendment protects independent contractors from having at-will contracts with the government terminated or not renewed simply because they exercise their rights to free speech. She added that the *Pickering* balancing test, which has to be adjusted to weigh the government's interest as a contractor and as an employer, determines the extent of an individual's protection.

Restrictions on Speech

An African-American deputy sheriff in South Carolina sought further review of a grant of summary judgment in his suit that alleged his dismissal violated his right to free speech under the First Amendment. The former deputy lost his job after he joined an association of Black officers and spoke out about perceived discrimination in his department. Relying in large part on *Pickering*, the Fourth Circuit reversed in finding that racial discrimination within a public law enforcement agency is a matter of public concern.[4] As such, the court analyzed the interests of the parties and declared that those of the deputy outweighed the government's.

In California, a staff member of the state Department of Education appealed a grant of summary judgment in his challenge to a policy that

---

[2] 116 S. Ct. 2353 (1996).
[3] 116 S. Ct. 2361 (1996).
[4] Cromer v. Brown, 88 F.3d 1315 (4th Cir. 1996).

forbade employees from engaging in oral or written religious advocacy in the workplace and displaying religious artifacts, tracts, or materials outside of their offices or cubicles. Further, the policy directed employees to refrain from religious discussions during the work day unless they took place at lunch or on breaks away from the office. The Ninth Circuit reversed in asserting that since the government was attempting to regulate speech, it failed to justify the restrictions.[5] More specifically, the court rejected the state's claim that the policy helped to advance its interest in maintaining and promoting an effective and efficient workplace.

A former intern with the Utah Department of Corrections appealed a grant of summary judgment in her suit that alleged she lost her position for exercising her First Amendment right to free speech. The student was released after she made a statement to a television reporter that was critical of a change in the law with regard to sex offenders. The Tenth Circuit reversed in favor of the intern.[6] According to the court, the intern was entitled to the protections of the First Amendment in commenting upon matters of public concern because she was considered a paid state employee insofar as she received a stipend in return for working twenty hours a week.

Public Forum Doctrine

A religious group in Indiana sought further review of the denial of their request to enjoin a policy adopted by a public agency that banned all private displays, religious or otherwise, from its lobby. The Seventh Circuit affirmed that since the lobby was a nonpublic forum, and the policy was content neutral, it was reasonable under the circumstances.[7]

In a similar suit from Nebraska, a welfare rights organization sued a department of social services after it was not permitted to distribute literature and discuss welfare reform in the lobby of a public building. The department had an informal policy that permitted groups providing a "direct benefit" to welfare recipients to meet in the lobby. Yet, under the policy, advocacy groups were never allowed access regardless of their position or message. The federal district court held in favor of the department but the Eighth Circuit reversed.[8] The court observed that since the unwritten policy was neither clear nor consistently applied, and was subject to arbitrary enforcement, it violated the group's First Amendment rights.

---

[5] Tucker v. California Dep't of Educ., 97 F.3d 1204 (9th Cir. 1996).
[6] Andersen v. McCotter, 100 F.3d 723 (10th Cir. 1996).
[7] Grossbaum v. Indianapolis-Marion County Bldg. Auth., 100 F.3d 1287 (7th Cir. 1996).
[8] Families Achieving Independence and Respect v. Nebraska Dep't of Soc. Servs., 91 F.3d 1076 (8th Cir. 1996).

Opponents of abortion in Iowa who were denied a permit to parade and picket the house of a doctor alleged that the city infringed upon their protected free speech rights. A federal district court dismissed the section 1983 action filed by the protestors as moot because the doctor no longer lived in the house where they wanted to picket. On further review, the Eighth Circuit agreed that the ordinance did not violate the First Amendment.[9] However, the court reversed on the ground that since the ordinance required applicants to file for a permit five days in advance of an event, it was insufficiently narrowly tailored to achieve the government's goal because it was not structured in such a manner that avoided delegating broad licensing discretion to individual officials.

A federal district court in Oklahoma granted a motion by a teenage Republican club to enjoin a city from enforcing a policy that would have prohibited it from displaying a sign in a public park during an annual Christmas festival. Subsequently, the court granted the club's motion for summary judgment on its First Amendment claim. On further review, the Tenth Circuit affirmed.[10] The court pointed out that since the event took place in a public forum, the city's content-based restriction was insufficiently narrowly tailored to serve a compelling governmental interest.

Freedom of Religion

Despite its general policy of prohibiting large unattended objects on public property, a city allowed an oversized, unattended menorah to be constructed in a public park during Chanukah season. After a federal district court in California granted the city's motion for summary judgment, the American Jewish Congress appealed. The Ninth Circuit reversed.[11] The court stated that the city violated the Establishment Clause of both the federal and state constitutions because the government is precluded from conveying a message that a particular religious belief is favored.

An inmate in Wisconsin unsuccessfully filed a section 1983 action against the department of corrections alleging that it violated his First Amendment rights by requiring him to attend a religious-based narcotics rehabilitation program. The Seventh Circuit reversed in favor of the inmate.[12] Based in part on the tripartite *Lemon v. Kurtzman*[13] test, the court maintained that requiring the inmate to attend the sessions on the risk of being classified as a higher security risk or possibly be denied parole if he did not do so violated the Establishment Clause.

---

[9] Douglas v. Brownell, 88 F.3d 1511 (8th Cir. 1996).
[10] Eagon v. City of Elk City, 72 F.3d 1480 (10th Cir. 1996).
[11] American Jewish Congress v. City of Beverly Hills, 90 F.3d 379 (9th Cir. 1996).
[12] Kerr v. Farrey, 95 F.3d 472 (7th Cir. 1996).
[13] 403 U.S. 602 (1971).

Fourteenth Amendment

Fourteenth Amendment claims can be grounded in the Equal Protection Clause and the Due Process Clause. The Equal Protection Clause assures equitable protection for all citizens. Once a state offers protection to its citizenry, then those rights may not be denied to any member. Moreover, governmental action must bear a rational relationship to a legitimate legislative goal and may not place an undue burden on an individual's fundamental rights or on members of a suspect class. The Due Process Clause, on the other hand, requires adequate notice and representation before an individual can be deprived of a property interest.

Equal Protection

Where a trial court terminated a mother's parental rights to her two minor children and granted custody to their natural father and his second wife, the Supreme Court of Mississippi denied her application to proceed in forma pauperis. The court contended that since the mother could not afford to pay for legal services, she did not have a right to use that status in a civil appeal. In a six-to-three decision delivered by Justice Ginsburg, the Supreme Court, in *M.L.B. v. S.L.J.*,[14] reversed in favor of the mother. She indicated that even though the constitution does not guarantee the right to appellate review, once a state offers it to some, equal protection dictates that a state may not deny the same to others due to poverty. Ginsburg added that in a parental rights case such as this, a state must provide access to judicial processes without regard to a person's ability to pay court fees.

The State of Colorado enacted an amendment to its constitution through a statewide referendum. Amendment 2 precluded all governmental action designed to protect the status of individuals based upon their homosexual, lesbian, or bisexual orientation, conduct, practices, or relationships. Further, the amendment was formulated in response to local ordinances that banned discrimination based on sexual orientation in housing, employment, health and welfare services, education, and public accommodations. A state trial court permanently enjoined the enforcement of the amendment and the Supreme Court of Colorado affirmed. On further review, in *Romer v. Evans*,[15] the Supreme Court affirmed that the amendment failed to have an identifiable legitimate purpose or objective. Justice Kennedy, writing for the Court in its six-to-three ruling, noted that Amendment 2 was too narrow and too broad in

---

[14] 117 S. Ct. 555 (1996).
[15] 116 S. Ct. 1620 (1996).

defining people by one trait and then denying them protection across the board. Further, he judged that refusing to allow individuals to seek protection under law is a denial of equal protection since statutes cannot burden a fundamental right or a suspect class. Kennedy concluded that the amendment was unconstitutional because it failed to bear a rational relationship to a legitimate legislative goal.

Due Process

Taxpayers challenged adverse rulings in their class action suit that alleged a county's occupational tax violated state and federal law. The Supreme Court of Alabama affirmed that the claims were barred in light of a previous suit by three other taxpayers. Writing for a unanimous Court in *Richards v. Jefferson County*,[16] Justice Stevens reversed in favor of the taxpayers on the basis that they had neither received notice of nor sufficient representation in the prior case. He posited that the prior litigation over the viability of the tax was neither binding on different parties nor barred their suit dealing with the constitutionality of the tax. Stevens ascertained that there was no evidence suggesting that the lower courts took the taxpayers' interests into account in a manner consistent with an entire group of individuals.

A woman sought further review of a public nuisance law under which a car that she jointly owned with her husband was forfeited to the state after he engaged in illegal sexual activity in it with a prostitute. The Supreme Court of Michigan reasoned that the state's failure to provide the innocent co-owner with a defense to the taking did not violate her federal right to due process. On further review in *Bennis v. Michigan*,[17] a closely divided Court affirmed. Writing for the majority in a five-to-four decision, Chief Justice Rehnquist held that a long line of cases supports the proposition that an individual may lose interest in property even when the owner is unaware of how it would be put to use. As such, he affirmed that the forfeiture order did not violate the Due Process Clause of the Fourteenth Amendment or the Takings Clause of the Fifth Amendment.

Fourth Amendment

The measure of the reasonableness of a search continues to be the benchmark utilized by the courts in evaluating Fourth Amendment claims. The courts continue to eschew establishing a bright-line standard for reasonableness; instead, they rely on an objective assessment of the totality

---

[16] 116 S. Ct. 1761 (1996).
[17] 116 S. Ct. 994 (1996).

of a situation based on the experience and knowledge of an investigator. The courts have recognized that subjective intentions may not be considered to invalidate a legal search if a suspect was detained through a justifiable objective assessment. Moreover, the judiciary has asserted that private individuals may conduct legal searches as long as they are not acting as state agents.

After a deputy sheriff stopped a driver for speeding and assessed him a verbal warning, he asked for and was granted permission to search the vehicle and discovered a small amount of marijuana. The Supreme Court of Ohio ruled that the search was illegal based upon the unlawful detention and the officer's failure to inform the subject that he was free to go. On further review in *Ohio v. Robinette*,[18] the Supreme Court, in an eight-to-one decision authored by Chief Justice Rehnquist, reversed. In evaluating the legality of a search, he noted that the totality of the situation must be assessed in light of its reasonableness. He decided that the police officer was not required to advise the suspect who was stopped lawfully that he was free to go prior to conducting a voluntary search. Rehnquist acknowledged that courts cannot second-guess police officers who rely on their judgment and experience in making objective determinations.

When a plainclothes police officer stopped a vehicle for a traffic violation in an area frequented by drug traffic ers, he observed that the driver had plastic bags of cocaine. A trial court and the Circuit Court of Appeals for the District of Columbia rejected the suspect's allegation that the traffic stop was a pretense for making the drug arrest and that he was detained illegally. On further review in *Whren v. United States*,[19] a unanimous Supreme Court, in a judgment authored by Justice Scalia, affirmed. He asserted that the temporary detention of a motorist whom police had probable cause to believe committed a traffic violation was consistent with the Fourth Amendment's prohibition against unreasonable searches and seizures regardless of whether the officer would have stopped the driver based on his desire to enforce the traffic laws.

Where a passenger denied ownership of a knapsack containing a gun that was discovered by police officers, a federal trial court denied his motion to suppress the evidence and to obtain the name of the confidential informant. Consequently, the suspect was found guilty of unlawful possession of firearms by a convicted felon. The Circuit Court for the District of Columbia affirmed on the basis that the scope and duration of the investigative stop of the car was reasonable.[20] The court added that there was no reason to disclose the name of the informant.

---

[18] 117 S. Ct. 417 (1996).
[19] 116 S. Ct. 1769 (1996).
[20] United States v. Mangum, 100 F.3d 164 (D.C. Cir. 1996).

The federal district court in Wyoming addressed whether an individual who searches a package independent of police authority is acting as a government agent. Where a bus station manager accepted a sealed package for shipping that appeared to be suspicious in light of his observations and experience, he called the police asking for advice on whether he could open it due to his concern for the safety of others on the bus. A police officer was present when the package was opened, but did not initiate or participate in the search. The defendant challenged the rejection of his motion to dismiss charges for conspiracy to possess, manufacture, and distribute methamphetamine and for carrying a firearm during a drug trafficking offense. Based on the totality of the circumstances, the Tenth Circuit affirmed that the Fourth Amendment was inapplicable since the search was conducted by a private individual who was not acting as a government agent.[21]

Religious Freedom Restoration Act

The Religious Freedom Restoration Act[22] (RFRA) was enacted by Congress in 1993 in response to the Supreme Court's holding in *Employment Division v. Smith*.[23] In *Smith*, the Court maintained that a facially neutral, generally applicable law may apply to religiously motivated conduct. As such, Congress passed the RFRA in order to assure that any law that substantially burdens the exercise of religion must pass the compelling interest test as designated in the RFRA. Additionally, the RFRA prohibits conduct that has the effect of burdening the free exercise of religion or discriminating against particular faiths or religion in general.

After a city in Texas enacted an ordinance to protect historic landmarks and to safeguard its heritage, a church challenged the denial of its request for a building permit to enlarge its structure. Even though the designation applied only to the church's facade, the city considered the entire building to be within the historic district. A federal district court stated that the RFRA was unconstitutional, but the Fifth Circuit reversed.[24] The court contended that the RFRA did not violate the First Amendment, Tenth Amendment, or Fourteenth Amendment because the government itself did not advance religion.

In Wisconsin, an inmate relied upon the RFRA in challenging a regulation that banned the wearing of jewelry, including religious symbols

---

[21] United States v. Smythe, 84 F.3d 1240 (10th Cir. 1996).

[22] Religious Freedom Restoration Act of 1993, 42 U.S.C.A. § 2000bb.

[23] 494 U.S. 872 (1990).

[24] Flores v. City of Boerne, 73 F.3d 1352 (5th Cir. 1996), *cert. granted* 117. S. Ct. 293 (1996).

such as crucifixes, that could be used as weapons, unless they were made of cloth. A federal district court posited that the policy violated the RFRA and the Seventh Circuit affirmed.[25] According to the court, since wearing symbols of this nature is religiously motivated, it could be considered religious behavior. The court reflected that the policy did not satisfy the state's burden of establishing the presence of a compelling interest in protecting inmates and staff from risk of injury. Among the factors that the court considered in striking down the policy were that the religious jewelry was too light and too small to be used as weapons, was too inexpensive to be bartered for a weapon, and was not a gang symbol or easily confused with one.

The Red Cross refused to certify an instructor who was going to work with individuals who had AIDS/ HIV even though he completed all of his written and practical examinations. The Red Cross would not certify the instructor based on its concern that he would be unable to separate his religious beliefs concerning the transmission of AIDS from his teaching duties. A federal district court in California dismissed for failure to state a cause of action and the Ninth Circuit affirmed.[26] The court indicated that the Red Cross was not a government entity because it was neither created to further objectives of the state nor did the government retain authority to appoint directors to its board. The court concluded that the Red Cross was not subject to the RFRA because the law applies only to governmental agencies or those involved in state action.

Charged with conspiracy to possess marijuana with the intent to distribute it, a suspect in Wyoming claimed that since he belonged to the Church of Marijuana, he was protected under the RFRA. On appeal from his conviction, the Tenth Circuit affirmed.[27] As part of its decision, the court examined a list of factors related to what constitutes a religion including ultimate ideas, metaphysical beliefs, moral or ethical systems, comprehensiveness of beliefs, and accoutrements of religion to determine whether the Church of Marijuana qualified as a faith. The court held that since the Church of Marijuana was unable to meet the threshold determination of a religion, the conviction did not violate the Free Exercise Clause.

A Muslim prisoner in Illinois unsuccessfully claimed that prison officials infringed upon his rights by refusing to accommodate his needs during a holy period. On further review, the Seventh Circuit affirmed.[28] The court noted that the prison rebutted the prisoner's prima facie case

---

[25] Sasnett v. Sullivan, 91 F.3d 1018 (7th Cir. 1996).
[26] Hall v. American Nat'l Red Cross, 86 F.3d 919 (9th Cir. 1996).
[27] United States v. Meyers, 95 F.3d 1475 (10th Cir. 1996).
[28] Mack v. O'Leary, 80 F.3d 1175 (7th Cir. 1996).

that his rights were violated. It offered that the denial of the prisoner's request to have a banquet to celebrate the birthday of his sect's founder did not violate the RFRA because communal eating was the standard for most of the approximately 300 such groups in the facility.

Discrimination in the Workplace

In order to fight discrimination, several federal laws safeguard the interests of individual employees. Title VII[29] is the primary statute utilized in these cases. The Age Discrimination in Employment Act[30] (ADEA), Pregnancy Discrimination Act[31] (PDA), section 504 of the Rehabilitation Act of 1973,[32] and the Americans with Disabilities Act[33] (ADA) provide additional protections for specific populations. These acts proscribe adverse employment activities directed at individuals based upon their membership within a specific group. In order to prevail, an aggrieved employee must establish a prima facie case by demonstrating that he or she is a member of a protected class, suffered from an adverse employment action, had met the demands of the job when the action occurred, and was replaced by an individual who was not a member of the protected class.

Age Discrimination in Employment Act

Where a fifty-six-year-old employee was fired and replaced by a forty-year-old, a federal district court in North Carolina granted his company's motion for summary judgment. The Fourth Circuit affirmed on the basis that the employee failed to establish a prima facie case of age discrimination under *McDonnell Douglas Corporation v. Green*[34] because he did not demonstrate that he was replaced by someone outside of the group that was protected by the ADEA. On further review, in *O'Connor v. Consolidated Coin Caterers,*[35] a unanimous Supreme Court, in an opinion by Justice Scalia, reversed in favor of the employee. He reasoned that even assuming that the title VII *McDonnell Douglas* framework applied to the ADEA, there at least had to have been a logical connection between each element of the prima facie case and the illegal discrimination. Scalia added that being replaced by someone under the

---

[29] 42 U.S.C. § 2000.
[30] 29 U.S.C. § 621.
[31] 42 U.S.C. § 2000.
[32] 20 U.S.C. § 794
[33] 42 U.S.C. § 12102 *et seq.*
[34] 411 U.S. 792 (1973).
[35] 116 S. Ct. 1307 (1996).

age of forty did not make such a logical connection. He pointed out that as long as the displaced worker lost his position because of age, regardless of how old the new employee was, then his rights under the ADEA were violated. Scalia decided that the employee's loss of his position to another member of the protected class was irrelevant.

In the first of two cases from Texas, a former contracts administrator challenged a grant of summary judgment in favor of his employer. The administrator sued under the ADEA claiming that his being released as part of a reduction-in-force was actually a pretext for age discrimination. The Fifth Circuit affirmed on the ground that the administrator was unable to refute his employer's contention that he was dismissed because his job performance was, at best, average.[36]

The Equal Employment Opportunity Commission (EEOC) questioned a grant of summary judgment in favor of an electronics company in a suit alleging that the manufacturer discharged six supervisors as part of a reduction-in-force because of their ages. The Fifth Circuit affirmed that statements made on behalf of the company were not probative of discrimination as they were not directly and unambiguously related to age.[37] In addition, the court ascertained that the EEOC was unable to undermine the company's legitimate, nondiscriminatory, and individualized reasons for dismissing the employees.

In Wisconsin, a pharmaceutical sales representative appealed a grant of summary judgment in favor of his employer where he claimed that his transfer to a position in a coaching program violated his rights under the ADEA. The Seventh Circuit affirmed that the transfer did not amount to an adverse employment action under the ADEA.[38] The court ruled that a lateral transfer that does not involve a reduction in pay and creates no more than a minor change in working conditions is not an adverse employment action. The court recognized that while the representative's earnings did decrease, his commission percentage rate remained the same after the transfer.

A former fire captain with thirty-three years of experience filed suit against the city for allegedly violating his rights under the ADEA and the ADA when he was dismissed from his job. The captain was released because he was unable to pass a physical fitness test required for approval to wear a self-contained breathing apparatus. After a federal trial court in Iowa granted the city's motion for summary judgment, the Eighth Circuit affirmed.[39] The court asserted that the city demonstrated a business

---

[36] Nichols v. Loral Vought Sys., 81 F.3d 38 (5th Cir. 1996).
[37] Equal Employment Opportunity Comm'n v. Texas Instruments, 100 F.3d 1173 (5th Cir. 1996).
[38] Williams v. Bristol-Myers Squibb Co., 85 F.3d 270 (7th Cir. 1996).
[39] Smith v. City of Des Moines, 99 F.3d 1466 (8th Cir. 1996).

necessity, in the form of the physical fitness test, as a defense to the ADEA claim. Turning to the ADA charge, the court found that the captain was not qualified under the ADA simply because he was unable to perform his duties as a firefighter.

Sexual Harassment

A former employee unsuccessfully sued a gas company under title VII alleging both that his supervisor had created a sexually hostile work environment and that he lost his job in retaliation for filing his complaint. The federal district court in Maryland granted the gas company's motion for summary judgment and the Fourth Circuit affirmed.[40] The panel acknowledged that even though the lower courts were divided over whether title VII applied to same-sex gender harassment, the employee failed to demonstrate that the conduct in question was sufficiently severe to create a hostile work environment. Moreover, the court stated that the worker was unable to show that he was the victim of an adverse employer action.

A male heterosexual who had worked as a waiter and cook sued a restaurant chain claiming that a homosexual supervisor and other gay male employees created a hostile work environment. A federal district court in North Carolina dismissed the employee's title VII claim for failure to state a cause of action. On further review, the Fourth Circuit reversed on the basis that the creation of a hostile work environment does not require the harassment to occur between persons of the opposite sex.[41] The court observed that a hostile work environment can result where a male or female homosexual supervisor either discriminates against a worker of the same sex or permits other workers to do so.

As illustrated by a case from Ohio, one incident may not meet the standard needed to demonstrate the creation of a hostile work environment. A male employee unsuccessfully filed suit under title VII against a soap manufacturing company alleging that it was liable when he was sexually harassed by a male coworker. The Sixth Circuit affirmed that alleged activity by one coworker was insufficient to impose liability.[42] The court declared that the employer was not responsible since managers took sufficient steps with regard to the harassment by reprimanding the employee who behaved inappropriately.

In Missouri, a supermarket appealed a ruling in favor of a seventeen-year-old floral worker who filed a title VII claim after it failed to respond

[40] Hopkins v. Baltimore Gas and Elec. Co., 77 F.3d 745 (4th Cir. 1996), *cert. denied,* 117 S. Ct. 70 (1996).
[41] Wrightson v. Pizza Hut of Am., 99 F.3d 138 (4th Cir. 1996).
[42] Fleenor v. Hewitt Soap, 81 F.3d 48 (6th Cir. 1996), *cert. denied,* 117 S. Ct. 170 (1996).

to her reporting two incidents of sexual harassment by a fifty-one-year-old male coworker. The Eighth Circuit affirmed.[43] The court rejected the supermarket's claim that the young woman failed to utilize the reporting procedures listed in her employee manual and did not exhaust administrative remedies in her collective bargaining agreement before initiating her suit. The panel noted that the young woman did not have to exhaust other channels before filing suit and that the primary issue was whether the employer knew or should have known of the harassment. Further, the court judged that the supermarket failed to take corrective action even after the young woman notified her supervisors about the harassment.

Four female restaurant employees brought sexual harassment claims under title VII against their supervisors and company. A federal district court in Alabama granted the restaurant's motion for summary judgment as to one of the employee's quid pro quo allegations but held for the workers on the hostile work environment. On appeal, the Eleventh Circuit affirmed that since the restaurant had at least constructive knowledge of the hostile environment, it was liable.[44] The court pointed out that the extent of the hostile environment was so pervasive that the employer knew or should have known of it yet failed to take prompt remedial action. At the same time, the court reversed in adding that insofar as the restaurant did not act with malice or recklessness, it was not responsible for punitive damages.

Pregnancy Discrimination Act

The first of two cases from Michigan involving the PDA was filed by a hotel worker who claimed that she was fired because she contemplated having an abortion. In fact, the woman carried the baby to term. The hotel appealed a ruling in favor of the woman on the basis that she was released because she had become a subject of controversy among hotel staff. The Sixth Circuit affirmed that the hotel violated the PDA since the decision to discharge the young, unwed mother because she contemplated having an abortion was not clearly erroneous.[45] The court also agreed that the woman was entitled to compensatory, but not punitive, damages.

A mail handler in Michigan challenged a grant of summary judgment in favor of the United States Postal Service in her suit that claimed her supervisors violated her rights under the PDA when they did not provide her with a light-duty assignment. The Sixth Circuit reversed in favor of the mail handler.[46] The court indicated that the woman established a prima

---

[43] Varner v. National Super Markets, 94 F.3d 1209 (8th Cir. 1996).

[44] Splunge v. Shoney's, 97 F.3d 488 (11th Cir. 1996).

[45] Turic v. Holland Hospitality, 85 F.3d 1211 (6th Cir. 1996).

[46] Ensley-Gaines v. Runyon, 100 F.3d 1220 (6th Cir. 1996).

facie case of pregnancy discrimination since similarly situated limited and light duty employees received more favorable treatment than she did.

In Illinois, a former sales representative who was dismissed weeks after informing her supervisor that she was pregnant sought further review of a grant of summary judgment in her suit which claimed that her rights under the PDA had been violated. The Seventh Circuit affirmed that the sales representative had not established a prima facie case as she was not qualified for her position.[47] Further, the court offered that comments by a supervisor were not discriminatory since nonpregnant employees were not treated any more favorably than the representative.

Section 504 and the Americans with Disabilities Act

A systems engineer in Texas who was fired due to his inability to meet deadlines on projects unsuccessfully filed suit under the ADA. The engineer, who had diabetes, claimed that he suffered from fatigue caused by renal failure. On further review, the Fifth Circuit reversed.[48] The court contended that summary judgment was precluded where there were material issues of fact as to whether the engineer's fatigue was a disability within the meaning of the ADA, whether his missing the deadlines was an essential function of his job, and whether he could have been accommodated reasonably by adjusting the due dates for the assignments or by being transferred to another position.

A marine drilling company in Texas appealed the denial of its motion for summary judgment in a suit filed by a former rig mechanic with asbestosis who claimed that his not being rehired violated the ADA. The Fifth Circuit reversed.[49] The court reasoned that asbestosis is not a disability within the meaning of the ADA because it did not substantially limit one of the mechanic's life activities insofar as his condition was transitory and only occurred occasionally while he was climbing the stairs.

Both parties sought further review where a railroad car inspector foreman with thirty-six years of experience was shifted from his position after it was discovered that he suffered from diabetes even though there was no evidence to suggest that his condition impaired his work performance. The Sixth Circuit affirmed that since the rail carrier is a recipient of federal financial assistance within the meaning of the Rehabilitation Act, it was liable for discriminating against the inspector.[50] At the same time, the court agreed that punitive damages are unavailable under section 504 since Congress neither intended to permit such awards

[47] Geier v. Medtronic, 99 F.3d 238 (7th Cir. 1996).
[48] Riel v. Electronic Data Sys., 99 F.3d 678 (5th Cir. 1996).
[49] Robinson v. Global Marine Drilling, 101 F.3d 35 (5th Cir. 1996).
[50] Moreno v. Consolidated Rail, 99 F.3d 782 (6th Cir. 1996).

nor did it wish to create remedies beyond the scope of existing mechanisms of the Rehabilitation Act.

In the first of two cases from Florida, an unsuccessful applicant for a position as a custodian claimed that county officials violated her rights under the ADA when they denied her request to have someone read her the questions on an examination. The applicant admitted that she did not have a high school diploma but was considered for the job since she indicated that she had taken special education classes. The woman then claimed that the officials knew that she was unable to read or write since she had taken special education courses. A federal trial court granted the county's motion for summary judgment. On further review, the Eleventh Circuit affirmed that the county had no reason to know that the woman was illiterate just because she had taken special education courses.[51] As such, the court concluded that the woman was not covered by the ADA.

Where a night supervisor of a camera department developed visual problems following brain surgery, he was reassigned to a clerical position and was ultimately dismissed from his job working for a newspaper. Subsequently, the supervisor appealed a jury verdict in favor of his employer. The Eleventh Circuit reversed in ruling that the supervisor could recover under the ADA without showing that his disability was the sole cause of his dismissal.[52] The court added that the jury form erroneously limited the supervisor's ability to recover only for his firing where he alleged, and there was evidence of, a variety of adverse employment actions that stopped short of dismissal.

Religious Discrimination

An evangelical Christian who worked in a temporary capacity for a telecommunications services company filed suit under title VII claiming religious discrimination when her application for full-time employment was rejected. A federal district court in Oklahoma found in favor of the applicant but denied relief on the basis that she submitted forged letters of reference. On further review, the Tenth Circuit affirmed that the woman failed to establish a prima facie case of discrimination since she did not present any direct evidence that religion played a part in the company's action.[53] The court determined that statements by a manager about the inappropriateness of expressing religious views during an interview or in the workplace were not indicative of a bias against religion.

---

[51] Moriskey v. Broward County, 80 F.3d 445 (11th Cir. 1996).

[52] McNely v. Ocala Star-Banner, 99 F.3d 1068 (11th Cir. 1996).

[53] Equal Employment Opportunity Comm'n v. Wiltel, Inc., 81 F.3d 1508 (10th Cir. 1996).

Collective Bargaining

Employment issues related to the collective bargaining process continue to be litigated. These complex matters typically examine a wide range of topics on the nature of the relationship between an employer and a bargaining unit. An added dimension in this area of law comes from the fact that the National Labor Relations Board (NLRB) closely monitors bargaining and is frequently involved in federal cases wherein the courts look to ensure that the parties have negotiated in good faith.

After a shoe company announced the closing of a factory in Missouri, a union unsuccessfully filed suit under the Worker Adjustment and Retraining Notification Act (WARN).[54] WARN requires certain employers to notify their workers or their unions of plant closings or mass layoffs at least sixty days prior to the planned action. A federal district court dismissed the union's complaint and the Seventh Circuit affirmed. However, in *United Food and Commercial Workers Union Local 751 v. Brown Group,*[55] a unanimous Supreme Court, in an opinion by Justice Souter, reversed and held that the union could sue for damages on behalf of its membership. He ascertained that the union could sue because it satisfied WARN requirements insofar as its members would otherwise have had standing to act on their own; the interests that it sought to protect were germane to its purpose; and neither the claim asserted nor the relief requested required individual members to participate in the suit.

The NLRB found that an iron works company in Massachusetts committed an unfair labor practice when, after the union of its employees accepted an outstanding proposal, its management refused to sign the agreement and withdrew its recognition of the union. The company allegedly disavowed the agreement based on its good faith doubt, in light of information acquired before the offer was accepted, about whether a majority of members supported the union. The First Circuit enforced the NLRB's order that required the company to cease and desist the unfair labor practice and, a unanimous Supreme Court, in *Auciello Iron Works v. NLRB,*[56] affirmed. Writing for the Court, Justice Souter maintained that the NLRB's actions were consistent with the National Labor Relations Act.[57] He posited that since the company's pre-contractual, doubt about the majority status of the union was inadequate to support its request for an exception to the good faith presumption of its majority status at the

---

[54] 29 U.S.C. § 2101 *et seq.*
[55] 116 S. Ct. 1529 (1996).
[56] 116 S. Ct. 1754 (1996).
[57] 29 U.S.C. § 158 (1994).

time that the contract had been accepted, the employer committed an unfair labor practice.

A dispute from New York City focused on whether a delicatessen committed an unfair labor practice by entering into negotiations with a rival union. The second union had attempted to file a notice with the NLRB claiming that a majority of employees desired a change in representation. When the contract between the parties expired, they agreed to continue negotiations since a majority of employees expressed a legitimate interest in retaining the incumbent union. The Second Circuit granted the NLRB's petition for an order of enforcement based on its finding that the delicatessen committed unfair labor practices by negotiating with the unions.[58] The court acknowledged that since the incumbent union's petitions were valid indications of its majority position, the delicatessen could not claim to have reasonable good faith doubt about its status. In addition, the court agreed that the NLRB properly ordered the delicatessen and nonincumbent group to reimburse employees for dues and fees that they had paid to the second union.

Employment Retirement Income Security Act

The Employment Retirement Income Security Act (ERISA),[59] which protects employees and their benefits packages from mismanagement, applies to employers who act as fiduciaries for their workers. Under ERISA, employers have a fiduciary duty to manage plans by acting in the best interests of their employees.

Former employees and retirees filed suit under ERISA where their employer encouraged them to change benefits plans when they transferred between subsidiaries of the corporation. The employees alleged that the corporation violated its fiduciary duty when, within two years of the transfer, the subsidiary dissolved into receivership and they lost their nonpension benefits. The corporation appealed after a federal district court in Iowa and the Eighth Circuit decided in favor of the employees. Justice Breyer wrote the Court's opinion in its six-to-three affirmation in *Varity Corporation v. Howe.*[60] He agreed that since the firm acted as an ERISA fiduciary when it misled the employees about the security of their benefits, the aggrieved workers had the statutory right to seek individualized equitable relief.

In 1979, an aerospace corporation rehired a sixty-one-year-old employee who had left to work for a competitor. However, based on

---

[58] National Labor Relations Bd. v. Katz's Delicatessen of Houston St., 809 F.3d 755 (2d Cir. 1996).

[59] 29 U.S.C. § 1001 *et. seq.* (1988).

[60] 116 S. Ct. 1065 (1996).

exclusions that were permitted under ERISA, the corporation modified its plan by excluding individuals over sixty from participating in its retirement plan. Even though these exceptions were subsequently eliminated, the corporation did not provide credit for service time between the date when the employee was hired and when its revised plan went into effect in 1988. After the plaintiff retired without obtaining the additional benefits, he filed suit claiming that the corporation violated his rights under ERISA and the ADEA. A federal trial court in California dismissed in favor of the employer and the Ninth Circuit affirmed in part. On further review in *Lockheed Corporation v. Spink*,[61] Justice Thomas, in a seven-to-two opinion declared that since the corporation and its board were not acting as fiduciaries within the meaning of the law when they amended the retirement plan, they did not violate ERISA. Moreover, he observed that because amendments to ERISA and the ADEA which prohibited aged-based reductions in benefit accrual rates did not apply retroactively, the employee was not entitled to service credit between 1979 and 1988.

Voting Issues

The Secretary of Commerce is charged with conducting an actual enumeration of the American public every ten years in order to apportion Congressional representation among the states. Yet, based on the 1990 census data, the Secretary elected not to use a statistical adjustment to account for an undercount. Consequently, several states, cities, citizens groups, and citizens unsuccessfully filed suit in New York seeking to compel the Secretary to apply a post-enumeration survey as a statistical adjustment to the census data. After the Second Circuit reversed and re-manded, the Supreme Court, in turn, reversed. Writing for a unanimous Court in *Wisconsin v. City of New York*,[62] Chief Justice Rehnquist stated that because it was reasonable to conclude that an actual count could best be achieved without the post-enumeration survey based on statistical adjustment, the Secretary's choice not to do so was well within the bounds of his discretion. Rehnquist offered that distributive accuracy is more important than numerical accuracy in utilizing the census data for the purposes of representative apportionment.

The first of three cases involving the Voting Rights Act of 1965 (VRA)[63] arose when the Republican Party in Virginia invited all registered voters who were willing to support their nominee for a Senate seat to

---

[61] 116 S. Ct. 1783 (1996).
[62] 116 S. Ct. 1091 (1996).
[63] 42 U.S.C. § 1973.

participate in the delegate selection process by paying a registration fee. When two voters who were qualified to become delegates were rejected because they refused to pay the fee filed suit, a federal district court dismissed their claims. On appeal in *Morse v. Republican Party of Virginia*,[64] the Supreme Court reversed. Justice Stevens' majority opinion in the Court's five-to-four judgment ruled that fees such as this limit the opportunity of voters to participate in conventions and ultimately weaken the effectiveness of the votes cast in the general election.

Residents in North Carolina challenged the existence of a voting district with irregular boundaries that was created after the 1900 census. A federal district court decreed that the redistricting plan passed constitutional muster, but the Supreme Court disagreed. Writing for the Court in another five-to-four holding, Chief Justice Rehnquist noted that the plan in *Shaw v. Hunt*[65] violated the Equal Protection Clause of the Fourteenth Amendment since it was not narrowly tailored to further a compelling state interest. He added that creating a district inhabited by a majority of African-Americans neither justified redistricting nor was required under the VRA.

The Court reached a similar result where registered voters sought declaratory and injunctive relief from a redistricting plan that was adopted after the 1990 census. Based on the census, Texas was entitled to three additional seats. Under the plan, the state disregarded city limits, local election precincts, and voter tabulation district lines in creating two districts where the majority of voters were African-American and one where residents were primarily Hispanic. A three judge panel in a federal trial court struck the districts down as unconstitutional. On further review in *Bush v. Vera*,[66] a closely divided Supreme Court affirmed. Justice O'Connor's plurality opinion in the five-to-four decision determined that since the three new districts were drawn with race as the predominant factor, they were subject to strict scrutiny. Further, she asserted that the racially gerrymandered districts violated the Fourteenth Amendment because they were not narrowly tailored to serve a compelling state interest. O'Connor added that the creation of the districts violated the results test of the VRA.

Psychological Privilege

The Court has recognized the importance of confidentiality between patients and psychotherapists, licensed social workers, psychiatrists, and psychologists. When a conflict arises over confidentiality, the Court

---

[64] 116 S. Ct. 1186 (1996).
[65] 116 S. Ct. 1894 (1996).
[66] Bush v. Vera, 116 S. Ct. 1941 (1996).

utilizes a balancing test to weigh a patient's right to privacy against the need for disclosure.

Where a police officer shot and killed a citizen, the officer's psychotherapist relied upon privilege in refusing to disclose information to the family of the deceased about their discussions. At trial, a judge in a federal district court in Illinois instructed a jury that the psychotherapist's refusal to divulge the information was legally unjustified and could be construed as containing unfavorable information about the officer. As such, the jury returned a verdict in favor of the family. However, the Seventh Circuit reversed in favor of the police officer and the Supreme Court, in *Jaffee v. Redmond*,[67] affirmed. Writing for the Court in its seven-to-two ruling, Justice Stevens pointed out that Federal Rule of Evidence 501 allows courts to use reason and experience in deciding whether confidential conversations between patients and therapists should be privileged. He maintained that in light of the significant privacy interest at stake, federal law recognizes the privilege that protects confidential communications between patients and psychotherapists. Stevens added that protecting psychotherapists from compelled disclosures will help to ensure the standardized treatment of both therapists and patients.

Damages Awards

Given the growing number of excessive jury awards, the Court examined three cases in an attempt to provide guidance for future disputes. The Court asserted that punitive damage awards should not be based upon a bright-line standard. Rather, the Court posited that judgments of this type should be based on the totality of circumstances where assessments are based on the reprehensibility of the conduct of the parties.

A customer who purchased a new car from an authorized BMW dealership later filed suit for compensatory and punitive damages when he discovered that the vehicle had been repainted without his knowledge. A jury awarded the customer $4,000 in compensatory damages and $4,000,000 in punitive damages. The Supreme Court of Alabama affirmed but reduced the punitive damage award to $2,000,000 based on a calculation that should have been restricted to car sales within the state. On further review in *BMW of North America v. Gore*,[68] the Supreme Court reversed in favor of the dealer. Writing for the court in its five-to-four decision, Justice Stevens observed that the punitive damages award was grossly excessive in light of the low level of reprehensibility displayed

---

[67] 116 S. Ct. 1923 (1996).
[68] 116 S. Ct. 1589 (1996).

by the car dealership and the 500 to 1 ratio between the award and the actual harm to the customer.

In New York, a photographer filed suit after officials at a center lost original transparency sheets that he loaned them for use in an education video. Although conceding liability, the center challenged a jury verdict which, relying on the "industry standard," awarded the photographer $450,000 for the lost transparencies. Based on a state law that permits appellate courts to review jury verdicts to determine whether they "materially deviate" from reasonable compensation, the Second Circuit vacated and ordered a new trial unless the photographer agreed to an award of $100,000. On appeal, in *Gasperini v. Center for Humanities*,[69] the Supreme Court vacated and remanded. Justice Ginsburg's opinion in the Court's five-to-four ruling offered that the statute controlling compensation awards for excessiveness or inadequacy can be given effect without detriment to the Re-examination Clause of the Seventh Amendment. She acknowledged that both state and federal interests can continue to be accommodated as long as federal trial judges apply the "deviates materially" standard and appellate courts continue to base their reviews on whether there has been an abuse of discretion.

The widower and family of a woman who died from toxic shock syndrome received $1,525,000 in actual damages and $10,000,000 in punitive damages from the manufacturer of the product that caused her death. The family paid taxes on the punitive damages but immediately filed for a refund. The federal district court in Kansas granted the spouse a refund and dismissed the government's suit aimed at recovering taxes from the children. However, the Tenth Circuit reversed in favor of the government. On further review in *O'Gilvie v. United States*,[70] the Supreme Court affirmed. Justice Bryer's opinion in the six-to-three ruling declared that since the family did not receive the punitive damages "on account of" the deceased's personal injuries, they were taxable. He reasoned that punitive, unlike compensatory, damages are not subject to the gross-income-exclusion provision. The ambiguous nature of the wording in the Internal Revenue Code notwithstanding, he contended that Congress only intended to make compensatory awards tax free so that injured parties could restore their lost "capital."

---

[69] 116 S. Ct. 2211 (1996).
[70] 117 S. Ct. 452 (1996).

Conclusion

First Amendment protections guarantee employees significant freedom of speech. Public employees may voice opinions about matters of public concern as long as their employers are unable to establish that such speech interferes with the effective and efficient operation of their organizations. In resolving such disputes, the courts continue to rely on the balancing test in *Pickering* to determine whether the burden on protected speech outweighs the rights of the employees. In fact, the Supreme Court has stated that any restrictions that the government places on free expression must be narrowly tailored and serve a compelling state interest. Moreover, independent contractors are afforded similar rights as employees in their relationship with the state.

Governmental restrictions on free speech and expression in nonpublic fora should be content-neutral and reasonable, even if they are not necessarily the most reasonable alternative. Further, the government must provide notice of the restrictions to all interested parties and rules should be enforced consistently. If content is used as a measure of regulations, then a policy should be narrowly tailored to further a compelling governmental interest. If time, place, and manner restrictions apply, alternative opportunities for expression must be provided.

The courts continue to apply the *Lemon* test in cases involving the First Amendment and religious freedoms. Under *Lemon*, the government violates the First Amendment any time that a state agent attempts to coerce an individual to support or participate in religiously oriented behavior.

The Due Process Clause and the Equal Protection Clause of the Fourteenth Amendment are evaluated under the three tiers of strict, intermediate, and rational basis scrutiny. Once a state provides a benefit to its citizens, policies may not deprive them of their rights unless they are narrowly tailored to further a substantial governmental interest.

Reasonableness is the standard applied by the courts in evaluating claims under the Fourth Amendment. At the same time, searches conducted by private individuals are not constrained by the Fourth Amendment as long as the person is not acting as an agent of the state.

The RFRA subjects any governmental action that infringes upon religiously motivated behavior to strict scrutiny. Under the RFRA, the government's actions must further a compelling state interest in the least restrictive manner. The RFRA also proscribes restraints on religiously motivated behavior, compelling individuals to act in a manner that is contrary to their beliefs, and prohibiting conduct or expressions of religious views.

Insofar as employment discrimination claims based on age only require a new staff member to be younger than the aggrieved party, the new employee need not be a member of the protected class of workers over the age of forty. Disparate impact claims are actionable under the ADEA and facially neutral tests must demonstrate that an employer had a business necessity in acting. Lateral transfers are not typically considered adverse employment actions under the ADEA and reductions-in-force may be legitimate, nondiscriminatory reasons for discharging employees.

Title VII requires employers to take prompt corrective action once they are notified of alleged sexual harassment by their employees. Constructive knowledge may be adequate to demonstrate that the employer knew or should have known of the illegal activity. Moreover, an aggrieved party does not have to exhaust administrative remedies prior to filing a suit. A policy that does not require supervisory personnel to report alleged incidents of sexual harassment that is brought to their attention is unlikely to survive judicial review. Policies should be communicated to employees and should require them to report sexual harassment by immediate supervisors to central office personnel. Further, same-gender sexual harassment is actionable under title VII guidelines.

In cases involving adverse employment actions for special classes, an injured party may demonstrate the presence of discrimination by showing that someone who is similarly situated was treated more favorably. Determinations must be made as to what conditions constitute a disability under the terms of the Rehabilitation Act and the ADA. Employees must demonstrate that they were qualified for their positions, that they were able to meet the essential requirements of the job, and that they were able to meet these standards with or without reasonable accommodations that did not unduly burden their employers.

Collective bargaining requires both parties to negotiate in good faith. When labor disputes arise, the NLRB has broad discretionary authority to resolve disputes. Employers may act as fiduciary representatives for their employees under the ERISA. Fiduciary responsibility mandates that administrators of benefit plans must act in the best interests of the employees.

Psychological privilege covers licensed social workers, psychiatrists, and psychologists during the course of psychotherapy since confidential communication between patients and therapists is a cornerstone of treatment. The courts will continue to balance the privacy interests of individuals against those of the government on a case-by-case basis.

Case law and opinions in actions not directly involving education may offer implications for educational institutions. Understanding these relevant decisions should allow educational leaders to apply these standards in their own settings.

TABLE OF CASES

CASES BY JURISDICTION

This section organizes cases by jurisdiction presenting federal cases first. Following U.S. Supreme Court cases are circuit cases and district cases for states within each circuit. State court cses follow the federal cases.

Federal Court Cases

United States Supreme Court

Board of Educ. of Hendrick Hudson Cent. Sch. Dist. v. Rowley/151, 160
Board of Educ. of Kiryas Joel Village Sch. Dist. v. Grumet/51, 175
Burlington Sch. Comm. v. Department of Educ., Commonwealth of Mass./166
Bush v. Vera/374
Cleveland Bd. of Educ. v. Loudermill/14
Dellmuth v. Muth/166
Florence County Sch. Dist. Four v. Carter/ 166, 168
Honig v. Doe/151,164
Hopwood v. Texas/296
Hsu v. Roslyn Union Free Sch. Dist. No. 3/ 76, 95
Immediato v. Rye Neck Sch. Dist./107
Irving Indep. Sch. Dist. v. Tatro/164
Krapf v. United States/335
Lovell v. Poway Unified Sch. Dist./34, 97
McDonnell Douglas Corporation v. Green/3
Moore v. Ingebretsen/96
Pickering v. Board of Educ. of Township High Sch. Dist. 205/356
Rivers v. Roadway Express/4
Rowinsky v. Bryan Indep. Sch. Dist./99, 210
School Bd. of Nassau County v. Arline/177
Seminole Tribe of Fla. v. Florida/249
Smith v. Robinson/166
Southeastern Community College v. Davis/ 177
Younger v. Harris/18

District of Columbia

Board of Regents of Univ. of Wash. v. Environmental Protection Agency/256
Bridgeforth v. District of Columbia/171
Career College Ass'n v. Riley/297
Equal Employment Opportunity Comm'n v. Catholic Univ. of Am./279

Holland v. District of Columbia/148, 168
Lemon v. District of Columbia/154
Park v. Howard Univ./264
United States v. Mangum/362
Washington v. Smith/224, 327

First Circuit

Cohen v. Brown Univ./221
David D. v. Dartmouth Sch. Comm./160
TI Fed. Credit Union v. Delbonis/300
Winnacunnet v. National Union Fire Ins./ 199
Wojcik v. Town of N. Smithfield/107, 207

Puerto Rico

Gonzalez v. Torres/111
Nogueras v. University of P.R./293
Ombe v. Fernandez/276
Reyes-Pagan v. Benitez/16

Massachusetts

Andrew S. v. Massachusetts Dep't of Educ./160
Armstrong v. Lamy/206
McLaughlin ex rel. McLaughlin v. Boston Sch. Comm./90
Morgan v. Gittens/119
Richard V. v. City of Medford/165
Zehner v. Central Berkshire Regional Sch. Dist./114

Second Circuit

Catlin v. Sobol/176
Danneskjold v. Hausrath/290
Dennin v. Connecticut Interscholastic Athletic Conference/158, 177, 180, 215
Donata v. Plainview-Old Bethpage Cent. Sch. Dist./14
Hsu v. Roslyn Union Free Sch. Dist. No. 3/ 76, 95
Immediato v. Rye Neck Sch. Dist./107
National Labor Relations Bd. v. Katz's Delicatessen of Houston St./372
Skubel v. Sullivan/173

Michigan

Divergilio v. Skiba/103, 208

Hudson v. Bloomfield Hills Pub. Sch./162

Nelson v. Almont Community Sch./78, 104, 209

Willing v. Lake Orion Bd. of Trustees/56

Ohio

Davis v. Kent State Univ./222, 313

Equal Open Enrollment Ass'n v. Board of Educ. of Akron Sch. Dist./91

Reed v. Rhodes/121

Rhodes v. Ohio High Sch. Athletic Ass'n/ 157, 178, 180

Wise v. Ohio Dep't of Educ./146

Tennessee

Doe v. Metropolitan Nashville Pub. Sch./ 169

Morgan v. Chris L./165, 170

Rynes v. Knox County Bd. of Educ./170

Seventh Circuit

Beck v. University of Wisc. Bd. of Regents/ 273

Board of Educ. of Downers Grove Grade Sch. Dist. No. 58 v. Steven L./155, 171

Charlie F. v. Board of Educ. of Skokie Sch. Dist. 68/157, 167

Clay v. Fort Wayne Community Sch./67

Equal Employment Opportunity Comm'n v. State of Ill./7

Geier v. Medtronic/369

Grossbaum v. Indianapolis-Marion County Bldg. Authority/358

Helland v. South Bend Community Sch. Corp./12

Hindo v. University Health Sciences/The Chicago Med. Sch./258

Illinois High Sch. Ass'n v. GTE Vantage/ 241

Johnson v. Duneland Sch. Corp/148

Johnson v. University of Wisc./267

Kerr v. Farrey/359

Knapp v. Northwestern Univ./179, 222

K.R. v. Anderson/145

Kuhn v. Ball State Univ./271

Mack v. O'Leary/364

Muller *ex rel.* Muller v. Jefferson Lighthouse Sch./96

Nabozny v. Podlesny/100

Rodiriecus L. v. Waukegan Sch. Dist. No. 60/151, 165

Sasnett v. Sullivan/364

Smart v. Ball State Univ./268

United States v. Ross/260

USA Group Loan Serv. v. Riley/298

Waid v. Merrill Area Pub. Sch./4

Weisbrot v. Medical College of Wisc./288

Williams v. Bristol-Myers Squibb Co./366

Illinois

Barbara Z. v. Obradovich/159, 167

Board of Educ. of Community High Sch. Dist No. 218, Cook, County, Ill. v. Illinois State Bd. of Educ./155, 156, 159, 172

Board of Educ. of Oak Park & River Forest High Sch. Dist. 200 v. Illinois State Bd. of Educ./150

County Collector of County of Winnebago, Ill., *In re* /64

Davis v. McCormick/11

Dell v. Board of Educ., Township High Sch. Dist. 113/171

Knapp v. Northwestern Univ./179, 222

Mary P. v. Illinois State Bd. of Educ./146, 170, 169

Monticello Sch. Dist. No. 25 v. Illinois State Bd. of Educ./162

Indiana

D.F. v. Western Sch. Corp./162, 178, 180

Harless *ex rel.* Harless v. Darr/97

Heller v. Hodgin/115

Hines *ex rel.* Oliver v. McClung/108

Linda W. v. Indiana Dep't of Educ./175

Robbins v. Indiana High Sch. Athletic Ass'n/93, 217

Smith v. Indianapolis Pub. Sch./153

Wisconsin

Heather S. v. State of Wis./161

Eighth Circuit

Agyei *ex rel.* Jenkins v. State of Mo./120

Batra v. Board of Regents of the Univ. of Neb./278

Brine v. University of Iowa/268

Canada v. Thomas/234, 321

Clay v. Board of Educ. of St. Louis/54

Dishnow v. School Dist. of Rib Lake/9

Douglas v. Brownell/359

Edgerson *ex rel.* Edgerson v. Clinton/120

Tomlinson v. Board of Educ. of Lakeland
 Cent. Sch. Dist. of Shrub Oak/132
Tout v. Erie Community College/265
Tremblay v. Riley/299
Van Derzee v. Board of Educ. of Odessa-
 Montour Cent. Sch. Dist./30
Vanmaenen v. Hewlett-Woodmere Pub.
 Sch./25, 71
Vartanian v. Research Found. of State Univ.
 of N.Y./291
Washington v. Baruch/297
Welcher v. Sobol/41
Weller v. Colleges of the Senecas/318
White Plains City Sch. Dist. Bd. of Educ. v.
 Merchants Mut. Ins./199
Wilson, *In re* /291
Wohlleb v. Board of Educ. of
 Bridgehampton Union Free Sch. Dist./
 19
Wolff & Munier v. New York City Sch.
 Constr. Auth./75
Womack v. Duvernay/189
Yastion v, Mills/34
Zayas v. Half Hollow Hills Sch. Dist./233
Zima v. North Colonie Cent. Sch. Dist./191

North Carolina
Aune v. University of N.C. at Chapel Hill/
 289
Ballard v. Weast/94
Barringer v. Caldwell County Bd. of Educ./
 13, 70
Bowlin v. Duke Univ./323
Caldwell v. Linker/281
Craven County Bd. of Educ. v. Boyles/49
Craven County Bd. of Educ. v. Willoughby/
 176
Dare County Bd. of Educ. v. Sakaria/242
Dorsey v. UNC-Wilmington/289
Evans v. Cowan/287
Hallman v. Charlotte-Mecklenburg Bd. of
 Educ./194
Harris v. County of Forsyth/211
H.B.S. Contractors v. Cumberland County
 Bd. of Educ./58
Leandro v. State/47
Long v. University of N.C. at Wilmington/
 297
Newton v. New Hanover County Bd. of
 Educ./83, 190
North Carolina v. Merritt/260

North Carolina Bd. of Examiners for
 Speech and Language Pathologists and
 Audiologists v. North Carolina State
 Bd. of Educ./39
North Carolina Chiropractic Ass'n v. North
 Carolina State Bd. of Educ./45, 243
Simonel v. North Carolina Sch. of Arts/277
Slater v. Marshall/293
Vester v. Nash/Rocky Mount Bd. of Educ./
 200

North Dakota
Borr v. McKenzie County Pub. Sch. Dist.
 No. 1/29
Lapp v. Reeder Pub. Sch. Dist. No. 3/153,
 171
Stratton v. Medical Ctr. Rehabilitation
 Hosp./325
Thompson v. Peterson/276
Wishnatsky v. Bergquist/257

Ohio
Darnell Painting Co. v. Toledo Bd. of
 Educ./74
Davis v. Lousiana *ex rel.* Charity-Delgado
 Sch. of Nursing/314
Doe v. Ohio State Univ. Hosps. and Clinics/
 324
Edwards v. Buckley/288
Elebrashy, *In re* /301
Fox, *In re* /300
Frabotta v. Meridia Huron Hosp. Sch. of
 Nursing/309
Furlong v. Alpha Chi Omega Sorority/330
Gebhart v. College of Mt. St. Joseph/315
Hackathorn v. Preisse/185
Hara v. Montgomery County Local
 Vocational Sch. Dist./35
James v. Trumbull County Bd. of Educ./22
Kellon v. Cleveland Marshall College of
 Law/310
Kemerer v. Antwerp Bd. of Educ./202
Lakota Local Sch. Dist. v. Brickner/205
Lucas v. Gee/252
Malley v. Youngstown State Univ./317
Marcum v. Talawanda City Sch./188
Ohio Civil Rights Comm'n v. Case W.
 Reserve Univ./296
Peaspanen v. Board of Educ. of Ashtabula
 Area City Sch. Dist./200
Pichardo, *In re* /300
Prete v. Akron City Sch. Dist. Bd. of Educ./
 27

INDEX